The shifting border

MANCHESTER
1824

Manchester University Press

CRITICAL POWERS

Series Editors:
Antony Simon Laden (University of Illinois, Chicago),
Peter Niesen (University of Hamburg) and
David Owen (University of Southampton).

Critical Powers is dedicated to constructing dialogues around innovative and original work in social and political theory. The ambition of the series is to be pluralist in welcoming work from different philosophical traditions and theoretical orientations, ranging from abstract conceptual argument to concrete policy-relevant engagements, and encouraging dialogue across the diverse approaches that populate the field of social and political theory. All the volumes in the series are structured as dialogues in which a lead essay is greeted with a series of responses before a reply by the lead essayist. Such dialogues spark debate, foster understanding, encourage innovation and perform the drama of thought in a way that engages a wide audience of scholars and students.

Published by Bloomsbury

On Global Citizenship: James Tully in Dialogue
Justice, Democracy and the Right to Justification:
Rainer Forst in Dialogue

Published by Manchester University Press

Cinema, democracy and perfectionism:
Joshua Foa Dienstag in dialogue
Democratic inclusion: Rainer Bauböck in dialogue
Law and violence: Christoph Menke in dialogue

Forthcoming from Manchester University Press

Autonomy gaps: Joel Anderson in dialogue
Toleration, power and the right to justification:
Rainer Forst in dialogue

The shifting border

Legal cartographies of migration and mobility

Ayelet Shachar in dialogue

Ayelet Shachar
with responses from:
Sarah Fine
Jakob Huber
Chimène I. Keitner
Noora Lori
Steffen Mau
Leti Volpp

Manchester University Press

Published by Manchester University Press
Altrincham Street, Manchester M1 7JA

www.manchesteruniversitypress.co.uk

British Library Cataloguing-in-Publication Data
A catalogue record for this book is available from the British Library

ISBN 978 1 5261 4531 4 hardback

First published 2020

The publisher has no responsibility for the persistence or accuracy of URLs for any external or third-party internet websites referred to in this book, and does not guarantee that any content on such websites is, or will remain, accurate or appropriate.

Typeset by
Sunrise Setting Ltd, Brixham

In memory of Arie Shachar

Urban geographer, atlas maker, rooted cosmopolitan, beloved mentor, and, beyond all else, eternal optimist

Contents

Illustrations

Contributors

Sarah Fine is Senior Lecturer in Philosophy in the Department of Philosophy at King's College London. She is also a Fellow at the Forum for Philosophy, LSE. She co-edited (with Lea Ypi) *Migration in Political Theory: The Ethics of Movement and Membership* (Oxford University Press, 2016). She has published widely on questions in the ethics of migration. She also has interests in methodology, and in work at the intersection of philosophy and the arts. Recent publications include 'Refugees, Safety, and a Decent Human Life', *Proceedings of the Aristotelian Society* 119, no. 1 (2019): pp. 25–52, and 'Migration', in Serena Olsaretti, ed., *The Oxford Handbook of Distributive Justice* (Oxford University Press, 2018).

Jakob Huber is Postdoctoral Fellow at the Cluster of Excellence *The Formation of Normative Orders* at Goethe University Frankfurt am Main. Having studied political science and political theory at Berlin, London, and Oxford, he obtained his PhD in political theory from the LSE in 2017. His work, which has been published in journals such as *Political Studies, European Journal of Philosophy*, and *Politics, Philosophy & Economics*, aims to make themes from Kant's philosophy fruitful for a variety of debates and issues in contemporary political philosophy. In his current research, he seeks to develop an account of the nature, norms, and value of hope in democratic politics.

Chimène I. Keitner is Alfred and Hanna Fromm Professor of International and Comparative Law at the University of California Hastings College of the Law in San Francisco. She has taught at law faculties including the University of California, Berkeley, the University of Southern California, the University of Alabama, and Tel Aviv University. She is the author of *The Paradoxes of Nationalism* (2007) and *International Law Frameworks* (4th edn, 2016), among other works. Her research focuses on questions surrounding the relationship between law, communities, and borders, including issues of jurisdiction, extra-territoriality, foreign sovereign and foreign official immunity, and the historical understandings underpinning current practice in these areas.

Noora Lori is Assistant Professor of International Relations at the Pardee School of Global Studies, Boston University. She was previously a scholar at the Harvard Academy for International and Area Studies and received the Best Dissertation Award from the Migration and Citizenship Section of the American Political Science Association (2014). She has published numerous works on citizenship and migration including in the *Oxford Handbook on Citizenship* (2017). Her first book, *Offshore Citizens: Permanent 'Temporary' Status in the Gulf*, is published by Cambridge University Press (2019).

Steffen Mau is Professor of Macrosociology at Humboldt-Universität zu Berlin. For ten years, he was Professor of Political Sociology at the University of Bremen. His most recent books include *The Metric Society: On the Quantification of the Social* (Cambridge: Polity, 2019), *Inequality, Marketization and the Majority Class: Why Did the European Middle Classes Accept Neoliberalism?* (Basingstoke: Palgrave Macmillan, 2015), and *Liberal States and the Freedom of Movement: Selective Borders, Unequal Mobility* (with Heike Brabandt, Lena Laube, and Christof Roos, Basingstoke: Palgrave Macmillan, 2012).

Peter Niesen is Professor of Political Theory at Hamburg University and Speaker of the Association of Political Theory in Germany (*Theoriesektion*). He has a PhD in philosophy and an Habilitation in political science from Goethe University Frankfurt am Main. His research interests lie in international political theory, enlightenment political philosophy (Kant, Bentham), and animal politics. Recent papers have appeared in *Behemoth*, *Kantian Review*, *Journal of International Political Theory*, *Journal of Bentham Studies*, and *Journal of Common Market Studies*.

Ayelet Shachar, FRSC, is Director at the Max Planck Institute for the Study of Religious and Ethnic Diversity and Professor of Law and Political Science at the University of Toronto. Her research focuses on citizenship theory, immigration law, cultural diversity, gender equality, talent migration, and new bordering regimes. She is the prizewinning author of *Multicultural Jurisdictions: Cultural Differences and Women's Rights* (Cambridge: Cambridge University Press, 2001), *The Birthright Lottery: Citizenship and Global Inequality* (Cambridge: Harvard University Press, 2009), and the lead editor of *The Oxford Handbook of Citizenship* (Oxford: Oxford University Press, 2017). Shachar is the recipient of excellence awards in four different countries (Canada, Israel, Germany, and the United States). Most recently, she was awarded the Gottfried Wilhelm Leibniz Prize—Germany's most prestigious research award.

Leti Volpp is the Robert D. and Leslie-Kay Raven Professor of Law at the University of California, Berkeley. She is also the director of the UC Berkeley Center for Race and Gender. Recent publications include 'Protecting the Nation from "Honor Killings": The Construction of a Problem', *Constitutional Commentary 133* (2019); 'Refugees Welcome?', *Berkeley La Raza Law Journal 28* (2018); and the co-edited volume (with Marianne Constable and Bryan Wagner) *Looking for Law in All the Wrong Places: Justice beyond and between* (New York: Fordham University Press, 2019).

Series editor's foreword

The crossing of borders is generally recognized as a key phenomenon in international political theory and in international law today—and the literature on the mobility of money, goods, and humans, and on migration and on the claims of asylum seekers, refugees, and non-citizen residents is exploding. Yet many contributions to the literature are unaware of a hidden presupposition they share. They assume that while people will try to move, borders will remain constant.

The original insight in Ayelet Shachar's lead essay is that states have made their borders a moving target, such that the crossing of borders is no longer frustrated only by making them physically insuperable. States can keep unwanted people out by moving the borders themselves, outward or inward, depending on the desired effect. Shachar argues that the shift from a "movement of people across borders" to "the movement of borders to regulate the mobility of people" (p. 7) amounts to a transformation from a physical/territorial conception to a functional view of jurisdiction.

The "shifting border," Shachar's felicitous term for the new phenomenon, is part of a process of modernization of border regimes, a mechanism for the managing of would-be migrants who can be rejected in transit or deported before they are deemed to have arrived. At the same time, the "portable" wall of the new type of border "changes form depending on how it is approached and by whom" (p. 13): while advances in technical infrastructure have enhanced the mobility of the global middle classes, they have at the same time strengthened the potential for control and arbitrary exclusion of unwanted applicants.

Although the phenomenology of the shifting border, as Shachar shows, is protean and complex, its logic follows a single aim: to keep unwanted arrivals out. In using new technology, co-opting third parties, or outsourcing control to private collaborators, it adds to the informalization and arbitrariness of the measures, and caters to the changing needs of states. Its productivity results from the fact that it breaks up the traditional nexus between territorial presence and the ability to trigger legal procedures.

While in an earlier, "Westphalian," age, refugees could by their physical presence on the territory exercise rights of claiming asylum or *non-refoulement* status, this can no longer be taken for granted in a world in which states disown their territorial boundaries and treat new arrivals "as though they had never reached [the country], despite having physically landed on its shores," and where undocumented migrants are chased well into the heartland. In an echo of Kant's distinctions in *Toward Perpetual Peace*, "access" is no longer considered "entry," "entry" is no longer co-terminous with "admission," and, where possible, "access" is blocked by legal fictions, technological innovations, or sheer physical force.

Ayelet Shachar is perhaps the best-placed person to diagnose the physiognomy of the shifting border, as its characteristic features have been at the center of her research in law, political science, and political theory for many years. She has discussed immigration law, cultural diversity, and structural inequality in her book *The Birthright Lottery: Citizenship and Global Inequality* (Cambridge: Harvard University Press, 2009), which confronts inherited citizen status with demands of justice such as the principle of equality of opportunity. In the lead essay of the current volume, the "birthright lottery" provides a continuing orientation point for her, in that it continues to demarcate the "persisting fault line" between those privileged and those disadvantaged by the phenomenon of the shifting border. In her forthcoming book, entitled *The Transformation of Citizenship: Territorial, Cultural, and Wealth-Based* (Oxford University Press), she again highlights selective inclusion. She has also made seminal contributions to the debate on the marketization of citizenship, another stratifying trend of immigration regimes—for example, in her article 'Citizenship for Sale', in *The Oxford Handbook of Citizenship* (Oxford: Oxford University Press), which she spearheaded as lead editor in 2017.

In the current volume, Ayelet Shachar shows how the border regimes of countries such as the United States, Canada, or Australia, or of supranational federations like the European Union, have become insuperable for some by extending outward or inward. In the case of the United States, borders effectively moved inward when officials were empowered to perform an "expedited removal" (p. 20) of undocumented migrants within a 100-mile zone within US territory. Both Canada and Australia have pushed their borders outward, deep into the points of embarkation in the states of origin or departure. Australia's "excision zone" creates the legal fiction that refugees who have arrived on Australian soil have never set foot there and can thus be returned to extraterritorial sites without violating the *non-refoulement* clause of the 1951 Refugee Convention. Perverting the logic of modern asylum law, the very presupposition for making asylum claims—touching soil—disqualifies applicants peremptorily from admission. The European Union, "tak[ing] a leaf out of Australia's playbook" (p. 56) in its pilot project iBorderCtrl, uses technology to permanently screen individuals before and after crossing territorial borders, effectively making them "carry" the border when moving about.

But Shachar does not restrict herself to diagnosing how borders "migrate," nor does she stop at criticizing the various manifestations and exclusionary consequences of current border regimes. She carefully outlines a normative proposal that is both constructive and radical. The constructive element is her sketch of various institutional responses to the shifting-border phenomenon, using her intimate familiarity with the workings of international law but infusing them with the forward-looking energies of legal and political philosophy. The radical element is the principled decoupling of state obligations from the criterion of the physical presence of applicants, enabling her to provocatively question the "overrated premium of territorial arrival" (p. 71). Although her suggestions never lose sight of what is pragmatically achievable, they demand nothing less than the beginnings of a "conceptual and paradigm shift that is long overdue" (p. 96).

The key element in countering the shifting realities remains the power to trigger claims for asylum or refugee status, thus activating "the protection machinery of host states." Shachar is clear that "recourse to territorial arrival must remain available to those seeking safety" (p. 72), while we also should not blind ourselves to the "unequal distributional effects of the current system" (p. 73). This entails that territorial recourse should no longer constitute the universal, or only, mechanism for processing mobility and migration claims. In her reconceptualization of the relationship between law and territory, Shachar therefore accepts the new reality of the shifting border, only to subversively turn it against itself. The first move is to see states assuming legal obligations toward individuals as soon as those are subjected to "effective control" by state agents or their delegates (p. 16). Whenever potential migrants encounter state authority in a functional sense, however far removed from state territory, this fact ought to trigger rights to have their claims processed. A second strategy is to bring the border to those seeking refuge. In functional terms, borders can be extended to process, review, and grant refuge and asylum extraterritorially—for example, in overseas refugee camps, as in the pioneering Welcome Refugees initiative by the Canadian government. This goes some way toward "de-territorializing" borders, which could be further strengthened by giving the United Nations High Commissioner for Refugees (UNHCR) a stronger role in the global re-allocation of refugees. None of these strategies, Shachar contends, can be achieved without significant political mobilization.

The contributions to this volume reflect the disciplinary strands that Shachar draws together in her lead essay. They come from international relations, political philosophy, political sociology, and international law. Acknowledging the innovation that a shifting-border framework brings to redescribing the confrontation between humanitarian needs and repressive state politics, they address all elements of Shachar's lead essay, from her diagnosis of the phenomenon and her focus on democratic systems, via her interpretation of public international law as it stands, to the coherence and desirability of her normative recommendations. They insist that any progressive developments in migration and mobility law will depend as much on the correct diagnosis of trends in global governance as on the legal intricacies of national and international court decisions, and will be put to the test in the electoral politics of the host states.

The responses section is kicked off by Sarah Fine, who likens Shachar's "magnificent and terrifying" idea of the shapeshifting state to Hobbes's vision of Leviathan, and challenges Shachar's strategy of "taming" the new beast. Noora Lori stresses the temporal transformations of borders and migration, arguing that they parallel the processes of spatial transformation highlighted by Shachar. She stresses that current developments threaten to incorporate autocratic migration policies in the heart of democratic systems. Steffen Mau agrees with Shachar that the ability to control an "outer shell" (p. 141) of borders will remain a central feature of statehood. He is skeptical about the attempt at de-territorializing sovereignty obligations such as the extraterritorial processing of asylum claims—in his view, the planned EU asylum centers in Africa represent an attempt to outsource such obligations. Chimène Keitner, from an international-law perspective, formulates a realist challenge to Shachar's diagnosis and recommendations, accentuating the constraints of state power on progressive designs, while Leti Volpp embeds Shachar's diagnosis into a larger legal history of the "manipulation of . . . legal salience" (p. 169), and criticizes Shachar's attempted conceptual separation of rights from territory. Jakob Huber, finally, reads Shachar's proposal from the perspective of Kant's philosophy of cosmopolitan right, and likewise argues that the link between territorial presence and legal entitlement should be strengthened, not suspended. In response, Shachar makes a passionate case for a critical methodology in interpreting today's institutional and legal frameworks, as well as their underlying normative commitments. She develops the analogy of a "hospital on the hill" to illustrate the limitations of pegging access to protection to close-to-impossible territorial arrival, offering instead the image of mobile field hospitals to demonstrate that we can constructively translate abstract ideas into concrete, actionable measures. Her reply further emphasizes the links between shifting-border policies and illiberal domestic policies, the complex relations between social and legal change, and, finally, the potential for political action and transnational solidarity to alleviate human suffering and injustice. She sides with the philosophers in having faith in the power of ideas to change the world. With the lawyers, she shares a belief in the value of institutional design and a commitment to holding governments to account. In the best tradition of critical theory, she believes the solutions lie within the contradictory social and political processes she has so eloquently ascertained.

Peter Niesen

Part I

Lead essay

The shifting border: legal cartographies of migration and mobility*

Ayelet Shachar

From the Great Wall of China to the Berlin Wall, fortified manifesta-tions of the border have long served as a powerful symbol of sover-eignty, real and imagined.[1] In 1989, the fall of the Berlin Wall led many to predict that barbed wire and sealed entry gates would become relics of a bygone era. Over a quarter of a century later, we find a very

---

* Earlier versions of this work were delivered as endowed lectures or keynote presenta-tions at conferences held in Berlin, Boston, Frankfurt, Hamburg, Cambridge, and New York. I owe a debt of gratitude to the audiences attending these inspiring events and to the organizers who generously invited me to participate in them: Danielle Allen, Seyla Benhabib, Rainer Forst, Ute Frevert, Klaus Günther, Mattias Kumm, Peter Niesen, Vlad Perju, and Joseph Weiler. I would also like to extend my thanks to Arthur Applbaum, Alex Aleinikoff, Chris Armstrong, Irene Bloemraad, Benjamin Boudou, Hauke Brunkhorst, Cathryn Costello, Derek Denman, Richard Fallon, Matthew Gibney, Tom Ginsburg, Ali-sha Holland, Dan Kanstroom, Cristina Lafont, Katerina Linos, Philip Liste, Hiroshi Motomura, Christoph Möllers, David Owen, Jaya Ramji-Nogales, Sarah Song, Tracy Strong, Leti Volpp, Katie Young, and especially Ran Hirschl, for their insightful com-ments and suggestions. Abigail Herrington, Thoby King, Karlson Leung, Matthew Milne, Teraleigh Stevenson, Gabe Thompson, and Chantelle van Wilenberg provided outstanding research assistance. All errors are mine.
[1] For a critical exploration of border walls, see Wendy Brown, *Walled States, Waning Sov-ereignty* (Cambridge: Zone Books, 2010). Definitions of sovereignty may vary, but legally there are three enduring constituent features: people, territory, and political authority exercised over that territory and its people. As Robert Jackson observes, "[s]overeignty is an idea of authority embodied in those bordered territorial organizations we refer to as 'states.'" Robert Jackson, *Sovereignty: The Evolution of an Idea* (Cambridge: Polity Press, 2007), pp. ix, 1. In international law, Convention on the Rights and Duties of the State (Montevideo Convention) art. 1, 26 December 1933, 165 L.N.T.S. 19 echoes the tradi-tional Westphalian view, stating that: "The state as a person of international law should possess the following qualifications: (a) a permanent population; (b) a defined territory; (c) government; and (d) capacity to enter into relation with other states." In international politics, the centrality of territory to sovereignty is acknowledged as a basic norm of the Westphalian order. See Michael Zürn, Martin Binder, and Matthias Ecker-Ehrhardt, 'International Authority and Its Politicization', *International Theory* 4 (2012): pp. 69–106.

different reality. Today, new walls are erected at an unprecedented pace the world over.[2] Around Spanish enclaves in Morocco, between South Africa and Zimbabwe, India and Bangladesh, Hungary and Turkey, and along the US–Mexico border and Norway's arctic border barrier with Russia, menacing border walls and steel fences continue to signal that even in a supposed post-Westphalian era physical barriers are still considered powerful measures to regulate migration and movement.

At the same time, a new and striking phenomenon—the *shifting border*—has emerged. The notion that legal circumstances affecting non-members change substantively only *after* they "pass through our gates" is well entrenched in both theoretical debates and regulatory practice.[3] The remarkable development of recent years is that "our gates" no longer stand fixed at the country's territorial edges. The border itself has become a moving barrier, an unmoored legal construct. As I will show in this essay, the fixed black lines we see in our world atlases do not always coincide with those comprehended in—indeed, created by—the words of law.[4] Increasingly, prosperous countries utilize sophisticated legal tools to selectively restrict (or, conversely, accelerate) mobility and access by detaching the border and its migration-control functions from a fixed territorial marker, creating a new framework that I call the *shifting border*.

When it comes to migration control, the *location* of the border is shifting: at times penetrating deeply into the interior, at others extending well beyond the edge of the territory. And in other contexts, fixed territorial borders are "erased" or refortified. This is part of a shifting-border

---

[2]   Ron E. Hassner and Jason Wittenberg, 'Barriers to Entry: Who Builds Fortified Boundaries and Why?', *International Security 50* (2015): pp. 157–190.

[3]   *Shaughnessy v. United States ex rel. Mezei*, 345 U.S. 206 (1953) (United States); *Zadvydas v. Davis*, 533 U.S. 678 (2001) (United States). For a critical exploration, see, for example, Linda Bosniak, 'Being Here: Ethical Territoriality and the Rights of Immigrants', *Theoretical Inquiries in Law 8* (2007): pp. 389–410; Leti Volpp, 'Imagining of Space in Immigration Law', *Law, Culture and the Humanities 9* (2012): pp. 456–474.

[4]   This is so even as politicians frequently revert to images of a fixed legal spatiality when it comes to the rhetoric surrounding the exercise of sovereign authority, as in Donald Trump's election promise to build an "impenetrable, physical, tall, powerful, beautiful . . . border wall."

strategy that strives, as official government policy documents plainly and tellingly explain, to "'push the border out' as far away from the actual [territorial] border as possible."[5] The idea, enthusiastically endorsed by governments in relatively rich and stable regions of the world, is to screen people "at the source" or origin of their journey (rather than at their destination country) and then again at every possible "checkpoint along the travel continuum—visa screening, airport check-in, points of embarkation, transit points, international airports and seaports."[6] The traditional static border is thus reimagined as the *last* point of encounter, rather than the first.[7] In this way, the shifting-border strategy makes it harder and harder for unwanted and uninvited migrants to set foot in the greener pastures of the more affluent and stable polities they desperately seek to enter. Conversely, wealthy migrants wishing to deposit their mobile capital in these very same countries find fewer and fewer restrictions to fast-tracked admission.[8] The shifting border is the key pillar in a wholesale agenda to strategically and selectively sort and regulate mobility as prosperous countries seek to "regain" control over a crucial realm of their allegedly waning sovereign authority.

This shifting border, unlike a reinforced physical barrier, is not fixed in time and place. It relies on law's admission gates rather than a

[5] Canada Border Services Agency, *Department Performance Report 2008–09, Section II: Analysis of Program Activities by Strategic Outcome* (Ottawa: CBSA, 05 November 2009); Office of the Auditor General of Canada, *Report of the Auditor General of Canada to the House of Commons, Ch. 5: Citizenship and Immigration Canada—Control and Enforcement* (FA1-2003/1-5E, 2003), ch. 5.8.

[6] Government of Canada, Preamble, Canada US Statement of Mutual Understanding (SMU) (Canada), online www.canada.ca/en/immigration-refugees-citizenship/corporate/mandate/policies-operational-instructions-agreements/agreements/statement-mutual-understanding-information-sharing/statement.html.

[7] My reference here is to the current legal situation which holds, in the words of the ECtHR, that "[s]tates enjoy an undeniable sovereign right to control aliens' entry into and residence in their territory." *Saadi v. UK*, App. No. 13229/03, Eur. Ct. H.R. (2008), sec. 64 (internal references omitted). Contemporary political theorists have, however, questioned the justice and legitimacy of this current legal situation. For this fast burgeoning literature, see, for example, Sarah Fine, 'The Ethics of Immigration: Self-Determination and the Right to Exclude', *Philosophy Compass 8* (2013): pp. 254–268.

[8] I discuss these developments in detail elsewhere. See Ayelet Shachar, 'Citizenship for Sale?', in Ayelet Shachar *et al.*, eds, *The Oxford Handbook of Citizenship* (Oxford: Oxford University Press, 2017), pp. 789–816.

specific frontier location. Just as the shifting border extends the long
arm of the state, ever more flexibly, to regulate mobility half the world
away, it also stretches deeply into the interior, creating within liberal
democracies what have been variably referred to as "constitution free"
zones or "waiting zones" (*zones d'attente*), where ordinary constitutional rights are partially suspended or limited, especially in relation to
those who do not have proper documentation or legal status.[9] Each of
these spatial and temporal contractions and protrusions bears dramatic
implications for the scope of rights and protections that migrants and
other non-citizens may enjoy, revealing the violence that may be
deployed through legal acts that ascribe meaning to bodies in relation
to (shifting) borders, prescribing or denying them access and setting
people in new relations of power in political spaces of im/mobility.[10] In
a world of mounting inequality and migration pressures, governments
frantically search for new ways to expand the reach of their remit, both
conceptually and operationally, inward and outward, in the process
reinventing one of the classic dimensions of sovereignty in the modern
era: namely, territoriality.

Philosophers and jurists are only now beginning to come to terms
with these deep currents, which are reshaping the terrain of law and
mobility in ways we might not yet fully recognize or understand. When
it comes to today's shifting border, we are, to borrow a metaphor from
Seyla Benhabib, like travelers navigating a new terrain with the help of
old maps; while the terrain has radically changed, our maps have not.
Thus, we stumble upon streams we did not know existed, and climb
hills we have never imagined.[11]

Despite its striking implications for human dignity, democratic
accountability, and disparities in attaining access to territory and

---

[9] For a concise overview, see Tugba Basaran, 'Legal Borders in Europe: The Waiting Zone',
in J. Peter Burgess and Serge Gutwirth, eds, *A Threat against Europe: Security, Migration
and Integration* (Brussels: VUB Press, 2001), pp. 63–74.

[10] The theme of legal interpretation occasioning the imposition of violence upon others is
central to the work of Robert Cover. See, for example, Robert M. Cover, 'Violence and
the Word', *Yale Law Journal 95* (1986): pp. 1601–1629.

[11] Seyla Benhabib, *The Rights of Others: Aliens, Residents, and Citizens* (Cambridge: Cambridge
University Press, 2004).

membership, the "near obsession" of wealthier countries with reimag-
ining migration and reinventing border control through sophisticated
legal (not extralegal) shifting-border techniques and innovations, we
currently lack the basic conceptual language to capture, describe, and
critique these rapid changes.[12] This book begins to fill this lacuna.

The theoretical landscape and the road ahead

The shift in perspective I propose—from the more familiar locus of
studying the *movement of people across borders* to critically investigating the *movement of borders to regulate the mobility of people*—reveals a
paradigmatic and paradoxical shift in the political imagination and
implementation of the sovereign authority to screen and manage global
migration flows in a world filled with multiple sources of law: formal and
informal, hard and soft, local, national, supranational, transnational, and
international. Scholars in multiple disciplines have creatively explored
borders as processes or methods.[13] My analysis builds on some of these
insights but seeks to both deepen and sharpen them by emphasizing
the core role of law and legal institutions in reconfiguring the border in
the brazen exercise of governmental authority. I further explore whether

---

[12] The "near obsession" term is drawn from James Hathaway and Thomas Gammeltoft-
Hansen, 'Non-Refoulement in a World of Cooperative Deterrence', *Columbia Journal of
Transnational Law 53* (2015): pp. 235–284. For a theoretical framework in which to
locate the shifting-border phenomenon and a nascent description thereof, see Ran
Hirschl and Ayelet Shachar, 'Spatial Statism', *International Journal of Constitutional Law
17* (2019): pp. 387–438.

[13] Borders-studies scholars have creatively explored borders as processes or methods. See,
for example, Thomas Nail, *A Theory of the Border* (Oxford: Oxford University Press,
2016); Sandro Mezzadra and Brett Neilson, *Border as Method, or, the Multiplication of
Labor* (Durham: Duke University Press, 2013). My analysis complements these accounts
by emphasizing the legal dimension of the reinvention of the border and the key challenges posed by these developments. Placing greater emphasis on territoriality and borders is part of a broader spatial turn in the social sciences, humanities, and law, to which
critical and progressive geographers have significantly contributed. See, for example,
Stuart Elden, *The Birth of Territory* (Chicago: The University of Chicago Press, 2013);
Edward W. Soja, *Postmodern Geographies: The Reassertion of Space in Critical Social Theory*
(London: Verso, 1989).

there are limits on such authority, and if so, how to activate them and who should do so.[14]

In a world where borders are transforming, but not dissolving, I will aim to show that the question of legal spatiality—*where* a person is barred from onward mobility and by *whom*—bears dramatic consequences for the rights and protections of those on the move, as well as the correlating duties and responsibilities of the countries they seek to reach and the transit locations they pass through. And here lies the deep paradox of the shifting border: when it comes to controlling migration, states are willfully *abandoning* traditional notions of fixed and bounded territoriality, stretching their jurisdictional arm inward and outward with tremendous flexibility; but when it comes to granting rights and protections, the very same states snap back to a narrow and strict interpretation of spatiality which limits their responsibility and liability, by attaching it to the (illusionary) static notion of border control. This duality is perhaps most profoundly pronounced in the case of asylum seekers who trigger protection obligations only once the destination country's soil is firmly under their feet, yet access to these territorial spaces of protection is increasingly unreachable. Those on the move are shut out long before they reach the gates of the promised lands of migration and asylum.[15]

By charting the logic of a new cartography (or legal reconstruction) of borders and membership boundaries I seek to show both the

---

[14] In legal and political theory, recent years have witnessed significant debates about whether—and if so, according to what grounds—states have the right to exclude. For influential accounts, see, for example, Arash Abizadeh, 'Democratic Theory and Border Coercion: No Right to Unilaterally Control Your Own Borders', *Political Theory* 36 (2008): pp. 37–65; Fine, 'The Ethics of Immigration' (n 7); Joseph H. Carens, *The Ethics of Immigration* (Oxford: Oxford University Press, 2013). For a wide-ranging and illuminating analysis, see Sarah Song, 'Why Does the State have the Right to Control Immigration?', in Jack Knight, ed., *NOMOS: Immigration, Emigration, and Migration* (New York City: NYU Press, 2017), pp. 3–50.

[15] There is some disagreement in the literature regarding whether the exclusion of asylum seekers is an indirect and unintended side effect of these new bordering techniques or one of its causes. Most scholars writing in the vein of human rights law and protection tend to express the latter view, as reflected in the work of Cathryn Costello, James Hathaway, Thomas Gammerltoft-Hansen, Matthew Gibney, Guy Goodwin-Gill, Jane McAdams, and Violeta Moreno-Lax, to name but a few. The contending view is articulated, among others, by legal academics and political theorists such as Kay Hailbronner and David Miller.

tremendous creativity and risk attached to these new legal innovations and the public powers they invigorate and propagate. I further seek to establish that debates about migration and globalization can no longer revolve around the dichotomy between open and closed borders. Instead, the unique and perplexing feature of this new landscape is that countries simultaneously engage in *both* opening *and* closing their borders, but do so *selectively*, indicating, quite decisively, whom they desire to admit (those with specialized skills, superb talents, or, increasingly, deep pockets), while at the same time erecting higher and higher legal walls to block out those deemed unwanted or "too different."[16]

This dialectical relationship between restrictive closure and selective openness is what makes the study of the new legal gates of admission ever more vital; this is also where the reformulation of basic democratic conceptions of membership boundaries become entangled with profound questions of justice and distribution about how, by whom, and according to what principles access to membership should be allocated, whether at birth or later in life. It further reveals, quite vividly, the recalibration of new immigration and border regimes as "public statements," as a recent study put it, "about who we are now, who we want to become, and who is 'worthy' to join us."[17] This idea of a border that is in flux— operating in a quantum-like fashion, simultaneously both fixed and fluid, stationary and portable, exerting influence over those coming under its kaleidoscopic dominion—is at the heart of my inquiry. This reinvention of the border facilitates unequal access to desired destinations and the life chances they offer. As such, it touches on some of the

[16] Ayelet Shachar and Ran Hirschl, 'On Citizenship, States and Markets', *Journal of Political Philosophy 22* (2014): pp. 231–257; Ayelet Shachar, 'Selecting by Merit: The Brave New World of Stratified Mobility', in Sarah Fine and Lea Ypi, eds, *Migration in Political Theory: The Ethics of Movement and Membership* (Oxford: Oxford University Press, 2016), pp. 175–202; Shachar, 'Citizenship for Sale?' (n 8). On the unequal mobility effects of such selective visa and admission policies, see, for example, Steffen Mau *et al.*, 'The Global Mobility Divide: How Visa Policies Have Evolved over Time', *Journal of Ethnic and Migration Studies 8* (2015): pp. 1192–1213.
[17] David Cook-Martin and David FitzGerald, 'Culling the Masses: A Rejoinder', *Journal of Ethnic and Racial Studies 38* (2015): pp. 1319–1327. See also Cass R. Sunstein, 'On the Expressive Function of Law', *University of Pennsylvania Law Review 144* (1996): pp. 2021–2053.

most delicate and contentious issues that must be addressed by any membership regime that falls short of a global reach: defining who belongs (or ought to belong) and on what basis.

The shifting border is not a disappearing border, however. Although theorists and activists have prophesied the imminent demise of states and borders, the new reality explored in this study tests and challenges such conclusions. The examples I provide throughout the discussion show quite vividly that sovereign authority over migration is neither dissipating nor vanishing. Today's brusque encounters of moving bodies and shifting borders provide concrete illustrations of both deeper and broader tensions, such as those between sovereignty and human rights, statists and cosmopolitanists, local and global obligations, and the right of the state to exclude and its duty to protect. Instead of rehearsing these influential debates, I wish to initiate a discussion that disrupts some of these familiar dichotomies while simultaneously investigating the grounds on which they stand, literally and conceptually. My intervention adds a crucial legal dimension to these pressing debates, focusing on the often neglected dimension of how the spatial and regulatory reinvention of borders matters dramatically to how we think about justice, equality, and the "crisis" of migration.[18] In a rapidly changing system, freeing up sovereignty from a rigid and static "Westphalian" understanding of fixed territoriality is a powerful transformation.

This is the case because relaxing the relationship between law and territoriality and blurring the distinction between "inside" and "outside"

---

[18] The term "crisis" is charged, but I have chosen to use it here to follow the current reference in most academic and public debates. Standard accounts in international migration point to the untenable life conditions in countries of origin as push factors, whereas the promise of a better life in destination countries is perceived as a pull factor, yet this analysis does not focus specifically on forced migration or the plight of refugees, who are entitled to international protection, whereas others fleeing dire circumstances, such as extreme poverty (as defined by the UN), for example, are not. Furthermore, it is not entirely clear what precisely is meant by the crux of the present "crisis" as it manifests in Europe: is it the very act of irregular entry by potential asylum seekers, which formally breaches states' border controls and standard documentary requirements for international travel? The size and volume of the inflow? The failure of member states to devise and implement a shared policy, which can be seen as a governance crisis, or a value crisis (as some EU officials have labeled it)? Another interpretation is that we are witnessing a crisis of solidarity and governability. Depending on how the crisis is defined, both politically and legally, we can expect different interpretations of its best resolution.

opens up a whole new purview for exercising power in the name of securing the integrity of the home territory and vigilantly protecting its membership boundaries. The sheer reach and magnitude of the shifting border thus calls for revisiting the age-old question of how to tame menacing governmental authority. Today, states, localities, and supranational entities such as Frontex (Europe's border and coastguard agency) increasingly rely upon a complex web of national, subnational, supranational, transnational, and international instruments to profoundly reconceptualize and "de-territorialize" the classic Westphalian manifestation of sovereignty as an activity that may potentially take place *anywhere* in the world.[19]

The shifting border is at once multidirectional and slippery, but not in the transnational, open, and tolerant variant that demise-of-the-state or post-Westphalian theories had foreseen. Instead, a darker, more restrictive, orientation has emerged. Far from the dream of a borderless world that emerged after the Berlin Wall came down, today we find not only more border walls erected on the global fault lines that divvy up the "have" and "have nots," but also the rapid proliferation of moveable legal barriers, which may appear anywhere but are applied selectively and unevenly, with fluctuating degree, intensity, and frequency of regulation, as prosperous countries turn to increasingly sophisticated measures of pre-emption, containment, and control in their quest to prevent "spontaneous" migrants, including asylum seekers, from accessing their bounded legal spaces of rights protection and relative safety and stability.[20]

The rise of the shifting border is contemporaneous with growing anxiety over immigration domestically and a surge in the numbers of

[19] On the legal authorization establishing the new European Border and Coast Guard Agency as an enhanced variant of Frontex, see Regulation (EU) 2016/1624 of the European Parliament and of the Council on the European Border and Coast Guard, O.J. (L 251/1) September 16, 2016 (EU). See also Home Office, *Securing the UK Border: Our Vision and Strategy for the Future*, March 2007 (United Kingdom), point 1.4; Canada Border Services Agency, *Department Performance Report* (n 5), p. 1; Department of Homeland Security, Designated Aliens for Expedited Removal, 69 Fed. Reg. 58.877, 11 August 2004 (United States).

[20] I owe the phrasing of this point regarding the fluctuating degree, intensity, and frequency of regulation to Derek Denman.

"people out of place" globally.[21] This new constellation gives added impetus to addressing some of the most profound and arduous questions of our time. Is it legitimate for states to exclude non-members? If so, on what basis? Does the nascent multilevel architecture of global law assist, or paradoxically constrict, the protected rights available to people out of place? In a world of growing interdependence and strife, whose duty is it to assist those who are escaping harm's way? Do such obligations extend to providing safe passage and temporary protection, or do they entail a right to resettlement and to embark on the road to citizenship? How much of a role should accidents of geography, such as a country's proximity to war zones or regions of civil strife, play in determining which political communities are asked to shoulder the greatest responsibilities to "people out of place"? The arrival of the migration crisis (as it is known) at Europe's borders has exposed the urgency of addressing these very questions, but this same crisis also immediately reveals the impossibility of formulating any easy answers.

---

[21] I intentionally use the term "people out of place," which is broader than the legal definition of asylum seekers and refugees. See Alison Brysk and Gershon Shafir, eds, *People Out of Place: Globalization, Human Rights, and the Citizenship Gap* (New York: Routledge, 2004). The legal definition of a "refugee" under the 1951 Convention Relating to the Status of Refugees, article 1, is a person who: "owing to well-founded fear of being persecuted for reasons of race, religion, nationality, membership of a particular social group or political opinion" is fleeing his or her country of nationality, or if stateless, is unwilling or unable to return to the country of his or her former habitual residence (UN General Assembly, *Convention Relating to the Status of Refugees*, July 28, 1951, United Nations, Treaty Series, vol. 189, p. 152, online www.refworld.org/docid/3be01b964.html). Today, migration scholars and international agencies readily acknowledge that the existing definitions, such as "voluntary" verses "forced migration" fail to recognize the more complex reality of human mobility across borders, which is better captured by terms such as "mixed migration" or "people out of place," which aim to highlight the mixed motives and multiplying drivers of mobility and displacement (escaping persecution, political instability, hunger, dire poverty, extreme environmental conditions, and so on). A debate is now brewing about whether the privileged legal protection granted to those fleeing a well-founded fear of persecution (the pinnacle of the internationally recognized definition of a refugee, emanating from the 1951 Refugee Convention) captures the full range of just claims for asylum, and whether additional instruments of international cooperation should be introduced in order to address the plight of displaced persons who do not meet the legal definition of refugee. For further elaboration, see Jill I. Goldenziel, 'Displaced: A Proposal for an International Agreement to Protect Refugees, Migrants, and States', *Berkeley Journal of International Law 35* (2017): pp. 47–89; Alexander Betts, *Survival Migration: Failed Governance and the Crisis of Displacement* (Ithaca: Cornell University Press, 2013); Matthew Price, *Rethinking Asylum: History, Purpose, and Limits* (Cambridge: Cambridge University Press, 2009).

A new road map is required to decipher the emerging code of the shifting border in a world in which prosperous "islands" of high standards of human rights, affluence, and democratic governance are increasingly protected through the operation of "portable" legal walls that may appear, disappear, and reappear in variable coordinates of space and time. This shifting border changes form depending on how it is approached and by whom. The better we comprehend the new logic and codebook informing these conceptual changes and policy instruments, the better positioned we will be to develop counter narratives and to carve out new theoretical and applied pathways to oppose their deleterious effects. I seek to fill an important gap in the refined scholarly and policy discourse by offering a grounded analysis, a fine-grained inquiry into the causes and consequences, explanatory and interpretive resources required to grasp the constitutive features of this new paradigm. After exploring the core implications of these recent transformations, I will develop innovative, real-world democratic and institutional responses to counter the rights-restricting dimensions of the shifting border.

The discussion proceeds in three parts, and it operates on three inter-related levels: diagnostic, interpretive, and prescriptive. I begin by painting a picture of the complex, multilayered, and ever transforming border, one that is drawn and redrawn by the words of law. To comprehend the novelty of the shifting border, I will contrast it with contending models: the classic, clearly demarcated, territorial border that serves as the frontline for setting barriers to admission; and the alternate, globalist, vision of a world in which extant borders are, or soon will be, traversed with the greatest of ease, to the extent that they become all but meaningless. In combination with the sheer number of people on the move, this has led some scholars to argue that the grip of borders, or the even the fundamental principle of territoriality itself, is waning in a world "where agency (individual choice) takes precedence over structures (the laws and rules of territorial states)."[22] As a corollary, it has been argued that in

---

[22] James F. Hollifield, 'Sovereignty and Migration', in Matthew J. Gibney and Randall Hansen, eds, *Immigration and Asylum from 1900 to the Present* (Santa Barbara: ABC-CLIO, 2005), pp. 574–576, p. 575.

the current age of globalization, sovereignty is waning and states are losing control over their authority to determine whom to include and whom to exclude.[23] The actual legal practices and exercise of authority by governments operating under the shifting-border framework, alas, refute this narrative of global, unidirectional progression toward a borderless world. Instead, we witness a more dynamic process of change whereby states—acting alone or in concert—are reinventing and reinvigorating their borders and membership boundaries in profound ways.[24] By locating the shifting border as an alternative to the established theoretical poles of "static" and "disappearing" boundaries, I aim to show that the proposed framework of analysis more fully captures and accounts for the profound patterns of change that we are witnessing in the world around us. To substantiate these claims about the multidirectionality of the shifting border, I will focus on the legal innovations adopted by the world's leading immigrant-receiving countries that have spearheaded the shifting border paradigm: the United States, Canada, and Australia. I will also demonstrate how the European Union and its member states have also rewritten pages—if not chapters—of the

[23] Among those defending the post-national claim that universal personhood has surpassed the significance of national belonging, see Yasemin N. Soysal, *Limits of Citizenship: Migrants and Postnational Membership in Europe* (Chicago: University of Chicago, 1994); David Jacobson, *Rights across Borders: Immigration and the Decline of Citizens* (Baltimore: Johns Hopkins University Press, 1996). Political theorists have advanced a justice argument for more open borders as a challenge to the prevailing legal situation, according to which states may legitimately exercise their authority to restrict mobility and control access to their territorial jurisdiction. The full list is too vast to cite. For an early influential article, see Joseph H. Carens, 'Aliens and Citizens: The Case for Open Borders', *The Review of Politics 49* (1987): pp. 251–273. See also Abizadeh, 'Democratic Theory and Border Coercion' (n 14). For contrasting views justifying the right of states to exclude, see Christopher Heath Wellman, 'Immigration and Freedom of Association', *Ethics 119* (2008): pp. 109–141. More critical accounts have emphasized the themes of immobilization, entrapment, the tightening of entry controls, and the emergence of a paradigm of suspicion. The last term is drawn from Ronen Shamir, 'Without Borders? Notes on Globalization as a Mobility Regime', *Sociological Theory 23* (2005): pp. 197–217. For rich empirical evidence to support these claims, see, for example, Eric Neumayer, 'Unequal Access to Foreign Spaces: How States Use Visa Restrictions to Regulate Mobility in a Globalized World', *Transactions of the Institute of British Geographers 31* (2006): pp. 72–84, 2006; Mau, 'The Global Mobility Divide' (n 16).

[24] While in some cases operating unilaterally, states are also devising increasingly complex and multilayered mobility-control regimes that require extensive interstate cooperation. For an excellent exploration of bilateral cooperation in the North American context, see Matthew Longo, *The Politics of Borders: Sovereignty, Security, and the Citizen after 9/11* (Cambridge: Cambridge University Press, 2018).

shifting-border book in the context of re-bordering mobility through extensive "externalization" strategies. These case studies provide a rich empirical foundation upon which the rest of the discussion relies.

Next, I place the analysis within a broader range of pressing debates, from the recent "methodological turn" in political theory to revisiting the demise-of-the-state thesis to evaluating how the ability of major actors to "shift" the level and timing of regulation in the service of the every-where-and-nowhere border strains earlier predictions that supranationalism and transnationalism will, almost necessarily, contribute to emancipatory developments. I further highlight the role of private third parties and the growing reliance on cooperation agreements with transit and host countries that create "buffer zones" around affluent democracies in exchange for material and infrastructure investments. Such processes of externalization are enthusiastically pursued by the European Union and its member states, raising real concerns about human rights abuses and "outsourcing" responsibility. Any attempt at theory building that seeks to move beyond idealized discussions of borders and membership boundaries must engage more directly with these empirical observations. This is vital if we want our non-ideal theories of migration, mobility, justice, multilevel governance, and democratic legitimacy to have relevance to the here and now.

Lastly, I revisit the relationship between law and territoriality, space and political responsibility, including the classic writings of Hannah Arendt, before engaging in the always perilous act of seeking pragmatically minded responses to seemingly intractable dilemmas. This part of the discussion brings together insights from law, political philosophy, and institutional design to explore innovative ways in which to "internalize" the costs of the extraterritorial dimensions of migration control. Moving from the interpretive to the aspirational, I will argue that the dramatic reconception of the border requires an equally radical reinvention of our responses to these new realities on the ground. To realign the almost boundless reach of migration control in the age of shifting borders with adherence to human rights norms by state actors (or their delegates, public and private), this final section will explore fresh ideas for crafting participatory and contestatory political responses to, as well as legal remedies for, today's new paradoxes of border control. In order to tame the rights-restricting tendencies documented in this study, we must not only decipher but also seek to "rewrite" the code of the everywhere-and-nowhere shifting border, infusing it with a migrant- and mobility-centered perspective that recognizes that states will continue to be key players in the current world order while at the same time de-centering them. One such promising direction for change is to amend the bases for attributing responsibility in a world of de-territorialized migration control. Instead of focusing on *where* the act of border regulation takes place, a more consistent and fair approach requires adopting a functional or jurisdictional test according to which obligations to protect are activated as soon as "effective control" occurs by official agents of states, acting alone or in concert, or their delegates.[25] The idea is to acknowledge the restless agility and multi-scalar operations of the shifting border as eliciting a set of rights-enhancing protections from the restricting states, which hitherto have relied on this new "technology" of governance and spatiality to escape accountability and constrain rights. This line of response incorporates the very logic of de-territorialized migration control that lies at the heart of the shifting border, while at the same time subverting it, and relies on two prongs: expanding the extraterritorial reach of human rights and relaxing the fixation on territorial access. While not a panacea, the endeavor is to break the current deadlock and refute the claim that applicable solutions are beyond reach or impossible to imagine.

1. Locating the shifting border: neither static, nor disappearing

To understand the tremendous resources and creativity invested in the shifting border in a world of conflicting demands of openness and

[25] This position is shared by many human rights organizations and is also the theory that guided the ECtHR in the landmark *Hirsi v. Italy,* [GC], App, No. 27765/09, Eur. Ct. H.R. (2012). For an early defense of the position that "[n]arrow territorial interpretation of human rights treaties is an anathema to the basic idea of human rights, which is to ensure that a state should respect human rights of persons over whom it exercises jurisdiction," see Theodor Meron, 'Extraterritoriality of Human Rights Treaties', *American Journal of International Law* 89 (1995): pp. 78–82, p. 82.

closure, we need to go back to basics, to revisit the dimension of territoriality, a core facet of the modern conception of sovereignty and its geography of power. In the world created in the image of the Westphalian system, "[s]overeignty is an idea of authority embodied in those bordered territorial organizations we refer to as 'states.' . . . [It] is one of the constituent ideas of the post-medieval world: it conveys a distinctive configuration of politics and law that sets the modern era apart from previous eras."[26] In the post-Westphalian literature, by contrast, the core prognosis is that the relevance of borders is declining, sovereignty is diminishing, and states as territorially bounded "containers" of power and authority are dissipating.[27] Neither of these perspectives captures the new paradigm shift we are witnessing.

The classic Westphalian ideal of statehood sees the border as a permanent and *static* barrier that stands at the frontier of a country's territory. This formidable border serves a crucial role in delimiting (externally) and binding (internally) a nation's territory, jurisdiction, and peoplehood, correlating with a notion of fixed "legal spatiality."[28] For many years, this concept permeated our thinking about mobility, borders, and sovereignty, pushing us into what political geographers refer to as the "territorial trap."[29] This trap, and the assumption undergirding it, reifies and naturalizes the global grid of lines demarcating states as

---

[26] Robert Jackson, *Sovereignty: The Evolution of an Idea* (Oxford: Polity Press, 2007), pp. ix, 1.

[27] On states as "power containers," see Anthony Giddens, *The Nation-State and Violence: Volume Two of A Contemporary Critique of Historical Materialism* (Berkeley: University of California Press, 1985), p. 13. An influential and sophisticated articulation of this argument, from a sociological perspective, is found in Saskia Sassen, *Losing Control? Sovereignty in an Age of Globalization* (New York: Columbia University Press, 1996).

[28] Kal Raustiala, 'The Geography of Justice', *Fordham Law Review 73* (2005): pp. 2501–2560, p. 2503. See also John H. Herz, 'Rise and Demise of the Territorial State', *World Politics 9* (1957): pp. 473–493, pp. 480–481.

[29] John Agnew, 'The Territorial Trap: The Geographical Assumptions of International Relations Theory', *Review of International Political Economy 9* (1994): pp. 53–80. The term "territorial trap" seeks to raise otherwise buried assumptions that treat the state's territory as if it were forever fixed and insulated—a "frozen geography" (a term also coined by Agnew)—camouflaging the fact that territory, in the context of sovereign exercise of power over it, is not natural or pre-political but rather constructed and reconstructed through law and politics. Another closely related image is that of states and borders operating as "containers." See also Giddens, *The Nation-State and Violence* (n 27); Peter J. Taylor, 'The State as Container: Territoriality in the Modern World-System', *Progress in Human Geography 18* (1994): pp. 151–162.

though they represent bounded territorial units with mutually exclusive borders. States are envisioned as having a monopoly over the legitimate exercise of power and authority in their clearly demarcated domains, thereby politicizing space and bringing it under juridical control.

Under the Westphalian lens and lexis, the modern state *is* a territorial state. Territoriality, or the territorial principle, here understood as the proposition that a legitimate government has ultimate authority over a defined territory and its population, is a central feature of the classic understanding of the current international world order.[30] The territorial principle plays, on this familiar and "naturalized" account, a key role in constituting respect for international borders and justifying their operation to demarcate "places, territories, and categories," thereby producing a cartographic image of the world as a "jigsaw puzzle of solid color pieces fitting neatly together."[31] Borders, according to this perspective, are the black lines we draw on our maps to divide up the world, with dramatic ramifications for the scope of rights and protections offered to individuals, depending on where said individuals stand in relations to these divvying lines. This process distinguishes between member and non-member, insider and outsider, the interior and the exterior, in the world's jigsaw-puzzle map. Only citizens have a guaranteed right to enter and remain within the jurisdiction of the territorial state; all others require permission to gain such access.[32] For the bulk of humanity, then,

[30] For an illuminating conceptual and historical overview, see Matej Avbelj, 'Theorizing Sovereignty and European Integration', *Ratio Juris* 27 (2014): pp. 344–363.
[31] Alexander C. Diner and Joshua Hagan, *Borders: A Very Short Introduction* (Oxford: Oxford University Press, 2012), p. 1; Karen Knop, 'Statehood: Territory, People, Government', in James Crawford and Martti Koskenniemi, eds, *The Cambridge Companion to International Law* (Cambridge: Cambridge University Press, 2012), pp. 95–116, p. 95.
[32] Human rights provisions guarantee individuals a right to exit their home countries but do not provide them with a right to enter other countries. See, most famously, UN General Assembly, *Universal Declaration of Human Rights*, 217 [III] A, Paris, 1948, Article 13(b). The exceptional limitation to this otherwise "plenary power" (in the terminology of US law) or "royal prerogative" (as it is known in the United Kingdom) of states over borders and migration control is vested in individuals at risk who seek protection by claiming asylum, which in the "ordinary situation will require a state to suspend its rules of immigration control and undertake an asylum procedure or equivalent to determine if such a risk is present." See Thomas Grammeltoft-Hansen, 'Extraterritorial Immigration Control and the Reach of Human Rights', in Vincent Chetail and Céline Bauloz, eds,

gaining lawful admission to desired destination countries remains "a privilege granted by the sovereign."[33] This makes control of the border the liminal and legal linchpin of migration regulation.

Given the intricate connection between sovereign authority, territory, and legal spatiality, it was logically assumed, under the Westphalian model, that it is precisely *at the border* that agents of the state are permitted to exercise the utmost control over access, including the power to make the decision "to turn back from our gates any alien or class of aliens."[34] US immigration and nationality law, for example, has long held that an alien who is stopped at the border enjoys far less protection than a person who is already within the country.[35] Such rights remain unavailable to would-be immigrants, so long as they remain outside the geographical borders of the United States.[36] The notion that legal circumstances affecting non-members substantively change after they cross "our gates" is a manifestation of the vision of a world order that imagines hermetically sealed legal spatiality alongside delineated and permanent borders. Yet these assumptions are increasingly strained. While continuing to formally rely on the fixed conception of the border, with rigid binary distinctions between the exterior and the interior, law-and-order agencies situated at multiple levels and junctures of governance simultaneously expand the actual (largely unchecked) scope and reach of their migration and border control activities far beyond the edges of the territory and deep into the interior.

This spatial and operational aggrandizement of regulatory power has not yet been matched by a corresponding expansion of responsibilities *beyond* borders, especially in relation to those who are most

---

Research Handbook on International Law and Migration (Cheltenham: Edward Elgar, 2014), pp. 113–131, p. 114.

[33] This is the classic formulation articulated by the United States Supreme Court in the case of *United States ex. rel. Knauff v. Shaughnessy*, 228 U.S. 537 (1950) (United States). In rule-of-law societies, which are the subject of inquiry here, such determinations are made by authorized officials based on rules, regulations, and provisions stipulated in domestic and international law.

[34] *United States ex rel. Knauff v. Shaughnessy*, 338 U.S. 537 (1950) (United States) (dissenting, Jackson, J.).

[35] This dates back to the early twentieth century. See, for example, *Kaplan v. Tod,* 267 U.S. 228 (1925) (United States).

[36] *United States v. Verdugo-Urquidez*, 494 U.S. 259 (1990) (United States).

directly and adversely affected by the shifting border of migration regulation: undocumented, unauthorized, smuggled, trafficked, or otherwise "irregular" migrants , including those seeking refuge and asylum.[37]
Before I turn to a more detailed assessment of these new shifting-border measures, and how to potentially tame their sting, it is imperative
to establish the foundation upon which the shifting border lies: the creation of a "moveable," transportable legal wall that variably shrinks,
expands, disappears, and reappears across space and time in the service
of managed and selective migration and mobility regimes.

The shifting border in action: bleeding inward, stretching outward

Consider the following examples, from near and far.[38] As part of a
major reform to US immigration regulation, a procedure called "expedited removal" was introduced into law.[39] This legal provision permits
frontline officers and border agents both to expeditiously return undocumented migrants at the border and to review the legal status of individuals detected up to 100 miles away from any US land or coastal
border, in effect "moving" the border from its fixed location at the
country's territorial edges into the interior (Map 1.1).[40]

---

[37] I return to this point in the final part of the discussion. On these tensions, see, for example,
      Andrew Brouwer and Judith Kumin, 'Interception and Asylum: When Migration Con-
      trol and Human Rights Collide', *Refuge 21* (2003): pp. 6–24.

[38] These examples were selected for illustrative purposes; they are not exhaustive. This sec-
      tion draws upon and adapts arguments developed in Ayelet Shachar, 'Bordering Migra-
      tion/Migrating Borders', *Berkeley Journal of International Law 37* (2019): pp. 93–147.

[39] This procedure was ushered in as part of the Illegal Immigration Reform and Immigrant
      Responsibility Act of 1996 ('IIRIRA'), Pub. L. No. 104–208, 110 Stat. 3009-546. Expedited
      removal grants the Attorney General (now the Secretary of Homeland Security) "sole and
      unreviewable discretion" to apply expedited removal to any class of aliens who "[have]
      not been admitted or paroled into the United States." See Immigration and Nationality
      Act, 8 USC. § 1225(b)(1)(A)(iii)(II) (United States). The only exception to this rule is that
      an arriving non-citizen who indicates an intention to apply for asylum and establishes
      "credible fear" of persecution is detained and referred to an asylum officer who must
      determine whether the individual will be permitted access to the US asylum system.
      The spatial and temporal reach of expedited removal was further expanded in 2019.

[40] As one scholar succinctly put it, this removal procedure "sharply redefined—downward—
      what process is due an individual who arrives at [the] border and is deemed not to have
      proper documents to enter." See Stephen M. Knight, 'Defining Due Process Down: Expe-
      dited Removal in the United States', *Refuge 19* (2001): pp. 41–47, p. 41.

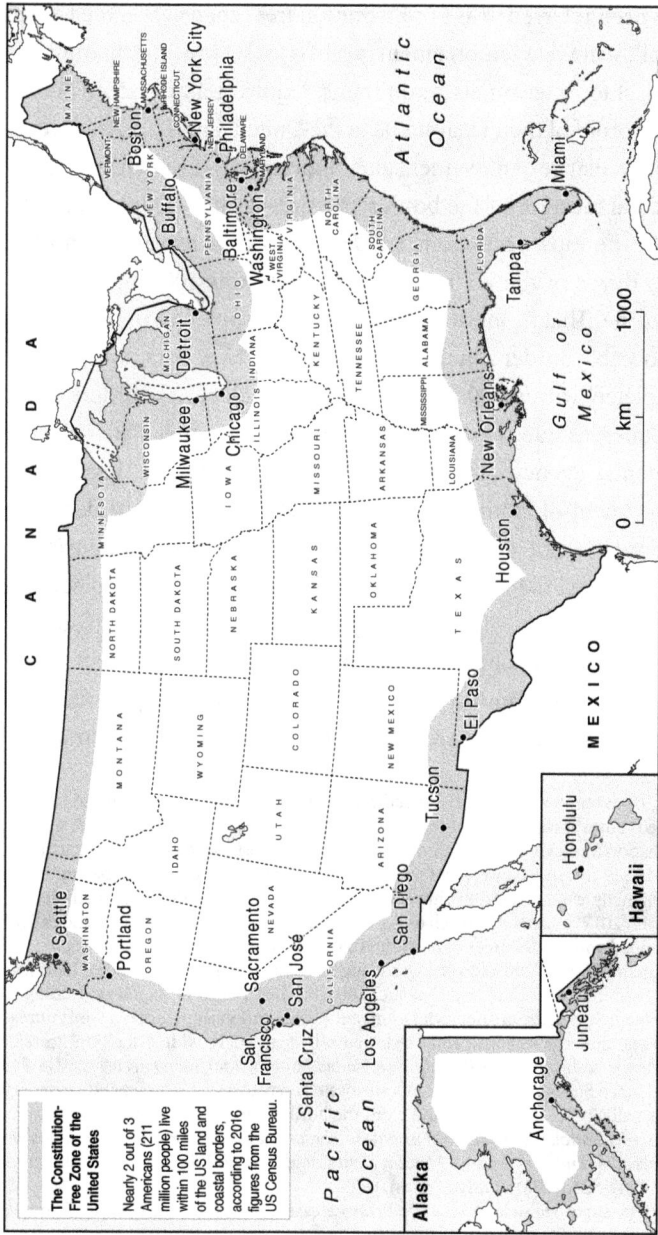

Map 1.1 United States: the shifting border—bleeding into the interior (redrawn from ACLU: www.aclu.org/know-your-rights-constitution-free-zone-map)

The Constitution-Free Zone of the United States

Nearly 2 out of 3 Americans (211 million people) live within 100 miles of the US land and coastal borders, according to 2016 figures from the US Census Bureau.

This legal maneuver not only relocates the border but also creates what has been referred to as a "constitution free" zone *within* the United States—allowing law-enforcement agents to set up checkpoints on highways, at ferry terminals, or on trains, requiring any random person to provide proof of their legal status in the United States.[41] Such governmental surveillance of movement and mobility—traditionally restricted to the actual location of the border crossing—is now seeping into the interior.[42] The most recent official US census data reveal that no less than two thirds of the US population lives in this 100-mile constitution-lite zone. That is, more than 200 million people live in the malleable or moveable border zone. The whole state of New York, for example, lies completely within 100 miles of the land and coastal borders of the United States, as does Florida, another migrant-magnet state. And the governmental agency responsible for managing the shifting border, the Department of Homeland Security, has gone on record declaring that its border-enforcement measures may well expand "*nationwide.*"[43]

Until recently, the prospect of nationwide implementation seemed to belong squarely in the realm of the futuristic and the implausible. However, in today's political environment of "getting tough" on immigration, the current administration's commitment to "using all statutory authorities to the greatest extent possible" has the potential to translate

[41] These current temporal and spatial specifications appear in the Federal Register. In 2002, expedited removal was extended to all those who had entered the United States without authorization by water and could not establish to the satisfaction of a border agent that they had been continuously present in the country for at least two years. Cuban nationals were originally exempted from this class. However, that exemption was rescinded on January 17, 2017. In 2004, the reach of expedited removal was expanded to include aliens apprehended within 100 miles of a US international border within 14 days of entry. See Department of Homeland Security, Designated Aliens for Expedited Removal (n 19).

[42] The US Supreme Court has held that such internal checkpoints on highways leading to or away from the border are not a violation of the constitutional guarantee against unreasonable searches and seizures, and border-patrol agents "have wide discretion" to refer motorists for additional questioning. See *United States v. Martinez-Fuerte*, 428 US 543 (1976) (United States). Such checkpoints are located on major US highways and secondary roads, usually 25 to 100 miles inland from the border. See Government Accountability Office, *Border Patrol: Checkpoints Contribute to Border Patrol's Mission, but More Consistent Data Collection and Performance Measurement Could Improve Effectiveness* (Washington, DC: GAO 09-824, 2008) (United States), p. 7.

[43] US Department of Homeland Security, Press Release, *Fact Sheet: Secure Border Initiative* (November 2, 2005) (emphasis added), p. l.

into a massive spatial and temporal expansion of expedited removal.[44] Supplemented by multiple executive orders and accompanying memos, expedited removal could potentially reach "*any* immigrant *anywhere* in the United States who can't prove that they've been in the country for two or more years."[45] A simple notice in the Federal Register is all that is required to make this sweeping augmentation of the border into a legal reality. With the strike of the pen, the "interior" could be recast as the "exterior" for the purposes of immigration control under the shifting-border paradigm. Turning the whole area of the United States into an expedited-removal zone sounds like science fiction. It is not. In 2019, the Trump administration issued a new rule authorizing just such massive, nationwide expansion.[46]

In addition to conjuring mirror-house-like stretching and contracting movements, the shifting border also distinguishes between *physical entry* into the country (which does not count for immigration purposes)

[44] On January 25, 2017, President Donald Trump issued Executive Order 13767, Border Security and Immigration Enforcement Improvements, 82 Fed. Reg. Presidential Documents 8793, January 27, 2017 (United States) and Executive Order 13768, Enhancing Public Safety in the Interior of the United States, 82 Fed. Reg. Presidential Documents 8799, January 30, 2017 (United States), which cumulatively hold the potential to dramatically expand the reach of expedited removal. Subsequently, Department of Homeland Security Secretary John Kelly issued two memos on the implementation of the aforementioned executive orders. Read together, the memos committed to using all "statutory authorities to the greatest extent possible" and promised a new Notice Designating Aliens Subject to Expedited Removal to be published in the Federal Register. Based on the language of the executive orders and memos, some observers have concluded that the Secretary intends to utilize his discretion to the fullest extent authorized, both spatially (nationwide) and temporally (two years).

[45] Parties in *Castro* and *Peralta-Sanchez* raised the likelihood of such expansion in their arguments (emphasis added). See interview with ACLU lawyers for *Castro*, Esther Yu Hsi Lee, 'Immigrant Families Aren't Getting Their Day in Court', online https://thinkprogress.org/immigrant-families-arent-getting-their-day-in-court-f7edc1026c2c/; source for *Peralta-Sanchez*: Bob Egelko, 'Court Denies Immigrants Right to Attorney in Expedited Deportations', *SFGate*, February 7, 2017, online www.sfgate.com/nation/article/Court-denies-immigrants-Sright-to-attorney-in-10915296.php.

[46] In July 2019, as this book was sent for publication, the US government authorized just such a nationwide expansion, enabling the Department of Homeland Security to apply expedited removal to aliens encountered *anywhere* in the United States for up to two years after their arrival. See Department of Homeland Security, Designated Aliens for Expedited Removal, 84 Fed. Reg. 35409, 23 July 2019 (United States). A preliminary injunction issued by the courts prohibits the enforcement of this policy change, pending the outcome of litigation challenging it. I thank Alex Aleinikoff and Jaya Ramji-Nogales for helpful discussions regarding these developments and the various legal scenarios that may follow.

and *lawful admission* through a recognized port of entry (which makes one's presence in the territory permissible, and therefore visible, in the eyes of the regulatory state).[47] In this legal maneuver, entry into the territory—the material act of crossing the geographical border and physically being present within the jurisdiction of the United States—does *not* equate with legally "being here."[48] This change in the meaning is formalized into law: "an alien present in the United States without being admitted," to recite the somewhat cryptic language of the Immigration and Nationality Act, is treated as though she (who is already present on the territory) had never really crossed the border into the country.[49] This legal fiction has serious consequences for those aliens "present in the United States without being admitted." For instance, their unlawful admission also effectuates the preclusion of status regularization or the application of waivers during the removal process, thereby causing them to forfeit their prospect of future lawful admission to the United States.[50] Moreover, the very act of crossing without inspection and permission (the otherwise unrecognized presence of the non-citizen in the territory) is turned into the "main substantive charge used to remove them."[51]

[47] The notion that legal circumstances affecting non-members change dramatically after the latter "pass through our gates" is well established, as canonical case law from *Shaughnessy* to *Zadvydas* attests. *Shaughnessy v. United States ex rel. Mezei*, 345 U.S. 206 (1953) (United States); *Zadvydas v. Davis*, 533 U.S. 678 (2001) (United States). See also *Kaplan v. Tod*, 267 U.S. 228 (1925) (United States).

[48] The term "being here" is drawn from Linda Bosniak's critical investigation into the ethical significance of territorial presence of unauthorized migrants. See Linda Bosniak, 'Being Here' (n 3). Other circumstances whereby "reaching what appears to be the territorial border may not constitute being 'inside'" are creatively explored by Leti Volpp, 'Imagining of Space in Immigration Law', *Law, Culture and the Humanities 9* (2012): pp. 456–474, p. 459. This spatial and legal blurring of the inside and the outside challenges a binary framework of "hard edges and soft interior," as Bosniak memorably put it. See Linda Bosniak, *The Citizens and the Alien* (Princeton: Princeton University Press, 2008), p. 4. With the shifting border we witness the emergence of a combination of hard–hard, both inside and outside, for some (for example, those who enter without permission) and soft–soft for others (for example, those who purchase access to citizenship without even stepping foot on the inside). See Ayelet Shachar, 'The Marketization of Citizenship in an Age of Restrictionism', *Ethics and International Affairs 32* (2018): pp. 3–13.

[49] Immigration and Nationality Act, 8 U.S.C. § 1182(a)(6)(A)(i) (United States). These individuals will have certain constitutional protections while in the country.

[50] Immigration and Nationality Act, codified as 8 U.S.C. § 1182(a)(6)(A)(i) and § 1227 (United States). See the waivers from removal specified in 8 C. § 1227(a)(1)(H), which are easier to establish than those appearing in 8 U.S.C. § 1182(i).

[51] There is also a ten-year bar to readmission.

Another such ramification is that those on the "inside" deemed to be on the "outside," including the hundreds of thousands of people expeditiously removed each year, find themselves in a parallel universe of "nonexistent procedural safeguards."[52] As a recent court decision put it, for those facing expedited removal, "[t]here is no right to appear in front of a judge and no right to hire legal representation. There is no hearing, no neutral decision-maker, no evidentiary findings, and no right to appeal."[53] When such far-reaching denial of basic procedural fairness occurs in an established democracy such as the United States, it tests not only our notions of territoriality but legality as well. Recent figures show that a "staggering 83% of the people removed from the United States ... were [expeditiously] removed without a hearing, without a judge, without legal representation, and without the opportunity to apply for most forms of relief from removals."[54] The traditional constitutional and human rights arsenal of responses has proven toothless in the face of these new realities. To begin to counter this reality, we must familiarize ourselves with the shifting legal ground upon which this immense, and almost unrestricted, governmental power to determine whom to exclude or remove now stands.

In creating the legal distinction between "entry" and "admission," US immigration law effectively treats individuals present in the country without authorization as though they had been stopped *at the border*—depriving them of the traditional protections enjoyed by non-citizens who have actually made it into the interior. Such a legal maneuver can only occur by "redrawing the traditional exclusion–deportation line" under a shifting conception of the border.[55] The exclusion–deportation line has become *de-territorialized*: the key factor for the legal analysis is

---

[52] *U.S. v. Peralta Sanchez*, 868 F.3rd 852 (9th Cir. 2017) (United States), p. 35 (dissenting, Pregerson, J.).

[53] Ibid., pp. 34–35.

[54] Ibid., p. 35. The 83 percent figure comes from Department of Homeland Security immigration-enforcement data for fiscal year 2013 and covers expedited and reinstatement of removal procedures, both of which are grounded in the IIRIRA reform and fast-tracked.

[55] T. Alexander Aleinikoff *et al.*, eds, *Immigration and Citizenship: Process and Policy*, 5th edition (Eagan: West, 2003), p. 428.

not whether the person has passed through the territory's physical frontiers; rather, the question for immigration-regulation purposes is whether the person has crossed at any time or place through *the law's gates of admission*, which, as the authorizing legislation proclaims without hesitation, are not territorially fixed but rather "designated" by the executive branch of government.[56]

Just as the shifting border bleeds into the interior, it extends the long arm of the state outward, ever more flexibly, to regulate mobility at a distance. To provide but one example, travelers who wish to embark on a US-bound flight now regularly encounter the US border or its authorized guardians—US officials located on foreign soil—in places as diverse as Freeport and Nassau in the Bahamas, Dublin and Shannon in Ireland, and Abu Dhabi in the United Arab Emirates.[57] Thanks to a legal carve-out known as the preclearance system, these procedures regularly take place in foreign transit hubs that are sometimes located tens, hundreds, or even thousands of miles away from the "homeland" territory.

This reinvention of the border and the kind of legal framework it relies upon—allowing the United States to exercise sovereign control over its border, far away from its territory, on the home turf of *another* nation-state—is "a really big deal," explained the Secretary of the

---

[56] Immigration and Nationality Act, 8 U.S.C. § 1182(a)(6)(A)(i) (United States).

[57] After 9/11, the Department of Homeland Security was established. It combined the functions of the former Immigration and Naturalization Service (INS) and the former US Customs Service. Currently, several agencies within the Department of Homeland Security perform the duties of border patrol and interior enforcement. The US Customs and Border Protection (CBP) is the largest uniformed federal law-enforcement agency in the country. Its agents have the authority to safeguard America's borders at officially designated ports of entry in the United States as well as a growing number of preclearance locations outside the country. See US Customs and Border Protection, 'Preclearance Locations', online www.cbp.gov/border-security/ports-entry/operations/preclearance. The US Border Patrol (BP) is part of CBP, which is responsible for patrolling the areas at and around US international borders: namely, the 100-mile zone in which expedited removal takes place, where BP agents have the jurisdiction to detect, apprehend, investigate, and detain "illegal aliens and smugglers of aliens at or near the land [and coastal] border." Lastly, US Immigration and Customs Enforcement (ICE) is responsible for locating persons who are within the remaining areas of the United States without authorization and removing them where relevant. The combined budget of these immigration-enforcement agencies is larger than all other federal enforcement agencies combined.

Department of Homeland Security in an interview with the *New York Times*:

> it would be like us saying you can have a foreign law enforcement operating in a US facility with all the privileges given to law enforcement, but we are going to do it on your territory and on our rules . . . So if you flip it around, you realize it is a big deal for [another] country to agree to that.[58]

Currently, more than 600 US customs and border-control and agricultural specialists are deployed in airports around the world, processing over 18 million US-bound passengers per year *before* they embark on their air-travel journey toward the United States. An ambitious expansion program for such preclearance and pre-inspection procedures was launched in 2015 with the goal of preclearing, on foreign soil, at least a third of all US-bound air travelers by 2040. Such expansion is expected to promote US interests by facilitating international trade and travel, while at the same time countering global security threats by allowing the "United States and our international partners to jointly identify and address threats at the earliest possible point" (conflating priority in time with location and distance), as the official publication of the US border-protection agency simply and elegantly summarizes the thinking behind this manifestation of the shifting border, highlighting its outward expansion.[59] Strikingly, such pre-inspection decisions bear the full weight of US law, as though their determinations were made "at the border"—although the territory of the United States is very far from sight. The border has instead been replanted as a legal construct on non-US soil.

While no other country operates its immigration control on US soil, the United States has now entered advanced negotiations to build more preclearance capacity at airports overseas, seeking to further expand its reach

[58] Janet Napolitano, then Secretary of the Department of Homeland Security (quoted in Michael S. Schmidt, 'US Security Expands Presence at Foreign Airports', *The New York Times*, July 13, 2012).
[59] US Customs and Border Protection, 'CBP Releases Fiscal Year 2015 Trade and Travel Numbers' (March 4, 2016), online www.cbp.gov/newsroom/national-media-release/cbp-releases-fiscal-year-2015-trade-and-travel-numbers.

into new regions and continents.[60] The rationale for such expansion is drawn straight from the playbook of the shifting border. As the government's highest officials readily pronounce, the intent is to "take every opportunity we have to push our [operations] out beyond our borders so that we are not defending the homeland from the one-yard mile."[61]

Critics, for their part, have decried such developments, arguing that coupled with increasingly intrusive reporting and monitoring requirements for international travel, the heightened risk of privacy violations reflects a "dystopian vision of a 'transatlantic security space' involving an exchange of [passenger] records, fingerprints and personal data."[62] Despite initial skepticism and concerns about compliance with the European Convention on Human Rights, key European countries such as Belgium, the Netherlands, Norway, Spain, Sweden, and the United Kingdom now permit, or are in the process of finalizing, approval for US officials to obtain "quasi-operative competences at European airports" so as to perform security checks on passengers before they embark on transatlantic flights.[63] Iceland and Italy are the latest countries to have joined this list.[64]

---

[60] In addition to extending migration control for air travel, the United States also has a long history of interdiction at sea, which has engendered the controversial US Supreme Court *Sale* precedent, according to which the summary return of migrants, including asylum seekers, interdicted on the high seas does not engage the *non-refoulement* obligation to which the United States, like other rich democracies, has committed through both its domestic and international law obligations. *Haitian Centers Council, Inc. v. McNary*, 807 F. Supp. 928 (E.D.N.Y. 1992). *cert. granted, Haitian Centers Council v. McNary*, 506 U.S. 814 (1992) (United States).

[61] Department of Homeland Security Press Office, Press Release, 'DHS Announces Intent to Expand Preclearance to 10 New Airports' (May 29, 2015), online www.dhs.gov/news/2015/05/29/dhs-announces-intent-expand-preclearance-10-new-airports (quoting Secretary of Homeland Security, Jen Johnson). See also Ron Nixon, 'Homeland Security Goes Abroad. Not Everyone Is Grateful', *The New York Times*, December 26, 2017 (estimating that over 2,000 Homeland Security employees, including immigration- and customs-enforcement special agents, are now deployed to more than seventy countries around the world).

[62] Philip Oltermann, 'UK May Allow the US Security Checks on Passengers before Transatlantic Travel', *The Guardian*, September 11, 2014, online www.theguardian.com/uk-news/2014/sep/11/uk-us-security-checks-passengers.

[63] Department of Homeland Security Press Office, 'DHS Announces Intent to Expand' (n 61).

[64] Department of Homeland Security Press Office, Press Release, 'DHS Announces 11 New Airports Selected for Possible Preclearance Expansion Following Second Open Season' (November 4, 2016), online www.dhs.gov/news/2016/11/04/dhs-announces-11-new-airports-selected-possible-preclearance-expansion-following.

Such measures for screening individuals before their arrival at a desired destination may well prove to be the wave of the future; they are arguably a regulator's dream tool for deterring unwanted admission. As the International Organization for Migration (IOM) noted in a recent report, "[m]any states which have the ability to do so find that intercepting migrants before they reach their territories is one of the most effective measures to enforce their domestic immigration laws and policies."[65] This insight has not been lost by the architects of the shifting border. The governing legislation in the United States, the Immigration and Nationality Act, now authorizes US customs and immigration-protection officers to examine and inspect the passengers and crew of "any aircraft, vessel, or train proceeding directly, without stopping, from a port or place in foreign territory to a port-of-entry in the United States" at its point of origin.[66] Such decisions made by US officers stationed at these non-US locations are *final* determinations of admissibility. A fine example is found in the arid, bureaucratic words of US immigration law, which hold that inspection made "at the port or place in the foreign territory . . . shall have the same effect under the Act as though made at the destined port-of-entry in the United States." This radical "re-location" of the border—placing it in a foreign territory's jurisdiction—is made possible through a combination of domestic authorization and transnational cooperation (typically bilateral agreements with the countries on whose territory US agents are permitted to conduct the preclearance).

The United States' shifting border is part of a larger transformation involving legislative and regulatory actions undertaken by other leading destination countries. The Canadian government, for example, proclaims itself a "world leader in developing interdiction strategies against illegal migration."[67] Apart from Canada's massive shared land border with the United States, it is otherwise surrounded by large bodies of

[65] Human Rights Watch *et al.*, *NGO Background Paper on the Refugee and Migration Interface* (2001), online www.hrw.org/report/2001/06/28/ngo-background-paper-refugee-and-migration-interface.
[66] Code of Federal Regulations, 8 C.F.R. § 235.5(b) (2014) (United States).
[67] Janet Dench, 'Controlling the Borders: C-31 and Interdiction', *Refuge 19* (2001): pp. 34–40, p. 37.

water and ice. Given its geopolitical location, Canada relies heavily on overseas interdiction. Over the years, it has perfected the technique of interdiction abroad, effectively relocating much of its migration-regulation activities to overseas gateways, located primarily in Europe and Asia, where migration-integrity officers, or liaison officers (as they are now called), conduct border-control activities as a matter of course, although they are nowhere near the formal edge or frontier of Canadian territory. Instead, as a key component of the shifting-border strategy, these government officials are strategically located in "key foreign embarkation, transit and immigration points around the world."[68] As official documents put it, this part of Canada's border strategy strives to "'push the border out' as far away from the actual [territorial] border as possible."[69] And as the Canadian Border Service Agency explains, "moving the focus of control of movement of people away from [the territorial] border to overseas, where potential violators of citizenship and immigration laws are interdicted prior to their arrival" has become a core feature of the country's "multiple border strategy," as Canada has branded its extensive variant of the shifting-border strategy (Figure 1.1).[70]

As is traditionally the case in the United States, in Canada the act of "touching base" on the territory has significant legal consequences for the scope of rights and protections granted to asylum seekers, according to domestic and international legal obligations.[71] In 1985, one of the earliest and most revered cases of the Supreme Court of Canada during the era of the Charter of Rights and Freedoms dealt with the

---

[68] CBSA, Department Performance Report (n 5).

[69] Government of Canada, Customs and Broder Management, 'Border Management in Canada', online www.canadainternational.gc.ca/eu-ue/policies-politiques/border-douanes. aspx?lang=eng.

[70] The quotation is drawn from the preamble to the Canada–US Statement of Mutual Understanding (SMU) signed between Canada and the United States in the aftermath of 9/11 to enhance information sharing, reflecting the premise that "border security and border management are based upon cooperation and collaboration."

[71] The 1951 Refugee Convention "does not deal with the question of admission, and neither does it oblige a state of refuge to accord asylum as such." See Guy Goodwin-Gill, 'The International Law of Refugee Protection', in Elena Fiddian-Qasmiyeh *et al.*, eds, *The Oxford Handbook of Refugee and Forced Migration Studies* (Oxford: Oxford University Press, 2014), pp. 36–45, p. 45. Commentators have emphasized that the fact that there is

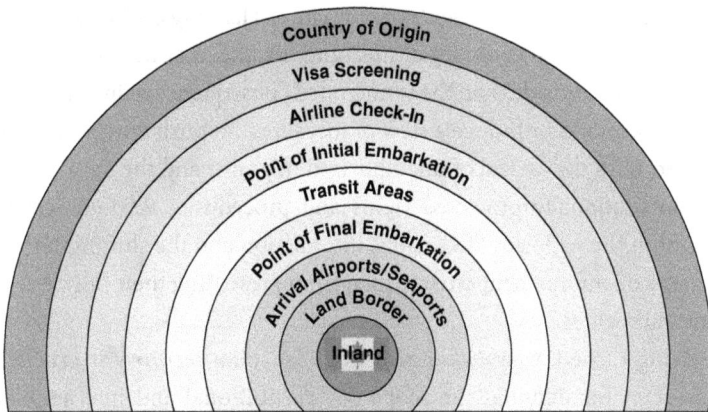

Figure 1.1 Canada: the shifting border—stretching outward (Canada Border Service Agency: Multiple Border Strategy)

rights of refugees. In *Singh v. Minister of Employment and Immigration*, the Court held that if undocumented or irregular migrants reach Canadian territory, they are entitled to the protection of the Charter, and as such, have a consecrated right to a refugee-status hearing before facing potential removal from the country. No similar substantive protections and procedural guarantees are automatically triggered if one is interdicted or intercepted *before* reaching Canada's shores. As part of a comprehensive study on immigration-triggered detention and removal, Canada's Senate Standing Committee on Citizenship and Immigration concluded that the "interdiction abroad of people who are inadmissible to Canada is the most efficient manner of reducing the need for costly, lengthy removal processes."[72] Under this scheme, Canada can avoid triggering the constitutional provisions that it had previously

limited legal guidance regarding access to protection is not accidental; states have discretionally left these questions open when drafting domestic and international protection regimes. Today, the common state practice is that physical presence on the territory is required for claiming asylum there. See Matthew J. Gibney, *The Ethics and Politics of Asylum: Liberal Democracy and the Response to Refugees* (Cambridge: Cambridge University Press, 2004).

[72] Standing Committee on Citizenship and Immigration, *Immigration Detention and Removal* (June 1998), Recommendation No. 18 (Canada), online www.ourcommons.ca/DocumentViewer/en/36-1/CITI/report-1/page-2.

established to protect the rights of non-citizens landing on Canadian territory.[73] Investing such legal meaning in the distinction between "inside" and "outside" had the unintended consequence of incentivizing policymakers to introduce a slew of measures to push out the border" to avert both the arrival of unauthorized migrants and the engagement of constitutionally protected rights and procedures. Asylum seekers caught in the wide net of Canada's interdiction and the shifting-border strategy of enforcement are impeded from presenting their full cases to state authorities.[74]

Being turned away *before* reaching Canadian territory is crucially important for defining the scope of constitutional and international protections to which these non-citizens are entitled. For if the very same individuals were to land on Canadian soil, by virtue of *Singh* they would be entitled to a full oral hearing to determine the merits of their claim to stay, even if they are carrying improper documents. No similar rights apply to them if they are interdicted prior to reaching Canada. Here again, we see an example of the tension between human rights protections and border-control measures that occur beyond the reach of the national territory, purportedly to "combat global irregular migration" (as official government documents put it). From a human rights perspective, measures to outwardly "relocate" the border to skirt legal obligations are deeply objectionable, as they reveal sophisticated governmental attempts to evade rights protections, confining them to the classic boundaries of the *static* Westphalian vision of territory in a world where mobility is increasingly cross-border and international.[75] The dynamism of the shifting border—its flexible and alternating

[73] *Singh v. Minister of Employment and Immigration* [1985] 1 S.C.R 177 (Canada).
[74] For illuminating analysis, see James Hathaway, 'The Emerging Politics of "Non-Entrée"', *Refugees 91* (1992): pp. 235–284; François Crépeau and Delphine Nakache, 'Controlling Irregular Migration in Canada: Reconciling Security Concerns with Human Rights Protection', *Immigration and Refugee Policy Choices 12*, no. 1 (2006).
[75] In response to the shifting-border technique, the scope and application of international refugee and human rights laws should not be determined, from a moral and legal point of view, by the question of *where* the encounter with state officials (or their delegates) has occurred. What matters is that such an encounter took place and effective control was exercised, a point to which I return later in the analysis, in the final part of the discussion.

inward and outward mobility—thus actively contributes to the *immobility* of those who seek to cross it. By barring certain bodies and populations from territorial arrival at the shores of well-off countries, the shifting border not only redraws the geography of power but also exacerbates the influence inequality and accidents of birthplace have on access to life-saving protection regimes. At-a-distance control measures play a vital role in the process as they prevent would-be immigrants and asylum seekers from activating the range of legal entitlements that they are owed in the destinations they seek to reach, while shielding well-off countries from otherwise binding human rights obligations toward those escaping persecution.[76] Nevertheless, it is not difficult to appreciate why such legal fictions and the idea of a shifting border more broadly are so attractive to policymakers under increasing pressures to act decisively in the face of growing uncertainty, as they ever more frequently find themselves in "crisis control" mode.

Canada, along with many other wealthy nations, relies heavily on private-sector third-party actors, in particular airline carriers, as "enforcers" of its immigration-regulation and border-control provisions.[77] As many seasoned travelers will know, it is usually airline personnel who take pains to verify that the required documents and visas are in place prior to permitting embarkation on international flights.[78] They do so,

---

[76] If a legal duty to protect arises only when a potential refugee has reached the actual, territorial border, pre-entry controls that draw on the cooperation of countries of origin and transit, place migration agents abroad in major transit hubs, or rely on safe-third-country agreements block the activation of state responsibility toward those stopped en route, unless effective control has been established by the state or its agents. I elaborate this in Section 3.

[77] For an early and still influential discussion of such transfer of responsibility to third parties and private actors, see Virginie Guiraudon and Gallya Lahav, 'A Reappraisal of the State Sovereignty Debate: The Case of Migration Control', *Comparative Political Studies 33* (2000): pp. 163–195. See also Michael Samers, 'An Emerging Geopolitics of "Illegal" Immigration in the European Union', *European Journal of Migration and Law 6* (2004): pp. 27–45. For a comprehensive account of "outsourcing" migration control, see Thomas Gammeltoft-Hansen, *Access to Asylum: International Refugee Law and the Globalization of Migration Control* (Cambridge: Cambridge University Press, 2011).

[78] Canada and other countries have also signed memoranda of understanding with airline carriers that permit immigration officials abroad to refuse permission to individual passengers to board flights in return for indemnity from the administrative fines these airline carriers would be obliged to pay if found carrying inadmissible passengers.

at least in part, because their companies face steep financial penalties from the receiving countries if they transport improperly documented persons into their territories. Canadian law permits the government to seek reimbursement from airline carriers for "costs of detention, return, and, in some cases, medical care" associated with irregular migrants who arrived aboard their flights.[79] Similarly, the Schengen Implementation Agreement obliges all members of the European Union to implement carrier sanctions.[80] Allowing airline personnel to perform such passport-control activities in effect contributes to the growing role of private-sector intermediaries in conducting what is arguably a central plank of sovereign authority: deciding whom to admit and whom to keep at bay.

The United Kingdom, New Zealand, and Australia have developed comparable mechanisms of migration regulation and control abroad, working in close cooperation with US and Canadian overseas migration-integrity and liaison officers, resembling the collaborative model of the "five eyes" alliance (FVEY, as it is known), a wide-ranging intelligence and data-sharing network with extensive surveillance capabilities, which focuses, among other things, on "remote control" border and migration control.[81] Since the early 2000s, member states of the European Union have followed suit, creating an expanded transnational network of immigration liaison officers operating under an EU directive framework that binds them all. As a result, today's interdiction programs have proliferated into massive information-gathering operations among trusted partners in offshore locations through a "network of

---

[79] Brouwer and Kumin, 'Interception and Asylum' (n 37), p. 10.

[80] In the same vein, the 1990 Schengen Implementation Agreement obliges all members of the European Union to implement carrier sanctions. This mandate was further enhanced in 2001 by a European Council Directive that aims to harmonize these financial sanctions as a powerful regulatory tool, used here by member states in concert, to diminish the prospects of arrival on their shores of unauthorized migrants.

[81] The term "remote control" is drawn from Aristide R. Zolberg, 'Matters of State: Theorizing Immigration Policy', in Charles Hirschman, Philip Kasinitz, and Josh DeWind, eds, *The Handbook of International Migration: The American Experience* (New York City: Russel Sage, 1999), pp. 71–93. However, it is here used to relate to translational, multilateral measures that extend far beyond that term's original reference to unilateral visa control and related measures.

contacts with host-country officials, officials from other governments in the designated region, airline personnel and law-enforcement agents" along the travel continuum to identify and interdict improperly documented travelers at the earliest point at which their identity can be verified, as remotely as possible from the actual border, before they stand a chance of reaching their territorial boundaries.[82]

No less significant for our discussion, these overseas government agents operate under the recommended guidelines developed by the International Air Transport Association (IATA). The existence of this *non-state* organization representing the global airline industry reveals not only the shifting *location* of the border but also the increased collaboration between private *and* public actors in regulating the de-territorialized "edges" of well-off polities seeking to prevent admission of persons they deem unwanted.[83] The ongoing expansion of the involvement of for-profit intermediaries in the task of regulating irregular migration blurs the line between state and market, providing yet another brick in the multidimensional re-bordering of access to territory and membership.[84]

Stretching and contracting space and time: the individualized border

In disrupting the Mondrian-like precision of clearly delineated and jurisdictionally exclusive territorial states that has undergirded (at least in principle) the Westphalian international system of nation-states, the

---

[82] See Canada Border Services Agency, '2008–2009 Report on Plan and Priorities', online www.tbs-sct.gc.ca/rpp/2008-2009/inst/bsf/bsf02-eng.asp. Citizenship and Immigration Canada, *Comparable ICO Network Models, Review of the Immigration Control Office Network— Final Report* (2001), Appendix A (archived, on file with author).

[83] See UN High Commissioner for Refugees [UNHCR], Standing Committee, *Interception of Asylum-Seekers and Refugees: The International Framework and Recommendations for a Comprehensive Approach* (10, U.N. Doc. EC/50/SC/CPR.17, June 9, 2000), online www.unhcr.org/4aa660c69.pdf.

[84] New federal legislation in the United States, to provide but one example, now allows state and local government as well as the private sector to get involved in the funding of port-of-entry infrastructure and staffing, allowing the business community and non-governmental organizations to partake in advancing border security and efficiency. See Erik Lee and Christopher Wilson, eds, *The US–Mexico Border Economy in Transition* (Washington, DC: Wilson Center, 2015), pp. 2–3. Other examples of semi-privatization of immigration enforcement and policymaking in the United States include the proliferation of detention centers, private prisons, and the like.

shifting border tacitly and covertly redefines the relationship between membership, territory, and sovereignty. Governments, for their part, are quick to assert that the core motivation for "dispatching" the shifting border outward is functional: to "identity and intercept illegal and undesirable travelers" as remotely as possible *before* they embark on their journey toward the lands of migration and prosperity.[85] As the Canadian Border Service Agency explains, the ubiquitous shifting border can, in principle, operate at "*any* point at which the identity of the traveler can be verified," giving full meaning to the notion of a border that is simultaneously nowhere and everywhere. The integrated border-management strategy, devised by the European Union, similarly relies on a multi-tiered control model that seeks to track the movement of non-EU citizens, known as third-country nationals, "from the point of departure in countries of origin, all throughout transit, and to arrival in the EU."[86] Within the European Union, inland control measures, including detection, investigation, and return, are applicable to third-country nationals deemed to lack status (they are regularly referred to as illegal immigrants), as are futuristic iBorder control strategies that "re-engineer" the system of border crossing and migration control.[87] Pilot projects funded by the European Union will enable "automatic control" procedures, as they are known, which involve pre-registration, whereby "[t]ravelers preform a short, automated, non-invasive interview with an avatar, undergo a lie detection and are linked to any pre-existing authority data." This data will be stored in large databases and connected with "portable, wireless connected

---

[85] Canada Border Services Agency, *Department Performance Report* (n 5), p. 1. For a comprehensive and comparative analysis, see Bernard Ryan and Valsamis Mitsilegas, eds, *Extraterritorial Immigration Control: Legal Challenges* (Leiden and Boston: Martinus Nijhoff, 2010).

[86] Violeta Moreno-Lax, *Accessing Asylum in Europe: Extraterritorial Border Controls and Refugee Rights under EU Law* (Oxford: Oxford University Press, 2017), p. 3. For further discussion, see Council of the European Union, Integrated Border Management: Strategy Deliberations, 13926/06 Rev 3, November 21, 2006.

[87] See, for example, Return Directive 2008/115/EC of the European Parliament and of the Council, O.J. (L 348/98) December 16, 2008 (EU) on common standards and procedures in member states for returning illegally staying third-country nationals. For an early analysis of these trends, see Samers, 'An Emerging Geopolitics' (n 77).

iBorderCtrl units that can be used inside buses, trains or any other point [to] verify the identity of the travelers . . . [and] calculate a cumulative risk factor for each individual."[88] Here, the once fixed territorial border is not only shifting but also multiplying and fracturing into an operational individual-control system, where each person "carries" the border with her as she moves across space and place. The border attaches to her pre-arrival, at crossing stations, and wherever she travels within the protected and surveilled territorial space—today, within the area of free movement in Europe; tomorrow, potentially the world.[89]

The underlying objective of ensuring that all legal requirements are met by entrants here takes on a new social, political, and technological meaning, transforming not only the regulation of movement prior- and post-arrival but also potentially sliding toward and morphing into a "society of control," where *everyone* (non-citizen and citizen alike) is tracked and encoded.[90] A further concern is that these new surveillance techniques, while in theory "blind" and universal, may end up producing divergent and discriminatory results—for example, by reaffirming and intensifying practices of racial profiling and uneven

---

[88] L3 Research Center, 'iBorderCtrl', online www.l3s.de.

[89] I am indebted to Irene Bloemraad for suggesting that I explore the imagery of the shifting border as "transported" to individual bodies. There is a growing line of research in feminist geography that emphasizes the body as a site of bordering and migration control. See, for example, Rachel Silvey, 'Borders, Embodiment, and Mobility: Feminist Migration Studies in Geography', in Lise Nelson and Joni Seager, eds, *A Companion to Feminist Geography* (Oxford: Blackwell, 2015), pp. 138–149; Alison Mountz, 'Embodying the Nation State: Canada's Response to Human Smuggling', *Political Geography 23* (2004): pp. 323–345, 2004; Robyn Sampson, 'Embodied Borders: Biopolitics, Knowledge Mobilization, and Alternatives to Immigration Detention', PhD dissertation, La Trobe University (2013).

[90] The term "society of control" is drawn from the work of Gilles Deleuze but has since been applied more broadly in the literature. See, for example, Shamir, 'Without Borders?' (n 23), p. 201ff. The loss of civil liberties is not restricted to non-citizens. In the United Kingdom, for example, draconian "control orders" that provided the state with legal authority to indefinitely detain non-citizens without trial, if a trial put secret or sensitive intelligence information at risk, were challenged before the courts as discriminatory. In response, the UK government did not rescind such powers. Instead, it equally applied them to citizens. For related examples whereby the deprivation of rights of non-citizens foreshadows a similar deprivation of the liberties of citizens, see Eric A. Ormsby, 'The Refugee Crisis as Civil Liberties Crisis', *Columbia Law Review 117* (2017): pp. 1191–1229.

geographies of policing, through a combination of algorithmic machine learning and human vetting.[91]

Such global ID systems have long been the dream of law enforcers, but they are now closer to becoming a reality. Even the United Nations has teamed up with leading technology firms to explore plans for creating a digital ID network running on blockchain technology to provide tamper-resistant legal documents for refugees and other displaced persons who lack them, creating a "'stamp'—a unique identifier between the refugee and the data on the servers—that proves they have been authenticated for each service they receive" at refugee camps or from official aid organizations.[92] While informed by benevolent intentions, such initiatives may violate privacy and restrict the freedom of mobility of such global ID bearers, especially if their "stamp" indicates passage through a third country deemed safe but which may prohibit onward travel or trigger return if it signs readmission agreements with the ID bearers' countries of origin.

Sought-after destination countries, then, beyond reinventing and replanting the "moveable" border while selectively opening and closing its multi-tiered gates of admission, are developing and implementing futuristic surveillance technologies that cross time and space as well as bilateral and multilateral agreements with countries of origin and transit that treat the latter as migration "buffer zones" (often in exchange for capacity building and material assistance in the form of development aid). This new conception of the shifting border has coincided with the rise of "big data" and propagated the creation of enormous databases that store biometric information and electronic passenger-name records—a treasure trove for artificial intelligence analytics.[93] Sharing these records prior to

---

[91] This set of concerns is receiving growing attention in the literature. See, for example, Margaret Hu, 'Algorithmic Jim Crow', *Fordham Law Review 86* (2017): pp. 633–696; Alpa Parmar, 'Policing Belonging: Race and Nation in the UK', in Mary Bosworth, Alpa Parmar, and Yolanda Vázquez, eds, *Race, Criminal Justice, and Migration Control: Enforcing the Boundaries of Belonging* (Oxford: Oxford University Press, 2018), pp. 108–124.

[92] BBC Technology, 'Accenture and Microsoft Plan Digital IDs for Millions of Refugees', *BBC*, June 20, 2017, online www.bbc.com/news/technology-40341511.

[93] Following a protracted political and legal battle between Brussels and Washington about levels of data protection, a new US–EU PNR agreement was signed in 2011 and approved

travel has replaced traditional interactions between the individual and state officials at the actual, territorial border, because, as the UK Home Office revealingly put it, this encounter "can be too late—they [unauthorized entrants] have achieved their goal of reaching our shores."[94] To achieve this ambitious yet Orwellian vision, the location, operation, and logic of the border has to be redefined through a complex conceptual and operational framework that allows government officials or their delegates (increasingly operating transnationally and in collaboration with third parties and private-sector actors) to screen and intercept travelers at continuous and multiple eBorders, iBorders, or "automated gates," en route to their desired destinations and within their territories as well.[95] Pre-travel electronic clearance is now required as a matter of course, even for those in possession of "high-value" passports, including travelers hailing from EU member states.[96] It must be applied for and approved by the government of the destination country *before* the traveler embarks on their journey, and it is linked electronically to the traveler's passport.[97]

and adopted by the European Parliament in 2012. The Agreement between the United States of America and the European Union on the use of transferred passenger-name records to the United States Department of Homeland Security came into effect on July 1, 2012. In 2016, after years of debate, the European Parliament approved the Directive (EU) 2016/681 of the European Parliament and of the Council, O.J. (L 119/132) May 4, 2016 (EU).

[94] Home Office, *Securing the UK Border* (n 19), point 1.4.

[95] For a now classic article that observed some of these transformations, see Guiraudon and Lahav, 'A Reappraisal of the State Sovereignty Debate'. A "network of state organizations for whom immigration enforcement is a central or defining part of their purpose" increasingly operates collaboratively at the local, national, or supranational levels. Third-party actors also play a role. Beyond the familiar example of airline carriers that have come to serve as "surrogates" for border control and migration screening, successive governments have further "'deputized' third parties for immigration enforcement, such as trade unions, employers, landlords, school teachers, doctors, labor inspectors, police officers, universities and welfare service. Those actors do not have immigration control as defining purpose, but have increasingly been brought into the control matrix." For further discussion, see Lea Sitkin, 'Coordinating Internal Migration Control in the UK', *International Journal of Migration and Border Studies 1* (2014): pp. 39–56; Ana Aliverti, 'Enlisting the Public in the Policing of Immigration', *British Journal of Criminology 55* (2015): pp. 215–230.

[96] On high-value passports and migrants, see Shachar, 'Citizenship for Sale?' (n 8).

[97] As Australia's Department of Immigration and Border Control explains, the next generation of border security will require further analytics-based capabilities, including "a state-of-the-art risk scoring engine developed by departmental analysts [that] uses complex statistical models to process large amounts of data in real time, to identify higher than acceptable levels of risk" as well as "a real-time risk identification system that scans information collected through the department's advance passenger processing system.

Without such authorization, it is impossible to board a plane heading to the United States, Canada, Australia, or to enter these countries. This additional layer of preclearance and information gathering creates a powerful yet invisible electronic border that applies everywhere (adjusting itself to the location and risk-profile of the traveler) and is intentionally detached from and sequentially precedes the act of territorial admission, facilitating mobility for approved or trusted travelers while denying access to all others.

While these high-tech borders are designed to keep out unwanted and uninvited entrants, even trusted travelers—those who benefit from the highest level of flexibility and mobility in crossing borders—must now have their identities verified before embarking on international travel and again at airports and other regulation points. "Smart" and automated-entry gates have iris scans or other biometric readers that run through multiple national and global databases which cross-reference and authenticate the trusted traveler's identity, low-risk status, and un-flagged profile. In an increasing number of airports, the initial decision on whether the golden gates of admission will open wide or shut tight is determined not by a human agent but by "smart machines" and automated eGates that are coded to identify risk factors based on sophisticated algorithms (themselves hardly ever the subjects of open, democratic review).[98] The "open sesame!" incantation in the age of big data and shifting borders has given Ali Baba's phrase a new magic and mythos.

Yet only those with a golden key know this magic formula; the shifting-border strategy makes it increasingly hard for those disadvantaged by the birthright lottery to lawfully set foot in the more affluent polities

All inbound travelers are screened and travelers representing potential risk are more closely examined."
[98] Such transformations are explored by Costica Dumbrava, 'Citizenship and Technology', in Shachar *et al.*, eds, *The Oxford Handbook of Citizenship* (Oxford: Oxford University Press, 2017), pp. 767–788. The transfer of responsibility to machines in lieu of human border guards is extensively elaborated by Longo, *The Politics of Borders* (n 24). Such regulation is more intertwined with and partly dependent upon private-sector providers and developers of sophisticated biometric-data-collection and verification technologies.

they desperately seek to enter.[99] This raises serious questions of justice in allocation, not only of membership affiliations but also mobility opportunities.[100] Coupled with restrictive admission categories and limited travel visas, especially for those entering from poorer and less stable countries, the shifting border may have the unintended effect of pushing unauthorized mobility further "underground." This, of course, triggers concerns about the rise of a lucrative black market for increasingly sophisticated human-trafficking and smuggling networks.[101] These concerns may help explain (although they do not justify) why and how governments seek to sever the knot that has traditionally tied a fixed territorial border to migration control: by attempting to cover the globe with "transportable" regulation and surveillance they may head off asylum seekers, refugees, and other uninvited entrants before they begin their journey.[102]

"Erasing" territory

Australia, even more explicitly than Canada or the United States, has officially *relocated* its border through words of law, creating—as its

---

[99] Ayelet Shachar, *The Birthright Lottery: Citizenship and Global Inequality* (Cambridge: Harvard University Press, 2009). Some have argued for open borders as the solution. For a classic account, see Joseph Carens, 'Aliens and Citizens' (n 23). As critics have noted, even adopting a policy of open borders (which is still a pipedream in most parts of the world) may not be sufficient to provide equal opportunity given structural and economic barriers to mobility that go beyond border controls. See, for example, Aveek Bhattacharya, 'Does Justice Require a Migration Lottery?', *Global Justice 5* (2012): pp. 4–15.

[100] Such a "global mobility divide" is evident in the context of visa-free travel, for example. For an innovative and comprehensive study, see Steffen Mau *et al.*, 'The Global Mobility Divide: How Visa Policies Have Evolved over Time', *Journal of Ethnic and Migration Studies 8* (2015): pp. 1192–1213. On the unequal value of passports, see Shachar, 'Citizenship for Sale?' (n 8).

[101] Anne T. Gallagher and Fiona David, *The International Law of Migrant Smuggling* (Cambridge: Cambridge University Press, 2014). See also David Kyle and Rey Koslowski, eds, *Global Human Smuggling: Comparative Perspectives*, 2nd edition (Baltimore: Johns Hopkins University Press, 2011).

[102] It is part of broader suite of measures to "quarantine" wealthy countries from the quicksand of civil strife, disease, abject poverty, or environmental crises frequently associated with mass mobility from the world's less developed countries. See Bimal Ghosh, 'Toward a New International Regime for Orderly Movements of People', in Bimal Ghosh, ed., *Managing Migration: Time for a New International Regime?* (Oxford: Oxford University Press, 2000), pp. 6–26, p. 10. This has led some commentators to suggest that we are

government readily admits—a distinction between the country's
"migration zone" and "Australia" as we know it on the map. This "excision" policy was created through the Migration Amendment Act of
2001, which was expanded in 2005 and then again in 2013.[103] This legislation authorizes Australia's immigration officials to remove asylum
seekers that have managed to reach its now "excised" territory, as
though they had *never reached* Australia, despite having physically
landed on its shores.[104] Put differently, those who reach the excision
zone cannot make a valid asylum claim in Australia, because they never
entered it in a legally cognizable way—the territory they reached is no
longer "Australia" for immigration-law purposes.[105] This legal fiction
further limits the procedural and substantive rights that asylum seekers
and other irregular migrants are entitled to under domestic and international law.[106] It also eliminates the possibility of judicial review, thus
not only redrawing the territorial border but also attenuating legality in
the process.[107] In 2013, the excision zone was expanded, through

witnessing the creation of the building blocks of a global regime of human immobility
precisely at the time when other trans-border flows, such as trade, knowledge, capital,
and the like, are flourishing. See Shamir, 'Without Borders?' (n 23).

[103] Migration Amendment (Excision from Migration Zone) Act 2001 (Australia). For background, see Australian Government, *Department of Immigration and Multicultural
Affairs, Fact Sheet 71: Border Measures to Strengthen Border Control (Consequential Pro-
visions Act)* (2001). See also Minister for Immigration and Multicultural Affairs, Press
Release, *Joint Statement with Minister for Justice and Customs: Government Strengthens
Border Integrity* (MPS 161/2001, September 17, 2001); Parliament of Australia, Depart-
ment of Parliamentary Services, *Excising Australia: Are We Really Shrinking?* (Research
Note No. 5, 2005–2006, August 31, 2005).

[104] Instead, they are immediately directed to third countries declared safe, such as Nauru
and Papua New Guinea (until the latter's court ruled the practice unconstitutional
according to Papua New Guinea law) where Australia has funded detention centers.
Even if found to be refugees, such unauthorized arrivals cannot be settled in Australia
and must remain in Nauru or Papua New Guinea, or be resettled elsewhere.

[105] We witness the almost incomprehensibly copious power of the words of law in this
example.

[106] Even before the creation of the excision zone, Australia introduced a mandatory detention policy for all arrivals without valid visas. See Migration Act 1958 (Australia), s. 196.

[107] The terms "legality" and "rule of law" are notoriously difficult to define and are used
interchangeably in my discussion, referring to "a number of ideas, among them constitutionalism, due process, legality, justice, that make claims for the proper character and
role of law in well-ordered states and societies . . . Appeal to the rule of law [or legality]
signals the hope that law might contribute to articulating, channeling, disciplining, constraining and informing—rather than merely serving—the exercise of power. I[t] refers

legislation, to include the entire Australian mainland. In effect, this means that the border applies *everywhere* and *nowhere* at the same time.

The legal consequences of arrival at Australia's "erased" territory are both far-reaching and irreversible; those falling under the spell of excision are denied the opportunity to secure status in Australia, even *after* their claims are adjudicated. Excision provides a hocus-locus-pocus way to keep out those who were never wanted or invited. This legal fiction makes them ineligible to claim protection under Australian immigration laws. By erecting an unlimitable line of defense against unauthorized maritime arrivals, excision creates a legal barrier that makes illusionary the possibility of passing through the proverbial entry gates, even for those who have managed to reach the country's (actual) territory. This logic is reminiscent of the rights-restricting inward "bleeding" of the US border into the interior, but with the unique Australian twist of "erasing" from the map, with the stroke of a pen, certain segments of territory for migration-regulation purposes (Map 1.2).[108]

Australia has gone further than any other country in the world in its quest to deter irregular migration. Creating "zones of exception," as in the Australian practice of excision, whereby a country effectively erases certain parts and eventually *all* of its territory, as it were perforating itself geographically, may appear to undermine "the very elements of national sovereignty that immigration controls seek to bulwark."[109] But, as both critics and advocates of this extreme manifestation of the shifting border agree, redrawing the boundaries of inclusion and exclusion through the tools of public law with a clear intent to restrict and deter

collectively to such contributions as *tempering* power." See Martin Krygier, 'Transformations of the Rule of Law: Legal, Liberal and Neo-', in Ben Golder and Daniel McLoughlin, eds, *The Politics of Legality in a Neoliberal Age* (Abingdon: Routledge, 2018), pp. 19–43, pp. 19–20.

[108] This unprecedented act was prefaced by a governmental clarification that the excised zones were not altogether removed from Australian sovereign territory. This legal interpretation is widely accepted by constitutional lawyers and other relevant experts in Australia.

[109] Robert A. Davidson, 'Spaces of Immigration "Prevention": Interdiction and the Nonplace', *Diacritics 33* (2003): pp. 3–18, p. 6.

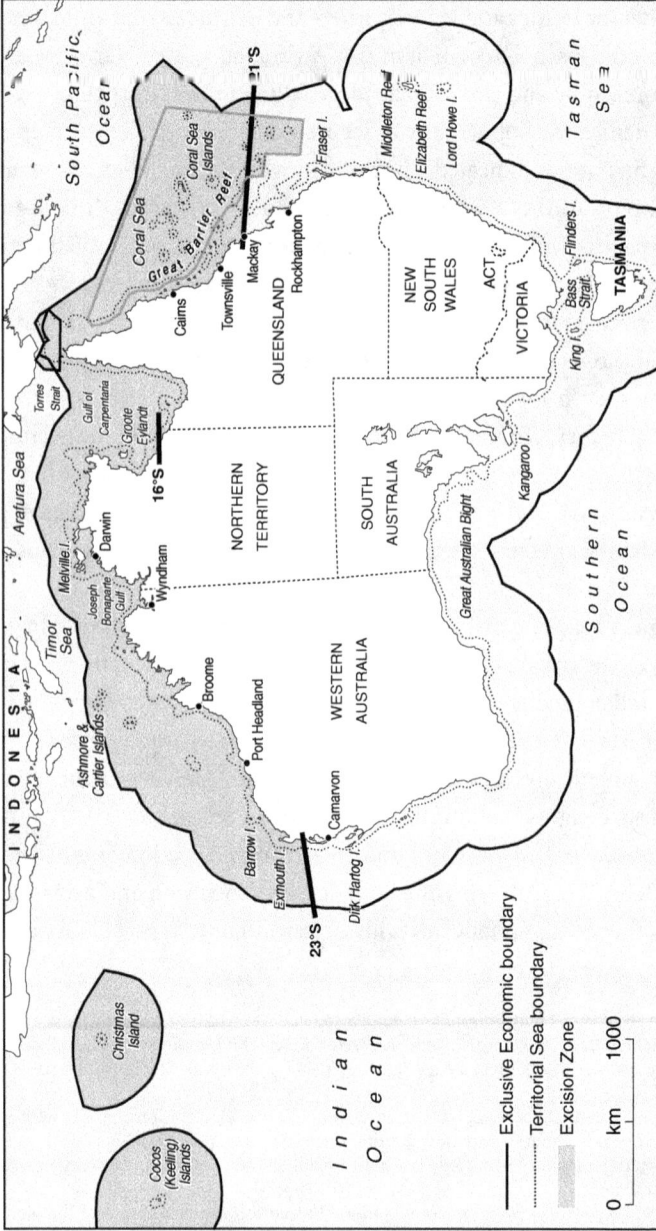

Map 1.2 Australia: the shifting border—"erasing" territory (redrawn from Parliament of Australia, Department of Parliamentary Services, *Excising Australia: Are We Really Shrinking?* Research Note, No. 5, 2005–2006)

unauthorized arrivals, including controversial policies to proactively "stop the boats" and turn back asylum seekers and other irregular migrants, can hardly be seen as a loss of control—although it may well be described as a glaring failure of both legality and morality. This process provides a textbook example of pressured governments seeking to *regain* control over cross-border movement in the age of globalization by exercising—upon securing the cooperation of third countries or private contractors—the naked power to determine whom to include and whom to exclude. As the Australian prime minister whose government initiated the excision policy, John Howard, famously declared: "We will decide who comes to this country and the circumstances in which they come."[110] The act of self-erasure of territory is paradoxically expressed here as a manifestation of self-determination and resolve.[111]

More limited versions of excision once operated in several high-traffic airports in European countries, which declared certain parts of these airports, physically located in their national territories, as extraterritorial "international zones," or "transit zones," where the standard protections of domestic and international law did not apply.[112] These transit zones were treated as legal "grey zones," operating in a limbo space, "in which officials '[we]re not obliged to provide asylum seekers or foreign individuals with some or all of the protections available to those officially on state territory.'" This practice was eventually challenged in the European Court of Human Rights (ECtHR), which concluded that

---

[110] Critics have pointed out that this is not the first time such assertions of national sovereignty, asserted in stark "us/we versus them" terms, have been part of the political discourse in Australia. As early as 1934, just a few years before Jews, who faced annihilation by Nazi Germany, were forced to wander from port to port, as no country accepted them and they were forbidden disembarkment even after escaping the horrors of Europe, the grammar of the modern state's control over immigration was expressed loud and clear in Australia (just as it was in the United States and elsewhere): "We have, as an independent country, a perfect right to indicate whether an alien shall or shall not be admitted within these shores." See Anne McNevin and Klaus Neumann, *Who Is Speaking?* (quoting Australia's Attorney-General Robert Menzies), paper presented at the 2017 APSA Annual Meeting, San Francisco.

[111] When passing the excision legislation, the Australian government was careful to clarify that the excised zones were part of the country's migration-control regime; they were not removed altogether from Australia's sovereign territory.

[112] On airports, seaports, and train stations as "grey zones," see Basaran (n 9); Mark B. Salter, 'Governmentalities of an Airport: Heterotopia and Confession', *International Political Sociology 1* (2007): pp. 49–66.

"[d]espite its name, the international zone does not have extraterritorial status," thus bringing border-control actions taking place in these transit zones back into the fold of legality.[113]

The creation of these legal "grey zones" is not entirely new, then; and the US navy base in Guantanamo Bay, before it became infamous for serving as the detention place for hundreds of foreign nationals suspected of terrorism links, was used as a repository for asylum seekers (particularly from Haiti) whose shattered boats were intercepted on the high seas by US navy ships in order to prevent those on-board from claiming refuge at "our gates."[114] Again, we witness the craftsmanship of legal definitions and categories to interdict unwanted entrants before they can reach the actual border (unless, as in Australia's extreme variant of the shifting border, that territory itself is "excised").

Along with the spatial expansion of the zone of excision, Australia has adopted another measure of shifting. Since 2013, *all* "asylum seekers who unlawfully arrive *anywhere* in Australia" must be transferred to third countries for offshoring processing.[115] The latter refers to what the Australian government calls "regional processing," which, in practice, means that those who have reached the excision zone are then transferred to offshore locations in remote islands in the Pacific, such as Nauru, a tiny microstate island nation 4,500 kilometers away from Australia, or Manus Island in Papua New Guinea, where asylum seekers may languish for years while their claims are being processed and assessed. Australia is currently the only country in the world that uses

---

[113] *Amuur v. France*, App. No 19776/92, Eur. Ct. H.R. (1996), sec. 52.

[114] These strategies of "containment" of irregular mobility through foreign maritime enforcement have long been employed by the United States, which has entered bilateral agreements with the Bahamas, the Dominican Republic, and other countries in the Caribbean; these signatory countries regularly interdict boats and summarily return unauthorized travelers heading toward the United States to their place of embarkation. For an exposition of the governmental practice of detention without trial of Haitian refugees at Guantanamo in the 1990s, and the legal challenges that followed, see Harold Hongju Koh, 'The Haitian Refugee Litigation: A Case Study in Transnational Public Law Litigation', *Maryland Journal of International Law 18* (1994): pp. 1–20.

[115] Migration Amendment (Unauthorised Maritime Arrivals and other Measures) Act 2013 (Australia). For a concise overview of these legislative changes, see Refugee Council of Australia, 'Australia's Offshore Processing Regime', online www.refugeecouncil.org.au/getfacts/seekingsafety/asylum/offshore-processing/briefing/.

other countries to process asylum claims, although the United States may soon follow suit. Close to 80 percent of those transferred to such offshore processing centers have been proven to have credible claims and were on average detained in offshore centers for 450 days (almost one quarter spent more than two years in the facilities).[116] Yet even those recognized as refugees are forbidden for life from settlement in Australia due to the "original sin" of arriving on its excised territory. The erased territory thus becomes a legal black hole, a gravitational field so intense that no unauthorized migrant can ever escape it. This ironclad policy—the one-way ticket *away* from Australia—has recently attracted the interest of European policymakers desperately seeking answers to the challenges of responding to uninvited migration flows, and it has fueled discussion of building migrant "reception" centers in North Africa and deeper into the heart of the continent.

By legally re-charting the area of Australian territory upon which asylum claims can be made, and by removing and "emplacing" any intercepted irregular migrants to offshore processing centers in remote locations in poorer and less stable third countries, Australia has invented one of the most striking manifestations of the shifting border. Australia's restrictive policy offers remarkable testimony to the lengths to which otherwise international law-abiding countries are willing to travel in their quest to deter unauthorized migration flows, even at the cost of blatantly breaching basic rights-protection obligations to which they have committed, both domestically and internationally. To complicate the picture even further, there are some early indications that Australia's wildly problematic interpretation of its refugee-protection obligations is proving effective in advancing in its stated policy mission: to stop the "boat people."[117] As a representative of the United Nations Human Rights Council (UNHRC) in Indonesia (a major transit hub in the region for asylum seekers and human smugglers heading for

---

[116] Elibritt Karlsen, Parliament of Australia, Research Paper Series 2016–2017, *Australia's Offshore Processing of Asylum Seekers in Nauru and PNG: A Quick Guide to Statistics and Resources* (Canberra: Parliamentary Library, December 19, 2016).

[117] Australian Government, 'Australia by Boat? No Advantage', online http://malaysia. highcommission.gov.au/files/klpr/No%20Advantage%20flayer.pdf.

Australia) has noted: "[w]ord that the prospects of reaching Australia by boat . . . are now virtually zero appears to have reached smugglers and would-be asylum seekers in countries of origin." This focus on deterrence and "reclaiming" border protection is in turn used politically to justify the tough policies adopted by Australia in the first place. Despite domestic contestation and international condemnation, the major political parties in Australia have refused to reverse the policy of offshore processing. This raises a host of pressing democratic queries about how to avert the denial of constitutional and human rights by the very institutions and processes designed to protect them, and about *whose* voices and interests ought to be heard and counted when challenging such policies, just as it reveals the blurring lines between law and politics in the age of shifting borders.[118] In the era of resurgent populism, Australia is not alone in facing such quandaries. The world over, incumbent leaders and their contenders try to appease the anxieties of voters fearing loss of control over borders and membership boundaries. The lethal combination of perceived loss of control and the apparent deterrence effect of restrictive policy forces us to rethink the complex relationship between agency and coercion, official and unofficial routes of passage, voice and power, as well as the uneasy interactions among countries of origin, transit, destination, and offshoring locations—a dynamic constellation that has largely been overlooked in the literature.

If we conceptualize borders as "crucial sites from which the nation state is narrated and constituted,"[119] Australia's all-out approach brings into sharp relief several important quandaries, not least who guards our legal guards? Australia's High Court has been called upon on several occasions to review various aspects of Australia's excision policy and offshore-processing framework. Importantly, in several landmark decisions, the High Court favored the claims of those in excised territories. These include the case known as *Plaintiff M61/2010* and *Plaintiff*

---

[118] There is a rich body of literature exploring these questions, which goes beyond the scope of my discussion here.
[119] Anthea Vogl, 'Over the Borderline: A Critical Inquiry into the Geography of Territorial Excision and the Securitisation of the Australian Border', *University of New South Wales Law Journal* 38 (2015): pp. 114–145, p. 117.

M69/2010, in which the High Court found unanimously that two Sri Lankan asylum seekers detained on Australia's Christmas Island were denied procedural fairness, leading the government to amend certain aspects of the processing of claims off mainland Australia.[120] In another case, *Plaintiff M70/2011 v. Minister for Immigration and Citizenship*, the High Court struck down the government's so called Malaysian solution, which would have seen a "swap" of asylum seekers from Australia with refugees from Malaysia, reasoning that Malaysia is neither a signatory to the Refugee Convention nor recognizes the status of refugees under its domestic law.[121] However, the very same justice system that protects all refugees but those arriving without authorization by boat has ultimately upheld some of the most controversial aspects of the country's excision and offshoring tactics.[122] As Robert Cover observed in his now classic *Justice Accused*, judges operating under unjust regimes (his analysis focused on antebellum America, where anti-slavery judges nevertheless issued pro-slavery decisions according to "neutral" rules) do not always find the courage to speak out against the most salient breaches of the rights and dignity of individuals who are most in need of legal protection. For those excised and offshored, the words of law clearly failed to provide solace or safety; they imposed violence instead.[123]

---

[120] *Plaintiff M61/2010E v. Commonwealth; Plaintiff M69 of 2010 v. Commonwealth* [2010] 243 CLR 319 (Austl).

[121] *Plaintiff M70/2011 v. Minister of Immigration and Citizenship* [2011] 244 CLR 144 (Austl). Most recently, the High Court raised questions about the legality of maritime interception and turn-back operations, but in a tight 4:3 decision eventually upheld the government's policies. See *CPCF v Minister for Immigration and Border Protection* [2015] 255 CLR 514 (Austl). Human rights lawyers have argued that despite this High Court decision, which focused on domestic law, Australia is still in breach of its *non-refoulement* international obligations. In a previous decision, *Plaintiff S156/2013 v. Minister for Immigration and Border Protection* [2014] HCA 22 (Austl), the High Court unanimously rejected a challenge to the constitutional validity of sections 198AB and 198AD of the Migration Act 1958 (Australia), as amended by the Migration Legislation Amendment (Regional Processing and Other Measures), Act 2012 (Australia), which gives the immigration minister the power to designate regional (offshore) processing countries. These amendments were introduced into law in response to a previous ruling of the High Court, Plaintiff M70, in which the Court struck down the government's "Malaysian solution."

[122] Mary Crock, ed., *Migrants and Rights* (Abingdon: Routledge, 2015).

[123] Robert M. Cover, *Justice Accused* (New Haven: Yale University Press, 1975); see also Robert M. Cover, 'Violence and the Word', *Yale Law Journal 95* (1986): pp. 1601–1629.

An unexpected twist in this saga occurred when the Supreme Court of Papua New Guinea, unlike the High Court of Australia, ruled that the practice of transferring and detaining asylum seekers on Manus Island was both illegal and in violation of the right to personal liberty. The Court held that because the "asylum seekers held [on Papua New Guinea's Manus Island] did not arrive . . . of their own volition, they had not broken any immigration law," and "keeping them in indefinite detention, where they face frequent acts of violence and suffer from poor health care, therefore, violated their constitutional protections."[124] The Court ordered that immediate steps be taken to end the detention, and the government of Papua New Guinea requested Australia make alternative arrangements. Those asylum seekers remaining on Manus Island are currently in a state of limbo. In the wake of the center's closure, they have lost access to running water, electricity, medicine, and working toilets, and their food supplies are dwindling, but out of fear for their safety many have refused relocation to other sites in Papua New Guinea, such as Port Moresby, the country's capital. The United Nations High Commissioner for Refugees (UNHCR) has warned of an "unfolding humanitarian crisis" and has called on Australian authorities to act, based on their responsibility for the original offshore transfer and eventual internment. The Australian government continues to refuse entry to the asylum seekers it has offshored, with the exception of those facing life-threatening medical circumstances. Litigation is before the High Court of Australia and in Papua New Guinea alleging a breach of the duty of care and requiring that these offshore refugees and asylum seekers be brought back to Australia or resettled in third countries such as the United States; the legal proceedings are expected to be lengthy. A growing choir of voices from civil society and human rights organizations, both local and global, has called on the Australian government to take accountability for the escalating situation, demanding "an end to this cruelty."[125] Such democratic protests have had some effect in

---

[124] *Blenden Norman Namah v. Rimbink Pato* (2016) SC 1497.

[125] See, for example, Refugee Council of Australia, 'Turnbull and Dutton Must Guarantee the Safety of the Men They Have Kept Trapped on Manus', *Relief Web*, November 23, 2017,

the past—for example, by pressuring the government to bring back to Australia some of the detained who required medical attention.[126] The jury is still out determining the impact of such contestation and protest on finding a humane resolution to the current deadlock.

Europe selectively closing its (multiple) gates

If we shift our gaze to Europe, we find that, unlike the situation in Australia, where national jurists have by and large approved the government's hardline policies, the ECtHR has on several occasions ruled against the creation of "black holes," or "grey zones," in which jurisdiction and European human rights provisions categorically do not apply. Arguably, "erasing territory" to avert rights protection would meet the definition of such areas.[127] These legal precedents from the ECtHR have drawn an important line in the quicksand of the shifting border. Europe, however, has its own multiple and ultra-sophisticated variants of the shifting border, stretching "both far beyond and deep inside the EU's territory."[128]

One aspect of such shifting that has become acutely charged in the context of the migration crisis is the question of how to share and divide responsibility for the protection of refugees that reach Europe's shores. The Dublin system allocates responsibility to the first country of entry to the European Union.[129] Accordingly, a registered and finger-printed

online https://reliefweb.int/report/australia/turnbull-and-dutton-must-guarantee-safety-men-they-have-kept-trapped-manus. Such democratic protests have made a dent in the past, for example, by pressuring the government to bring back to Australia some of the detained who required medical attention; their impact in this instance remains to be seen.

[126] In 2019, a new Australian law, the "medevac law," entered into force. This legislation authorizes transfer from remote processing facilities back to Australia on the recommendations of two independent Australian doctors. However, the law has been subject to calls for repeal since its adoption, and its future remains unclear.

[127] The landmark case here is *Hirsi v Italy* (n 25). See also *Khlaifia and others v. Italie*, App. No 16483/12, Eur. Ct. H.R. (2015) (official judgment in French).

[128] Raphael Bossong and Helena Carrapico, 'The Multidimensional Nature and Dynamic Transformation of European Borders and Internal Security', in Raphael Bossong and Helena Carrapico, eds, *EU Borders and Shifting Internal Security: Technology, Externalization and Accountability* (Berlin: Springer, 2016), pp. 1–21, p. 9.

[129] European asylum legislation applies to all who apply "at the border" or "on the territory." For a concise overview of the Common European Asylum Policy and its impact on

"Dublin" asylum seeker engaged in onward mobility (or "secondary movement," as it is technically known) will be *barred* from claiming refugee status in the country she has reached in her onward mobility, shifting the responsibility back to the frontline member state, unless her situation falls under a narrow set of exceptions.[130] Critics have argued that, "due to the way the system is structured, the Dublin Regulation seems less about burden-sharing and more about externalization of responsibilities from the northern to the southern [and eastern] member states."[131] In 2015, when a record of over 1 million asylum applications were lodged in the European Union, the unequal-distribution implications of this protection system became blatantly clear.[132] Italy and Greece in particular, already overwhelmed by the migrant influx, bore the brunt of responsibility for addressing the escalating European crisis. The European Commission eventually admitted as much, stating that "the current system is not sustainable. . . . [W]e have

asylum policy outcomes in the member states, see, for example, Dimiter Toshkov and Laura de Haan, 'The Europeanization of Asylum Policy: An Assessment of the EU Impact on Asylum Applications and Recognitions Rates', *Journal of European Public Policy 20* (2013): pp. 661–683.

[130] A claim for family reunification is one such exception. Upon application for asylum, the Dublin procedure is used to determine "which country is responsible for making a decision on [the] application." See Regulation (EU) 604/2013 of the European Parliament and of the Council, O.J. (L 80/31), June 29, 2013 (EU); Commission Implementation Regulation (EU) No 118/2014, O.J. (L 39/1), February 8, 2014 (EU). Each applicant's fingerprints are taken and stored in a central European database (Eurodac), which helps identify the country responsible for the asylum application. The goal of the Dublin system is to establish clear, objective criteria for responsibility "to prevent and discourage forum shopping, to prevent and discourage secondary movements, and to avoid the phenomenon of asylum seekers 'in orbit.'" Opinion of Advocate General Sharpston in *A.S. v. Slovenia*, Case C-490/16, EU:C:2017:585, Eur. Ct. Justice (2017), sec. 100. Member states are permitted to rely on the sovereignty clause under the Dublin regulation, which allows states to voluntarily assume responsibility for processing asylum applications for which they are not otherwise responsible, as was the case with Germany's unilateral decision in summer 2015.

[131] Anna Triandafyllidou and Angeliki Dimitriadi, 'Migration Management at the Outposts of the European Union', *Griffith Law Review 22* (2013): pp. 598–618, p. 616.

[132] Despite cracks in the reach and implementation of this system in the wake of the mass influx of 2015, the European Court of Justice ruled in 2017 that the regulation still stands. See *A.S. v. Slovenia* (n 129). For analysis of the overall EU data and per-state numbers of registered first-time asylum seekers, see Eurostat, *Record Number of over 1.2 Million First Time Asylum Seekers Registered in 2015* (Eurostat News Release 44/2016, March 4, 2016), online http://ec.europa.eu/eurostat/documents/2995521/7203832/3-04032016-AP-EN.pdf/790eba01-381c-4163-bcd2-a54959b99ed6.

seen in the ongoing crisis that the Dublin rules have placed too much responsibility on just a few Member States."[133] While an EU-wide relocation program was introduced to relieve some of these pressures, it could not quell nor erase the multifaceted tensions and political backlash that the mass influx has wrought in Europe.[134] The relocation program, designed to express European solidarity by relieving the pressure from Greece and Italy, was met with stiff opposition by the Visegrad governments (Czech Republic, Hungary, Poland, and Slovakia) and lukewarm compliance by other member states, ultimately failing to achieve its goals. Today, immigration continues to top the list of voters' concerns in Europe, fueling the sharp ballot-box success of populist anti-immigrant leaders and parties that galvanize the narrative of "loss of control."[135]

When it comes to devising new measures to regulate mobility, the European Union and its member states have borrowed more than one page from the shifting-border book. The Court of Justice for the European Union (CJEU) has recently ruled that border and migration enforcement activities can stretch inward *beyond* the actual, territorial border of members states; it has authorized "border officials responsible for border surveillance and the monitoring of foreign nationals" to

[133] European Commission, Migration and Home Affairs, 'Reforming the Common European Asylum System and Developing Safe and Legal Pathways to Europe', online https://ec.europa.eu/home-affairs/what-is-new/news/news/2016/20160406_2_en (quoting EC first vice-president Frans Timmerman).

[134] This program refers to the "relocation" of 160,000 asylum seekers, based on a key that takes into account several features of the respective member states. The progress of the plan is reported by https://ec.europa.eu/home-affairs. The resistance of countries such as Hungary, Poland, and the Czech Republic to the terms of the relocation plan has led to the issuance of "letters of formal notice" against this failure to adhere to solidarity measures, and is seen as indicative not only of the refugee crisis but also a crisis of European Union's political unity. It is less well known, however, that many other member states were foot-dragging its implementation.

[135] Demonstrating a dramatic shift in rhetoric from the earlier emphasis on granting access for those who need international protection, Angela Merkel recently stated that Europe's goal is to "replace *illegal* migration with legal migration" (emphasis added), thus accepting the "regaining control" narrative. This point was made even more explicitly by the President of the European Council, Donald Tusk, who insisted that, "Europe itself needed to do more to secure its borders," and further warned that if the external borders of Europe are not protected, then the Schengen free-movement zone, which was established by the removal of internal borders, "will become history." See James Kanter and Andrew Higgins, 'EU to Offer Turkey 3 Billion Euros to Stem Migrant Flow', *The New York Times*, November 29, 2015.

carry out their activities within an area of 20 kilometers away from the border, crafting a European variant of the United States' "constitution free" zone, here translated to the denser continental geography.[136] In 2017, the CJEU reviewed the matter again, holding that "random" and "baseless identification checks" cannot be used as a way to circumvent free mobility within Europe. However, so long as such checks are proportional and done "to prevent unauthorized entry," identity checks can take place not just within in the 20-kilometer zone, as previously ruled, but within a broader territorial range: 30 kilometers of the land border and a radius of 50 kilometers of the sea border, as well as in train stations nationwide and on-board trains *anywhere*.[137] Again, we find the same inland "stretching" dynamic that we have witnessed elsewhere. What is perplexing in this context, however, is that such shifting-border measures are exercised *within* Europe's free-movement zone.[138]

In addition to the above-mentioned measures of tightening *inland* control and shifting responsibility and accountability (as well as finger pointing) among European countries, the European Union and its member states have adopted an extensive outward-looking strategy, known as "externalization," which extends beyond the boundaries of

---

[136] *Melki and Abdeli*, Cases C-188/10 and C-189/10, ECLI:EU:C:2010:36, Eur. Ct. Justice (2010) and *Adil*, Case C-278/12 PPU, ECLI:EU:C:2012:508, Eur. Ct. Justice (2012).

[137] Case C-9/16, ECLI:EU:C:2017:483, Eur. Ct. Justice (2017), reference on preliminary ruling. This case challenged the intra-Schengen border-checks practice of the German Bundespolizei under Articles 20 and 21 of Regulation 562/2006 of the European Parliament and of the Council of March 15, 2006, establishing a Community Code on the rules governing the movement of persons across borders (Schengen Borders Code), 2006 O.J. (L 105) 1 (EU), and Article 2 of the German Bundespolizeigesetz [BPolG] [Federal Police Law], October 19, 1994, BGBl. I at 2987, § 2, last amended by Art. 3 of Gesetz, July 26, 2016, BGBl. I at 1818 (Ger.).

[138] Beyond such invisible, moving borders, several Schengen member states also temporarily re-erected their marked and visible border controls at Europe's internal borders in the wake of the migration crisis, pursuant to the requirements of Article 25 of the Schengen Borders Code (n 136), online https://ec.europa.eu/home-affairs/sites/homeaffairs/files/what-we-do/policies/borders-and-visas/schengen/reintroduction-border-control/docs/ms_notifications_-_reintroduction_of_border_control_en.pdf. The reintroduction of border controls within the Schengen area is a last-resort prerogative of member states, which is subject to the requirement of proportionality and must be limited in time.

[139] These agreements have been criticized for failing to provide sufficient human rights safeguards and for the unfair bartering tactics used by the European Union to achieve such agreements with third countries, which effectively become Europe's "dumping" ground

the continent and shifts focus to migrants' countries of origin or transit. This has led the European Union to establish one of the world's most complex, inter-agency, multi-tiered visions of the shifting border, comprised of *pre-entry* controls at countries of origin and transit all the way through to removal of irregular migrants *after* they have reached EU territory. This removal procedure is facilitated by the shared European Return Directive and a growing list of bilateral and multilateral "readmission agreements" negotiated with poorer and less stable non-EU countries to which irregular migrants can be returned, even if they merely passed through such countries en route to Europe.[139]

Europe's externalization policy creates a "ring of protection" outside the European Union. It involves a "close partnership" with non-EU states from near and far through programs such as the Neighborhood Policy, Euro-Mediterranean Partnership, the Balkan Stability Pact, the Africa–EU Partnership, the Valletta Action Plan, the Global Approach to Migration and Mobility, and so on. These policies are designed to enforce migration control in collaboration with countries of origin or transit "at the earliest possible stage"; they combine readmission agreements with development incentives and asylum-system capacity building for the signatory third-countries, as well as enticements such as promises of easier visa processing for their citizens, highlighting the unequal bargaining power of the European Union and its member states.[140] The controversial agreement between the European Union and Turkey, which involves the transfer of billions of euros and other inducements in return for Turkey's assistance with "'keep[ing] people

in exchange for promises of development aid, eased procedures for visa processing, and the like.

[140] Red Cross, *Shifting Borders: Externalising Migrant Vulnerabilities and Rights* (Brussels: Red Cross EU Office, 2013), p. 28, online https://redcross.eu/uploads/files/Positions/Migration/Shifting%20borders%20booklet/shifting-borders-externalizing-migrant-vulnerabilities-rights-red-cross-eu-office.pdf. The external dimension of EU asylum and migration policy dates back to 2005 (Council of European Union, *A Strategy for the External Dimension of JHF: Global Freedom, Security and Justice* (14366/1/05, 24 November 2005) (EU)), although in practice this policy follows up on earlier iterations and frameworks that emphasized the importance of cooperation with non-EU third countries as a way to "push out" the border and its migration-control functions. For comprehensive analysis, see Ryan and Mitsilegas, *Extraterritorial Immigration Control* (n 85).

in the region' and out of Europe" is a classic example of outsourcing migration and border control.[141]

Earlier bilateral and multilateral agreements have been criticized as absolving EU countries of their otherwise binding human rights obli gations by insisting that non-EU states provide protection to forced migrants, including asylum seekers, as soon as possible after the initial displacement and as close as possible to countries of origin or transit. Such agreements recast countries of origin or transit as "gatekeepers to the developed world," in the process allowing wealthier countries to insulate themselves from legal responsibility toward refugees and other persons entitled to international protection.[142] In the aftermath of 2015's migration crisis and with the rise of populist, anti-immigrant sentiments, calls to establish regional disembarkation centers outside Europe have grown louder. Such proposals remain murky on the details, but it is crystal clear that they take a leaf out of Australia's play-book: they are designed to offshore refugees and divert legal responsi-bility away from EU member states. While responding to political pressures to "regain" control and halt uninvited arrivals, such proposals do little or nothing to provide safe passage or lawful channels for EU entry for those identified as in need of protection, wherever they happen to have encountered the long arm of the mobility-inhibiting shifting border.

This need not be the case, however. I believe this shift in the "tech-nology" of governance and spatiality of migration regulation must be matched by a reconceptualization of the relationship between law and territory, stratification and (im)mobility, space and political will, so as to facilitate rights protections and access options that begin to match the restless agility of the shifting border. I argue that an understanding of borders as *mobile* constructs provides an important

---

[141] Kanter and Higgins (n 134), quoting Chancellor Angela Merkel of Germany. The most far-reaching variant of the externalization policy, which has been proposed but not implemented, would involve "outsourcing" the processing of asylum claims of those who attempt to reach the territory of the European Union to non-EU countries, along the lines of Australia's controversial offshore-processing practice.

[142] Hathaway and Gammeltoft-Hansen, 'Non-Refoulement' (n 12), pp. 9, 17.

corrective to prevalent theoretical accounts. I return to elaborate these ideas, and how they might be put into action, in the final section of the discussion.[143]

2. Some implications of the shifting border: thinking beyond the binary

Before turning to explore potential remedies and reforms, we must ask: why this flurry of activity, and why now? As Bimal Ghosh aptly observes, "no other source of tension and anxiety has been more powerful [in the global north] than the fear, both real and perceived, of huge waves of future emigration from poor and weak states in the years and decades to come."[144] Migration experts have persistently argued that these fears are inflated and remain empirically unfounded, emphasizing that the number of refugees that reach the greener pastures of the world's more affluent countries is dwarfed by the share of burden borne by the countries in poorer and less stable regions that host approximately four fifths of the world's refugees. In Europe, economists and others, adopting a bird's eye perspective, have claimed that it should not be impossible for a union of 500 million people to successfully absorb 1 million asylum seekers. While such opinions that emphasize scale and capacity may be descriptively accurate, as a matter of political expediency they miss the

---

[143] Theorists and activists concerned with the imbalance of power across borders and the complicity of actors in one political community in harms that are manifested in another (what economists would term negative externalities) have provided excellent arguments for moving beyond the current stalemate. In the political-theory literature, authors such as Iris Marion Young and Catherine Lu have advanced broader understandings of structural injustice that cover such situations. Related concerns are addressed in the vast literature on global justice and environmental justice. In the normative scholarship on migration, see, for example, Benhabib, *The Rights of Others* (n 11); David Owen, 'In Loco Civitatis: On the Normative Basis of Refugeehood and Responsibilities for Refugees', in Sarah Fine and Lea Ypi, eds, *Migration in Political Theory: The Ethics of Movement and Membership* (Oxford: Oxford University Press, 2016), pp. 269–289.

[144] Bimal Ghosh, 'Toward a New International Regime for Orderly Movements of People', in Bimal Ghosh, ed., *Managing Migration: Time for a New International Regime?* (Oxford: Oxford University Press, 2000), pp. 6–26, p. 10.

emotive mark: it is the public's *perception* of threat or a looming crisis of loss of control over borders that matters.[145]

In the wake of the refugee crisis, images of large waves of people desperately marching on foot or crossing the sea on dangerous dinghies—seeking any possible pathway to Europe—are now etched in our collective memory. These images feed into already protracted debates, accentuating positions in both the human rights camp and the need-to-"regain"-control constituency. The fear of loss of control, along with xenophobic and anti-immigrant sentiment, has proven powerful in unleashing a backlash and nourishing the rise of populist nationalism. Political opportunists have latched on to this perception of loss of control—the sense that governments are clueless, toothless, or both. Such sentiments have prevailed in the past but have become more pronounced following the sharp surge in global displacement due to protracted situations of civil strife, war, climate emergency, famine, and oppression amplifying forced migration and international protection pressures. All of this led the United Nations High Commissioner for Refugees to issue a stern warning that "the world is facing a staggering crisis" as the number of refugees and displaced people has reached "the highest level ever recorded" since the aftermath of World War II.[146]

As member states continue to bicker about responsibility and burden-sharing, treating refugee-protection obligations as a "'hot potato'. . .[for] which nobody wants to bear the costs," the push to further restrict access

---

[145] Even at the height of the refugee crisis in Europe, the vast majority of Syrian refugees were, and still are, hosted in neighboring Turkey, Lebanon, Jordan, Iraq, and Egypt. Together these latter countries carry the brunt of this refugee crisis: 4.8 million have now fled to them, according to 2017 UNHCR figures. About a quarter of the population of Lebanon now consists of displaced Syrians. More affluent parts of the world are not the major recipient-states for refugees; in fact, no country in Europe or North America has made the top-ten list of the UN High Commissioner for Refugees in recent years. The problem, however, is that simply reciting and relaying these facts and figures is unlikely to alleviate the deep sense of anxiety surrounding questions of migration, especially in countries facing the resurgence of populist nationalism, in no small part due to the politicization of the charged "loss of control" theme.

[146] UNHCR, 'Global Trends Report—Forced Displacement in 2014: World at War', online http://unhcr.org/556725e69.html; UNHCR, 'Worldwide Displacement Hits All-Time High as War and Persecution Increase', online www.unhcr.org/news/latest/2015/6/558193896/worldwide-displacement-hits-all-time-high-war-persecution-increase.html.

and to rely on ever more aggressive migration-management techniques increases. So does the human toll. Those who manage to pass through the cracks of the shifting border resort to the cavalier guidance of human smugglers who unscrupulously profit from their despair.[147] Data collected by the IOM reveal that since 2000, more than 45,000 migrants have drowned, mostly in the Mediterranean. As a recent report observes, "[t]his is despite the fact that this stretch of water is the most heavily surveyed and among the most tranquil in the world."[148] This glaring failure to provide safe passage is connected to, and indeed fueled by, the attempt to skirt responsibility in a global system whereby the standard interpretation of access to protection is tied to a fixed interpretation of territoriality: namely, it requires reaching the proverbial "gates."

When it comes to the obligation to protect—the so-called "trump card" or "blank cheque" held by those refugees who reach the frontier of desired destinations—the shifting-border paradigm, with its malleable legal spatiality, provides the required flexibility for borders to operate in a quantum-like duality, simultaneously static and diffuse. To limit their liability to humanitarian claims, states retreat to the narrowest and strictest application of the classic Westphalian notion of the sovereignty, placing the burden of "getting here" on individuals who are already displaced and vulnerable. Multiple layers and sources of law—administrative and constitutional, immigration and refugee, regional and international—require that, to claim protection, individuals must be on the territory of the state in question. Thus, when it comes to refugees, the old, static, and fortified border appears in full glory: to launch an asylum claim, it is vital to reach the territorial border. Until

---

[147] The "hot potato" quote is drawn from Didier Bigo, 'Frontier Controls in the European Union', in Didier Bigo and Elspeth Guild, eds, *Controlling Frontiers: Free Movement into and within Europe* (Aldershot: Ashgate, 2005), pp. 48–98. See also Gallagher and David, *International Law of Migrant Smuggling* (n 101).

[148] Migrant deaths also occur along the Mexico–US border. The major reported causes of death are dehydration and hyperthermia. Civil society groups such as border angels seek to prevent unnecessary deaths by providing "border water drops"—plastic jugs of water that are placed by volunteers in the desert along high-traffic migrant paths. Border Angels, 'Border Water Drop', online www.borderangels.org/desert-water-drops/.

the target country's soil is physically underfoot, which even then is sometimes insufficient (as in the case of excision or *zones d'attente*), a migrant's right to protection remains abstracted and un-actionable vis-à-vis a specific jurisdiction.

When states seek to *control* migration, the spatial and temporal understandings of the border shift, seeping the border inward or extending it outward, just as the same borders may be shrunk and/or folded back to create constitution-free zones. These maneuvers allow affluent societies to continue to present themselves as global beacons of democracy and human rights while engaging in ever more frantic efforts to avert such arrival in the first place, or, as Canada now does, following the lead of Australia, declaring those who actually reach the territory as "inadmissible" upon arrival. Government policymakers and other stakeholders, public and private, thus simultaneously uphold a conception of fixed territoriality when it comes to extending rights and protections to non-citizens, while at the same time switching to an unmoored and increasingly mobile conception of the border (contracting and expanding to wherever the enforcement need arises) when it comes to the rights-*restricting* dimension of migration-control activities.

What theoretical and pragmatic insights can be drawn from the more grounded analysis of the shifting-border paradigm that I have offered above? There are at least five interrelated lessons which I would like to emphasize. First, in today's world, understandings of mobility and globalization can no longer revolve around the dichotomy between open and closed borders. This binary misses the unique and perplexing features of the shifting-border landscape: states may simultaneously open *and* close their borders, depending on who is seeking passage, where the encounter takes place, and what security and identity credentials (or, conversely, algorithmic risks) the person is deemed to bear. Thus, we can no longer merely focus our debates on whether borders are, or should be, more porous or impermeable, as this misses the mark. The new paradigm rests on the logic of acquiring enhanced control over those passing through multiple checkpoints, *fracturing* the uniformity of impact of the border on those seeking to pass through its gates.

For some it offers a welcome mat, for others a locked barricade. Such selectivity is at heart of the shifting-border operations, fast-tracking desired entrants while at the same time erecting higher and higher legal walls, ever further away, to keep out the unwanted and uninvited migrants.[149]

In lieu of idealized and abstracted discussions, the framework offered here begins from the ground up, allowing us to see the nuances and dark corners of the evolving legal cartography and geography of power and (im)mobility. It thus avoids the trap of overlooking troublesome realities by making unrealistic assumptions about how borders operate in the world around us. The "high resolution" investigation of the shifting border offered in this study therefore fits comfortably with the recent "methodological turn" in political theory, which calls for more grounded theorizing against the background of non-ideal conditions.[150]

Second, the legal changes I have recounted in identifying and explaining the shifting-border phenomenon permit us to revisit the demise-of-the-state thesis, prevalent among humanists and activists, which engendered the influential "disappearing"-border and waning-sovereignty debate. The evidence shows that borders and migration control are not vanishing but are being reinvented. As we have seen, traditional Westphalian concepts of sovereignty and territoriality are being "reworked" and implemented in novel ways. Such revisions have contributed to the pressing and, as yet, unresolved tensions between these aggressive new measures of controlling mobility across ever shifting borders and rule-of-law countries' declared commitments to human rights. Indeed, as we have seen in the examples above,

---

[149] On the selectivity of migration under the shifting border, see, for example, Shachar and Hirschl, 'On Citizenship, States and Markets' (n 16); Ayelet Shachar, 'The Marketization of Citizenship in an Age of Restrictionism' (n 48).

[150] Recent collections focusing on the ethics and politics of migration in a non-ideal world share similar sentiments. See Crispino E.G. Akakpo and Patti T. Lenard, 'New Challenges in Immigration Theory: An Overview', *Critical Review of International Social and Political Philosophy* 5 (2014): pp. 493–502; Jan Brezger, Andreas Cassee, and Anna Goppel, 'The Ethics of Immigration in a Non-Ideal World: Introduction', *Moral Philosophy and Politics* 3 (2016): pp. 135–140, among others. Some of these discussions have antecedents in Carens, *The Ethics of Immigration* (n 14).

constitutional doctrine and human rights jurisprudence has yet to fully catch up with this new and far more creative exercise of plenary power in regulating access and control through the invention of the shifting border.[151] There is thus a deep irony embedded in the current situation: the idea of de-territorialized space and action, initially vaunted as progressive and human-rights-enhancing, has been skillfully (and arguably repressively) "hijacked" by law-and-order agencies seeking to restrict and police mobility.[152] What kind of normative and institutional implications does such capture entail, and how can it be countered or at least tamed?

With these concerns in mind, the final section of my discussion will advance the argument that, as part of a two-pronged response, the shifting-border technology and ideology must be matched by a reconceptualization of the relationship between law and territory that would entail that legal obligations become operative as soon as state agents (or their delegates) exercise "effective control." In other words, if states exert their power in an extraterritorial fashion, then claims of law and justice must similarly extend beyond borders.

Third, shifting the locus of governance structures—for example, by moving from the national to the supranational, or from the unilateral to the multilateral—does not necessarily improve the human rights protections and mobility options afforded to those seeking entry or who have been stopped en route. We have already seen, for example,

---

[151] Whereas typically we think of public law in the context of global constitutional or administrative law as focusing on rights and placing limits on the exercise of executive power, in the context of citizenship and immigration much of the work occurs through the regulatory side of law, with comparatively little judicial review involved. This is reflected, for example, in entrenched legal concepts such as the "plenary power doctrine" in US immigration law or the "royal prerogative" in the United Kingdom. The term "*plenary* power" itself comes to us from Latin, from the etymological root of "*plenus*," meaning full power or full authority. While a perennial subject of scholarly critique, plenary power still holds a significant sway in law, and it allows a great degree of discretion to power holders in the realm of controlling a nation's borders (real or imagined) and membership boundaries as expressions of sovereignty.

[152] Some of this idealism is still reflected in the literature on the transnational promise of higher law beyond the state. For a detailed account, see Turkuler Isikel, *Europe's Functional Constitution: A Theory of Constitution beyond the State* (Oxford: Oxford University Press, 2016).

the emphasis placed by the shifting-border architects on "policing at a distance."[153] In Europe, scholars have been fascinated with the multiple ways in which the "contemporary thought on visas developed in parallel to the reflection upon the abolition of border controls within the Schengen."[154] This juxtaposition of mobility and immobility, openness and closure, freedom in the interior and security threats from its exterior is part and parcel of the shifting-border paradigm as it finds expression at the transnational level. As official EU policy states, "the Union shall develop policy with a view to . . . the gradual introduction of an integrated management system for external borders."[155]

A key to fulfilling this mandate is the development and implementation of a common policy on visas, which was incorporated into consular instructions and manuals.[156] Even more significantly, it has facilitated the establishment of so-called blacklists of countries, whose citizens must obtain visas to EU member states in advance of travel.[157] Visa regulation of this kind is, of course, not new. It dates back to the nineteenth century, to the time of the "invention of the passport" (as John Torpey memorably put it), offering a prime example of *unilateral* national-generated and enforced techniques of "remote control."[158] Tracking the evolution of visa-free travel (or visa-waiver programs) from the 1950s onward, recent studies have documented a "global mobility divide," whereby visa-free travel and ease of mobility has

[153] As explained earlier, such measures recast the timeline of migration control to *pre*-arrival and spatially push such regulation outward to the jurisdiction of countries of origin and transit. This is part and parcel of Europe's ambitious, expansive, and multi-stakeholder integrated border-mobility strategy.
[154] Nora El Qadim, 'The Symbolic Meaning of International Mobility: EU–Morocco Negotiations on Visa Facilitation', *Migration Studies* 6 (2018): pp. 279–305, p. 282.
[155] Consolidated versions of the Treaty on European Union and the Treaty on the Functioning of the European Union, 2012/C 326/01 (EU) § 77(1)(c). For comprehensive analysis of the development of these legal measures, see Moreno-Lax, *Accessing Asylum in Europe* (n 86), pp. 47–69.
[156] Consolidated versions of the Treaty on European Union and the Treaty on the Functioning of the European Union, 2012/C 326/01 (EU) § 77(2)(a). For those hailing from the world's less stable and poorer regions, securing a visa is a mandatory first step to gaining lawful admission to Europe—and it must take place outside the continent, prior to travel.
[157] Qadim, 'The Symbolic Meaning of International Mobility' (n 154).
[158] John Torpey, *The Invention of the Passport: Surveillance, Citizenship and the State* (Cambridge: Cambridge University Press, 2000).

increased for citizens of well-off countries, while it has stagnated or even decreased for those hailing from poorer or less stable countries.[159] The creation of regional "blocks" such as the European Union has added yet another twist to the story. Shared or harmonized visa policies have paradoxically generated greater, not lesser, restrictions for those seeking admission from the outside, as "each member state must exhibit solidarity with the other member states and respect the presence on the blacklist of a country whose nationals do not necessarily present a problem for it."[160] The *cumulative* list is thus more extensive and robust. This pattern is repeated in other contexts: the power to enter into readmission agreements, once reserved to member states alone and now expanded to the European Union, provides another example of how the regional block can gain greater concessions from its bargaining partners (primarily countries of origin and transit in the world's poorer regions) than individual member states may have been able to, leading some commenters to dub such agreements as "repressive measures of pre-frontier control."[161]

Fourth, one of the major themes of renewal in comparative constitutional law over the past few decades has been the celebration of the "migration of constitutional ideas."[162] The gist of the argument is that apex courts in the world of new constitutionalism now regularly "borrow" progressive ideas from one another—for example, by citing precedents from comparable countries as a source of persuasive authority.[163] Through this transnational dialogue, judges are advancing a new and expanded catalogue of rights protections for citizens and non-citizens alike.[164] But there is another, darker, side to this increased cross-border

[159] The term "global mobility divide" is drawn here from Steffen Mau.
[160] See Didier Bigo and Elspeth Guild, 'Policing at a Distance: Schengen Visa Policies', in Didier Bigo and Elspeth Guild, eds, *Controlling Frontiers: Free Movement into and within Europe* (Ashgate, 2005), pp. 233–263, p. 245.
[161] Marion Panizzon, 'Readmission Agreements of EU Member States: A Case for EU Subsidiary or Dualism', *Refugee Survey Quarterly 31* (2012): pp. 101–133.
[162] For a concise overview, see Vlad F. Perju, 'Constitutional Transplants, Borrowing, and Migrations', in Michel Rosenfeld and András Sajó, eds, *The Oxford Handbook of Comparative Constitutional Law* (Oxford: Oxford University Press, 2013), pp. 1304–1325.
[163] H. Patrick Glenn, 'Persuasive Authority', *McGill Law Journal 32* (1987): pp. 261–287.
[164] See, for example, Anne-Marie Slaughter, *A New World Order* (Princeton: Princeton University Press, 2005).

dialogue. Just as progressive ideas about the scope and extent of rights protections can travel quickly, so can restrictive policies. We might call this the *constrictive precedent* problem, or emulating the "worst case" rather than following the "best case" precedent.

Just as human rights and constitutional ideas can travel across borders and organizational terrain, restrictive immigration measures, anti-constitutional or abusive constitutional measures can do so no less easily and effectively, if not faster. Once a reputable court or government adopts a highly restrictive policy toward unauthorized migrants, other governments facing similar predicaments may decide to follow that earlier restrictive decision or policy (even if legally and morally contentious) as a persuasive precedent, or "model," to justify *their* own subsequent choices limiting the substantive rights or procedural protections accorded to vulnerable migrant populations such as refugees, asylum seekers, and other humanitarian causes. A classic example of this pattern at work is found in the global influence of the US Supreme Court decision in *Sale*, which held that US Coast Guard ships can "push back" Haitian asylum seekers if they are interdicted on the high seas, based on the argument that *non-refoulement* obligations (derived from the French word *refouler* (to "turn back" or "repel")) do not apply extra-territorially. While criticized by migration scholars and legal experts, *Sale* stands for a restrictive interpretation of domestic and international refugee and human rights laws, according to which such obligations apply only at the border or within the territory.[165] Here again we witness how the shifting paradigms, or competing conceptions of the border, matter dramatically when it comes the geography of human rights and their implementation. The *Sale* court upheld an image of the border as static and fixed, standing at the territorial edges of the country. The interdiction of Haitian by US Coast Guard ships, which arguably operated as a functional equivalent of the border, applied far away from the

---

[165] *Sale v. Haitian Centers Council,* 509 U.S. 155 (1993). See Leila Nasr, 'The Extraterritoriality of the Principle of Non-Refoulement: A Critique of the Sale Case and Roma Case', *LSE Human Rights,* online http://blogs.lse.ac.uk/humanrights/2016/02/09/the-extraterritoriality-of-the-principle-of-non-refoulement-a-critique-of-the-sale-case-and-roma-case/.

protected territory and, accordingly, was not "visible" or legible to a court that examined it under the classic Westphalian lens.[166] The United States still upholds this legal position, as it firmly made clear in response to the UNHCR's Advisory Opinion on Extraterritorial Application of Non-Refoulement Obligations, released in 2007.[167]

The *Sale* ruling and the United States' permissive stance on pre-emptive interdiction have been rebuked by some national and international courts and tribunals. The English Court of Appeals, for example, broke the semi-sacred principle of international comity among courts when it referred to the case as "wrongly decided." Going a step further, the Inter-American Commission held, contra *Sale*, that the *non-refoulement* provision in the Refugee Convention "has no geographical limitations," thus interpreting legal responsibility and jurisdiction in a more robust fashion than ever before, no longer focusing solely on territorial location (as under the static model) but also on situations whereby a state exercises "effective control" or "public power" beyond its borders. A growing number of international-law and migration scholars echo this judgement call. However, these statements are non-binding, and *Sale* has proven more resilient than some predicted. It is seen as providing indirect guidance and legitimacy for comparable jurisdictions to adopt similarly obstructive interdiction policies—that "align in a control continuum . . . at several stages of the migrant's journey," appearing and reappearing "numerous times, in different guises"—while escaping the reach of their legal responsibility to offer access to international protection systems to those affected by these shifting-border measures by virtue of claiming that *non-refoulement* does not apply extraterritorially.[168] Australia is a case in point. The fact that the United States has already provided

---

[166] On the functional equivalent of the border argument in the *Sale* case, see Hiroshi Motomura, 'Haitian Asylum Seekers: Interdiction and Immigrants' Rights', *Cornell International Law Journal* 26 (1993): pp. 695–717.

[167] United States Department of State, *Observations of the United States on the Advisory Opinion of the UN High Commissioner for Refugees on the Extraterritorial Application of Non-Refoulement Obligations under the 1951 Convention Relating to the Status of Refugees and Its 1967 Protocol* (US Department of State Archive, January 20, 2001 to January 20, 2009, December 28, 2007), online https://2001-2009.state.gov/s/l/2007/112631.htm.

[168] Moreno-Lax, *Accessing Asylum in Europe* (n 86), p. 2.

justification for such a rights-restricting approach is seen as "license" to follow suit.[169] In a similar vein, the European Union's invention of the safe-third-country concept has traveled widely and globally, inspiring, among other examples, the safe-third-country agreement between the US and Canada, or Norway's recent designation of Russia as a safe third country to which asylum seekers can be returned, thus denying them access to Norway's (and, by extension, Europe's) asylum procedures.[170] In turn, the Australian policy of declaring maritime arrivals unauthorized by virtue of reaching the excision zone has inspired Canadian legislation to declare those arriving without authorization by boat as "irregular arrivals," thereby restricting their substantive and procedural rights and protections. Even if eventually recognized as refugees, such arrivals face a "freeze period" of five years before they can apply for permanent residency. This is quite a dramatic shift for Canada, which prides itself, perhaps in an overly self-congratulatory fashion, as maintaining one of the world's most generous immigration systems. In short, ideas travel fast and furiously across borderlines, especially when policymakers feel pressured to demonstrate action to counter the public perception of "loss of control." The result, for those en route or escaping harm's way, is further restrictions and the tightening of rights by precisely those premium democratic destinations that are globally perceived to be beacons of the rule of law, not rogue or lawless states. There is real room for concern that such behavior advanced by the leaders of the "free world" will justify infringements on protected rights by partner states that may have less than dazzling records on human rights.

Fifth, the sheer reach and magnitude of the shifting border also invites revisiting the age-old question of how to tame menacing governmental

---

[169] As in the United States, Australian courts have determined that practices of interdicting migrants and asylum seekers on the high seas does not violate *non-refoulement*. See *Ruddock v. Vadarlis* [2001] 110 FCR 491 (Austl).

[170] The transnational emulation of the practices of detention in the context of return is another prime example, as is the more general trend toward adopting more restrictive immigration policies, which, outside the European Union, is not tamed by binding regional human rights courts or minimum agreed-upon standards. For an illuminating analysis, see Hélène Lambert, Jane McAdam, and Maryellen Fullerton, eds, *The Global Reach of Europe's Refugee Law* (Cambridge: Cambridge University Press, 2013).

authority. As this power has now become almost boundless in its conceptual framing and spatial manifestation, it has become increasingly difficult to challenge with traditional legal tools and conceptions of human rights, both of which still rely on territoriality as their core grounding principle.[171] If we seek to develop fresh proposals to tame the rights-restricting consequences of the shifting border, we must rethink the relationship between law and territory, space and political organization, a task to which I turn momentarily.

3. Normative considerations and institutional redesigns: on "place" and political obligation

It is time now to explore strategies by which these pervasive patterns might be challenged or changed, taking into account the gravity of the problems addressed. Because it engages the basic building blocks of the modern state—territoriality, sovereignty, and legal spatiality—this transformation engages both norms and interests, raising some of the core legal and normative questions of our time.

Space and political organization: Hannah Arendt's intervention

Writing after the atrocities of World War II and the Holocaust, Hannah Arendt astutely observed:

> [s]uddenly, there was no place on earth where migrants could go without the severest restrictions, no country where they would be assimilated, no territory where they could found a new community of their own. This

---

[171] The presumption against extraterritoriality is deeply ingrained. In the United States, for example, even a federal act that explicitly permits non-nationals to sue in US courts against the breach of human rights in other countries was eventually construed narrowly by the United States Supreme Court on the basis of the presumption against extraterritoriality, which, the Court ruled, was not displaced in the case at stake, which involved a human rights violation that occurred outside the United States. See *Kiobel v. Royal Dutch Petroleum*, 569 U.S. 108 (2013) (United States). For a critical account, see Philip Liste, 'Transnational Human Rights Litigation and Territorialized Knowledge: *Kiobel* and the "Knowledge of Space"', *Transnational Legal Theory* 5 (2014): pp. 1–16.

moreover, had nothing to do with any material problem of overpopulation; it was a problem not of space but of political organization.[172]

While the world has changed dramatically since the publication of *The Origins of Totalitarianism*, in 1955, the plight of refugees and displaced persons still remains one of the biggest and most pressing human rights issues of our time. For Arendt, explains Benhabib, the "right to have rights" could only be realized in the context of a political community in which we are political equals who are judged "through our actions and opinions, by what we do and say," not on account of ascriptive factors such as ethnic lineage or descent.[173] No less significant, for Arendt the tragedy of the migrants and refugees was that they had "no place on earth where [they] could go to without the severest restrictions," a problem itself wholly entrenched in the Westphalian system, which accords exclusive sovereignty to national jurisdictions over every habitable space on earth. For Arendt, the fulfillment of political equality could only take place within a particular kind of territorially demarcated political community: the modern state. Despite her radicalism and groundbreaking ideas, Arendt's writing, a product of her own historical period, manifests a rather fixed and rigid vision of territoriality.

As we have already seen, today it is paradoxically states themselves that are reinventing sovereignty and territoriality, showing a remarkable capacity to adapt to new environments. As border control is increasingly portrayed as "either or both a security imperative and a life-saving humanitarian endeavor," doing nothing in the face of large-scale global mobility pressures counters the basic sovereign instinct to control the border, wherever it is placed and replaced through the words of law and the assistance of "big data" and sophisticated technocratic-biometric surveillance.[174] Irregular movement of people is perceived by governments,

---

[172] Hannah Arendt, *The Origins of Totalitarianism* (New York: Schoken, 2004), pp. 372–373.

[173] Seyla Benhabib, 'Political Geographies in a Global World: Arendtian Reflections', *Social Research* 69 (2002): pp. 539–566, p. 557.

[174] Bill Frelick, Ian M. Kysel, and Jennifer Podkul, 'The Impact of Externalization of Migrant Controls on the Rights of Asylum Seekers and Other Migrants', *Journal on Migration and Human Security* 4 (2016): pp. 190–220, p. 193.

and by growing sectors of their populations, as risking the stability and security of the international order, informing discussions of contemporary migration as a "crisis" for a multitude of actors: those seeking mobility across borders but denied access to legal channels of entry, for neighboring countries on the brink of insolvency and political instability, for transit countries endowed with growing responsibilities to "stop the flow," for governmental and non-governmental humanitarian agencies bearing the brunt of meeting the fundamental needs of migrants and refugees stranded in "temporary" situations that seem to never end, for destination countries and supranational bodies fearing loss of control, and, ultimately, for the Westphalian order itself, if sovereignty is (unrealistically) expected to generate unbridled control over cross-border movement. In Europe, the failure to offer adequate responses to the sharp increase of asylum applications in the summer of 2015 under a common framework also led to the return of internal borders, not as moveable and invisible, but as visible, physical barriers manifesting statist attempts to "regain" and display potent sovereign authority.

At present, established regimes of rights and protections help ensure that those who "make it"—those who manage to defy the shifting border and touch base on the soil of desired destination countries—will enjoy more vigorous protections. None of this, however, addresses the plight of those who do not arrive, who cannot gain access, who are not safe and who are unable to defeat the geopolitical rifts and global inequalities that make arrival in the vicinity of our admission gates a pipedream. They are the contemporary embodiment of the displaced and dispossessed that Arendt so powerfully places at the heart of her analysis. Recall that for Arendt the problem was "not of space, but of political organization." I beg to differ. Based on the analysis of the shifting border and the reinvention of borders for the purposes of migration control by governments seeking to admit the few but not the many, selectively deterring or encouraging mobility, the challenges posed by current migration flows encompass *both* our notions of space *and* political organization, and, as a result, any new answers will require addressing these combined factors in tandem.

The overrated premium of territorial arrival

Today's harsh realities reveal the inadequacy of seeking legal cover under the static conception of the border while persistently breaching it by devising far more dynamic, multifaceted and de-territorialized techniques of governance that rely largely on the flexible variability of the shifting border. It is in this tension—between states' skirting their constitutional and human rights obligations and their declared commitment to upholding them—that an opening might be found to challenge the darker corners and unresolved contradictions embedded in the shifting border.

What are the implications of this massive yet still under-theorized change of the *locus* of the exercise of the so-called last bastion of sovereignty—migration control—that no longer takes place exclusively or primarily in the confines of a bounded territory? Does it shed new light on the range of possibilities for resistance and creative openings for action (whether by states, individuals, non-governmental actors, or the international community at large) that were impossible to imagine under the classic, static, view of the border? I believe the answer is affirmative and that it need not fall back on the competing yet no longer stable poles of the "static" and "disappearing" narratives. Nor should we limit our imagination to another either/or choice: the confines of neo-refortification, as in the populist promise to erect impenetrable border walls, versus neoliberal concepts of a borderless world, whereby the lowest common denominator of rights and protections under a market economy may end up replacing whatever shred of solidarity and distribution is available under our current, imperfect political structures.[175]

Still, the skeptic might argue that despite the proliferation of new forms of law, identity, and transnational political activism, some fault lines persist: those seeking entry into Europe (or any other promised or imagined land of immigration) typically arrive from poorer and less stable regions of the world and are racialized, feared, and often

---

[175] I discuss these concerns in Shachar, 'Citizenship for Sale?' (n 8).

stigmatized as security risks.[176] For those subscribing to the "neo-impe-rialism" school of international relations, refugees' desperation at home is seen, in part, as the result of larger geopolitical interests and armed conflicts that are the fallout of global power politics. Whatever the cause, it is undeniable that for the "huddled masses yearning to breathe free" the gates of orderly admission are increasingly bolted shut. Remarkably, the limit to this otherwise "plenary" power is vested in individuals at risk who seek protection by claiming asylum, which in the "ordinary situation will require a state to suspend its rules of immi-gration control and undertake an asylum procedure or equivalent to determine if such a risk is present."[177] Those refugees who reach the frontiers of affluent countries thus hold the unique legal capacity to "activate" the protection machinery of host states by virtue of territorial arrival. This grants both agency and protection to the lucky few who can overcome barbed wires or the equally powerful (though less visible) hurdles of the shifting border.

In a world marked by borders, the refugee thus stands in a special position: by reaching the frontier of a safe country (so long as its terri-tory is not legally "erased" or "excised"), the almost unlimited power of states to install and enforce migration controls bows, at least in theory, to the individual. In practice, however, states are proving endlessly enterprising in trying to "release" themselves from the domestic, regional, and international legal protection obligations they have undertaken, *without* formally withdrawing from them. This disjuncture is vitally important, as it opens up a space for democratic resistance and contes-tation. It also supports the conclusion that recourse to territorial arrival must remain available to those seeking safety who have somehow—usually at great risk and with the backing of callous human smugglers—managed to comply with the rigid requirement of "touching base." However, if we wish to find fresh prescriptions fit for a world of shifting borders, where human mobility is a regular target of blockade and

---

[176] For a powerful articulation of this point, see Leti Volpp, 'The Citizen and the Terrorist', *UCLA Law Review 49* (2002): pp. 1575–1600.
[177] Gammeltoft-Hansen, 'Extraterritorial Immigration Control' (n 32), p. 114.

policing from afar, then additional routes for acquiring rights and protections must be envisioned.

As several authors have noted, the fact that a significant premium is placed on territorial arrival—the requirement that in order to gain a chance to activate the asylum-seeking process moving bodies must first arrive at our shores—is not surprising, for "[t]his interpretation . . . poses a negligible threat (if any) to the sovereignty" of states under the traditional Westphalian image of bounded and exclusive legal spatiality.[178] Efforts to extend the applicability of human rights beyond fixed territoriality are more disruptive, yet they are urgently called for, as we cannot blind ourselves to the unequal distributional effects of the current system. The requirement to have the soil of the recipient country firmly under one's feet, after "eluding the frontier guards," is soaked in a hefty dose of arbitrariness, as it grants some safety and others "hard luck."[179] Given that the frontier guards themselves are no longer physically restricted to operating only on the edges of the protected territory, and that the most needy are frequently those least able to embark on dangerous and costly travel to affluent countries, the traditional notion of "touching base" cannot exhaust the routes for protection.

A new approach

Amid a backdrop of governments who bicker and shirk responsibility for receiving and protecting the inflow of migrants who have managed to reach their territory, and fear-mongering politicians proclaiming that Europe is on the brink of "invasion," can we not envision more creative and humane approaches to addressing the plight of people out

---

[178] Randall Hansen, *Constrained by Its Own Roots: How the Origins of the Global Asylum System Limit Contemporary Protection* (Washington, DC: Migration Policy Insitute, 2017), p. 7.

[179] Nehemiah Robinson, *Convention Relating to the Status of Refugees: Its History, Contents and Interpretation; A Commentary* (New York: Institute of Jewish Affairs, World Jewish Congress, 1953), p. 163. See also Shachar, *The Birthright Lottery* (n 99); Moria Paz, 'The Law of Walls', *European Journal of International Law 28* (2017): pp. 601–624. It is also unfair to countries that bear a disproportionately heavy burden of humanitarian responsibility toward refugees and displaced persons due to geographic proximity to conflict zones or escape routes.

of place? To overcome the current impasse, we need to return to the basics—to the conception of sovereignty, territory, and legal spatiality—which, like Arendt's analysis, still rely heavily on the static conception of borders in which access to territory is the crucial component.

We have already seen the manifold ways in which the shifting border disrupts these traditional notions. Now I wish to take the argument a step further and argue that instead of ignoring this reality, as most accounts of migration do, whether positive or normative, it is more promising to borrow a page from the shifting-border book, albeit subversively. The basic idea, currently more aspirational than applied, is to take advantage of the shifting border's advanced techniques of spatial and temporal expansion in order to *counter* its stated goals of restriction. Such a transformation may take many forms. Instead of having to reach Europe (or any other desired destination) through irregular and increasingly deadly routes of passage, humanitarian-visa applications can in theory be accepted anywhere en route: in countries of origin or transit, via embassies, upon encounter with official agents of border enforcement or their delegates, even if the latter are privately employed or operate under the flag of a third country. Humanitarian corridors that temporary seal off conflict zones to permit vulnerable refugees to be airlifted to safety or escape harm's way by crossing the territories of several countries can be drawn and redrawn through joint action by states, migrants, non-governmental organizations, and international bodies such as the UNHCR. Another range of possibilities opens up when new technologies are taken into account. Just as countries can pre-authorize entry electronically, they may permit non-emergency applications to be transmitted digitally from anywhere in the world. These various examples manifest a human-rights-enhancing vision of responsibility and accountability that does not stop at the territorial edges of states, much like their migration-regulation activities no longer stop there either. Where a country intentionally delinks migration-control activities from its geographical borders, a correlated expansion of rights and protections for the individual must follow. Two complementary methods would achieve this result: (1) expanding the extraterritorial reach of human rights, on the one hand, and (2) relaxing the fixation on territorial access as a precondition for securing refuge and protection, on the other. These changes in law and thought would place the burden on wealthier destination states to deploy border representatives on intake missions to countries of origin and transit, effectively mobilizing the machinery of the shifting border in service of human mobility and rights-protection rather than as a mere tool for exclusion. This shift is necessary if we are to respond to the reality of borders that move. Both components of this hinge-like strategy warrant further elaboration.

Human rights follow the shifting border

The first method would function to "rein in" the shifting border by ensuring that core human rights and constitutional provisions that regulate and constrain the exercise of executive power will apply *irrespective* of the location of border-control activities, whether on land, sea, or in the air. The goal is to close, or at least significantly minimize, the gap between a shifting border—which escapes the standard limits on the exercise of authority—and to act *as if* such power had been exercised within the domain of the territorial state or its actual, physical frontiers, inviting the range of legal instruments and norms that constrain the state and its agents in the act of exercising governmental authority.[180] This does not mean that migration regulation would "resettle" at the fixed border. Rather, the approach I propose may bring about an equally radical shift toward safeguarding legality and legitimacy in the exercise of power, according to the basic rule-of-law principle that the "presence of authority does not entail the absence of constraint."[181]

[180] This approach is grounded in the jurisprudence of national and supranational courts as well as human rights tribunals. The ECtHR has articulated the basic principle according to which the European Convention on Human Rights "cannot be interpreted so as to allow a state party to perpetrate violations of the Convention on the territory of the other state which it could not perpetrate on its own territory." See *Issa and others v Turkey*, App. No 31821/96, Eur. Ct. H.R. (2004). This principle originally focused on military action but was gradually expanded to other contexts.

[181] Adam B. Cox, 'Three Mistakes in Open Borders Debates', in Jack Knight, ed., *NOMOS: Immigration, Emigration, and Migration* (New York City: NYU Press, 2017), pp. 51–68, p. 54.

This restraining principle is accepted in most other fields of law, and there is no inherent reason why the sovereign authority to control borders ought to entail that the "government must have virtually unrestricted power over immigration—power largely immune from constitutional constraint, judicial oversight and even moral objection."[182] From the perspective of the individual, bringing constitutional and human rights constraints to bear on the shifting-border exercise of authority would entail that whatever procedural and substantive protections would have applied to the encounter with a border agent at the territorial edges of the country should similarly apply if equivalent movement-control authority is exercised in a remote location or like fashion.[183]

The operative logic, then, is not to "undo" the flexibility of the shifting border but to bring it under the normative umbrella of regulatory and democratic oversight. Accordingly, if we adopt more flexible interpretations of jurisdiction, effective control, and the exercise of authority, following the actual geography of power of moveable legal walls, freed from the confines of a fixed territory, then instances of protection will begin to match the spatial and temporal acrobatics of the shifting border, becoming operative not only upon arrival at the territory but also upon contact with state officials or their delegates exerting binding migration-regulation authority, *whenever* and *wherever* such authority is implemented under color of law.[184] This first line of responses is based on the rationale of switching the basis for bringing the shifting border in check from the mere *territorial* to the *jurisdictional* and the *functional*, in line with human rights arguments in favor of relying on the

---

[182] Ibid., p. 53. In practice, such regulation is hard to achieve even within the domestic sphere, let alone at the transnational level.

[183] The implementation of such an edict is of course highly complex as the border itself has frequently been a special region of potentially less extensive rights protections.

[184] As with other fields of law in which law applies extraterritorially, important procedural and substantive details need to be worked out, but the principle remains clear: the exercise of legal authority cannot be free from review and accountability by virtue of operating from a distance. For an illuminating articulation of different legal bases or justifications for extending rights beyond borders, see Chimène I. Keitner, 'Rights beyond Borders', *Yale Journal of International Law 36* (2011): pp. 55–114. Although Keitner focuses exclusively on the extraterritorial application of constitutional rights by domestic courts, the models she develops can be applied to regional and international human rights.

concept of effective control as the relevant ground for establishing responsibility in such extraterritorial, or "grey zone," situations.[185]

There are important precedents pushing in this direction. In its recent case law, the ECtHR has imposed juridical limits on extraterritorial migration control on the high seas. In the early 2000s, facing a tide of irregular migrants arriving from Libya with the aim of reaching the Italian coast, Italy began to conceptualize the space of the Mediterranean Sea as an expanded "border zone" that could act as a buffer to mainland Italy.[186] To achieve its vision, Italy signed the innocently named Treaty of Friendship, Partnership and Cooperation with Libya, which stipulated a grandiose migration-control project: Italy would provide ships and staff to patrol the 2,000 kilometers of Libyan coastline. Several protocols put this plan into action. None mentioned explicitly the "push backs" of irregular migrants intercepted on the high seas. Nor did the protocols specify human rights provisions or protections for asylum seekers. In the landmark *Hirsi* case, decided in 2012, the ECtHR was called upon to determine whether Italy had breached its protection obligations by stopping a vessel with about 200 passengers on the high seas and sending these intercepted migrants back to Libya without affording them a chance to make their protection claim. To establish such responsibility, the ECtHR had to determine whether the group of irregular migrants who filed the claim (24 of the estimated 200 migrants who were on-board the interdicted boat) were at any stage under Italy's jurisdiction. Although the European Convention of Human Rights does not extend globally, in *Hirsi* the Grand Chamber held that human rights obligations do *not* necessarily stop at the traditional, territoriality-fixed, "Westphalian," border. Instead, such obligations can follow state action and thus become applicable in an extraterritorial fashion if and when state officials exercise "continuous and exclusive *de jure* and *de facto* control."[187] By focusing on the exercise of effective

---

[185] For a powerful elaboration of this claim, see Hathaway and Gammeltoft-Hansen, 'Non-Refoulement' (n 12).

[186] Valentina Aronica, 'Italy, the Mediterranean as a Political Space, and Implications for Maritime Migration Governance', PhD dissertation, Oxford: University of Oxford.

[187] *Hirsi v Italy* (n 25), sec. 81.

control, rather than asking where the act took place, the ECtHR was able to expand Italy's legal liability beyond its territorial border. Moreover, it was the failure to offer the interdicted-at-sea migrants an opportunity to make an asylum claim or challenge their removal—procedures they would have been entitled to had they actually "made it" to Italy's shores—that amounted to a breach of the Convention.

In this, the ECtHR rejected the narrow approach adopted by the US Supreme Court in *Sale*—which held that under domestic or international law the US coastguard is not obliged to *non-refoulement* if irregular migrants are interdicted on the high seas and then turned back—in favor of a more expansive interpretation of jurisdiction, responsibility, and effective control. We saw earlier that the ability to repeatedly change the locus of migration control and act through multiple levels of governance and with various actors, both public and private, gives the shifting border its edge. Refocusing on the *content*, not the *location*, of the shifting-border techniques adopted by states, acting alone or in concert, or under the auspices of supranational entities such as Frontex, helps close the gap, extend rights, and apply regulatory controls on otherwise "unruly" practices.

In another recent case, dealing with attempts to stop migrants from reaching the cities of Ceuta and Melilla, enclaves of Spain in Morocco, the ECtHR again emphasized that what matters is not how a member state defines its "operational border" or where it locates and relocates it, but whether those affected by such exercise of migration control are given basic procedural protections, such as the opportunity to raise a claim of credible fear and activate the protection process. Whereas the *Hirsi* case dealt with a policy of stretching the border outward, this case, *N.D. and N.T.*, followed in the tradition of bleeding the border inward, as we have seen in the US example of expedited removal. Guarding against uninvited entry, Spain erected an 11.5-kilometer barrier around Melilla by building three massive fences of barbed wire, fitted with sensors and cameras, separating the European Union from Africa. The barrier and the three fences constituting it were located on Spanish territory, not outside it. Reminiscent of the Australian concept of excised territory, Spain carved out a zone of Spanish territory in Melilla that was "non-Spain" for the purposes migration control—the so-called operational border—a zone in which the principle of *non-refoulement* did not apply.[188]

Representing the claims of two individuals, a Malian and an Ivorian national, identified as N.D. and N.T., who were part of a group of migrants who attempted to enter Spain via the Melilla barrier, human rights groups challenged Spain's practice before the ECtHR.[189] While there was some confusion about the precise chronology of the events at the enclosures, the two had succeeded in scaling the first two fences and climbed on top of the third fence. After several hours, they climbed down the third fence with the assistance of the Spanish police. They were immediately arrested by members of Spain's *Guardia Civil* and, without receiving procedural treatment or the opportunity to identify themselves and explain their circumstances, were transferred back to Morocco and subsequently deported.[190]

On Spain's account, the two were stopped at the operational border and thus never reached Spain. By extension, they never entered the region and "realm" of European human rights conventions and protections. The Strasbourg court flatly rejected this claim. Interestingly, however, the ECtHR avoided a determination on whether the applicants succeeded in entering Spain, sidestepping a confrontation with a national member state on a matter as sensitive as defining its own geographic and cartographic boundaries. Instead, it switched the jurisdictional

---

[188] Anyone caught trying to climb the fences, cross the area between the fences, or sit on top of the third fence closest to the city of Melilla was subject to a practice of "summary returns" to Morocco. These summary returns applied to third-country nationals who were "detected on the border line of the territorial demarcation of Ceuta or Melilla while trying to cross the border's contentive elements (fences) to irregularly cross the border." Article 10, Aliens Act 2000 (Spain), translated and cited by Christina Gortazar Rotaeche and Nuria Ferre Trad, 'A Cold Water Shower for Spain—Hot Returns from Melilla to Morocco: *N.D. and N.T. v. Spain*', online: http://eumigrationlawblog.eu/a-cold-shower-for-spain-hot-returns-from-melilla-to-morocco-n-d-and-n-t-v-spain-ecthr-3-october-2017/.

[189] *N.D. and N.T. v. Spain,* App. Nos 8675/15 and 8697/15, Eur. Ct. H.R. (2017), p. 1.

[190] Registrar of the Court, Press Release, European Court of Human Rights, *The Immediate Return to Morocco of Sub-Saharan Migrants who Were Attempting to Enter Spanish Territory in Melilla Amounted to a Collective Expulsion of Foreign Nationals, in Breach of the Convention* (ECHR 291 (2017), October 3, 2017) (EU), p. 2.

basis altogether: *from the territorial to the functional.* The court held that once the applicants climbed down the third fence, they were under the "continuous and exclusive control of the Spanish authorities."[191] By virtue of this exercise of effective control by uniformed state officials, jurisdiction arose—and with it came the whole slew of rights and protections enshrined in regional, international, and domestic human rights instruments and standards.

These legal precedents offer a glimpse into how effective control, as a functional rather than a territorially bounded interpretation of jurisdiction, can expand the spatial reach of human rights in ways that begin to mimic the creativity and flexibility of the shifting border itself. States cannot have their cake (rely on the shifting border) and eat it (be released from legal liability for their action). Governments seek the "gain" of excision, fortification, the creation of constitution- or human-rights-free zones, and the like; they cannot do so without constraints, however. The "pain" of judicial review and the application of constitutional and human rights and protections is slowly catching up with the dynamic reinvention of territorially unbounded border control.[192] This is one promising path on which to begin to close the gap between a mobile exercise of migration control and an outdated system of constraints on the exercise of authority that is imagined as immobile under the confines of a static vision of territoriality.

This is no panacea, however. Just as the attraction of this "jurisdictional turn" is established, so is its frailty exposed. In the cat-and-mouse game of extending the reach of the shifting border both inward and outward while seeking to skirt their constitutional and human rights responsibilities, governments may again prove more adaptive and savvy than the demise-of-the-state theory or globalization theories would

---

[191] *N.D. and N.T. v. Spain,* App. Nos 8675/15 and 8697/15, Eur. Ct. H.R. (2017), sec. 54 [translated from French].

[192] In theory, we can imagine a legal regime establishing such responsibility *wherever* and *whenever* border migration controls take place. In practice, the case law to date is more circumscribed. It holds that when the facts clearly establish that border guards or other official agents of the state exercise effective control and explicitly breach a basic norm of human rights, such as *non-refoulement,* or fail to offer core procedural protections, legal responsibility will follow.

predict. Post-*Hirsi*, Italy no longer sends its ships and personnel to interdict unwanted migrants on the high seas. Instead, with generous EU funding, it has trained Libyan coastguard officials to do Europe's dirty job of closing the border.[193] Such "outsourcing" of migration control to third countries makes it difficult to establish legal responsibility, as effective control—the requisite jurisdictional link with a member state—is technically broken.[194] Similar concerns arise with the growing reliance on carrier sanctions. Through a series of bilateral and multilateral agreements, airline companies and other private, for-profit actors are obliged to engage in what is essentially a quintessential act of public exercise of migration-control authority: pre-entry clearance. Frontline airline personnel or private security guards must check whether passengers have valid passports, visas, and any other required documentation prior to departure, operating as "surrogate border guards."[195] In many parts of the world, these private actors are "often assisted by immigration liaison officers, or other officials from the destination state stationed in the departure state."[196] This requires the cooperation of third countries, which must authorize the deployment on their territories of these stationed-abroad immigration or liaison officers. Remarkably, while stationed aboard and jointly implementing measures of migration control, these immigration liaison officers "maintain only an advisory role with regard to the controls carried out by airline staff," thus limiting the possibility of attaching liability to their home countries.[197] As these examples illustrate, the more layers of discretion that are

---

[193] The reports from Libya that migrants from West Africa are bought and sold in a modern-day slave trade is only exacerbating these concerns of complicity with unspeakable abuse of human rights.

[194] Thomas Gammeltoft-Hansen emphasizes this point in *Access to Asylum* (n 77). A similar set of concerns was raised in the Report of the Special Rapporteur on the human rights of migrants, François Crepeau, *Regional Study: Management of the External Borders of the European Union and Its Impact on the Human Rights of Migrants* (UN Doc. A/HRC/23/46, 24 April 2013), p. 14, sec. 56.

[195] Moreno-Lax, *Accessing Asylum in Europe* (n 86), p. 6.

[196] Theodore Baird, 'Carrier Sanctions in Europe: A Comparison of Trends in 10 Countries', *European Journal of Migration and Law 19* (2017): pp. 307–334, p. 328.

[197] Gammeltoft-Hansen, *Access to Asylum* (n 77), p. 8; Moreno-Lax, *Accessing Asylum in Europe* (n 86), pp. 3, 6.

introduced and the greater the number and variation of the actors involved (public and private, at home and abroad, official and semi-official), the more difficult it becomes to attribute legal responsibility, even under the more expansive interpretation of effective control.

Affording protection extraterritorially: shifting the burden from the individual to the state

The second, complementary approach is to relax the connection between accessing territory and seeking asylum. If mobility is to be protected in the age of the shifting border, it is not enough for powerful destination countries merely to affirm the human rights of those under their effective control. Rather, these countries (and their enforcement partners along major migration routes) have an active role in facilitating mobility. A rights-affirming response to the shifting border implores domestic, regional, and international courts, governments, and engaged publics to dig new channels for migrants seeking protection, rather than leaving these migrants to rely exclusively on the act of "touching base." Instead, individuals in need of protection will be able to claim asylum or other forms of protection upon encounter with the shifting border, which will likely occur far away from the territory they wish to enter. When affluent states flex their legal muscle, the shifting border moves to avert uninvited entry. However, the very same techniques of reaching people before they encounter the territorial border can in theory also become rights-enhancing, just as they are presently rights-restricting.

An example may help explain this last point. In 2015, Canada emerged as one of the global "do-gooders" in swiftly airlifting and resettling over 25,000 Syrian refugees.[198] How did Canada achieve this humanitarian feat? Unlike Europe, these refugees did not reach its shores. Instead, *the border came to them*, conceptually and functionally. Canadian immigration officials were dispatched to refugee camps in

---

[198] By 2017, the number of resettled Syrian refugees in Canada had almost doubled, reaching approximately 50,000, many of whom benefited from the country's innovative private-sponsorship resettlement program.

Jordan, Turkey, and Lebanon, where they conducted pre-screening interviews and identity verification of asylum seekers. Within a matter of weeks, these reviews were completed, and successful refugee claimants were given not only temporary travel documents to Canada but also permanent-resident visas, placing them on the road to citizenship, instead of putting them through the years of insecurity that would otherwise have laid ahead of them if they had been made to wait for determination of their status in Europe—that is, if they were among the lucky ones who managed to reach its shores and comply with the requirements of the territoriality of asylum in the first place.[199]

Importantly, and unromantically, the Canadian initiative allowed the state to exercise powerful gatekeeping functions. It was revolutionary, however, in deploying the shifting border "machinery" in the service of *enhancing* rights and securing mobility, rather than inhibiting both.

This can be done by shifting the burden of "touching base," normally placed on asylum seekers, to states and their authorized agents, moving the determination process closer to the asylum seekers, *wherever* they are, so as to provide access from afar to opportunities that are otherwise open only to those who can afford to reach the actual border.[200] Much like Canada's reliance on the long arm of the shifting border when restricting mobility, this initiative allows decisions to occur prior to arrival and many thousands of miles away from the actual border. Conceptually, then, affording protection extraterritorially retains a statist logic, exerting sovereign control over admission and membership decisions.[201] However,

[199] Resettlement, voluntary repatriation, and local integration are the three durable solutions promoted by the UNHCR, although there is also growing discussion of incorporating labor migration into the durable-solutions framework as well as creating sustainable economies and self-sufficient "cities" in refugee camps in so-called haven countries in the vicinity of conflict zones. These latter suggestions are not uncontroversial.

[200] Resettlement facilitates relocation from refugee camps in conflict zones, where the vast majority of the world's displaced persons are presently hosted, to willing third countries that are often far removed from the conflict zone. For states, this "de-territorialized" procedure grants control and containment, in lieu of the chaos of spontaneous migration, in addition to facilitating a "tangible expression of international solidarity and a responsibility sharing mechanism."

[201] Pre-screening and admission from abroad also keeps the resettling government in the driving seat and allows it to combine international humanitarian assistance with a message of control communicated to the domestic population. As official documents

shifting the burden from the individual to the state here *bolsters*, rather than undermines, rights and protections for those who need them most.[202] At the same time, for the individuals selected, it provides hope, dignity, and a ticket to a new, permanent home.[203] By allowing for an expansion of the spaces of protection, people escaping from harm's way who are unable to comply with the territorial-arrival dictum will gain a chance to secure international protection according to priority criteria. Reversing expectations, geographically far-flung resettlement processing of permanent-residence permits or humanitarian visas that facilitate safe, dignified, and legal migration channels provide *greater* control over who gets in and under what conditions, even in the context of an unfolding crisis, than the classic insistence on exercising sovereignty through linking asylum claims to territorial access. The Canadian example thus shows us the potentially rights-enhancing possibilities buried underneath the restrictive tendencies of the shifting border. This inversion of roles tasks states with the responsibility to reach out to the individual in need of international protection and not, as current law has it, put the onus on the

put it: "protecting the safety, security and health of Canadians and refugees is a key factor guiding the Government of Canada's actions throughout this initiative." Compare this tone to the sense of loss of control and images of a mounting "invasion" manifested by leaders throughout Europe, and across the political spectrum, in the current refugee crisis. Not all countries have the luxury of pre-screening and resettlement.

[202] Of course, the number of refugees who are offered resettlement and the number of states involved in such relief efforts must rise significantly. Current recommendations, developed in the context of discussion surrounding the global compact on refugees, have called the global community to commit to the goal of resettling 10 percent of the world's refugees every year. This proposal is nested within a broader range of proposals to develop responsibility-sharing formulas to respond to large-scale movements of people out of place, as well as recommendations that call for greater cooperation between destination and transit countries to close gaps in the current refugee-protection system and the provision of asylum and due-process safeguards at borders. For a concise overview, see Kevin Appelby, 'Strengthening the Global Refugee Protection System: Recommendations for the Global Compact on Refugees', *Journal on Migration and Human Security* 5 (2017): pp. 780–799.

[203] Such resettlement determinations usually rely on UNHCR or country-specific priority criteria; they offer more immediate relief for those considered more vulnerable. Related programs have now been established by other countries, in different regions, providing greater protection for migrants, by establishing mechanisms to acquire visas in countries of origin or transit. In Brazil, for example, the government responded to a spike in human trafficking of Haitians seeking to escape the aftermath of the 2010 earthquake through a dangerous passage known as the "jungle route" by opening a visa processing facility in Port-au-Prince, Haiti, in cooperation with the IOM. The aim of this initiative is to allow potential migrants to apply for special humanitarian permanent visas on

already vulnerable and displaced individual to reach the territory of a protection-granting state.

This alternative turns the logic of the shifting border on its head by making the *severance* of the relationship between territory and the exercise of sovereign authority rights-enhancing rather than rights-restricting.[204] Past experience with international cooperation in planning and executing "orderly departure programs," which introduce legal channels for the departure of asylum seekers whose claims have already been processed overseas, relaxing the requirement of territorial "contact" prior to activating the refugee-determination process, has drastically reduced irregular migration and saved lives.[205]

The world has seen such initiatives before. There are two iconic historical precedents:[206] one was a tragic failure, the other an impressive success. The infamous Evian multilateral conference, convened by Franklin D. Roosevelt in 1938 after the *Anschluss* in response to the escalation in Nazi persecution of the Jews in Germany and in annexed Austria, brought together representatives of thirty-two countries, including the United States, the United Kingdom, France, Canada, Australia, New Zealand, and several other European and Latin American countries. The conference gave participating nations the opportunity to coordinate with one another higher rates of entry to Jews seeking to escape the Nazi regime; all of them paid lip service to the cause and expressed

location, rather than rely on smugglers to get them to Brazil without authorization via the deadly jungle route. The initial screening and processing in Port-au-Prince is conducted by the IOM and the ultimate visa decisions are made by Brazilian officials, offering another example of how a "humanitarian" shifting border that comes to the individual where and when she is in dire need may offer safety and security without requiring territorial arrival as a precondition. As with any such initiative, the intentions of the acting governments and related parties must be carefully scrutinized.

[204] Such initiatives could save lives, dry up the market for human smugglers, allow security screening of entrants prior to arrival, permit greater choice and agency for migrants themselves to select their destination country, and help alleviate fear of "loss of control" among voters in the recipient countries.

[205] See Judith Kumin, 'Orderly Departure from Vietnam: Cold War Anomaly or Humanitarian Innovation?', *Refugee Survey Quarterly 27* (2008): pp. 104–117. See also UNHCR, *Resettlement Handbook* (Geneva: UNHCR, 2011).

[206] See Patrick Weil and Itamar Mann, 'We Need a New Orderly Departure Program', Opinion, *Al Jazeera America*, September 9, 2015.

commiseration with the plight of the persecuted. But, one by one, they excused themselves from upholding these commitments by refusing to alter national immigration quotas or consular visa policies. The consequence was that just as the Nazis were increasing the crackdown on Jews, destination countries' gates of admission were being locked and sealed when it came to emigrants whose passports the Nazis stamped with the letter "J" (*Jude*=Jew). The conference did succeed, however, in creating the Intergovernmental Committee on Refugees (IGCR), with a mandate to negotiate with candidate countries the provision of places of refuge for those escaping Germany. The Dominican Republic was, alas, the only country that eventually heeded to the plea of the IGCR and agreed to resettle a small number of Jewish refugees before the Nazis shut down Jewish emigration altogether. Had the member nations followed on their promise to work out multilateral burden-sharing arrangements in the face of calamity, the number of survivors would have been significantly higher. Arendt might have then written a different essay from "We Refugees." But that never happened.

The more successful example flexed the muscles of protection beyond borders: the Orderly Departure Program, coordinated by the UNHCR in response to the alarming death toll among the massive exodus of so-called boat people—Vietnamese fleeing to the South China Sea after the end of the Vietnam War. Although the Program arose after the negotiation of the Refugee Convention and its 1967 Protocol, it was premised on participating countries' suspension of the principle of geographic proximity and the deadly ordinance of "touching base." This multilateral cooperation began in the late 1970s and involved more than thirty countries, none of which were in geographical proximity to the Indochinese refugee crisis. It is credited with saving more than 2 million lives over a fifteen-year period. An unknown number of those who departed clandestinely on rickety boats drowned and perished; others reached neighboring coastal states. As the flow of irregular migrants grew, countries in the region were fearful of the destabilizing effect. They refused to grant the boat people permission to land. Instead, they were pushed back to sea and then "denied permission to disembark in port after port."[207] There was literally no place on earth where they could go, the plight that Arendt so powerfully identified. The situation reached crisis proportions. In the midst of the Cold War, and against all odds, the UNHCR managed to broker a multilateral agreement to address this outflow of irregular migration. At the core of this orderly-departure program we find two elements: international cooperation and the *severance* of the linkage between territorial arrival and the granting of protection status. Vietnam agreed to offer regular channels of exit to those who wanted to leave the country, thus averting the resort to smugglers, unsafe boats, and unauthorized means of passage. No less significant, with international assurances that the refugees would benefit from onward mobility, the coastal countries that had previously closed their gates and refused to grant entry to the escaping Vietnamese refugees agreed to grant them temporary refuge until they were resettled under the international program. The United States alone resettled over 1.3 million individuals, with Canada, Australia, France, Germany, the Netherlands, Japan, Israel, and New Zealand, among other countries, taking in significant numbers of refugees. This program, while far from perfect and conceived in a geopolitical era quite different from today, nevertheless provides testimony that international cooperation is possible in a field where currently we mostly see states bickering and passing the buck of responsibility.

Adopting any or all of these steps would represent an advancement in comparison with the current situation, in part because they offer hope for the displaced, reduce the pressures on refugee-hosting societies in the region (some of which are on the brink of insolvency and turmoil), and draw a commitment from richer countries that are shielded by geography from the immediate impact of the current refugee crisis to help share responsibility for offering that hope—and a new home.[208]

---

[207] Kumin, 'Orderly Departure' (n 209), p. 106.
[208] The UNHCR helps in the process of identifying and prioritizing the urgency of individual protection needs; the resettlement country can also define the profile of vulnerable categories for resettlement, including those with urgent legal or physical-protection needs or life-threating medical conditions, survivors of torture and violence, women and girls at risk, and so on.

In a world where 85 percent of the global population of refugees and displaced persons are hosted by already struggling, resource-strapped countries in close proximity to active conflict zones, there is much to gain by breaking the current gridlock. The twofold strategy I have just described rests on the lexical priority of the first principle (human rights follow the border) over the second (relocating protection operations to where vulnerable migrants are, rather than vice versa), to ensure that governmental authorities do not use the latter as a fig leaf to extend the reach of the rights-restricting shifting border under the guise of humanitarian do-gooding, a result the former proviso aims to address.

Legal spatiality as a resource

So, while Arendt is correct that political organization is at the heart of the predicament we face, I want to suggest that a productive response will reverse the order of operations: scholars and activists might think about place and space as part of the solution and then muster the political organization to follow.[209] More importantly still, treating space as a resource, not a problem, can help avert the plight indentified by Arendt: that of there not being a place, *any* place, in the world in which the rightsless, the stateless, or the displaced can find refuge. Legal reliance on static, old-school, sovereigntist conceptions of "space" for relief and refuge prevents access to new worlds of opportunity for those who globally need them most; it condemns many of them to the Sisyphean fate of traversing and re-traversing terrains of shifting borders, in order, potentially, to be sent back to square one.

[209] Governments themselves now routinely amend and challenge fixed conceptions of territoriality—for example, by creating special economic zones within their jurisdictions in which distinctive legal regimes apply, or by the creation of jointly governed border regions in which cooperative governance is influenced by more than one set of legal norms emanating from multiple and multilevel sources. We have seen this creatively unleash itself in the name of neoliberal economic restructuring, but have witnessed almost a complete standstill when it comes to promoting safe passage or establishing jointly governed humanitarian zones for refugees and displaces persons to cross through the "gates" of several countries, let alone imagining, in a more out-of-the-box fashion, the allotment of designated parcels of land for "refugee nations" to rebuild their lost homes and political autonomy.

Moving the border closer to the individual to offer her protection may take various configurations. It can be the result of unilateral decision-making, as in the Canadian Welcome Refugees initiative, operating at the discretion of the resettling state, which is conditional upon the consent of the host country offering refuge to hold the interviews and screening procedures on *its* territory.[210] Here, we witness both the de-territorialization of legal space, as the process can in principle take place anywhere in the world, as well as its re-territorialization, as the interview must take place *somewhere* on the face of the earth, in this case in the place where temporary protection was granted. More comprehensive relief efforts would require involving a larger number of states pooling resources and collaborating on resettlement and responsibility sharing according to criteria relating to vulnerability, urgency, matching links, and so on. Rather than relying on geographical proximity to allocate responsibility—as is the current norm—placing the heaviest burden on poorer, neighboring countries in the Global South that are already stretched to capacity, more equitable distribution mechanisms would require harnessing significant cooperation across national and regional borderlines; so too will any feasible solution.[211] To increase the chances of success, such cross-border and multi-actor efforts would benefit from the active participation of, among others: civil societies, supranational entities, NGOs, regional and international organizations, transnational diasporas, and refugee representatives. In terms of institutional design, such programs will likely have to rely on embracing bilateral and multilateral burden- and responsibility-sharing initiatives, in line with the recent UN Global Compact for Migration recommendations.[212] If such a system were put

---

[210] Where relevant, the cooperation of the UNHCR is also elicited. The condition of consent by the country of asylum where migrants and refugees reside is vital. Otherwise, the humanitarian variant of the shifting border might be abused by states seeking to aggrandize their power in the name of protecting the vulnerable. I thank Tracy Strong for this point.

[211] The goal is to undo or at least tame the current linkage between arbitrary geographical proximity and bearing the brunt of humanity's dispossessed.

[212] In the 2016 New York Declaration for Refugees and Migrants, the world's leaders emphasized "the centrality of international cooperation" and further committed "to a more equitable sharing of the burden and responsibility for hosting and supporting the world's refugees, while taking account of existing contributions and the differing capacities and

in place, individuals in need of international protection would gain greater voice and agency in shaping their future. The political units participating in such global schemes, be they cities, nations, or regions, would gain an air of control over orderly mobility and the ability to plan for the arrival and absorption of newcomers. Future endeavors to break the exclusivity of the touching-base dictum will require daring political leadership, which is currently in short supply, but it is, contrary to populist and anti-immigrant rhetoric, in the *sovereigntist* interest of states to create a comprehensive action plan that will allow refugees to apply from afar, in addition to keeping open routes for protection that are activated upon territorial arrival.

Observing the dangers of inaction by Europe prior to the refugee crisis of 2015, François Crépeau, the United Nation Special Rapporteur on the Human Rights of Migrants, proposed at the time that EU member states, along with other Global North countries, such as Canada, Australia, New Zealand, and the United States, as well as a number of immigration countries in the South, such as Brazil, make a commitment to a meaningful refugee resettlement program that states could put into operation with the help of the UNHCR and civil society organizations according to priority criteria.[213] Such a proposal was never adopted. However, its principled and prudential justification rests precisely on the logic that I have advanced here: namely, extending protection through relocation or resettlement to a wider class of people fleeing oppression and involving more non-geographically proximate countries in the relief effort. Such programs reach out to "people out of place" in the countries to which they have fled. In this way, they encompass those

---

resources among [s]tates." See United Nations General Assembly, Resolution adopted by the General Assembly on September 19, 2016, New York Declaration for Refugees and Migrants, A/Res/71/1, October 3, 2016 (United Nations), Articles 7 and 11. The commitment to more equitable burden- and responsibility-sharing has long been pushed for by the world's developing countries, where the vast majority of the world's refugees are hosted. For a detailed analysis, see Rebecca Dowd and Jane McAdam, 'International Cooperation and Responsibility-Sharing to Protect Refugees: What, Why, and How?', *International and Comparative Law Quarterly* 66 (2017): pp. 863–892.

[213] François Crépeau, UN Human Rights Council, 29th Session, Geneva, Statement by Mr. François Crépeau, Special Rapporteur on the Human Rights of Migrants 5 (June 15, 2015).

who have *not* been able to comply with the survival-of-the-fittest "ordinance" demanding that they enter the territory of the affluent countries that simultaneously do everything within their powers to keep them out.[214]

As already mentioned, there are yet other creative possibilities to be considered within the context of the new approach I have defended. Beyond the obvious call to expand and deepen regional and international cooperation in relief and resettlement efforts, additional steps may include reclaiming the pre-1951 Refugee Convention legacy of facilitating safe passage and opportunities for lawful mobility by issuing international (rather than national) travel documents, following the tradition of the interwar Nansen passport issued by the League of Nations.[215] Issuing humanitarian visas and related emergency, single-journey entry permits would perform a similar function, allowing displaced people to lawfully cross borders at recognized ports of embarkation and entry rather than risk unauthorized passage and the survival-of-the-fittest requirement.[216]

---

[214] Although we have seen a breakdown of unity and division in response to the refugee crisis in Europe, it is easy to forget that in 2016 the world's leaders had already made the milestone commitment to a "more equitable sharing of the burden and responsibility for hosting and supporting the world refugees." Of course, declaration is one thing, implementation another. However, some initial progress is already under way. In 2017, the OECD International Migration Outlook reported that "[i]n response to the growing demand for international protection, many OECD countries have increased their resettlements programmes." OECD, *International Migration Outlook 2017, Summary* (Paris: OECD 2017), p. 1.

[215] Resettlement and procedural fairness are concrete responses that relate to the encounter at the border. They do not, and cannot, resolve much broader debates about the relationship between mobility and global inequality, self-determination and freedom of movement. Any sustainable solution or comprehensive response to migration pressures in an unequal world requires a wide-ranging approach that will facilitate development measures, expansion or addition of new definitions of people in need of protection, and the opening up of new legal channels of migration and mobility.

[216] Pushing the envelope ever further, economists have argued that "matching markets" do a better job than current regulations of reflecting and accounting for refugees' agency and expressed preferences about where they wish to live, considerations that are sorely lacking in the top-down vision of the European Union's planned "relocation" strategy. The argument advanced is that two-sided matching markets grant greater agency to refugees and allow states to include more variables in setting their priority criteria (severity of threat, degree of vulnerability, etc.) as well as regain control over what is perceived, politically and administratively, as a chaotic process. Such proposals have been advanced by scholars such as Hillel Rapoport, Will Jones, and Alex Teytelboym.

Paradoxically, a major obstacle is the current *in*flexibility of the refugee-protection legal framework, establishing a firm linkage between
territorial arrival and the obligation to protect, an obligation that, as we
have already seen, states seek to skirt and avert by almost any means
possible, including the invention of the shifting border. If there were a
constellation whereby countries could provide *some* relief and an
immediate safe haven, without necessarily attaching themselves to a
long-term commitment to arriving refugees, relying on the knowledge
that they are part of a larger system of fair and equitable international
response, where non-proximate countries commit to contributing to
assisting those in need with resettlement or other mobility-supporting
mechanisms, there is reason to believe that there would be many more
takers than deflectors.[217]

None of this will be easy to achieve. Decisions pertaining to the border will always be contested, as they are tied to access to territory and
membership, partaking in the definition of who belongs to the political
community—the last bastion of sovereignty. My account has proceeded on
the assumption that states currently have, and are likely to continue to have
in the foreseeable future, the authority to determine conditions of entry
and stay. It has emphasized, however, the constraints of law and justice that
come with the exercise of such authority in a world of shifting borders.
This new approach places center stage the obligation to respect and protect
the human rights of those who come into contact with the regulatory
power of the state, *irrespective* of the location of that encounter: on the
territory's edge, deep in the interior, in transit hubs, or in far-flung third
countries, where the function of border control increasingly takes place.

---

[217] Refugee-law and policy experts have drawn an analogy with the variable architecture of
international environmental law to overcome the current situation, whereby the allocation of responsibility to protect is "starkly imbalanced," with the vast majority of the
world's refugees hosted by poorer and less stable countries in the world's developing
regions. For further discussion, see Dowd and McAdam, 'International Cooperation and
Responsibility-Sharing' (n 205). Such a variable architecture would envision a mixture of
voluntary and mandatory contributions, temporary and permanent protection options,
relocation and resettlement as well as in-lieu instruments, and would also take into
account the socio-economic and political-stability considerations of refugee-hosting
countries. This new approach could be further placed within a broader framework of
authorized migration and development measures.

In a world of regulated mobility, migrants considered undesirable will continue to face significant obstacles. With this in mind, the two-pronged response I have outlined seeks to mitigate vulnerability and offer protection and empowerment to those who need it most. As with any proposed change, such a transformation cannot happen in a vacuum, nor can it rely exclusively on adjudication and advocacy. To stand a fighting chance of success, significant political mobilization is required of critical civil publics, acting locally, nationally, and transnationally, in order to resist what they see as unjust and unjustifiable acts of border control, especially those stretching inward and outward with no limit in sight, infringing the basic human rights and dignity of the migrants caught in the whirling kaleidoscope of the shifting border.

Governments and their voters detest irregular movements of people across borders. An idealist can ignore such realities, but the non-idealist cannot.[218] We are thus in search of a system that, under current conditions, recognizes states' *pro tanto* sovereign authority to regulate movement across borders, while at the same time re-spatializing their law and justice obligations in line with their ever more creative and multi-scalar migration-regulation operations. The path I have advanced emphasizes the jurisdictional link as a basis for expanding and extending responsibility beyond borders. This is complemented by the basic human rights idea that "[e]veryone has the right to recognition everywhere as a person before the law" (a formulation drawn from the New York Declaration for Refugees and Migrants), *especially* at the encounter at the border, wherever the capricious shifting border may reach her.[219] Such

---

[218] Here I share Rainer Forst's observation that "[i]f we do not understand how norms and interests intermesh to generate and reproduce power, we are condemned to failure" in our efforts to understand political, legal, and normative orders, let alone transform them. See Rainer Forst, *Normativity and Power: Analyzing Social Orders of Justification* (Oxford: Oxford University Press, 2017), p. 143.

[219] This formulation is drawn from the United Nations General Assembly, Resolution (n 205). The process for developing the global compact for migration and the global compact for refugees is well underway, under the auspices of the United Nations and the UNHCR respectively, and will be presented in 2018 with a view to their adoption. For a comprehensive discussion of the potential promises and pitfalls of such international instruments, see Klaus Günter, 'World Citizens between Freedom and Security', *Constellations* 12 (2005): pp. 379–391.

recognition is based on personhood, not membership, and thus applies equally to non-citizens irrespective of their legal status in relation to the given place or particular political community whose border, shifting or static, fortified or erased, they encounter.[220] It offers a minimal baseline of protection and dignity for each person, irrespective of place and time, when encountering the exercise of coercive governmental power that affects their basic interests.[221]

As the reach of the shifting border has expanded, so have new spaces for democratic contestation been created, stretching the boundaries of the political, both above and below the nation-state level. These changed scales provide room for resistance and protest, both local and transnational, against the encroaching shifting border in its various spatial manifestations.[222] As Michael Walzer recently observed, "[s]uddenly, everyone ... is talking about resistance."[223] In the United States, for example, we witness acts of resistance to sweeping migration enforcement measures by civil society activists, cities and municipalities, colleges and universities, local authorities, faith-based communities, various professional and non-governmental organizations, advocacy groups, and undocumented migrant networks, to name but a few examples, galvanizing their multiple voices into action, mobilizing protests, filing law suits, planning sit-ins, accompanying irregular migrants to their deportation hearings, offering shelter, food, legal aid, and medical care in houses of worship, and providing "sanctuary" in cities, campuses, and

---

[220] On this account, the rule of law "defines the parameters of permissible government action *wherever*, and toward *whomever*, the government acts." See Keitner, 'Rights beyond Borders' (n 182), pp. 66–67 (emphasis added).

[221] Similar conclusions can be drawn from a variety of theoretical perspectives, as developed in recent years by scholars focusing on the claims of non-domination, the right to justification, or the all-affected or all-subjected principles, to mention but a few such sources.

[222] For an excellent representative of this new line of scholarship, see Peter Niesen, 'Reframing Civil Disobedience: Constituent Power as a Language of Transnational Protest', *Journal of International Political Theory 15* (2019): pp. 1–48.

[223] Michael Walzer, 'The Politics of Resistance', *Dissent*, March 1, 2017, online www.dissent-magazine.org/online_articles/the-politics-of-resistance-michael-walzer. While offering a full account of these developments falls beyond the scope of this work, it is worth noting that we are witnessing such an awakening.

workplaces.[224] As the shifting border operates in increasingly invasive ways to identify individuals "out of place," local jurisdictions and sanctuary cities have developed counter-policies that limit cooperation with federal immigration authorities and offer protection for immigrants at the local level by issuing ID cards irrespective of legal status, creating a new spatiality of subnational membership informed by ideas of "rooted cosmopolitanism" and transnational human rights discourses. Across Europe, new networks and cross-border solidarities have emerged from pro-migrant groups resisting the production of a "Europe of borders."[225] In Australia and Canada, refugee advocates have taken the lead in challenging detention and contesting the rhetoric of bogus claimants and queue jumpers. The politics of contestation and resistance is on the rise, providing a vital companion and catalyzer for any progressive legal and conceptual change along the lines I have advocated here.

Coda

The train of extraterritorial border control has already left the station—the classic functions of regulating entry, admission, settlement, and membership demarcation are no longer contained within a fixed and clearly delineated geopolitical space and instead take place *beyond* territory and long *before* travelers can reach the political community in

---

[224] Time will tell the effects of the politics of resistance and its ability to reverse the course of harsh governmental action against immigrants in an age of resurgent populism and border-worshiping politicians. On this point, see Naomi Paik, 'Abolitionist Futures and the US Sanctuary Movement', *Race and Class 59* (2017): pp. 3–25. For critical and comparative accounts, see, for example, Randy K. Lippert and Sean Rehaag, eds, *Sanctuary Practices in International Perspectives: Migration, Citizenship and Social Movements* (Abingdon: Routledge, 2013); Robin Celikates, Regina Kride, and TiloWesche, eds, *Transformations of Democracy: Crisis, Protest and Legitimation* (London: Rowman & Littlefield, 2015).

[225] This vast body of literature includes, for example, Marco Giugni and Florence Passy, eds, *Political Altruism: Solidarity Movements in International Perspective* (London: Rowman and Littlefield, 2001); Helga Leitner and Christopher Struck, 'Spaces of Immigrant Advocacy and Liberal Democratic Citizenship', *Annals of the Association of American Geographers 104* (2014): pp. 348–356. For a "dual track" approach that incorporates official and unofficial spaces for and acts of contestation, see Seyla Benhabib, *The Claims of Culture: Equality and Diversity in the Global Era* (Princeton: Princeton University Press, 2002).

which they wish to settle or seek refuge. Yet these tools can be repurposed to help those they currently keep out.

The analysis I have offered—especially the emphasis on territory's malleability under the shifting-border conception, now routinely and instrumentally used to help states control migration and admit the few but not the many—points to a previously unexplored path. Instead of a menacing obstacle and tool to restrict access to asylum, we can rethink the shifting border as a creative resource in the service of advancing human rights across borders. As we have seen, the shifting border is a powerful tool, and states are unlikely to cede their authority over migration regulation any time soon—and especially not in the current political environment. Under such circumstances, the two-pronged change I have proposed would offer a more sanguine future: namely, extending the extraterritorial reach of human rights provisions while simultaneously relaxing the linkage between territory and asylum. It would lay the foundation for a conceptual and paradigm shift that is long overdue.

Part II

Responses

2

Monsters, Inc.: the fightback

Sarah Fine

This is the Generation of that great LEVIATHAN, or rather (to speake more reverently) of that *Mortall God*, to which wee owe under the *Immortal God*, our peace and defence. For by this Authoritie, given him by every particular man in the Common-Wealth, he hath the use of so much Power and Strength conferred on him, that by terror thereof, he is inabled to forme the wills of them all, to Peace at home, and mutuall ayd against their enemies abroad.[1]

> Can you pull in Leviathan with a fishhook
> or tie down its tongue with a rope?
> Can you put a cord through its nose
> or pierce its jaw with a hook?
> Will it keep begging you for mercy?
> Will it speak to you with gentle words?...
> ... Nothing on earth is its equal—
> a creature without fear.[2]

That great Leviathan

Early in a political-theory education, students are introduced to Thomas Hobbes's masterpiece, *Leviathan, or The Matter, Forme, and Power of a Common-Wealth Ecclesiasticall and Civill,* published in 1651.

---

[1] Thomas Hobbes, *Leviathan,* Richard Tuck, ed. (Cambridge: Cambridge University Press, [1651] 1996), pp. 120–121.
[2] Job, 41: 1–3, 33. *Bible,* New International Version.

In *The Shifting Border: Legal Cartographies of Migration and Mobility*, Ayelet Shachar delivers a *Leviathan* for the twenty-first century—fittingly, as we shall see, in more ways than one. First, *The Shifting Border* joins Hobbes's *Leviathan* on the list of essential reading about the nature of states and sovereignty. Yet there is more to the comparison than that.

Intriguingly, Hobbes named his "commonwealth, or state" and his text after a biblical monster which features in the books of Job and Isaiah. The biblical Leviathan has powerful limbs, a "double coat of armour" and "fearsome teeth." When it snorts, it "throws out flashes of light" and "flames stream from its mouth." So fearsome is this beast that "when it rises up, the mighty are terrified" and "they retreat before its thrashing."[3] What kind of strange creature is this? It is variously described as "a crocodile, a whale, a fish, a snake, or a dragon."[4] As Johan Tralau highlights, Hobbes mentions Leviathan three times in his book, and each time he offers a different image of it. First, Hobbes's Leviathan is the commonwealth, portrayed as an artificial man (*Leviathan*, the Introduction). Second, it is the commonwealth, described as a mortal god (chapter 17). Third, Leviathan is presented as the sovereign, the "governor," of man (chapter 28). Thus, remarks Tralau, Hobbes's Leviathan is "not only a beast, but also a man, a machine, a god, the state as a whole, and the sovereign, that part of the state wielding absolute power."[5] Given Hobbes's commitment to "conceptual clarity" and apparent suspicion of metaphor, the ambiguity and indeterminacy in his depiction of Leviathan is noteworthy.[6] Leviathan strikes the reader as protean. We are reminded of mythical shapeshifting creatures, with the power to change their physical appearance in different situations.[7] This seems even more perplexing when we note that large parts of *Leviathan* are dedicated to persuading readers that they do

---

[3]   Job, 41: 13–14, 18–19, 25. *Bible*, New International Version.
[4]   Johan Tralau, 'Leviathan, the Beast of Myth: Medusa, Dionysos, and the Riddle of Hobbes's Sovereign Monster', in Patricia Springborg, ed., *The Cambridge Companion to Hobbes's Leviathan* (Cambridge: Cambridge University Press, 2007), pp. 61–81, p. 62.
[5]   Ibid., pp. 61–62.
[6]   Ibid., p. 62.
[7]   Ibid., p. 68.

not need to believe in mythical creatures such as ghosts or fairies.[8] In fact, Richard Tuck contends that Hobbes's account serves to "liberate" us from "unnecessary fear."[9] But what about *necessary* fear? Tralau argues that the beastly imagery is a crucial piece in Hobbes's abso-lute-sovereignty puzzle: it "supplement[s] the rational account of sover-eignty with an image conducive to the kind of fear and awe necessary for absolute obedience to prevail."[10] In short, we are supposed to be scared of Leviathan.

Here enters Shachar's image of today's Leviathan. We have become accustomed to a "traditional" picture of the modern state, with sover-eign authority over the people and place clearly delineated by the fixed borders lying at its territory's edges. If this picture ever were accurate (and the history of empire and the slave trade gives us reason to doubt that it was), it certainly is not now. It is an illusion, as Shachar illus-trates. Borders are transforming to suit the evolving legal and political landscape, and with them states and sovereignty are morphing into different shapes too. Borders are not *disappearing* or losing their salience, as in the "globalist" hopes, dreams, or fantasies of post-nationalists (p. 13). Nor should the rising number of fortified walls and fences mislead us into thinking of twenty-first-century borders as mere static, physical boundaries which mark the sovereign state's beginning and end. Instead, borders are the modern-day shapeshifters. In lan-guage that calls to mind the protean beast Leviathan, Shachar writes of the shifting border as "at once multidirectional and slippery" (p. 11); it "changes form depending on how it is approached and by whom" (p. 13); it has "long arm[s]," which stretch outward beyond the state's physical territory, and inward to the state's interior (p. 6); it is "moving" and "unmoored" (p. 4); it operates in a "quantum-like fashion" (p. 9); and it is even "multiplying and fracturing" so that it can attach to indi-viduals, who then "carry" it with them as they go "across space and place" (p. 37). Terrifying.

---

[8] See Richard Tuck, 'Introduction', in Hobbes, *Leviathan* (n 1), p. xlii.
[9] Ibid.
[10] Tralau, 'Leviathan' (n 4), p. 76.

What is the appropriate response to this shapeshifting monster, the metamorphizing border? A first step is trying to understand why it is transforming and how it operates, because comprehending the whys and hows is essential for determining the next move. One of the most impressive and significant contributions of Shachar's brilliant essay is its illumination of the "dark corners of the evolving legal cartography and geography of power," and its critical analysis of how borders function in practice (p. 61). I will begin with a brief outline of that picture. Then I will explore three different responses to living among monsters. The first is to admit defeat. The second—the main thrust of Shachar's favored approach—is to try to tame the beast. The third is to fight back. I will argue that it is time to fight back, and I will explain why and how I think this can be done.

Shapeshifting borders

In his study of Hobbes's "sovereign monster," Tralau compares Leviathan to the Greek gods Proteus and Zeus, who are able to change shape at will. Tralau mentions Hegel's discussion of the kind of physical "metamorphosis" that happens "only when the particular god intends to do something immoral."[11] As Shachar illustrates, the border performs its best shapeshifting routine—from fluid to rigid—when the rights of migrants are implicated and a state is determined to avoid incurring obligations. To control the movement of people, she explains, "states are willfully *abandoning* traditional notions of fixed and bounded territoriality, stretching their jurisdictional arm inward and outward with tremendous flexibility." However, when the issue of granting protections arises, "the very same states snap back to a narrow and strict interpretation of spatiality which limits their responsibility and liability, by attaching it to the (illusionary) static notion of border control" (p. 8, emphasis in the original). Where migrant rights are concerned,

[11] Tralau, 'Leviathan' (n 4), p. 68.

the aim is never to be in the right place, at the right time, assuming the right form.

The shifting-border phenomenon is no random coincidence. As Shachar carefully explains, it has emerged in response to a particular combination of legal and political factors. On the one hand, it is generally assumed that migration control is an essential right of sovereign states. Indeed, it is often described as the "last bastion of sovereignty," because of the various ways in which many traditional, supposed sovereign rights are thought to have been weakened, eroded, or erased over time, particularly via developments in international, regional, and domestic law (p. 71). Moreover, states often are considered to enjoy "almost unlimited power" in the realm of migration control, where they are usually subject to fewer of "the standard limits on the exercise of authority" (pp. 72, 75). States that self-identify as "prosperous 'islands' of high standards of human rights, affluence, and democratic governance" are taking great lengths to repel "uninvited" entrants (including refugees, and low-skilled, low-income migrants), while remaining more open to the "desirable" migrants whom they wish to attract (p. 13). This means there are few if any legal routes to admission and settlement for those deemed "unwanted and unwelcome."[12] Their only migration options are "irregular."

On the other hand, the same states are supposedly committed to protecting the rights of refugees, including the human right to seek and enjoy asylum from persecution. In practice, though, a range of refugee-protection obligations are only activated when the person has "touch[ed] base" on a state's territory (p. 70). Hence, the onus is usually on refugees to cross borders in search of protection. Yet under the guise of controlling irregular migration, prosperous states are erecting more (and more sophisticated) obstacles to the movement of people across borders, making it increasingly difficult and dangerous for refugees to access the protection they need.

---

[12] See Ayelet Shachar, 'Selecting by Merit: The Brave New World of Stratified Mobility', in Sarah Fine and Lea Ypi, eds, *Migration in Political Theory: The Ethics of Movement and Membership* (Oxford: Oxford University Press, 2016), pp. 175–201.

In addition, migration is becoming ever more closely linked—in policy, in rhetoric, and in minds—with security concerns (pp. 69–70). Controlling movement (especially irregular migration) is presented as a crucial weapon in the battle against "global security threats" (p. 27). This legitimizes further restrictions on the movement of people across the world.

The by-product of this toxic mix is the shifting border. Prosperous, stable states have evolved imaginative techniques to "skirt" their protection obligations, by doing their best to prevent refugees arriving on their territory (p. 59). These states seek to seal themselves off from people trying to escape persecution, human rights abuses, conflict and political instability, poverty, the effects of climate change, and so on, elsewhere in the world. This selective closure intensifies existing global inequalities of all sorts—inequalities between individuals and also inequalities between states (p. 70). Those who bear the greatest costs of this system of control are refugees, displaced people, and other "unwanted" migrants: most glaringly, the thousands dying every year on "clandestine" migrant routes; those who have been tortured along their journeys; those trapped in atrocious conditions in detention centers and in makeshift camps; those subjected to police brutality; those separated from close family members; those on the receiving end of the racial discrimination that is endemic to migration control.[13] However, Shachar also highlights that the shifting border affects more or less everyone—citizens and non-citizens, the mobile and the immobile, those with and those without the relevant documents—as movement restrictions, surveillance, and data-gathering intensify and pervade countless aspects of our everyday lives.

In the course of her essay, Shachar offers a number of dramatic illustrations of the shifting border in operation: borders stretch inward and outward, attach to individuals, and sometimes perform a magical disappearing and reappearing act. To give the first of a few concrete

---

[13] On this, see Sarah Fine, 'Immigration and Discrimination', in Sarah Fine and Lea Ypi, eds, *Migration in Political Theory: The Ethics of Movement and Membership* (Oxford: Oxford University Press, 2016), pp. 125–150.

examples, there is the "expedited removal" provision in the United States which allows authorized personnel to remove and return irregular migrants detected on US territory within 100 miles of the borders. The border thus reaches inside the country, accompanied by its checkpoints and officials. This "constitution-lite zone" within the US interior is home to around 200 million people and may be rolled out "nationwide" (pp. 22–23).

At the same time, the US is determined to "push the border out" and "regulate mobility at a distance." For instance, there are hundreds of US officials operating in countries across the world, checking the documentation of travelers bound for the US, with the authority to determine whether people will be permitted to embark on their journey. As Shachar notes, these decisions "bear the full weight of US law as though their determinations were made 'at the border'," and in this way the border is "replanted as a legal construct on non-US soil" (p. 27).

These shifting border practices are replicated elsewhere. The European Union has developed sophisticated surveillance techniques designed to monitor the movement of non-EU citizens, not just once they are *within* EU territory, but from the *start* of their journey in their countries of origin (p. 36). In one of the more alarming passages of Shachar's essay, she introduces the reader to the European Union's pilot project for iBorderCtrl units (p. 37). The following excerpt is not from a work of science fiction. It is from the European Commission's website:

> iBorderCtrl ... leverages software and hardware technologies ranging from portable readers/scanners, various emerging and novel subsystems for automatic controls, wireless networking for mobile controls, and secure backend storage and processing. The two-stage procedure includes: (A) the registration before the travel to gather initial personal, travel document and vehicle data, perform a short, automated, non-invasive interview with an avatar, subject to lie detection and link the traveller to any pre-existing authority data. Utilizing multifactor analytics and risk-based approach, the data registered is processed and correlated with publicly open data or external systems such as the SIS II. Processing will

need the travellers consent as set in EU legislation and national law. (B)
the actual control at the border that complements pre-registered information with results of security controls that are performed with a portable, wireless connected iBorderCtl unit that can be used inside buses/
trains or any point. Multiple technologies check validity and authenticity
of parameters (for example, travel documents, visa, face recognition of
traveller using passport picture, real-time automated non-invasive lie
detection in interview by officer, etc.). The data collected are encrypted,
securely transferred and analysed in real time, providing an automated
decision support system for the border control officers.[35]

This is the border as all-seeing eye (or, more likely, as iSeeU). Once
again, Leviathan appears as beast, human, mortal god, and machine.

The model mobility-controlling shapeshifter is the Australian state,
which has performed the improbable conjuring trick of having its cake
and eating it, too (pp. 43–51). It officially "excised" some—then all—of
its territory from its "migration zone", though that territory still remains
as "Australia" on the map. Asylum seekers who arrive without authorization are treated "as though they had *never reached* Australia, despite
having physically landed on its shores" (p. 42, emphasis in the original).
Australia removes these asylum seekers to offshore detention centers
(which it designed and funded) without allowing them ever to submit
an application for asylum in Australia.

In case anyone remains under the illusion that such states really are
beacons of democracy, justice, and human rights, Shachar urges us to
think again. As part of the shifting border process, the European Union
has outsourced some of its migration control to countries with appalling
human rights records, such as Libya and Turkey, repaying Turkey with a
3.2 billion euros thank-you note for its troubles (p. 56). Furthermore, it is
not just other states that are drafted in to do the border dirty work. Countries also co-opt non-state actors, such as airlines and ferry operators, to
manage their borders for them—threatening them with stiff penalties if

---

[14] European Commission, 'Intelligent Portable Border Control System', online https://
cordis.europa.eu/project/rcn/202703_en.html.

they allow unauthorized travelers to use their services (p. 35). This use of financial incentives and coordination with private companies "blurs the line between state and market," illustrating yet another form assumed by the shifting border (hence the "Inc." in my chapter's title).

Importantly, Shachar emphasizes throughout her piece that the states in question are utilizing "legal tools," rather than "extralegal" methods, to refashion their borders and exert control (pp. 4, 7). They do not (or not usually) withdraw from the treaties, conventions, agreements, and compacts that supposedly signal their commitments to upholding human rights and protecting refugees (pp. 72–73). And why would they formally withdraw from the "refugee law regime," when, as Thomas Gammeltoft-Hansen and James Hathaway point out, it is in their interests for the regime to remain in operation?

> Simply put, migratory and other pressures on the developed world are significantly attenuated by the efforts of the less developed states in which the overwhelming majority of the world's refugees now live. If the global north were to withdraw entirely from refugee law, there would be no politically viable basis upon which to insist that poorer countries continue to shoulder their refugee law obligations under the current system of atomized responsibility and fluctuating charity from the wealthier world. . . . [W]hile refugee law matters to developed states today for a variety of reasons, the most important is that it conscripts less developed countries to act in ways that provide a critical support to the developed world's migration control project.[15]

A monstrous picture. So what, if anything, is to be done?

Admit defeat?

A tempting response to living among monsters is to throw up one's hands and admit defeat. Monsters are dangerous and frightening.

---

[15] Thomas Gammeltoft-Hansen and James C. Hathaway, 'Non-Refoulement in a World of Cooperative Deterrence', *Columbia Journal of Transnational Law 53*, no. 2 (2015): pp. 235–84, p. 240.

Perhaps we just have to try and coexist with them, hoping that they do not gobble *us* up. We might try to stay out of their way as far as possible. But now and then some of us will be forced to confront them and will come off the worse because we are no match for them. Consider the folktale *The Three Billy Goats Gruff*. The billy goats Gruff spot a meadow with fine grass on the other side of a river. They want to reach the meadow, and there is a bridge over the river, but a terrifying troll lives beneath it. According to the story, "people were afraid to cross the bridge because of the troll. Every time he heard footsteps on the bridge, he popped and gobbled up the person who was trying to cross."[16]

Perhaps the population of the story resigned themselves to living with the troll under the bridge and accepted him as an unfortunate but inescapable feature of their existence. However, an obvious problem with the model of "admitting defeat" is that sometimes people have to cross the proverbial bridge. As the billy goats Gruff asked themselves, must we really just accept that we confront a choice between missing out on the fine grass or being gobbled up by the troll? On top of that, the longer the troll is given free rein under the bridge, the more the myth of the troll's strength and invincibility grows, and the more people adapt their behavior to comply with the troll's real or imagined power.

Shachar shines a light on the trolls living under our own bridges, "pushing back" the boats of migrants traveling from Libya, returning migrants arriving in Greece back to Turkey, removing asylum seekers from "excised" Australian territory to detention centers in Nauru and Papua New Guinea, and so on. Their victims are the people with little choice but to cross the bridge, who do not have the luxury of just trying to coexist with the monster. As Shachar's essay makes abundantly clear, the costs of this status quo are unevenly distributed, falling most heavily on those with the fewest and least palatable options.

---

[16] *The Three Billy Goats Gruff*, retold by Vera Southgate (London: Ladybird Books, 2014), p. 6.

Taming the beast

Rather than admit defeat, a second reaction is to try to tame a monster. This domesticating strategy is a large part of Shachar's response to the shifting border. The language of "taming" recurs throughout the text. For example, Shachar invites us to consider "how to tame menacing governmental authority" (pp. 67–68), and how "to tame the rights-restricting consequences of the shifting border." (p. 68). She examines "how to potentially tame [the] sting" of these practices (p. 20), and how they can be "countered or at least tamed" (p. 62).

As Shachar understands the shifting border largely as a legal construct, it is perhaps no surprise that her proposed taming strategies primarily take legal forms too. If the border is unmoored from place, so legal protections should follow that de-territorialized model. When states exercise their authority over people, whether "at home" or beyond their territory's edge, their actions should be subject to appropriate legal oversight. The hope is that "instances of protection will begin to match the spatial and temporal acrobatics of the shifting border, becoming operative not only upon arrival at the territory but also upon contact with state officials or their delegates exerting binding migration-regulation authority, *whenever* and *wherever* such authority is implemented under color of law" (p. 76). Furthermore, one of the chief problems refugees encounter is the absence of safe, legal routes to places of genuine protection, and this predicament pushes them to embark on dangerous, clandestine journeys. So the obvious solution must be to make available more safe, legal routes. These can be provided by means of humanitarian visas, for example, which allow refugees to travel directly to the countries willing to admit them. The applications for such visas could be submitted anywhere, removing the requirement to remain in the region or to "touch base" on a country's territory first. Another option is to "bring the border" to refugees. For example, Shachar mentions Canada's decision to resettle over 25,000 Syrian refugees. In a short, efficient process, they were "pre-screened" in Jordan, Turkey, and Lebanon by Canadian officials, and soon offered permanent residency—no dangerous journeys or years of waiting required (pp. 82–83).

Why does Shachar adopt the taming strategy? She argues that a proper response cannot ignore "reality," which includes understanding that "governments and their voters detest irregular movements of people across borders," and that "states are unlikely to cede their authority over migration regulation any time soon" (pp. 93, 96). What is needed is a "non-idealist" approach to the shifting border that "recognizes states' *pro tanto* sovereign authority to regulate movement across borders" (p. 93). Shachar assumes that the shifting border is here to stay: that train "has already left the station" (p. 95). Given the state of play, the most effective tactic is "to borrow a page from the shifting-border book, albeit subversively" (p. 74). The challenge is to try to keep up with its twists and turns.

All of these "rights-enhancing" strategies would be welcome developments and would represent a dramatic improvement on the status quo. As Shachar points out, a number of them have precedents (such as the Canadian refugee-resettlement example). Interestingly enough, though, Shachar herself seems less than optimistic about the prospects of some of the proposed legal moves. While arguing that legal oversight should accompany the state's exercise of authority beyond its territory, Shachar urges caution: "[t]his is no panacea." She suspects that states will adapt to the new legal landscape, just as they have done so far (p. 80). That seems a reasonable concern. If we are dealing with shape-shifters, we can expect them to take a new form to fit their context. What is more, the trouble with borrowing a page from the shifting-border book is that states wrote it. They know it better and are at least one chapter ahead.

Ultimately, if the shifting border is as protean and Leviathan-like as Shachar's study has suggested, are we kidding ourselves to think that it can be tamed? Recall the biblical lines that Hobbes's seventeenth-century readers would have known well: "can you pull in Leviathan with a fish-hook or tie down its tongue with a rope? . . . Nothing on earth is its equal—a creature without fear." The twenty-first-century state is unlikely to speak to us with gentle words.

Moreover, while Shachar's proposed response would be much better than what we have now, it leaves many of the "dark corners" of migration control unlit. For instance, what happens to the refugees who do not secure humanitarian visas or any other form of "golden ticket to a life of safety" (p. 83)? How does this approach confront the growing systems of surveillance and data-gathering that accompany the shifting border? Shachar argues that the shifting border's "tools can be repurposed" and used creatively to de-territorialize rights and protections in the service of refugees and other migrants (p. 96). That sounds promising, but talk of repurposing tools calls to mind the famous words of Audre Lorde: "the master's tools will never dismantle the master's house. They may allow us temporarily to beat him at his own game, but they will never enable us to bring about genuine change."[17]

Fighting back

There is another option. This is my preferred option. Shachar gestures toward it at the end of her essay too. It is the fightback. She writes of the politics of resistance and contestation—the political and grassroots counterpart to the legal response. Civil society is rising to the challenge: people are "galvanizing their multiple voices into action, mobilizing protests, filing law suits, planning sit-ins, accompanying irregular migrants to their deportation hearings, offering shelter, food, legal aid, and medical care in houses of worship, and providing 'sanctuary' in cities, campuses, and workplaces" (pp. 94–95). This is a welcome reminder of Michel Foucault's celebrated line that "where there is power, there is resistance."[18] Therein lies the possibility for change.

[17] Audre Lorde, *Sister Outsider: Essays and Speeches* (Berkeley: Crossing Press, 1984), p. 112.
[18] Michel Foucault, *The History of Sexuality: The Will to Knowledge*, volume 1 (London: Penguin Books, [1976] 1998), p. 95.

But performing the tireless work of studying and unmasking the ignoble practices of states, and the violent functions of borders, can grind a person down. Again, Shachar gently cautions against too much optimism: we must wait to judge whether this resistance is able "to reverse the course of harsh governmental action against immigrants in an age of resurgent populism and border-worshiping politicians" (p. 95, n 224).

The shapeshifting border is a frightening phenomenon and it is difficult to remain hopeful when confronted with its monstrous form. However, I think we are overlooking one of the most effective, time-honored ways of responding to monsters. The power of monsters in large part depends on us *believing in them*. The power of the shifting border draws on one belief above all others: that migration control is a fundamental sovereign right of states—that states have the right to exclude non-members from their territory and from access to their political community. This is the belief that feeds the beast, gives it strength, and keeps us all in awe. On the back of this apparently unshakeable belief, states construct their prison-like detention centers at home and "offshore";[19] coordinate with other states and non-state actors to push back boats carrying migrants, resulting in needless deaths;[20] separate children from their parents at borders;[21] vow to send heavily armed troops to meet migrant "caravans";[22] threaten long-term-settled irregular migrants with deportation;[23] refuse to allow refugees to

[19] See Nadine Chemali, 'It's Great to Get Kids off Nauru, but Detention Centres in Australia Are Like Prisons', *The Guardian*, October 31, 2018, online www.theguardian.com/commentisfree/2018/nov/01/i-have-visited-detention-centres-in-australia-they-are-not-much-better-than-nauru.

[20] See Harret Agerholm, 'Italy Sued over Migrant 'Push Back' Deal with Libya after 20 Migrants Drown in Mediterranean', *The Independent*, May 8, 2018, online www.independent.co.uk/news/world/europe/italy-libya-migrant-refugee-push-back-deal-mediterranean-a8342056.html.

[21] Patrick Greenfield, 'Family Separation: Hundreds of Migrant Children Still Not Reunited with Families in US', *The Guardian*, July 27, 2018, online www.theguardian.com/us-news/2018/jul/26/trump-administration-family-separations-children-reunited.

[22] Tom Embury-Dennis, 'Trump Says up to 15,000 Troops Will Be Sent to US–Mexico Border to Counter "Migrant Caravan"', *The Independent*, November 1, 2018, online www.independent.co.uk/news/world/americas/us-politics/trump-migrant-caravan-mexico-us-border-troops-military-guatemala-central-america-a8611941.html.

[23] Sophie McBain, 'The Deportation Nightmare Haunting the Dreamers of the US', *New Statesman*, February 2, 2018, online www.newstatesman.com/world/2018/02/deportation-nightmare-haunting-dreamers-us.

transit through their territories, and repel them with riot police;[24] spend hundreds of billions of dollars on border infrastructure;[25] deliberately seek to foster a "hostile environment" for irregular migrants—in the process, causing grave harm to some residents who have the right to remain, stripping them of benefits and even deporting them;[26] charge migrants thousands of pounds for citizenship applications;[27] and so on, and so on, and so on. This is the astonishing, terrifying, mighty—even deadly—power of a simple idea. Every person who drowns in the sea, dies in the desert, suffocates in the back of a lorry, or freezes to death on clandestine migration journeys is a victim of this monster.

Why do we believe that states have this right to exclude non-members from their territory and from access to citizenship? Many of us just do not question it and feel as though we can go about our ordinary lives, not adversely affected by this particular troll under the bridge. People on the grassy side of the bridge may even appreciate the troll's presence, because it is seen to protect the meadow's rich, green grass. They might prefer the troll to behave more "humanely," with a bit less of the gobbling up, but they are prepared to accept that there will be casualties. Maybe they think that is the price that must be paid for protecting their "prosperous 'islands' of high standards of human rights, affluence, and democratic governance" from outsiders (p. 13). That is, at least, until they or the people they know have to confront the troll— as when they are prevented from employing workers from abroad because of immigration caps and points systems and salary thresholds,

[24] Adam Withnall, 'Hungary Opens Fire on Refugees with Tear Gas as It Steps Up Border Operation', *The Independent*, September 16, 2015, online www.independent.co.uk/news/world/europe/hungary-opens-fire-on-refugees-with-tear-gas-as-it-steps-up-border-operation-10503822.html.

[25] Katanga Johnson, 'Trump Budget Asks More than $200 Billion for Infrastructure, Border Security: Budget Director', *Reuters*, February 12, 2018, online www.reuters.com/article/us-usa-budget-mulvaney/trump-budget-asks-more-than-200-billion-for-infrastructure-border-security-budget-director-idUSKBN1FW03N.

[26] 'Government Knew for Years that Windrush Generation Hurt by "Hostile Environment"', *The Guardian*, April 23, 2018, online www.theguardian.com/uk-news/2018/apr/22/government-aware-for-years-that-hostile-environment-hurt-windrush-generation.

[27] See the details on the UK government's website: 'Fees for Citizenship Applications and the Right of Abode from 6 April 2018', online www.gov.uk/government/publications/fees-for-citizenship-applications/fees-for-citizenship-applications-and-the-right-of-abode-from-6-april-2018.

or their own friends and relations are stuck on the other side of the bridge, or they just want to cross the bridge with no trouble or bother.

Should we believe that states must enjoy this right to exclude, this wide degree of discretion when it comes to migration control and access to citizenship? Shachar is surely correct that states are unlikely to relinquish their claims to authority over migration control anytime soon, and so responding to the shifting border must take that reality seriously. But it is one thing to assume that states will keep doing what they are doing, for the foreseeable future. It is quite another to proceed as though what they are doing is *legitimate*. The air of legitimacy matters for all sorts of reasons, not least—as Max Weber pointed out— because ongoing political rule depends not only on the rulers having the means of "physical force" at their disposal, but also on people having the "disposition to obey those rulers who claim to be the bearers of legitimate force."[28] The disposition to obey comes from all kinds of sources (including "motives of fear and hope").[29] It seems clear, however, that we are more likely to obey voluntarily when we believe that the rulers have the right to behave as they do.

At this point one might think that the examples that Shachar highlights—such as the "push backs" of boats carrying migrants, Australia's reliance on offshore detention centers, and so on—as well as the policies of the Trump administration in the United States, or the recent experiences of the Windrush generation in the United Kingdom, are cases of illegitimate overreach. The reply may go: states have a right to exclude and so to control migration, but it is not unlimited. It must be constrained by respect for human rights, the rule of law, and other domesticating forces. However, Shachar's essay shows us that these striking cases are not rare aberrations. They are actually part of migration control's business-as-usual—albeit business that states often like to conduct behind closed doors. If one of President Trump's executive

---

[28] Max Weber, 'The Profession and Vocation of Politics', in Peter Lassman and Ronald Speirs, eds, *Political Writings* (Cambridge: Cambridge University Press, [1919] 1994), pp. 309–369, p. 313.

[29] Ibid., p. 312.

orders is successfully derailed or delayed by the courts, another will follow, and then another, and then another. Shachar's illumination of migration control's many dark sides—its deadly costs, the ways in which it infiltrating our lives—offers powerful ammunition in the fightback against the idea that the right to exclude is and must be a legitimate part of state authority.

Just as there are multiple ways in which a proponent might try to defend the idea that states have at least some kind of a right to exclude, so there are numerous means to challenge that idea.[30] I will focus on one challenge here. It is common to assume that the right to exclude non-members is just a fundamental component of state sovereignty. It is difficult to imagine states without their claiming this sort of entitlement. In fact, as Shachar emphasizes, this is often described as "one of the last bastions of sovereignty."

Where does that idea come from? Let us return to Hobbes, usually considered the defining theorist of the modern state. What did he have to say about the state's right to control migration? Notably, it is not one of the many items on his list of the essential rights of sovereigns (*Leviathan*, chapter 18). Of course, that is not to say he would not have argued in defense of the state's right to exclude. It is fair to assume that would have done so. This is simply to illustrate that the right to control movement across borders did not seem crucial to Hobbes. It was not, as it were, a *first* bastion of sovereignty.

Migration *into* the kinds of states Hobbes had in mind (rather than *out of* those states to go and secure and settle the colonies) has taken on a different level of political salience for governments and populations in

---

[30] I have tried to push back against the idea myself; for example, in Sarah Fine, 'Freedom of Association Is Not the Answer', *Ethics 120*, no. 2 (2010): pp. 338–356; and Sarah Fine, 'The Ethics of Immigration: Self-Determination and the Right to Exclude', *Philosophy Compass 8*, no. 3 (2013): pp. 254–268. Among other notable efforts, see Arash Abizadeh, 'Democratic Theory and Border Coercion: No Right to Unilaterally Control Your Own Borders', *Political Theory 36*, no. 1 (2008): pp. 37–65; Phillip Cole, *Philosophies of Exclusion: Liberal Political Theory and Immigration* (Edinburgh: Edinburgh University Press, 2000); Joseph H. Carens, *The Ethics of Immigration* (New York: Oxford University Press, 2013); and Christopher Bertram, *Do States Have the Right to Exclude Immigrants?* (Cambridge: Polity Press, 2018).

the centuries since Hobbes penned *Leviathan*. Hence, we might wish to argue that the right to exclude is an essential feature of sovereignty today. This is what states are and do.

However, just because states claim to do and be some form now does not mean we should accept that they must continue to do and be that form into the future. As I have emphasized elsewhere, modern states used to claim the sovereign right to prevent their subjects from leaving, or to restrict their movement within their own territory. We do not tend to accept those as essential "sovereign rights" now.[31] But belief in the state's right to exclude somehow endures. This is the power of unchallenged ideas.

Hobbes knew all about the immense power of ideas, of course. Recall that his Leviathan is presented as a *mortal* god. Like all other mortals, thought Hobbes, the commonwealth itself can succumb to disease, and the diseases can be fatal. The whole edifice can come crashing down. Among the causes of the dissolution of commonwealths are the diseases that "proceed from the poyson of seditious doctrines." Hobbes enumerates these at length (*Leviathan*, chapter 29). They include the beliefs "that he that hath the Soveraign Power, is subject to the Civill Lawes," and "that the Soveraign Power may be divided." For Hobbes, sovereignty had to be absolute and indivisible in order for it to endure over time and to work in the service of "peace at home, and mutuall ayd against their enemies abroad"—the ends for which it was established in the first place (*Leviathan*, chapter 17).

Yet it is now a commonplace of self-styled constitutional democracies that *no one* is above the law, and that sovereign power can and should be divided between executive, judiciary, and legislature—and can be divided between national state and smaller, regional units, too. In short, many of Hobbes's readers have refused to believe that we face a Hobbesian choice between absolute, indivisible sovereignty, on the one hand, and sowing the seeds for the dissolution of the commonwealth, on the other. More specifically, they have rejected the claim that

---

[31] See, for example, Fine, 'The Ethics of Immigration' (n 73).

indivisible sovereignty and sovereigns remaining above the law are essential components of functioning states, without which they will not be able to fulfill their purposes and may eventually decay. Here, then, is another seditious doctrine: we do not have to believe in the state's right to exclude. And to follow it up with one more: without the right to exclude, the whole edifice would not collapse, just as it has not collapsed in the absence of a belief in the state's sovereign right to prevent its own citizens from leaving and returning.

Is this response on the wrong side of the realistic/unrealistic or idealist/non-idealist divide in political philosophy? Does it fall foul of the injunction to take reality seriously? I do not know, and anyway that probably is not for me to judge. As lawyers must maintain some faith in the power of the law, so philosophers continue to have faith in the power of ideas (for good or ill). The difficulty when it comes to judging political "reality" is that we are peering through a glass, darkly. From this vantage point, it is hard to ascertain whether what we see is solid or ephemeral, material or myth.

Shachar's *The Shifting Border* is the most magnificent and terrifying text I have read in a long time. Anyone who wishes to understand the modern state must read her essay. Despite the unquestionable power of the shifting border, I maintain that a deeper kind of resistance to these forces is available to us—one grounded in a refusal to believe in the state's right to exclude. This refusal can empower the politics of contestation; it can fuel the fightback against the miseries of migration control. Ultimately, it can begin to liberate us from one of the unnecessary fears of our time.

3

Migration, time, and the shift toward autocracy

Noora Lori

National borders are territorial markers that bound a country's edges. We can locate these fixed black lines on our world atlases, and while there may be territorial disputes or ambiguity about the precise location of a specific border, the fact that borders are located *somewhere* on a fixed terrain appears to be a basic fact. In her lead essay, Shachar meticulously undermines this conventional wisdom by showing how national borders are shifting—expanding far beyond the edges of a particular territory and bleeding inward into the interior.

Shachar's essay provides us with the conceptual language to identify and critique the contemporary migration-enforcement practices of liberal states, while developing a framework for practicably countering the illiberal effects of these policies. She pushes the contemporary scholarship on migration by proposing a shift in the dominant perspective, "from the more familiar locus of studying the *movement of people across borders* to critically investigating the *movement of borders to regulate the mobility of people*" (p. 7). Others have pointed out that states deploy de-territorialized migration-enforcement practices (such as migrant interdiction and offshore detention) to evade responsibility and circumvent their own due processes. But the innovation of Shachar's contribution is that her response not only develops a common vocabulary for discussing a wide range of diverse practices to illustrate that the national border itself is moving—she also presents an agenda-setting plan for how legal protections and due processes might be made to move *with* it. The task at hand moving forward is thus "not to 'undo' the flexibility of the shifting border but to bring it under the normative umbrella of legal and democratic oversight" (p. 76). Her policy response captures the national border's expansions into space and incorporates "the very logic of de-territorialized migration control . . . while at the same time subverting it," by calling for an expansion in the extraterritorial reach of human rights while at the same time relaxing the fixation on territorial access (p. 16).

Shachar's essay functions as a road map for deciphering "the emerging code of the shifting border in a world in which prosperous 'islands' of high standards of human rights, affluence, and democratic governance are increasingly protected through the operation of 'portable' legal walls that may appear, disappear, and reappear in variable coordinates of space and time" (p. 13). While Shachar explains that the shifting border contracts and expands into time as well as space, most of the empirical examples in the lead essay focus on the spatial mobility of the shifting border. The first part of this response expands upon the temporal aspects of Shachar's argument, focusing on the legal maneuvers of contemporary migration enforcement that deploy time to police the boundaries of the national body politic. These legal innovations separate the chronological advancement of the clock from the counting of time under the mantle of the law.

What matters is not how much time a person has resided in a territory but rather how that time is counted by the state. By pegging legal rights to a specific legal status, and counting the time of different legal statuses differently, states can suspend, slow down, or speed up chronological time in order to exclude, delay, or (conversely) hasten the inclusion of particular non-citizens. Temporary legal statuses allow states to delay or suspend the time of undesirable migrants, while citizenship by investment schemes speed up time for desirable (wealthy) migrants.[1] These legal expansions of space and time in the

---

[1] Ayelet Shachar, *Citizenship for Sale?*, in Ayelet Shachar *et al.*, eds, *The Oxford Handbook of Citizenship* (Oxford: Oxford University Press, 2017), pp. 789–816.

name of migration enforcement have created states of exception that allow even the most established of liberal democracies to circumvent their own due processes and increase their discretionary power over who should or should not have access to the rights and protections associated with democratic governance.

In identifying the contours of the shifting border as a contemporary practice of liberal states and their migration-enforcement efforts, Shachar raises important underlying questions that are never explicitly posed: what is the relationship between effective migration enforcement and regime type? What does it mean to legally tamper with time and space and create domains where the rules of the game are suspended in order to increase the state's discretionary power? The second part of this response takes a step back to assess the larger implications of Shachar's findings for our understanding of the political continuum between liberal democracies and authoritarian or autocratic states. Like the enterprises of colonialism and imperialism during previous periods, the practices associated with contemporary migration enforcement highlight the contradictions between democratic ideals and the actual practices of liberal states.

The use of time to police national boundaries

The national border as a legal construct has shifted both outward from and inward into the territorial boundaries of liberal states. The border has shifted outward as wealthy democratic states like the United States and United Kingdom have developed mechanisms for screening people at "the source," or origin, of their journey rather than at the destination. Such legal constructs render the traditional static border one of the last points of encounter that migrants have with the state, rather than the first. Simultaneously, liberal democracies have also moved the border into the interior—developing special zones where normal laws are suspended in the name of migration enforcement. This has led to the creation, within liberal democracies, of what have been "referred to as 'constitution free' zones or 'waiting zones' (*zones d'Attente)*, where ordinary constitutional rights are partially suspended or limited, especially in relation to those who do not have proper documentation or legal status" (p. 6). These erosions of civil liberties are occurring through sophisticated legal (not extralegal) techniques and innovations that increase the state's discretionary power by circumventing the due processes in place for assessing whether an individual has the right to reside in a state.

If the national border as a legal construct has shifted in space to create legal ways of interdicting migrants before they even reach a territory, then the shifting border has also used the counting (and miscounting) of time to create legal ways of excluding migrants who have already accessed a territory's interior. In theory, democracies guarantee inalienable rights only for their own members (secure citizens). For all non-citizens, access to particular rights (like asylum assessments) can only be activated when an individual crosses the threshold into the territory; "legal circumstances affecting non-members change substantively only *after* they 'pass through our gates'" (p. 4). But in the eyes of the law, rights are not only tied to a particular geographic space: they also accrue over time.

Time, or duration of residency, is one of the predominant ways of accruing membership rights in a political community. States assign durations of time political value and use time as a form of exchange value to accord or deny rights.[2] As Elizabeth Cohen explains, time is widely accepted as a way of creating value in democratic processes because it is assumed to be impartial and equally available to all. As a result, time becomes a political currency that is exchanged for rights:

> That is, increments of time are used to represent different values, such as loyalty, civic knowledge, or cultural assimilation; and then these increments are inserted along with other variables into formulae that

---

[2] Elizabeth F. Cohen, *The Political Value of Time: Citizenship, Duration, and Democratic Justice* (Cambridge: Cambridge University Press, 2018).

confer or deny rights. The deployment of time in this way creates a
political economy of time in which durations of time are used as currency for states and citizens to transact over rights.[3]

The notion of membership rights accruing over time is central to democratic understandings of inclusive deliberation. This is why new arrivals and those on tourist visas are party to different rules and regulations
than those on short-term residency visas, and those on short-term
visas have fewer rights than permanent residents. In a number of liberal
democracies, permanent residents have even gained some political rights
(usually at the local level), in line with the understanding that long-
term residents have earned a voice through the time they have spent
residing in a democratic state.[4]

In theory, migrants are assumed to experience a transition from
being temporary to being permanent—migration is an act that should
recede into the background as the duration of residency progresses.
However, in practice this act (migration) becomes a noun (migrant)
that can cling to an individual over time (even over generations). In
other words, in practice the transition from temporary to permanent
must occur not only through the register of time as duration, but also
on the level of changing legal statuses and requisite rights. A disjuncture
between these registers of time occurs when political entities refuse to
count the "time spent" of some their residents, creating what Bridget
Anderson calls "asynchronicities between subjective experiences of
time and administrative requirements."[5]

States can withhold rights by refusing to recognize the time spent
by particular individuals or groups. In the realm of migration enforcement, this not only occurs through the criminalization of irregular
migrants (whose time does not count as authorized residency). It also

3   Elizabeth F. Cohen, 'The Political Economy of Immigrant Time: Rights, Citizenship, and
    Temporariness in the Post-1965 Era', *Polity 47*, no. 3 (2015): pp. 337–351, p. 337.
4   On the extension of voting rights to non-citizens in Japan, see Erin Chung, *Immigration
    and Citizenship in Japan* (Cambridge: Cambridge University Press, 2006). On Europe,
    see Tomas D. Hammar, *Democracy and the Nation State: Aliens, Denizens, and Citizens
    in a World of International Migration* (Aldershot: Gower Pub. Co., 1990).
5   Bridget Anderson, *About Time Too*, 2018 (manuscript on file with author), p. 13.

occurs through the innovation of developing legal statuses that render individuals temporary in the eyes of the law, even if their actual presence on the territory is protracted. This suspension of time of residency based on one's legal status is the temporal equivalent of spatially erasing territory in the name of migration enforcement. As Shachar explains, states like Australia are excising their own territory to exclude migrants by claiming that certain territorial zones do not *count* as the state under the mantle of the law. This legal maneuver makes the land itself a mirage:

> This legislation authorizes Australia's immigration officials to remove asylum seekers that have managed to reach its now "excised" territory, as though they had *never reached* Australia, despite having physically landed on its shores. Put differently, those who reach the excision zone cannot make a valid asylum claim in Australia because they never entered it in a legally cognizable way—the territory they reached is no longer "Australia" for immigration-law purposes. (p. 42)

In the same way that contemporary migration-enforcement laws can render the material act of crossing a geographical border invalid, legal categories are used to differentiate between being physically present in a territory and valid residency. Time of residency is suspended or delayed for different groups of individuals who inhabit temporary and ad hoc legal categories that are explicitly designed to prevent visa holders from acquiring citizenship. A large number of states deploy this maneuver, and two of the most common types of temporary statuses include categories designed for temporary work authorization and temporary humanitarian protection.

In the United States, temporary legal statuses are referred to as "nonimmigrant" visas. To be eligible for naturalization in the US, a migrant must be a resident for a minimum of five years, but time as a nonimmigrant visa holder does not count toward this requirement. Nonimmigrant visas began to proliferate at the turn of the twentieth century, in the aftermath of the Chinese Exclusion Act. Initially, these visa categories allowed US companies to continue to hire Chinese laborers without allowing their presence in the territory to count toward accruing citizenship rights.[6] This system was extended with the Bracero programs, which were designed to supply Mexican farmers to US farms from 1917–1921 and again from 1946–1967.[7] As is typical of temporary worker schemes, the employers' need for workers lasted longer and proved to be larger than originally expected, creating a permanent migration corridor. Today nonimmigrant visas account for a wide range of functions—allowing migrants to legally reside in the US for the purposes of education, temporary humanitarian protection, and temporary or seasonal employment, without allowing that time to count toward eligibility for permanent residency or naturalization. With the exception of H1-B visas (high-skilled specialized work visas) that can be adjusted to immigrant status, nonimmigrant visas are not numerically restricted in the same way that immigrant visas are.

In addition to temporary worker programs, many states have developed temporary statuses to respond to the fact that the vast majority of displaced people find themselves in "refugee-like" situations without being eligible for refugee status as defined under international law. In the United States, this is referred to as Temporary Protected Status (TPS), which Congress passed in 1990.[8] Temporary protection is also offered in Germany and Turkey, and, at least on paper, could be triggered in the European Union. TPS is a stopgap measure to protect designated nationalities from being deported during times of armed conflict, natural disasters, or other "temporary and extraordinary" conditions. While asylum is individually determined, TPS is granted to all nationals of a designated country, as a blanket form of relief for people who face reasonable threats but are not individually persecuted.

Under TPS, it does not matter how long an individual has resided in the United States; their time does not count toward accruing

---

[6]   Mae Ngai, *Impossible Subjects: Illegal Aliens and the Making of Modern America* (Princeton: Princeton University Press, 2004).
[7]   Philip L. Martin, *There Is Nothing More Permanent than Temporary Foreign Workers*, *Backgrounder* (Center for Immigration Studies, 2001).
[8]   Bill Frelick and Barbara Kohnen, 'Filling the Gap: Temporary Protected Status', *Journal of Refugee Studies* 8 (1995): pp. 339–363.

membership rights. Because TPS is not meant as path to permanent settlement, each extension of TPS works to lock beneficiaries into "a 'legal
limbo', rendering them unable to fully integrate into life in the United
States."[9] Migrants under TPS inhabit a liminal space—they are neither
"legal" nor "illegal," because they are neither fully recognized as economic migrants nor political refugees; at times they are treated as refugees and granted temporary relief from deportation, and at other times
their permits are not renewed and they fall into being "illegal" migrants
again.[10]

Note that non-citizen residents under TPS and other nonimmigrant
visas have fewer rights in the United States but not necessarily fewer
responsibilities. After five years of residency, any alien on a nonimmigrant visa is subject to the same taxes that apply to permanent residents
and citizens. When it comes to taxation, the law reverts to a strict chronological understanding of time. But when it comes to accruing "credit"
toward naturalization and citizenship, the law suspends or delays time.
This double movement is similar to the way legal maneuvers shift space
in the name of border control. When it comes to restricting rights, the
border shifts inward and outward from the territory, but when it comes
to granting rights, the border reverts back to a static boundary. As
Shachar explains, "here lies the deep paradox of the shifting border:
when it comes to controlling migration, states are willfully *abandoning*
traditional notions of fixed and bounded territoriality . . . but when
it comes to granting rights and protections, the very same states snap
back to a narrow and strict interpretation of spatiality" (p. 8). The

---

[9] Claire Bergeron, 'Temporary Protected Status after 25 Years: Addressing the Challenge
of Long-Term "Temporary" Residents and Strengthening a Centerpiece of US Humanitarian Protection', *Journal on Migration and Human Security 2* (2014): pp. 22–43.

[10] On the liminal statuses of TPS recipients, see Cecilia Menjívar, 'Liminal Legality: Salvadoran and Guatemalan Immigrants' Lives in the United States', *American Journal of
Sociology 111* (2006): pp. 999–1037. This oscillation between amnesty and illegality has
recently been illustrated by the case of El Salvadorans in the United States. President
Trump's administration has terminated El Salvador from the TPS list (effective September 2019) for the first time since it was place on the list of protected countries in 2001.
This move renders members of this community illegal and subject to deportation—
including people who have resided in the United States for eighteen years (over three
times the duration of what they would need to acquire citizenship formally if they were
counted as legal permanent residents).

manipulation of time and space in the name of migration enforcement is less about simply excluding migrants than it is about gaining greater discretionary power over who should be excluded or included and on what basis.

States are simultaneously opening and closing their borders "but do so *selectively*, indicating, quite decisively, whom they desire to admit (those with specialized skills, superb talents, or increasingly, deep pockets), while at the same time erecting higher and higher legal walls to block out those deemed unwanted or 'too different'" (p. 9). When it comes to undesirable migrants, exclusion from permanent rights and citizenship is justified on the grounds that certain temporal and spatial criteria have not been met. For example, the basis for exclusion can be that a migrant has not "touched" the territory or has not resided in the territory for the appropriate duration of time under the "right" legal status. However, when it comes to admitting desirable populations, those same temporal and spatial criteria are manipulated for the purposes of hastening admission.

As Shachar explains in her previous work, with the introduction of citizenship-by-investment schemes "a growing number of countries now offer tailor-made, exclusive, and expedited pathways for the world's super-rich to acquire citizenship" quickly and easily.[11] In the United States, new immigrants can gain permanent-residency status (a green card) without spending any time in the territory if they can provide a capital investment of 1 million US dollars (or 500,000 in some designated areas).[12] In this case, time is not suspended but sped up, and the fixation on territorial access and residency is waived entirely. An exceptionally wealthy migrant can legally "parachute" into a citizenship status, while a less desirable migrant who has been a resident of that state for a protracted period can be legally excluded from accruing citizenship rights.

In the contemporary language of migration enforcement in liberal states, subjective criteria like race or ethnic origin are replaced by

---

[11] Shachar, *Citizenship for Sale?* (n 5), pp. 789–90.
[12] Ibid., p. 791.

seemingly objective spatial and temporal criteria. However, as Shachar shows, legal maneuvers are used to separate the physical territory from what counts as the state's border by law, just as they can be used to separate the unfolding of time from what counts as time under the mantle of the law. While Shachar limits the scope of her argument to liberal democracies, especially those that are also traditional immigration states, like the United States, it is important to highlight that her findings are applicable to a much wider array of cases. The creation of legal statuses that delay or suspend the time of migrants is not unique to the United States or other democratic states. Most guest-worker programs are built on similar "nonimmigrant" schemes. For example, in the world's third largest migrant-receiving region, the Arab Gulf (including Bahrain, Kuwait, Oman, Qatar, Saudi Arabia, and the United Arab Emirates) all visas are considered temporary. Officially, the non-citizens residing in the Gulf are not "immigrants" but temporary contractual laborers with little to no recourse to permanent settlement or citizenship. They enter the country as guest workers under fixed-term employment contracts and are obliged to leave upon the termination of their work. Their stay is regulated through the *kafāla*, or sponsorship system, which makes an individual Gulf national citizen or company sponsor (known as the *kafīl*) legally and economically responsible for the foreign worker for the duration of the contract period.

Following the trend of most other guest-worker schemes, the *kafāla* has produced a structural dependence on foreign labor in the Gulf that has created a sizeable and permanent migrant community. Due to the massive inward flow of migrants, the region's aggregate population increased more than tenfold in a little over half a century (from 4 million in 1950 to 40 million in 2005), the highest growth rate of anywhere in the world during that period.[13] Migrants now outnumber citizens in

[13] Andrzej Kapiszewski, United Nations Secretariat, Population Division, Department of Economic and Social Affairs, *Arab versus Asian Migrant Workers in the GCC Countries* (Beirut: UN/POP/EGM/2006/02, United Nations Expert Group Meeting on International Migration and Development in the Arab Region, 2006), online https://pdfs.semanticscholar.org/6512/6c08bb15b1dfbd7c0951fc09e6f0bb8a50a3.pdf.

four out of the six Gulf Cooperation Council (GCC) states—the
United Arab Emirates (UAE), Qatar, Kuwait, and Bahrain. They represent between 37.8 percent (Saudi Arabia) to 87.4 percent (United Arab
Emirates) of the domestic labor forces and over 60 percent of the
region's aggregate workforce.[14] While the diverse migrant population
in the Gulf is formally described as "temporary," in reality a large seg-
ment of this population is durably settled in the region, often with
their families. Indeed, in some cases, family settlement is occuring
over generations.[15] This permanent residency is not officially acknowledged, which means that the time of long-term non-citizen residents
is suspended—it never counts toward the acquisition of membership
rights.[16]

While the regime type of these autocratic Gulf states may make the
exclusion of migrants seem like a foregone conclusion, this specific
mechanism of exclusion (the suspension of time) operates under the
mantle of the law and not through the assertion of dictatorial authority.
The legal maneuvers of contemporary migration enforcement raise
important questions about the political continuum between liberal and
illiberal states—and the way that the law can be used to create, sanc-
tion, and legitimize discretionary power. It is especially important to
address this focus on legal rather than extralegal innovations because
"one of the defining features of authoritarianism today is the extent to
which power is not purely discretionary, but is instead structured
fundamentally through the proliferation of legal forms and legal authorization as the basis of decision-making."[17] The next section explores
the relationship between regime type and migration enforcement by

[14] Estimates provided by the Gulf Labour Markets and Migration demographic database: https://gulfmigration.org/gcc-total-population-and-percentage-of-nationals-and-non-nationals-in-gcc-countries-national-statistics-2017-2018-with-numbers/.
[15] For example, in *Impossible Citizens: Dubai's Indian Diaspora* (Durham and London: Duke University Press, 2013), Neha Vora shows that the Indian community has been entrenched in Dubai for over a century, and its members are in their second, third, and, in some cases, even fourth generation.
[16] Qatar has recently announced the introduction of a permanent-residency status for long-term migrants, but at the time of publication this has yet to be implemented.
[17] Call for paper proposals from the Organizing Committee of the Yale Law School Middle East Legal Studies Seminar (April 17, 2017) (on file with author).

comparing the shifting-border practices of liberal states with the exclusionary citizenship polices of the Gulf states.

Migration enforcement and regime type

Shachar makes clear that the practices of the shifting border have "striking implications for human dignity, democratic accountability, and disparities in attaining access to territory and membership" (p. 6). For example, when it comes to expedited removal in the United States (which impacts 83 percent of migrants removed from the territory), migrants cannot access any of the procedural safeguards associated with democratic governance—they have no right to appear in front of a judge, no right to legal representation, no right to a hearing or evidentiary findings, and no right to appeal. "When such far-reaching denial of basic procedural fairness occurs in an established democracy such as the United States, it tests not only our notions of territoriality but legality as well" (p. 25). While Shachar highlights the illiberal effects of the shifting border, she never really questions whether (or when) this rise of discretionary power should make us stop calling the states who partake in these practices democratic. Is it only the nature of territoriality and legality that is changing with the new practices of the shifting border— or does the shifting border also change the character of the regime itself?

We are witnessing a massive shift in governance—from rule-bound to discretionary—that is occurring in a depoliticized way through the introduction of legal innovations that tamper with time and space. What is striking about these legal maneuvers is that they are not open claims about abolishing asylum or other immigration laws. The shifting border introduces circumlocutions that chip away at the core policy while allowing those same states to maintain claims about being "inclusive" and protecting human rights. In other words, "states are proving endlessly enterprising in trying to 'release' themselves from the domestic, regional, and international legal protection obligations they have undertaken, *without* formally withdrawing from them" (p. 72). Are democratic states more inclusive and rule-bound than their less democratic counterparts? Is creating zones where the law is suspended so different from not having those laws to begin with?

It is worth going beyond the scope of Shachar's findings to reflect on the migration and citizenship policies of non-democracies when assessing the larger implications of the shifting border on formal democracies. When it comes to the treatment of non-citizens, it is not necessarily the case that autocratic states fare worse than democratic ones. As a case in point, the vast majority of the world's displaced populations are hosted by states that are not considered developed democracies—far from it. The ten largest hosts of refugees are Turkey, Pakistan, Lebanon, Iran, Uganda, Ethiopia, Jordan, Germany, DR of the Congo, and Kenya. But beyond this fact, states are categorized as liberal or illiberal based on their treatment of citizens, not aliens. As a result, few have attempted to systematically compare migration and citizenship policies across regime types, but Joppke's recent comparative study provides a helpful point of departure for this discussion.[18] He argues that while Western migrant-receiving states may have variations among them, they are all essentially "inclusive," while the autocratic Gulf states are ultimately "exclusive." This inclusive/exclusive dichotomy emerges because "in a liberal-democratic constellation the natural tilt is toward more inclusiveness. Liberal democracy requires the 'congruence' between the subjects and the objects of rule (Dahl), and it shuns the existence of 'second-class' citizens (Walzer)."[19]

Grafting an inclusive/exclusive binary onto a regime-type difference is intuitive. After all, as Joppke rightly points out, none of the Gulf states can be considered democratic, and they all systematically foreclose citizenship from the vast majority of their foreign residents,

[18] Christian Joppke, 'Citizenship in Immigration States', in Ayelet Shachar *et al.*, eds, *The Oxford Handbook on Citizenship* (Oxford: Oxford University Press, 2017), pp. 385–406.
[19] Ibid., p. 387.

regardless of the length of residency. Moreover, the oil-rich Gulf states have created a criterion for citizenship that links it to those who can trace their lineage to a "cut-off" date, prior to the discovery of oil, in an effort to limit the group of beneficiaries who may profit from the rents of this resource. But this practice of foreclosing access to citizenship by creating legal statuses that allow certain groups to reside in a country without ever being eligible for naturalization is not limited to autocratic states, rentier states, or the Gulf region. Indeed, the strategy of tampering with the criteria of citizenship to exclude certain groups of residents is a practice that long precedes state formation in this region.

But an inclusive/exclusive democratic/autocratic binary only makes sense if we focus on liberal values rather than the actual practices of liberal states. Scholarship on liberal states has often reaffirmed the importance of inclusive/democratic values in undergirding laws even when they have coexisted with the exclusionary practices of those same states. Labeling democratic migrant-receiving states as inclusive would require ignoring a robust literature that has shown how democracies have almost always been simultaneously inclusive and exclusive, depending on the group in question.

The same states that are heralded as beacons of democracy have long histories of creating gradations of citizenship that allowed certain populations to reside in the territory without enjoying the full rights associated with citizenship. These include slaves, labor migrants, women, and racial minorities—all populations who were either excluded from the very definition of who is eligible for citizenship or allowed to exercise only partial citizenship rights in liberal democracies.[20] For example, the United States not only scores highly on almost every metric of democracy, but it is also a prime example of a traditional immigration state. And yet for the vast majority of its history as a nation—from 1790 to 1952—the opportunity for immigrants to naturalize was restricted to those

---

[20] David Fitzgerald, 'The History of Racialized Citizenship', in Ayelet Shachar *et al.*, eds, *The Oxford Handbook on Citizenship* (Oxford: Oxford University Press, 2017), pp. 129–152.

who came from a racially defined group (white) and denied to all others, even if they were allowed to reside in the territory.[21]

The institution of citizenship, since its earliest manifestations, has critically depended upon the labor of those who are outside the body politic while remaining inside that polity's territory and playing an integral role in its economy. Kasimis shows that the Athenian democracy was based on a political economy supported not only by slavery but also by a large class of resident aliens—the *metics* (*metoikoi*)—a free immigrant population that was assimilated but disenfranchised, on the basis of blood, generation after generation.[22] It may be tempting to dismiss the exclusive dimensions of citizenship as a bygone relic of earlier periods of imperialism, but there is evidence that (after a period of liberalization) liberal democracies are actually becoming more exclusionary rather than more inclusive.[23] Those who are deemed unworthy of full enfranchisement can be rendered as "aliens" who are not party to the laws or due processes that make democracies democratic.

The shifting of space and time to prevent certain subjects from accruing membership rights falls under what Uday Mehta has previously referred to as a "liberal strategy" of exclusion.[24] Mehta's work explores how liberal conceptions of rationality and deliberation sanctioned the exclusion of certain subjects from citizenship based on their perceived lack of rationality—including children (temporarily) and colonial subjects (more permanently). Liberal strategies of exclusion operate by tampering with the criteria of inclusion rather than through outright denial. The contemporary migration-enforcement practices of liberal states have largely replaced racial and civilizational criteria with geographic and temporal ones for legitimately excluding or including

---

[21] Ibid., p. 131; for the impact of these policies on different communities of Asian Americans, see Ngai, *Impossible Subjects* (n 13).

[22] Demetra Kasimis, 'The Tragedy of Blood-Based Membership: Secrecy and the Politics of Immigration in Euripides's Ion', *Political Theory 41*, no. 2 (2013): pp. 231–256.

[23] See, for example, Sara Goodman, *Immigration and Membership Politics in Western Europe* (Cambridge: Cambridge University Press, 2014).

[24] Uday Mehta, 'Liberal Strategies of Exclusion', in Frederick Cooper and Ann Laura Stoler, eds, *Tensions of Empire: Colonial Cultures In a Bourgeois World* (Berkeley: University of California Press, 1997), pp. 59–86.

migrants. But, as Shachar shows, new legal innovations shift the terrain to make both space and time malleable when it comes to policing the boundaries of the citizenry.

Rather than assuming that liberal states are more inclusive than autocratic ones, future scholarship can begin to measure inclusivity empirically. The Gulf states have been heavily criticized by the international community for the abysmal conditions that some migrants find themselves in across the region—especially in the sectors of construction and domestic work. These human rights concerns should certainly not be minimized, but the attention to human rights abuses associated with migration policies should be broadened to follow the shifting border and capture the human costs and collateral damage of de-territorialized migration-enforcement practices. If we take this more expansive view, then it is not readily clear that the *kafāla* system fares much worse when it comes to human costs than the current policies of the European Union, United States, and Australia. Instead, these different migration paradigms are producing different human costs. The Gulf does not receive large numbers of asylum seekers, because none of these states allow the physical act of reaching the territory to confer any additional rights like asylum. As a result, the security forces are involved in processing and vetting large numbers of employment applications from the developing world—but not large numbers of asylum seekers. This also means that these states do not take part in the same kind of costly large-scale migrant-interdiction and deportation efforts as some of their more democratic counterparts. As a result, they do not systematically detain migrants—without trial—either on offshore sites or in outsourced private prisons.

The current quantitative metrics we have for measuring how liberal a state is do not take the treatment of non-citizens into account. Freedom House's democracy-score index helps illustrate this point. When coding how democratic or free a state is this index tracks ten indicators for measuring political rights and fifteen indicators for measuring civil liberties (Table 3.1). These indicators are then scored on a scale of 0 (smallest degree of freedom) to 4 (greatest degree of freedom) across all countries.

Table 3.1 Freedom House democracy index

Domain	Subcategories of indicators (# of questions)
Political rights	Electoral process (3)
	Political pluralism and participation (4)
	Functioning of government (3)
Civil liberties	Freedom of expression and belief (4)
	Associational and organization rights (3)
	Rule of law (4)
	Personal autonomy and individual rights (4)

Source: Freedom House, 'Freedom in the World 2018: Methodology', online https://freedomhouse.org/report/methodology-freedom-world-2018.

The civil liberties metric (on the question of individual rights) takes into account discrimination against minorities and women, but this is limited to how a state treats those who already have citizenship. Democracies are measured based on how they treat members of the in-group, and we therefore lack a common language for comparing the treatment of non-citizens across regime types. In the same way that the political-science literature has mapped the empirics of electoral authoritarianism, future studies can and should measure the replacement of rule of law with discretionary power in the realm of migration enforcement. It is not only the procedures surrounding the question of who rules that determine how liberal a state is, but also the procedures that determine how the boundaries of the in-group are defined and policed.

Migration-enforcement practices can be empirically mapped and included in metrics that rank how liberal a state is. Factors that can be tracked in an index of migration enforcement might include:

1 The proportion of a resident population that has (or is eligible for) citizenship
2 Estimates of resident irregular populations
3 Estimates of resident trafficked populations
4 Estimates of resident indebted/bonded labor
5 Estimates of resident displaced persons (with and without refugee status)

6　Number of people interdicted by the officials of a specific territory (or their offshore affiliates) prior to reaching the state

7　Number of people detained for unauthorized entry or residence (and whether people can be detained without trial, as well as the average length of detainment)

The existing social science and legal scholarship on migration already documents and measures these and other indicators (especially for Organization of Economic Cooperation and Development (OECD) countries), but we have yet to adopt a systematic way of comparing these practices across regions in a holistic fashion. Such a metric would be useful not only for empirically mapping the differences between the treatment of migrants across regime type, but also for understanding how migration-enforcement practices can reshape the nature of the state for those who are secure citizens. I will make this final point by drawing on two illustrative examples from my research on the migration and citizenship policies of the UAE.[25]

In the summer of 2010, Dr Ali Al-Khouri, the Director of the Emirates Identity Authority (EIDA) in Abu Dhabi, gave a keynote lecture on "The Question of Identity in the Gulf" at a conference hosted by the University of Exeter. He explained that the exceptional demographic growth experienced by the Gulf region required its governments to develop new instruments of population management—including extensive surveillance and DNA imaging—to pre-empt the security threats associated with migrant populations. Al-Khouri explained that while forensics had typically been used in criminal investigations, they were now being applied to the field of population management. The EIDA was spearheading a DNA initiative in civil biometrics—the use of forensics to categorize the population into genealogical sub-groupings associated with different threat levels. Pre-empting possible objections from an audience located in the United Kingdom, Al-Khouri emphasized that in the Gulf the role of security and the nature of citizenship

---

[25] Noora Lori, *Offshore Citizens: Permanent 'Temporary' Status in the Gulf* (Cambridge: Cambridge University Press, 2019).

differed from that in other regions. He said that in the United Kingdom this would lead to "the fear of invasion of privacy, but in the GCC states we trust our governments. We can see that they are keeping us safe."[26] Although addressing the use of new technologies, Al-Khouri's claims about the purported acquiescence and allegiance of GCC citizens exemplify a common and long-standing narrative about the links between migration and national security in the UAE.

Even prior to the formation of the UAE in 1971, foreign and domestic political elites linked its migrant populations to national security threats, arguing that open borders required extensive domestic surveillance. National security, it is argued, must take precedence over individual rights and privacy in this context because of the high levels of immigrants—a reality that citizens must live with or (according to Al-Khouri) actively embrace. Just under fifty years earlier, a UK security official in Dubai made a similar point in his report on the security situation. In a letter to the Arabian Department of the Foreign Office in London in 1963, he elaborated on the rationale of linking migration with the need to privilege security over the protection of individual rights. He had been approached by Sheikh Rashid, the ruler of Dubai at the time, who "was very concerned about the police's habit of searching houses without a warrant" and wanted to know "what was the system in England and to advise what he ought to do in Dubai."[27]

Like Al-Khouri's, the security official's response was that the protections in place in the United Kingdom could not be applied to Dubai. He explained that in England the police had the right to search and arrest without a warrant only when there was a good reason to believe that a serious offence had been committed, or in pursuit of an individual evading arrest, or when an offence had been committed in the

---

[26] Ali Al-Khouri, 'The Challenge of Identity in a Changing World: The Case of GCC Countries', in *2010 Exeter Gulf Studies Conference* (Exeter: University of Exeter, July 7, 2010). These quotes from Al-Khouri's speech (which I attended) diverge from the written version of his conference paper. The speech was recorded and available for download by conference attendees using the following link: http://socialsciences.exeter.ac.uk/iais_old/all-events/audio/khouri1.php.

[27] Anita Burdett, ed., *British Records of the Emirates 1961–1965* (Slough: Archive Editions Limited, 1963), 3.5: 531.

presence of the police officer. However, Sheikh Rashid "should bear in mind that Dubai was not England, that the task of the police here was much more difficult and that it might therefore not be possible to attach *quite so much importance to the rights of the individual* as one did in a settled and orderly community."[28] According to the security official, the large number of immigrants in Dubai meant that it could not be considered a "settled" community.

These examples help illustrate how the specter of migration as a national security threat played a key role in the emergence and consolidation of autocratic rule in the UAE. The possibility of creating and protecting civil liberties in the new state was eroded, in a piecemeal fashion, by the obsession with migration enforcement. From the earliest manifestations of statehood, security concerns related to the regulation of migrants were used to legalize and legitimize authoritarian rule. The result of this is that surveillance capacities have prevailed over any notion of protecting the civil liberties of Emirati citizens (who are now a numerical minority in the country). When considering the example of how the border has bled inward into US territory with the creation of "waiting zones" 100 miles from the physical territorial border, Shachar warns that this jurisdiction could be extended nationwide so that "[w]ith the strike of the pen, the 'interior' could be recast as the 'exterior' for the purposes of immigration control under the shifting-border paradigm" (p. 23). We do not need to imagine a dystopian scenario in which the whole country is a "border"—this scenario is already the lived reality of those who reside in highly surveilled immigration states like the UAE. National IDs are not only checked at every port of entry but also internally across all public and private institutions. Today, one is unable to be employed, rent or buy a house or car, open a bank account, enroll in school, access medical care, or appear in courts in the UAE without undergoing an identity check on one's legal status. It is impossible to disentangle the role of migration enforcement from the growth of the surveillance state and consolidation of autocratic rule in the UAE.

---

[28] Ibid. (emphasis added).

Instead of assuming that autocratic states are more exclusionary toward migrants, it might be worth considering how the very factors that make a state more and more "effective" at migration enforcement can actually make it more autocratic. I conclude by posing questions about the relationship between migration enforcement and discretionary power rather than drawing any firm conclusions. Is it possible for democratic governments to enforce their own migration policies and remain democratic, or does effective migration enforcement necessitate the erosion of democratic governance and civil liberties? While Shachar points to concrete ways by which the illiberal practices of contemporary migration enforcement can be reined in, there may also be a constitutive tension between democratic governance and effective migration enforcement. This tension does not simply derive from the fact that right-wing and fascist groups have tended to tout anti-immigrant platforms in many liberal states. Rather, regardless of political platform, the very mechanisms of effective migration enforcement create the conditions for a descent into authoritarianism—a path paved by (often seemingly benign) laws that are framed as protecting the nation from non-citizens and "illegal" infiltrators. Migration enforcement requires more than an infrastructure for screening individuals at the physical border—to be effective, it requires a vast network of identity checks internally, with the engagement of virtually every public and private entity embedded as part of an identity-management infrastructure. In other words, to be effective, migration enforcement requires a deepening surveillance state that cannot simply target non-citizens but also necessarily impacts citizens and their civil liberties. The boundaries of citizenry and how these boundaries are enforced cannot be neatly disentangled from the substance of citizenship rights and how these rights are protected.

4

Borders that stay, move, and expand

Steffen Mau

Statehood, territoriality, and border control

In 1989, the Berlin Wall opened literally overnight after East German political functionary Günter Schabowski misspoke at a press conference. At the time, I was serving as a soldier in the East German National People's Army, and on that very night we soldiers were all huddled around a small radio that broadcast West German news. A speaker said: "The Wall has fallen: that is the end of the GDR." And that's what came to pass. Without the ability to effectively control its own borders, the GDR could no longer prevent people from leaving. It might be true for dictatorships that border functions are directed particularly strongly inward—that is, toward their own people—but the ability to control borders seems to be absolutely crucial for democracies, as well. Liberal principles may call for freedom of movement or openness,[1] but open and "borderless" states appear to be nothing but a utopia today. The ability to control territory is considered an important element of a state's capacity to act. States that have lost this ability—for political, military, or organizational reasons—or that were never able to secure their own borders and determine who or what crossed a border are viewed as "failed states."

This idea that there is a close link between a state's order and its territorial control, including monitoring and regulating its own borders,

[1] Joseph Carens, 'Aliens and Citizens: The Case for Open Borders', *Review of Politics 49*, no. 2 (1987): pp. 251–273.

has long been a core aspect of the concept of modern statehood. This is
the case even though we know that an internationalized passport and
border-control regime is a very modern invention.[2] In the nineteenth
century, for example, it was possible to cross many national borders
within continental Europe without travel documents or controls.[3] Not
until the twentieth century did a coherent and comprehensive system
develop that suppressed "informal" and non-authorized mobility and
gave states the possibility of comprehensively controlling and channeling cross-border mobility. Alluding to Weber, John Torpey calls this
monopolization of the "legitimate means of movement"[4] a key element
of modern state-building, whereby the territorial organization of statehood and the assignment of a specific membership to people (for example, with passports and citizenship) went hand in hand. The rise of
modern states can therefore be understood as a large-scale sorting process that was undertaken by drawing territorial and membership borders.

Territoriality can be described very generally as a "spatial strategy to
affect, influence, or control resources and people, by controlling area."[5]
The principle of territorially defined sovereign domains can only
become operational when the state has the possibility to effectively
monitor the domain by controlling the territory.[6] Jellinek's state theory,[7]
which is based on a congruence of territory, population, and exercise of
control, assumes that securing a state's spatial integrity is an important

2 John Torpey, *The Invention of the Passport: Surveillance, Citizenship and the State*
   (Cambridge: Cambridge University Press, 2000).
3 Andrea Komlosy, 'Migration und Freizügigkeit: Habsburger Monarchie und Europäische
   Union im Vergleich', in Joachim Becker and Andrea Komlosy, eds, *Grenzen Weltweit:
   Zonen, Linien, Mauern im historischen Vergleich* (Wien: Promedia und Südwind, 2004).
4 John Torpey, 'Coming and Going: On the State Monopolization of the Legitimate
   "Means of Movement"', *Sociological Theory 16*, no. 3 (1998): pp. 239–259, p. 256.
5 Robert David Sack, *Human Territoriality: Its Theory and History* (Cambridge: Cambridge
   University Press, 1986), p. 21.
6 John H. Herz, 'Rise and Demise of the Territorial State', *World Politics 9*, no. 4 (1957):
   pp. 473–493, p. 474. Herz summarizes the core physical and integrative capacities of the
   state "as an expanse of territory encircled for its identification and its defense by a 'hard
   shell' of fortifications. In this lies what will here be referred to as the 'impermeability', or
   'impenetrability', or simply the 'territoriality' of the modern state. The fact that it was
   surrounded by a hard shell rendered it to some extent secure from foreign penetration,
   and thus made it an ultimate unit of protection for those within boundaries."
7 Georg Jellinek, *Allgemeine Staatslehre* (Berlin: O. Häring, [1900] 1914).

issue for state action and that the spatial area of a state's territorial rule is clearly defined. In this Westphalian territorial model of state order, there is no consideration of overlapping authorities or an extension or externalization of state sovereignty. The border represents the outer shell, the outline of the state structure that separates an inside from an outside. For precisely this reason, states are given the right to fortify their own borders freely and to control and regulate border crossings at their own discretion. This approach to state order also assumes that the limiting function of borders is built on the border's external functions. The geographical border and border control are inextricably linked so that any discussion of borders always simultaneously includes both understandings.

The model of state and society as "containers" can be criticized both empirically and conceptually, however, because it may overemphasize borders' closing-off function. Borders do not only mean closing off: they also stand for a specific kind of permeability. The metaphors of borders as "semipermeable filters" or "membranes" suggest that borders are also always about regulating mobility or connectivity. Borders are not merely walls and fences but also gates, waterway locks, or bridges that create connections.

The discussion about "vanishing borders" or a "borderless world,"[8] which was strongly inspired by economics and for a time dominated the globalization discourse, came to a standstill several years ago. The dominating narrative for many years, possibly even decades, of disappearing borders has lost its persuasive power and finds itself confronted with serious counter-movements and objections. This is not only true on a political level, when thinking of demands for social closure, economic protectionism, or cultural borders. It also applies normatively—for example, when considering the topic of unequally distributed globalization returns, or the losers of globalization.

The question that arises from this is whether it is still possible under current conditions to use national borders to close a territory. The

[8]   Kenichi Ohmae, *The Borderless World* (London: Collins, 1990).

loss-of-control thesis claims that states' ability to control and close borders has gradually declined. Even if they want to, they are hardly able to counter the pressure of globalization. Even large migration movements cannot be stopped with tollgates. Wendy Brown argues, for example, that borders—especially border constructions, walls, and fences—may assert state sovereignty but it is an assertion they would have great difficulty backing up. In their materiality, new walls are meant to demonstrate state power, but their actual effectiveness as blockades or instruments of separation is not particularly significant. She writes: "Rather than resurgent expressions of nation-state sovereignty, the new walls are icons of its erosion." And she continues: "This landscape signifies the ungovernability by law and politics of many powers unleashed by globalization."[9]

The observation that walls are erected especially where states rely on strong symbols to counteract endangered sovereignty or territorial control has yet to be tested empirically, however. They are certainly not lines for halting the powers of globalization, but states may still benefit from them. Closing the route through the Balkans for the refugees that came to Europe in 2015 and 2016 is a prominent example of how border barriers can influence migration flows even if they cannot be completely stopped.

The new borders: disentangling territory and control

In her impressive and stimulating essay on the "shifting border," Ayelet Shachar points out that a fixed gaze toward the territorial borders on the edges of a country overlooks the actual transformation of borders in the age of globalization. She focuses on how border controls have become more flexible in terms of where they take place, not in terms of moving geographical borders. Or expressed in a different way: under the conditions of globalization, border functions and border lines are decoupled. While the former can move, the latter remain

[9]   Wendy Brown, *Walled States, Waning Sovereignty* (New York: Zone Books, 2010), p. 25.

in one location. We no longer, then, find borders where a state's territory ends but instead where control is exercised. This introduces a functional, not a territorial, definition of borders. What is important are the border functions of governance, control, and selection, not *where* the border is. In a similar manner, Balibar[10] emphasizes that borders exist "wherever selective controls are to be found." With this understanding, the term "border" is de-territorialized, as it is not the shifting border that is being discussed but instead shifting border control.

This change in perspective is only logical when thinking of borders from the viewpoint of mobile people. For them, borders are interventions in mobility: the authorization and enabling or hindering of mobility that influence the movement of people through territories. This influence can take place at the entry points to a territory, but it does not have to; when it does, it is often symbolized by barriers, walls, and barbed wire or control posts. Borders regulate territorial openings and closing, but they can also do this at various locations.

With reference to Ayelet Shachar's approach to the topic and our own previous work,[11] one can assume that in light of globalization and increasing mobility, a fundamental change in borders is occurring. The old, territorially fixed border both remains and changes, but other border locations are being added. Shachar's approach to the shifting border assumes that the border functions of selective closing and opening are being progressively displaced and becoming spatially flexible, and she provides convincing evidence of this. In general, control and entry into a state's territory are now becoming partially de-linked, and there are many interventions in migration and mobility movements before arrival at a border. Checks and controls at a very early stage—that is,

---

[10] Étienne Balibar, *Politics and the Other Scene* (London and New York: Verso, 2002), pp. 84–85.

[11] Steffen Mau *et al.*, *Liberal States and the Freedom of Movement: Selective Borders, Unequal Mobility* (Basingstoke: Palgrave Macmillan, 2012). The paper also uses insights from a new project titled The Borders of the World: Processes of De- and Rebordering in a Global Perspective (part of the Collaborative Research Center 1265: Re-Figuration of Space, funded by the German Science Foundation DFG).

Table 4.1 Instruments of preventive border controls

Locations	Instruments of preventive border controls
In the countries of origin	— Allocation of visas in embassies and consulates — Sanctions against transport companies (controls at departure airport) — Liaison civil servants for immigration issues — Document advisors (controls at departure airports) — Collection, saving, and (international) exchange of travelers' data
During transit	— Readmission agreements with countries of origin and transit — Safe third countries' regulation — Logistical and financial support of third countries for expanding their border-control capacities — Control of EU external borders — Seizing refugee boats on the water — Controls in spaces close to the border
At the destination	— Pre-entry controls — Asylum applications in transit areas (airport procedure)

Source: Lena Laube, *Grenzkontrollen jenseits nationaler Territorien: Die Steuerung globaler Mobilität durch liberale Staaten* (Frankfurt am Main: Campus Verlag, 2013), p. 151.

when people are still far away from the territory—seem to be able to be traced back to greater degrees of legal freedom and greater effectiveness in steering mobility. On the other hand, the spatial flexibility of border controls combined with their increasing selectivity makes it more difficult even for mobile people desired by the state to recognize the border. When border controls shift, borders also become invisible for those not affected by the controls, while the 'rest' are still confronted with mobility barriers and are subject to controls.

Ayelet Shachar's approach is strongly supported by the work of my former doctoral student Lena Laube, who examined the movement of border controls outside of the territory. Based on comparative case studies, her study reconstructed the movement of border controls for Austria, Finland, and the United States since the 1970s.[12] She first differentiated between locations and instruments of control and then among controls in the country of origin, during transit, at the destination (Table 4.1). For the countries in the study, she was able to show that these instruments are increasingly being used and systematically expanded, so that today they make up an important part of the control repertoires of these three very different countries.[13] In addition, she showed new personnel, administrative, and legal conflations linked to this shift—for example, the use of national civil servants abroad, the delegation of control duties to private actors or other countries, and the creation of new control zones in which special rights apply.[14]

Ayelet Shachar focuses especially on the legal motivations and implications of shifting border controls, which require a different understanding of the relationship between law and territoriality discussed at the beginning of this article. If it is correct that legal obligations are strongly based on the principle of territoriality, then moving border controls offers states the opportunity to elude these. This is particularly evident in the case of flight and asylum, as both of these legal rights can only be claimed once a person has set foot in the territory of the country in which they are to be claimed.

For example, the safe-third-country rule in the European Union's Dublin Agreement creates a kind of "buffer zone" around those states that are surrounded by third countries declared to be safe.[15] Asylum seekers can now only submit an application if they do not travel through a safe transit country, and in combination with carrier sanctions this significantly increases the difficulty of reaching a specific territory. The attempt to declare North African countries as safe third countries

---

[12] See Lena Laube, *Grenzkontrollen jenseits nationaler Territorien: Die Steuerung globaler Mobilität durch liberale Staaten* (Frankfurt am Main: Campus Verlag, 2013).

[13] Ibid., p. 236.

[14] Ibid., p. 154.

[15] Sarah Collinson, 'Visa Requirements, Carrier Sanctions, "Safe Third Countries" and "Readmission": The Development of an Asylum "Buffer Zone" in Europe', *Transactions of the Institute of British Geographers 21*, no. 1 (1996): pp. 76–90.

means that boats full of refugees may be legally towed back to Africa. The European Union's efforts are increasingly moving toward handling refugees offshore, excluding access to EU states' territories. Transit procedures in international airports as applied by many countries fall into a similar category. The European Court of Justice decided that these special zones do not have an extraterritorial status, but special procedures are applied that give asylum seekers only limited rights and enable quick repatriation in cases that are seemingly without merit.[16] Asylum seekers are brought into a transit area of the airport before entering the country and may not leave the area until a decision has been made on their application.

Selectivity, internationalization, macroterritorialization, digitization

Four developments in the metamorphosis of borders can be outlined. All of these are already included in Shachar's contribution, but they can only be partially subsumed under the concept of the shifting border and may have a different momentum. It is possible that they should be viewed as independent dimensions because they are at least in part subject to different logics and also have different legal, political, and social consequences. This is why I believe it is necessary to emphasize them once again.

Increased selectivity and visa policies

In the context of the shifting border, the goal is not only to exercise control beyond the territory but, as stated by Ayelet Shachar, also increasingly to exercise selectivity. An important area for linking selectivity and "remote control"[17] is visa policy. The visa requirement enables the

---

[16] Sharon Oakley, 'Accelerated Procedures for Asylum in the European Union', Sussex Migration Working Paper No. 43 (Sussex: Sussex Centre for Migration Research, 2007).

[17] Aristide R. Zolberg, *A Nation by Design: Immigration Policy in the Fashioning of America* (New York: Russell Sage Foundation, 2006), p. 443.

selection of people based on various criteria—for example, for security-policy considerations or the social and economic status of the traveler. A visa may be denied without reason, meaning that states have a relatively free hand in deciding to whom they will grant entry. Typically, visas are issued as pre-arrival visas. This means they must be applied for in embassies and consulates abroad or in the country of origin—these are the decisive locations of control. In contrast to passport controls at the border, this allows for a longer examination period, since the person has not yet traveled. To close possible "gaps" in this system, private companies such as airlines are obligated to carry only passengers who have a valid entry visa for the destination country under threat of financial penalties (so-called carrier sanctions). As an entry requirement, the visa is therefore an instrument of extraterritorial control of people.

At the same time, the general visa requirement is a hindrance to global mobility. If it is assumed that there is a state interest in certain aspects of globalization and increasing mobility (after all, tourism is an important economic factor), then the general visa requirement is a cost-intensive and time-consuming instrument. It counteracts the permeability of borders and the increase in and simplification of mobility. Agreements and programs to eliminate visa requirements can serve as a key instrument to overcome the conflicting interests of a globalized world: on the one hand, the interest in enabling quick border movement for desired persons and, on the other hand, the aim of continuing to limit entry for undesired persons. Waivers from the visa requirement (and thus from extraterritorial control) are an expression of generalized trust that is only given to travelers from certain countries: the trust is that their stay will not cause any "damage" to the destination country. By waiving the visa requirement, entry is made easier, while those who are still subject to visa requirements can be controlled more carefully—both spatially and temporally before they attempt to cross the border.[18]

---

[18]　Didier Bigo and Elspeth Guild, eds, *Controlling Frontiers: Free Movement into and within Europe* (Aldershot: Ashgate, 2005).

We can observe how visa requirements have expanded over time—even becoming universalized—before again being selectively waived.[19] It can also be seen that the Western world has become increasingly selective with visa waivers. While concluding visa-waiver agreements was often part of foreign policy in the past—for example, to maintain good relations—today harder criteria are used for selection, such as those related to migration or security. Typically, those countries that receive visa waivers are similar to the waiving country in terms of economics, politics, and often culture, or they are assumed to be headed in that direction. At the same time, in the Western world we witness a convergence in waiving or applying the visa requirement. The lists of countries on visa-waiver lists are becoming more and more similar from country to country. This is true not only for the European Union—specifically for the Schengen European Union, which introduced a unified list of countries under the visa requirement and countries for which the requirement is waived—but also for other countries in the Western hemisphere. Even countries that did without explicit entry and residence laws in the past have introduced these with the consequence that across all Western countries there is now a significant standardization of permitting or refusing mobility. Similar problems, the diffusion of norms, and international and supranational cooperation are the driving forces of this standardization.

By and large, these findings support the assumption that borders in the age of globalization differentiate more strongly among people and groups of people.[20] For groups of people who are considered potentially dangerous, risky, or problematic, globalization means no growth in opportunities related to mobility but "closure, entrapment and containment."[21] Borders have therefore not disappeared. Instead, they have been categorically restructured in the OECD world. They have

[19] Steffen Mau and Heike Brabandt, 'Visumpolitik und die Regulierung globaler Mobilität: Ein Vergleich dreier OECD-Länder', *Zeitschrift für Soziologie 40*, no. 1 (2011): pp. 3–23; Mau *et al.*, *Liberal States and the Freedom of Movement* (n 11).

[20] Balibar, *Politics and the Other Scene* (n 10).

[21] Ronen Shamir, 'Without Borders? Notes on Globalization as a Mobility Regime', *Sociological Theory 23*, no. 2 (2005): pp. 197–217, p. 199.

become more permeable for citizens of wealthy democracies but have maintained their impermeability and intensive controls for other citizens and groups. One can even refer to a "global mobility divide."[22] When it comes to mobility rights or even a kind of "mobility citizenship,"[23] we must therefore assume there is an "unequal power of passports."[24]

Internationalization of border regime

Internationalization includes deeper cooperation among states when shaping borders, exchanging information, and exercising control. This could include bilateral agreements, for example, within which neighboring states agree to take back irregular migrants or which agree on assistance in expanding border control capacities. The European Union practices this regularly in its association policies, which it carried out actively before the eastern expansion in the 2000s. Forms of internationalized border policies also develop in the context of international organizations—for example, the IOM, the UNHCR, and the International Labour Organization (ILO).

The IOM offers services for its 120 member states that range from education on "border management" and carrying out repatriation and deportation to policy advice for governments on the topic of preventing irregular migration. It influences the discourse about legitimate forms of action while working as an operational actor in the policy field. It is therefore an integral part of a comprehensive border regime that is detaching itself from territorial borders. At the same time, it provides a forum for multilateral cooperation among states and organizations. Regional forms of integration with permanent supranational institutions and agencies go even further. Here, states often cooperate on border processes and security, exchange information, and

---

[22] Steffen Mau *et al.*, 'The Global Mobility Divide: How Visa Policies Have Evolved over Time', *Journal of Ethnic and Migration Studies 41*, no. 8 (2015): pp. 1192–2213.

[23] Steffen Mau, 'Mobility Citizenship, Inequality, and the Liberal State: The Case of Visa Policies', *International Political Sociology 4*, no. 4 (2010): pp. 339–361; John Urry, 'Globalization and Citizenship', *Journal of World-Systems Research 5*, no. 2 (1999): pp. 311–324.

[24] Mau *et al.*, 'The Global Mobility Divide' (n 22).

cooperate at the level of security agencies, creating common visa and entry regulations.[25]

Macroterritorialization

Macroterritorialization represents a specific kind of supranationalization. One can see that in the course of regional integration processes, forms of mutual opening toward other member states and closing and/or standardization of the external borders arise. Because regional integration is often based on building common markets and increasing mobility, internal borders are viewed as restricting those markets. Beyond freedom of movement for goods and services, many regional integration initiatives include the improvement of mobility for citizens of member states. This can mean improved freedom of movement for employees, residency rights, or specific mobility programs for individual groups. Research on visa policies has shown that granting visa-free travel is often a core element of progressing integration, and converging visa relationships with third countries is also often found.[26]

Another aspect of establishing "macro-regional borders" is the cooperation of several states using common border-security standards.[27] In the course of macroterritorialization processes, border-control functions are bundled and shifted to the outer borders while sometimes being eliminated along internal borders. The EU's Schengen Agreement is an excellent example of this.[28] Internal opening and external

[25] Malcolm Anderson and Didier Bigo, 'What Are EU Frontiers for and What Do They Mean?', in Kees Groenendijk, Elspeth Guild, and Paul Miderhoud, eds, *In Search of Europe's Borders* (Den Haag: Brill, 2002), pp. 7–26; James Anderson *et al.*, eds, *Culture and Cooperation in Europe's Borderlands. European Studies: An Interdisciplinary Series in European Culture, History and Politics* (Amsterdam: Rodopi, 2003); Mark B. Salter, 'Passports, Mobility, and Security: How Smart Can the Border Be?', *International Studies Perspectives* 5, no. 1 (2004): pp. 71–91.

[26] Fabian Gülzau, Steffen Mau, and Natascha Zaun, 'Regional Mobility Spaces? Regional Integration and Visa Waiver Policies', *International Migration* 54, no. 6 (2016): pp. 164–180.

[27] James Anderson and Liam O'Dowd, 'Borders, Border Regions and Territoriality: Contradictory Meanings, Changing Significance', *Regional Studies* 33, no. 7 (1999): pp. 593–604, p. 600.

[28] Steffen Mau, 'Die Politik der Grenze. Grenzziehung und politische Systembildung in der Europäischen Union', *Berliner Journal für Soziologie* 16, no. 1 (2006): pp. 115–132.

control enter into a reciprocal relationship, as reducing internal borders is linked to external borders being sufficiently protected and controlled so that the individual member states do not need to fear any negative consequences.[29] The expansion of mobility rights, which is one result of the de-institutionalization of internal border controls, and the increasing importance of external borders is that borders can no longer be understood from the perspective of the individual states but from the regional or supranational context—as a collective border. The European Union's external border in Poland or Hungary, then, is simultaneously the external border for all EU member states.

Macroterritorialization approaches can be found in many regions of the world—for example, in Africa (ECOWAS), Europe (European Union), and South America (Mercosur). The Nordic states of Denmark, Finland, Iceland, Norway, and Sweden founded the Nordic Passport Union in 1954 in the context of the Nordic Council. This enabled citizens of the Nordic states to travel without a visa and stay without a residency permit in the states that were party to the agreement. In addition, a common job market with far-reaching social rights was established. In the European Union, the Schengen agreement regulates the internal opening and common structure of the external borders. In South America, the development of Mercosur—made up of Argentina, Brazil, Paraguay, Uruguay, and Venezuela—meant the creation of a common internal market with freedom of movement for capital, goods, services, and people. Freedom of movement for employees was one of the stated goals of integration efforts from the very beginning, and in 2002 it resulted in the agreement on freedom of movement and residency in the Mercosur states and associated states. Across the world, there have been numerous attempts at regional integration, but in regard to macroterritorialization they have not progressed as far as in the European Union.

---

[29] Lena Laube and Andreas Müller, 'Warum die Kontrolle abgeben? Die Delegation von Migrationskontrolle aus der Prinzipal-Agent-Perspektive', *Berliner Journal für Soziologie* 25, no. 3 (2015): pp. 255–281.

Digitization and new border technologies

With digitization, data-based and algorithmic screening and scoring procedures are increasingly being used for controls.[30] And, as Shachar describes, control starts far beyond the border in these cases as well. That is, control is spatially expanded and relies on technology, data exchange, and biometric registration to classify people. If the evaluation of documents' validity and proof that a person and their passport belonged together used to be of key importance during controls, today the most important aspect is access to the information saved in databases. This includes not only information that people have submitted themselves but the aggregation of information from various databases to assess their trustworthiness. The assessment can include information about their previous travels, their financial status, or that has arisen about them on social media. This can also lead to negative selection, through which people are excluded from mobility opportunities. In contrast, one can also gain mobility rights based on a certain track record—for example, by moving up to the category of a trusted traveler. A trusted traveler is someone who has been categorized as trustworthy based on a pre-screening of movement and travel history that is considered unproblematic from the perspective of state agencies. The trusted traveler can then be processed quickly and without any additional checks. The programs currently being established advertise faster border-crossing processes for this group of trusted travelers.[31]

The primary goal is to develop "smart borders," which use new technology and database systems to filter travelers as efficiently as possible. By defining standard data formats and enforcing the use of certain technologies to exchange data, data repositories are created that can be used by various states and their control agencies. Biometric forms of identification—an iris scan or fingerprints—already ensure that people

---

[30] Steffen Mau, *Das metrische Wir: Über die Quantifizierung des Sozialen* (Berlin: edition suhrkamp, 2017).
[31] The United States developed the first trusted-traveler programs, which include a voluntary, extensive pre-screening of the applicant—a biographical background check. Those who pass this screening can cross the border faster.

are clearly identified. It is now technically possible to combine biometric information with digital footprints and voluntarily given personal data.[32] Biometrics and sociometry are thereby linked! Technologies for collecting biometric data without physical contact promise faster, more efficient controls in the future, which will hardly be perceived as troublesome by the positively filtered travelers. In the future, it can be expected that locational media and the data they generate—that is, data about a person's mobility—will be used more intensively for control purposes. Security agencies could then exercise control regardless of whether the person is passing a control point—for example, using authentication with facial recognition—thereby radically decoupling controls from a specific location. It is also possible that the creation of these kinds of information-technology-based possibilities should no longer be called shifting borders but viewed as a new form of permanent control. The border would then suddenly be everywhere and nowhere! Mobility controls would be embedded in a digital infrastructure and effective at any time and at any location.

The extent of this development's consequences is shown impressively in Ayelet Shachar's considerations of the shifting border. She warns that we must understand the dialectic of "disappearing borders" and newly arising or shifting borders. She warns that we must take changing constellations of territoriality, control, and law seriously, both diagnostically and normatively. She warns that we must better understand how to deal with the spatial flexibility of borders, which challenges the one-dimensional perspective of more or less state control. She warns that we must rethink the idea of clear (and possibly converging) borders of territoriality and membership. And, finally, she warns that we must put aside the idea of a Westphalian system of borders and territoriality. Her essay lays a remarkable base for the "rediscovery" of borders under conditions of technological developments, globalization, and perceived pressure from migration, thereby paying particular attention to the changing links among law, territoriality, and control.

---

[32] Louise Amoore, 'Biometric Borders: Governing Mobilities in the War on Terror', *Political Geography 25*, no. 3 (2006): pp. 336–351.

The world of nation-states no longer seems binary—that is, with clear external and internal areas or open or closed. Instead, it is a complex arrangement of overlapping forms of control that can be put together in various combinations. It is spatially flexible, with the goal of comprehensively regulating the cross-border mobility of people. This encompasses a categorical shift in perspective, which Shachar frames as moving away from the "movement of people across borders" and toward the "movement of borders to regulate the mobility of people." In a radicalized form, one could speak of individualized borders that only play a role for "border people" and allow everybody else to cross the border almost without impediment. "Border people" would then be controlled intensively and their mobility regulated by being recorded and addressed at the time when they start their movement. For a modern border regime based on information technology, this early identification and efficient immobilization of those who are not welcome will be a key goal. It goes without saying that this will also rely on the assistance of private actors as well as transit countries and countries of origin. A state's sovereign control, which up to now was located at its own borders, is thereby not given up but instead combined with other actors and subject to changing framework conditions. Governmental forms of control are arising that encompass many different actors, including private actors—from the airlines to the data-brokerage companies.

Liberal states and their interest in illiberal borders

In the final part of her essay, Ayelet Shachar argues that states that exercise extraterritorial border control and whose borders "migrate" are also confronted with normative-legal problems. If border controls are expanded and decoupled from a specific territory, then as a consequence an institutional-legal design must be developed that does justice to this change. Otherwise, those groups who—for whatever reason—have made it to a territory by avoiding the external border controls and can claim certain protective rights there could be privileged

(Shachar speaks of an "overrated premium of territorial arrival"), which is per se unjust and could also provide false incentives. Instead, she calls for protective rights to migrate that can be claimed from the state, together with the border controls. She does not argue for turning back the flexibilization of border controls but instead for placing these forms of control in a legal framework, ideally even in a common legal framework that does not differ significantly from the legal claims linked to the territory. State actors or those acting on their behalf would then take the legal obligations "with them."

Second, she recommends loosening the ties between access to a certain territory and rights, so that "touching the ground" is no longer the sole criterion. States can and should be prepared to help—for example, accepting refugee contingents—when the refugees have not even started traveling. The border could be brought to them to implement protective humanitarian measures. Ayelet Shachar even believes it is in the states' interest for refugees to work toward gaining recognition and protection from far away.

The asylum centers being discussed in the European Union represent such an approach. However, it becomes clear that it is difficult to extraterritorialize sovereign rights and connected legal procedures when using the typical standards. In these centers, humane and safe conditions must be ensured. In addition, the application process must be completed in a reasonable period of time. The primary motive behind the EU discussion, however, is to keep refugees from heading toward the European Union: there is to be remote screening instead of screening in the destination country. The hope is to keep those seeking protection at a distance—in the end, a stronger form of extraterritorializing control. In contrast, Shachar advocates for territorial access to remain open so that refugees and asylum seekers have both options.

Ayelet Shachar's suggestions for expanding the legal space or legal obligations refer first and foremost to the question of humanitarian migration but need to be extended. The areas of labor migration or tourism that are also significant for prior border controls are not discussed here. The question arises of how a legal context that limits arbitrariness can be ensured for these forms of mobility, as well. Here, states have considerable leeway. Of course, the topic of refugees is highly sensitive and politically controversial, but visa-overstayers—that is, people who arrive legally, usually with a tourist visa, and then stay— make up a significant number of migrants and influence the visa-refusal rates for some countries. The rejection rates for tourist visas are very high for some countries of origin, and in Europe it depends on the embassy a person visits to obtain a Schengen visa.

Moreover, the establishment of "smart borders" poses mounting problems. The protection of informational self-determination and the question of the reversibility of agencies' decisions are complex and have not been considered fully up to now. Should the state be allowed to classify us based on data without our knowledge and without us being able to object? And should it be allowed to grant mobility rights based on this? The question of the data basis for authorizing mobility is a sensitive topic when considering that more and more data are becoming available and could be included in the screening process. Initial plans to systematically use social-media accounts as a basis for allocating visas exist in the United States. What is particularly critical here is that many of the algorithms and the data upon which they are based produce systematic errors or are biased.[33] As soon as the allocation of mobility rights relies on big data, the problem arises of who will be able to control the digital controllers. But if the shifting border also implies the extensive use of technology and big data, this needs to be put on the agenda too.

There is one last serious objection related to the question of whether Shachar's conclusions are politically feasible. As necessary and norma- tively convincing as her call for corresponding legal responsibility and shifting border control might be, it seems to me highly improbable that this will actually come to pass. The extraterritorialization of border controls is driven not only by questions of the greater effectiveness of "remote control." Another key factor is the attempt on the part of liberal states to rid themselves of their normative self-obligations. Accepting

---

[33] Mau, *Das metrische Wir* (n 30).

human rights and international refugee rights into national constitutions has strengthened the individual as a legal subject vis-à-vis state powers. With national legislation derived from international obligations, the nation-state limits its ability to decide on entry into its territory.[34] The shifting border could be understood as a reaction to the challenge of doing justice to their own liberal ethics and related obligations, on the one hand, and, on the other, the interest of limiting and controlling migration and mobility. This would mean that states use legally under-determined control locations beyond their borders in creative ways precisely because they seek to circumvent their own legal obligations. It is an attempt to create illiberal leeway.

In light of this, one must ask whether and why states should have an interest in spatially expanding legal responsibilities that are hindrances to their control objectives. The price they would pay is a loss of pos-sibilities for controlling undesired migration and mobility. It is doubt-ful whether they would actually be willing to pay this price given the domestic political objections to obligations to migrants. The more recent debates in Europe and the United States give little reason to hope, at any rate. With these controls beyond their borders, states create leeway for defense and deterrence that they would not have within the territory of their liberal order. It is precisely this link between the liberal and illib-eral that makes the shifting border so interesting for Western states.

---

[34] Christian Joppke, 'Why Liberal States Accept Unwanted Immigration', *World Politics 50*, no. 2 (1998): pp. 266–293; James F. Hollifield, 'Offene Weltwirtschaft und nationales Bürgerrecht: Das liberale Paradox', in Dietrich Thränhardt and Uwe Hunger, eds, *Migra-tion im Spannungsfeld von Globalisierung und Nationalstaat* (Wiesbaden: Westdeutscher Verlag, 2003), pp. 35–57.

5

Pushing out and bleeding in: on the mobility of borders

Leti Volpp

The "shifting border" is what Ayelet Shachar identifies as a "new and striking phenomenon" (p. 4)—the detaching of migration control from a fixed territorial marker, via legal manipulation. This manipulation is undertaken by wealthy countries to either restrict or enable the access and rights of those who seek to enter. While nation-state borders are conventionally imagined as coterminous with territorial or carto-graphic frontiers, states engaged in these strategies can move the migra-tion border deep inside a territory or push it out far beyond its geographic edges. *The Shifting Border* examines these maneuvers, which turn the border into a "moving barrier—an unmoored legal con-struct" (p. 4), creating an unsettling legal topography.

Unsettling and striking, but is this entirely new? Shachar states: "The remarkable development of recent years is that 'our gates' no longer stand fixed at the country's territorial edges" (p. 4). Yet the disjuncture between territorial space and governance is not novel. There have always been specific exceptions to the Westphalian model of absolutely cotermi-nous sovereignty, territory, and jurisdiction.[1] These are spaces within territories where the territorial sovereign's power does not reach—as current examples of historic practice, we could think of Julian Assange in the Ecuadorian embassy in London and the many undocumented immigrants now claiming sanctuary from Immigration and Customs

---

[1] Leti Volpp, 'Imaginings of Space in Immigration Law', *Law, Culture and the Humanities 9*, no. 3 (2012): pp. 456–474.

Enforcement in churches across the United States. And there are spaces located outside the territory of the sovereign that have nonetheless been subject to sovereign authority, in the form of colonial governance and extraterritorial jurisdiction. Tugba Basaran reminds us that the distinction between physical presence and legal presence is not a new invention used for migration control, but an old legal tactic created to manage humans, economies, and resources.[2] Restating Shachar's claim only slightly, then, we might suggest that the fact that "our gates" no longer stand fixed at the country's territorial edges has *developed remarkably* in recent years.

As is characteristic of Ayelet Shachar's body of scholarship, this new work pushes thinking forward along multiple dimensions: descriptive, analytical, and normative.[3] While other scholars have certainly addressed how states deliberately manipulate their borders to limit the rights claims of those who are positioned outside, Shachar's thorough and synthetic approach will help direct future conversation. *The Shifting Border* pulls together a rich array of case studies drawn primarily from Europe, Canada, Australia, and the United States, importantly drawing connections between governmental practices often studied in isolation. These examples are then used to develop a conceptual road map to explain the delinking of law and territoriality, clarifying the consequences for both scholarly thought and policy debates. Shachar also embraces the normative question of what is to be done about this moving border, proposing two remedies: first, that the extraterritorial reach of human rights be expanded via an approach to the acts of states that attends to function rather than location; and, second, that the relationship anchoring asylum to territory be relaxed.

In this response, I focus first upon Shachar's discussion of the "shifting border in action" (p. 20) and her analysis of state techniques that both "bleed" (p. 20) the border inward and stretch it out in order to

---

[2] Tugba Basaran, *Security, Law and Borders: At the Limits of Liberties* (Oxford: Routledge, 2011), pp. 66–67.

[3] See, for example, Ayelet Shachar, *The Birthright Lottery: Citizenship and Global Inequality* (Cambridge and London: Harvard University Press, 2009); Ayelet Shachar, *Multicultural Jurisdictions: Cultural Differences and Women's Rights* (Cambridge: Cambridge University Press, 2001).

parse what might be distinctive about these politico-legal phenomena. I then turn to her two normative proposals and express measured skepticism as to Shachar's hope of eliciting greater state responsibility through affording extraterritorial protection.

Pushing out

Let us begin by examining how "the long arm of the state" (p. 6) can move. Vividly written, the text of *The Shifting Border* affords us a wealth of additional corporeal metaphors that depict the state's manipulation of borders. The border "contracts," "protrudes," "pushes out," "bleeds inward," and "penetrates deeply" (*passim*), as the state stretches its "jurisdictional arm inward and outward with tremendous flexibility" (p. 8), suggesting the tentacle of an octopus. Such representations enable Shachar to demonstrate the "flurry of activity" (p. 57) of the shifting border. Undeveloped in *The Shifting Border* are more explicit links between the state and body, or body politic, particularly in a context where the national body is described as invaded, penetrated, and violated by migrants. Such an exploration would help explain why governments assert limiting migration is necessary to take back control.

While the border may shift in order to accelerate the passage of desired immigrants welcomed by states, such actions are less a focus of *The Shifting Border* than are states' attempts at restrictive closure.[4] That there *is* a dialectic between this double gesture of closure and selective openness, which operates, as Shachar puts it, in a "quantum-like fashion, simultaneously both fixed and fluid" (p. 9), so that states exercise a "kaleidoscopic dominion" (p. 9), is an important observation, as most scholarship in this area focuses solely upon restriction.

---

[4] Shachar has written extensively elsewhere about what she has described as "Olympic citizenship," or "citizenship for sale," referring to visa, admission, and naturalization policies that privilege the desired few. See, for example, Ayelet Shachar, 'Citizenship for Sale?' in Ayelet Shachar *et al.*, eds, *The Oxford Handbook of Citizenship* (Oxford: Oxford University Press, 2017), pp. 789–816.

Turning to its restrictive capability, the long arm of the state can extend outward to bar would-be immigrants from reaching the state's territory and its concomitant legal protections. Such protections arise from both international and domestic law. Article 33 of the UN Refugee Convention prohibits any contracting state from expelling or returning a refugee to territories where her life or freedom would be threatened, in what is called *non-refoulement*, or non-return. Compliance with the duty of non-return requires an asylum claim to be examined in its substance, which is why once a territorial frontier is accessed, states have the responsibility to afford migrants access to asylum procedures.[5] It is similarly the case that the legal claim any person might make for rights recognition by the United States is in most cases a territorial one. This is not just because of the Refugee Convention, but also because of judicial interpretations of the US Constitution, which recognize territorially present persons as the relevant category of humanity entitled to due process and equal protection.[6] But if a person has not yet reached the territory of a state, she cannot then be "expelled" or "returned," nor is she territorially present, and thus we see states pushing out the location of their borders beyond the territorial frontier.

This pushing out is known as interdiction, the interception and prevention of movement. We could classify three types of interdiction depending upon mode of travel. The first, which Shachar calls "overseas interdiction" (p. 30), involves extraterritorial screening of those seeking to travel by air. This interdiction can take place at the origin of a journey, accomplished either by airline employees as private delegatees of border policing, who can face sanctions for not having properly sorted

[5] Alice Edwards, 'Human Rights, Refugees, and the Right "to Enjoy" Asylum', *International Journal of Refugee Law 17*, no. 2 (2005): pp. 293–330.
[6] One might think that the recognition that the US Constitution's Suspension Clause applies to non-citizens held at Guantánamo Bay, Cuba, would correlate with holding that the Due Process Clause also applies, but courts have been reluctant to embrace this idea. See, for example, *Kiyemba v. Obama*, 555 F. 3de 1022, 1026–27 (D.C. Cir. 2009). For a discussion of this relationship between due process and habeas, see Jonathan Hafetz, 'Due Process and Detention at Guantanamo: Closing the Constitutional Loopholes', *Just Security*, November 4, 2014, online www.justsecurity.org/17076/due-process-detention-guantanamo-closing-constitutional-loopholes/.

out travelers, or by destination-country officials located on foreign soil. This "regulator's dream tool" (p. 29) can push the border of the destination country all the way to the country of origin, sometimes thousands of miles from the territorial border.

The second type of interdiction involves the limiting of mobility of those who seek to travel by land. The United States has now outsourced border control to Mexico with the creation of Mexico's Programa Frontera Sud, essentially shifting the US–Mexico border 1,864 miles south. Concerned about the 2014 "surge" of unaccompanied children and women fleeing violence in Guatemala, Honduras, and El Salvador, the United States pressured Mexico to stem migration flows. Mexico agreed to undertake increased policing along its southern border in exchange for 86 million US dollars to train security forces and to purchase new communication, protection, and inspection equipment. This program added layers of new controls that stretch up through Chiapas (at the border with Guatemala) to the states of Oaxaca and Veracruz, to the skinniest portion of Mexico, where the movement of migrants is easiest to control.[7]

As is apparent in the example of Programa Frontera Sud, interdiction over land can be accomplished through externalization of a destination country's border policies to a contiguous bordering country. Such cooperation agreements between transit countries and destination countries, exchanging funds for assistance in border policing, similarly occur when interdiction is accomplished at sea. *The Shifting Border* points to Italy's training of Libyan coastguard officials to "do Europe's dirty job of closing the border." (p. 81).

Maritime interdiction, the third type of interdiction, generally involves two phases: physically intercepting and boarding a vessel, and then either deflecting the vessel or taking the vessel and/or its passengers to another location.[8] The United States is often credited with having pioneered this tactic with its policy directed at Haitian migrants,

---

[7] Stephanie Nolen, 'Southern Exposure: The Costly Border Plan Mexico Won't Discuss', *Globe and Mail*, June 16, 2016, online www.theglobeandmail.com/news/world/the-costly-border-mexico-wont-discuss-migration/article30397720/.

[8] Daniel Ghezelbash, *Refuge Lost: Asylum Law in an Interdependent World* (Cambridge: Cambridge University Press, 2018), p. 74.

beginning in 1981 under President Ronald Reagan. The US Coast Guard would board vessels, question those aboard, and return to Haiti all those who had no valid entry documents or who failed to indicate a fear of persecution upon return to Haiti. Between 1981 and 1990, 22,940 Haitians were interdicted at sea; of that number the then Immigration and Naturalization Service determined that only eleven were qualified to apply for asylum in the United States.[9]

After the coup against Jean Bertrand Aristide in 1991, the number of Haitians trying to flee the country escalated. In a period of six months, 34,000 Haitians were interdicted. Some were held in a camp at the US naval base on Guantánamo, Cuba, for screening. This was the first foray of the United States into holding what have been called rightless detainees or prisoners in this particular place, a place selected for its geographic location far from US judicial oversight.[10] With the camp on Guantánamo full, and Coast Guard cutters overwhelmed, President George H. W. Bush opted—rather than allowing Haitians into the United States while their cases were screened—to return them to Haiti with no consideration of their qualifications for asylum.

This brutal policy of interdiction was challenged, unsuccessfully, as being in violation of the *non-refoulement* obligation of Article 33 of the Refugee Convention, implemented into US law through the Immigration and Nationality Act. The US Supreme Court, in *Sale v. Haitian Centers Council* (1993), held that the prohibition on returning refugees to a place where their life or freedom would be threatened only referred to those on the threshold of initial entry at a border, and not to those who are transported away before they could reach that border.

As we see in the example of US policy toward Haitian migrants, interdiction often leads to yet another form of borders stretching outward: extraterritorial processing. This processing refers to screening of

[9] Ruth Ellen Wasem, *U.S. Immigration Policy On Haitian Migrants*, Congressional Research Service (RS2149, January 15, 2010, online http://trac.syr.edu/immigration/library/P4230.pdf.
[10] A. Naomi Paik, *Rightlessness: Testimony and Redress in U.S. Prison Campus since World War II* (Chapel Hill: University of North Carolina Press, 2016).

asylum claims conducted well outside a state's geographic boundaries, typically in order to shield that processing from judicial scrutiny and to limit the access of those being screened to legal protection. The United States inaugurated this practice when it commenced screening Haitians at sea and then began to do so at Guantánamo Bay.[11] *The Shifting Border* refers to extraterritorial processing as "offshoring processing" (p. 16) in describing Australia's notorious policies, by means of which asylum seekers who arrive in Australia by boat are removed to detention centers entirely outside of Australia's territory, on the islands of Manus and Nauru. Later in Shachar's discussion, she describes this decoupling of refugee processing from territory as "processing-at-a-distance" (p. 84) and does not condemn it but rather advocates it as a possible response to the shifting border. I return to this proposal below.

Bleeding in

The border can also "bleed in." The primary example discussed by *The Shifting Border* to illustrate this metaphor is that of "expedited removal" in the United States, so this practice requires close examination.[12] Expedited removal is a creation of the Illegal Immigration Reform and Immigrant Responsibility Act of 1996. It was invented as a form of summary exclusion for non-citizens who are inadmissible for one of two reasons: they either lack valid immigration documentation or have made a misrepresentation in an attempt to attain immigration status.[13]

---

[11] Ghezelbash, *Refuge Lost* (n 21), p. 100.

[12] Shachar also briefly discusses recent rulings by the Court of Justice for the European Union on the question of whether border- and migration-enforcement activities can stretch inward beyond the actual territorial border of member states. Identity checks can now take place within 30 kilometers of the land border and a radius of 50 kilometers of the sea border, as well as in train stations nationwide and on-board trains anywhere (p. 42).

[13] Immigration and Nationality Act, 8 USC. § 1225(b)(1) (United States). This is thus a more specific category of non-citizens than the more general category of 'undocumented migrants' described in *The Shifting Border* as potentially placed in expedited removal (p. 20).

Routine removal proceedings provide far more process for the non-citizen than do these expedited removal proceedings. In ordinary removal proceedings, the non-citizen is entitled to a hearing before an immigration judge; she may present and cross-examine evidence, may call witnesses, may be represented by an attorney or another person of the non-citizen's choosing, may demand reconsideration or reopening of the case, and may file for administrative and judicial review of adverse decisions.[14]

But expedited removal provides none of these protections. Those subject to expedited removal receive no judicial hearing and are mandatorily detained.[15] They are not statutorily provided the privilege of being represented, and the Ninth Circuit—the most immigrant-friendly of all federal appellate courts in the United States—recently held that they are also not guaranteed a constitutional right to counsel under the Fifth Amendment's Due Process Clause.[16]

By law, expedited removal may not be applied to US citizens, lawful permanent residents, or refugees, asylees, or asylum seekers.[17] Thus, the only way out of summary exclusion for most non-citizens facing expedited removal is through expressing a fear of persecution or torture, in which case the non-citizen is to be screened by an asylum officer to determine whether she may stay in the United States to pursue a claim for protection. If she is determined to pass a certain threshold, she will be placed in a removal proceeding, and is typically detained while she waits.[18] In June 2018, former Secretary of Homeland Security Kirstjen Nielsen referred to non-citizens expressing fear in these screenings as "well-coached applicants ... uttering the magic words indicating

---

[14] Immigration and Nationality Act, 8 USC. § 1229 (a) (United States). This guarantee of judicial review is not available to all: note that in 1996 the US Congress identified certain categories of immigration decisions as no longer eligible for judicial review, in a practice known as "court stripping."

[15] Certain categories of non-citizens in standard removal proceedings are also mandatorily detained.

[16] *U.S. v. Peralta Sanchez*, 868 F.3rd 852 (9th Cir. 2017).

[17] Cubans arriving by aircraft were also exempted from expedited removal, until January 2017.

[18] The screening threshold that non-citizens must pass is to show credible fear—or reasonable fear for non-citizens who have previously been removed—of persecution or torture.

a fear of returning home," and indicated that the Trump administration had requested Congress to render the screening process more difficult.[19]

From its inception in April 1997 until November 2002, expedited removal applied only to "arriving aliens" at US ports of entry. In 2002, the Bush administration expanded expedited removal to those arriving by sea.[20] In August 2004, expedited removal was additionally expanded to non-citizens present without having been admitted or paroled, who are encountered by an immigration officer within 100 air miles of the US international southwest land border and who cannot show that they have been present in the United States for more than two weeks.[21] This is still the current reach of the practice. However, the Secretary of Homeland Security has statutory authority to expand expedited removal to non-citizens anywhere in the United States who are present without being admitted or paroled and who cannot show they have been present in the United States for more than two years. In his first week in office, President Trump indicated his intent to expand expedited removal along these lines.[22] *The Shifting Border* illustrates the 100-mile zone where expedited removal can presently take place with a map from the American Civil Liberties Union (ACLU), depicting the "Constitution-Free Zone of the United States." We might note here that there are actually two interrelated policies with separate statutory and regulatory authority creating a 100-mile zone in the United States. One 100-mile zone is that of expedited removal; the second is that shown on the ACLU map, governing the actions of Customs and Border Patrol, invested with the statutory authority to stop and conduct

[19] Joseph Curl, 'Homeland Security Secretary Kirstjen Nielsen: "Well Coached" Illegal Aliens Using Children to Pose as Families', *The Daily Wire*, June 18, 2018, online www.dailywire.com/news/31968/homeland-security-secretary-kirstjen-neilsen-well-joseph-curl.
[20] Parole refers to an administrative permission for a non-citizen to physically enter and temporarily remain in the United States, usually for urgent humanitarian or significant public benefit reasons.
[21] Department of Homeland Security, *Designated Aliens for Expedited Removal*, 69 Fed. Reg. 58.877 (August 11, 2004) (United States).
[22] This plan was expressed thus: "Pursuant to section 235(b)(1)(A)(iii)(I) of the Immigration and Nationality Act, the Secretary shall take appropriate action to apply, in his sole and unreviewable discretion, the provisions of section 235(b)(1)(A)(i) and (ii) of the Immigration and Nationality Act to the aliens designated under section 235 (b)(1)(A)

searches on vessels, trains, aircraft, or other vehicles within "a reasonable distance from any external boundary of the United States" for the purposes of "preventing the illegal entry of aliens into the US."[23] As first announced in the Federal Register in 1957, "reasonable distance" is defined through regulation as "100 air miles," although a distance of more than 100 miles may also be considered reasonable due to unusual circumstances.[24]

In choosing to adopt the 100-mile zone for expedited removal, the Federal Register declared that this was "in the interests of focusing enforcement resources upon unlawful entries that have a close spatial and temporal nexus to the border" and that the government "anticipates expedited removal will be employed against those who are apprehended immediately proximate to a land border" and have "negligible ties or equities" in the United States.[25] Nevertheless, "this designation extends to a 100-mile operational range because many aliens will arrive in vehicles that speedily depart the border area, and because other recent arrivals will find their way to near-border locales seeking transportation to other locations within the interior of the US."[26] As justification, the notice points out that the 100-mile range already has been established by regulation as a "reasonable distance" from the external boundary of the United States for the search activities of Customs and Border Patrol.[27]

Both of these interrelated 100-mile zones illustrate Shachar's shifting border, treating what is physically in the interior as though it were on the territory's frontier. *The Shifting Border* notes that this bleeding inward of the border has also occurred through another legal maneuver, which

---

(iii)(II)"; see Executive Order 13767, Border Security and Immigration Enforcement Improvements, 82 Fed. Reg. Presidential Documents 8793, January 27, 2017, sec. 11(c) (United States).

[23] Immigration and Nationality Act, 8 U.S.C. § 287(a)(3) (Unites States); see Chris Rickerd, 'Customs and Border Protection's (CBP's) 100-Mile Rule', online www.aclu.org/sites/default/files/assets/14_9_15_cbp_100-mile_rule_final.pdf.

[24] Code of Federal Regulations, 8 C.F.R. § 287.1 (b) (United States); see 22 Fed. Reg. 9.739-9.828 (December 6, 1957).

[25] 69 Fed. Reg. 48.877, 48.880 (2004).

[26] Ibid.

[27] Ibid.

it calls "creating the legal distinction between 'entry' and 'admission'" (p. 25). This is a distinction made between physical entry and lawful admission, so that the bodily act of entry does not equate to legal entry. One can thus be what US immigration law calls "present without admission." Shachar asserts that "in addition to conjuring mirror-house-like stretching and contracting movements, the shifting border also distinguishes between *physical entry* into the country (which does not count for immigration purposes) and *lawful admission* through a recognized port of entry (which makes one's presence in the territory permissible, and therefore visible, in the eyes of the regulatory state)" (p. 24). In so writing, Shachar suggests that this legal distinction between physical entry and lawful admission is a product of the shifting border. But when one recalls the long history of disjuncture between territorial presence and the application of territorial jurisdiction mentioned above, this claim appears inapt insofar as the shifting border is characterized as a "new" phenomenon.

Even if we confine our inquiry to the migration context, what might it mean to say that the legal distinction between physical entry and lawful admission is a product of the shifting border? A distinction between physical entry and lawful admission crystalized in US immigration law in 1882, when Congress first empowered the federal government to deport immigrants via the Chinese Exclusion Act and the statutory directive to remove "any Chinese person found unlawfully within the United States."[28] The legal distinction between entry and admission seems not so much a product of the shifting border as a product of *the border itself*, so long as the very idea of the border logically contains within it state powers of exclusion and deportation.

---

[28] Chinese Exclusion Act 1882, sec. 12 (United States): "That no Chinese person shall be permitted to enter the United States by land without producing to the proper officer of customs the certificate in this act required of Chinese persons seeking to land from a vessel. And any Chinese person found unlawfully within the United States shall be caused to be removed therefrom to the country from whence he came, by direction of the President of the United States, and at the cost of the United States, after being brought before some justice, judge, or commissioner of a court of the United States and found to be one not lawfully entitled to be or remain in the United States."

If the idea of the border does not contain these powers—if Shachar seeks to argue that there should be no distinction made between physical entry and lawful admission, suggesting that territorial presence should always equate with legal presence—then we need to hear more on precisely this point. One could certainly imagine a state that chose to use only its exclusionary authority and not its deportation power, so that all non-citizens would be sorted at the gates, but that once one passed those gates (whether lawfully or not) one could then never be deported.

So if the border itself, then, is responsible for the distinction between entry and admission, what is the particular contribution of the shifting border? More precisely articulated as a result of the shifting border would be the *manipulation of the legal salience* of the distinction made between physical entry and lawful admission. This is, in fact, what *The Shifting Border* describes when Shachar quotes an immigration casebook noting the "redrawing [of] the traditional exclusion–deportation line" (p. 25)—which Shachar restates as "[t]he exclusion–deportation line has become *de-territorialized*" (p. 25)—so that the key factor dividing exclusion from deportation in the United States is no longer entry but lawful admission.

This redrawing, or de-territorialization, refers to the statutory change enacted in 1996 to whether persons who were inside the United States but were never lawfully admitted would be placed in exclusion or deportation proceedings. Traditionally, pre-1996, the power of exclusion was reserved for those who had not effectuated an entry into the United States. The power of deportation was reserved for those who had. An "entry" is a legal construct; one may physically enter the United States but not be considered to have effectuated an entry (one needs to be physically inside—whether following inspection and lawful admission or after evading inspection—and must be free from official restraint). Thus, one may have entered physically but not be considered to have entered legally. Persons who did so were called EWIs, or persons who had "entered without inspection." Then in 1996, the line dividing exclusion and deportation shifted from entry to admission, so that persons who were never admitted (those who are called "present without admission") are now placed in removal proceedings on grounds of inadmissibility, not deportability. The current consequence of this, for most persons within the United States who have never been lawfully admitted, is not that they are placed in expedited removal, but that they are subject to a different set of statutory grounds for removal, with underlying lesser constitutional protections.[29]

This depiction of bleeding in in *The Shifting Border* is of the state subjecting those inside to legal control as though they were standing outside at the gates, treating those who should be in the "soft inside" as if they were at the "hard outside."[30] This raises some questions. Could one argue that the threat of deportation should also be considered the border bleeding inside, traveling inside the territory accompanying the body of the non-citizen? So long as the non-citizen faces potential deportation, she is arguably not able to enjoy the soft inside and cannot truly enjoy the personhood of territorial presence. In other words, is pushing in only about exclusion? If not, why not?

Lastly, if we follow Shachar in putting together these two modes of the shifting border in action, should bleeding in and extending out be considered equivalent forms of the shifting border? Which should we find more troubling: blocking initial access to territory or treating those who are territorially present as if they are outside? Here, I would draw upon Shachar's earlier writing on birthright citizenship and her critique of what she has termed the "birthright lottery" in an unjust world, as well as her proposal that citizenship be granted because of a connection to a particular location, via what she has termed *jus nexi*.[31] Shachar's

---

[29] We know this because most undocumented immigrants in the United States have resided there far longer than the time period that would render them vulnerable to being placed in expedited removal. An estimated two thirds have resided in the United States for over ten years. See Paul Taylor *et al.*, 'Unauthorized Immigrants: Length of Residency, Patterns of Parenthood', *Pew Research Center*, December 1, 2011, online www.pewhispanic.org/2011/12/01/unauthorized-immigrants-length-of-residency-patterns-of-parenthood/.

[30] On the hard edge contrasted with the soft interior, see Linda Bosniak, *The Citizen and the Alien* (Princeton: Princeton University Press, 2008).

[31] See Shachar, *The Birthright Lottery* (n 6).

earlier work might tell us that using interdiction to preclude those dis-advantaged through the lottery of birth location from accessing wealthy states, and categorizing those who live in a territory in which they have developed stakes and ties as if they are standing outside at the border, are equal affronts. But these are different modes of bordering. They could be distinguished as policies affecting non-citizens who are terri-torially present (bleeding in) versus policies affecting non-citizens who are not (extending out). This poses the normative question: are there different duties owed to those who are territorially present? What if we observe that pushing out the border impinges on the sovereignty of other states? Conceptually and normatively, these phenomena raise distinct questions.

Severing territory from the allocation of rights

Shachar's normative proposals for how we might counter the shifting border derive from her focus on the fact of territorial arrival giving rise to state obligations of protection. She seeks to delink territory from protection in a kind of *jiu-jitsu* move, taking advantage of the shifting border's tactics of expansion in an effort to counter its stated goals of rights-restriction. This move has two dimensions: expanding the extra-territorial reach of human rights so that rights follow the shifting bor-der, and relaxing the fixation on territorial arrival as a precondition for claiming refuge.

The first proposal would constrain the shifting border by ensuring that the human rights and constitutional provisions that govern execu-tive power apply regardless of where border control activities are exer-cised; if they are exercised at all, wherever this takes place, these constraints must apply. The precedent Shachar finds for this is in two cases of the ECtHR. In the 2012 *Hirsi* case,[32] the ECtHR rejected the approach of the US Supreme Court in *Sale* and found that Italy breached

---

[32] *Hirsi v. Italy*, [GC], App No. 27765/09, Eur. Ct. H.R. (2012).

its protection obligations by stopping a vessel with 200 passengers on
the high seas and sending those migrants to Libya, depriving them of
any chance to state their protection claim. In *Hirsi*, the ECtHR found
that human rights obligations become applicable if and when state officials exercise "continuous and exclusive de jure and de facto control"
regardless of whether this state action takes place extraterritorially. The
2017 *N.D. and N.T.* case[33] addressed Spain's attempt to bleed in the border by fencing an 11.5 kilometer barrier around Melilla on Spanish territory and then claiming that individuals who failed to completely
surmount this barrier were not in Spain and therefore not within the
realm of European human rights. The ECtHR held that the individuals
were in fact under continuous and exclusive control of Spanish authorities. As Shachar notes, this would be a functional rather than a territo-
riality-bounded interpretation of jurisdiction.

We could add here to *Hirsi* and *N.D. and N.T.* the US Supreme
Court's ruling in the 2008 *Boumediene* decision, when it endorsed a
functional approach to extraterritoriality in the context of applications
for a writ of habeas corpus filed by prisoners on Guantánamo. The
Supreme Court rejected a categorical or formal conception of sovereignty that would define the geographical scope of habeas protection.[34]
Another case to examine might be *Regina v. Immigration Officer at
Prague Airport*, which concerned preclearance procedures adopted by
UK immigration officers stationed at Prague Airport. These officers
refused six Roma who were Czech nationals—several of whom stated
they intended to claim asylum on arrival in the United Kingdom—
leave to enter before they boarded aircraft bound for the United Kingdom. Here, although the appellants could not successfully make a claim

---

[33] *N.D. and N.T. v. Spain*, [GC], App Nos. 8675/15 and 8697/15, Eur. Ct. H.R. (2017).
[34] *Boumediene v. Bush*, 553 U.S. 723 (2008). For discussion on the implications of Boumediene for the rights of non-citizens subjected to US government action outside the
Guantánamo context, see Christina Duffy Burnett, 'A Convenient Constitution? Extraterritoriality after Boumediene', *Columbia Law Review 109* (2009): pp. 973–1046;
Chimène I. Keitner, 'Rights beyond Borders', *Yale Journal of International Law 36* (2011):
pp. 55–114; Gerald L. Neuman, 'The Extraterritorial Constitution after *Boumediene v.
Bush*', *Southern California Law Review 82* (2009): pp. 259–290.

as refugees, as they were still inside their country of origin, they were able to show, according to the House of Lords, that they had been subjected to racial discrimination.[35]

As Shachar notes, the response of Italy to the *Hirsi* decision was to abandon Italian interdiction and to outsource enforcement operations to Libya, thus breaking the jurisdictional link to Italy and the European Union. If the shifting border is increasingly operationalized through outsourcing, there will be many questions as to how much and what types of contact with state officials or their delegates is considered sufficient to show effective control; literature on contracting out in other contexts might be helpful.

Shachar's second normative suggestion is to delink access to territory and asylum claims. Since states are pushing their borders outward from their physical territories, Shachar seeks to tie these shifting, non-territorial borders to the responsibility of states to hear asylum claims. As an illustration, the text provides the example of over 25,000 Syrian refugees resettled in Canada in 2015 who were not on-shore asylum seekers but who had been reached by the border regime in the form of Canadian immigration officials deployed to Jordan, Turkey, and Lebanon. Here, the shifting border was deployed in order to *enhance* rights. The "burden of 'touching base'" (p. 83) shifted from the asylum seekers to states and their authorized agents. This is "processing-at-a-distance" (p. 84), which resembles the shifting border, but as a "rights-enhancing" (p. 84), rather than rights-restricting, legal innovation would "mov[e] the border closer to the individual to offer her protection" (p. 89). The one other successful example of this approach that Shachar describes is the Orderly Departure Program coordinated by the UNHCR after the end of the Vietnam War, involving more than thirty countries, that was credited with ultimately saving more than 2 million lives.

There are still other, less dramatic examples of processing-at-a-distance that give a more textured sense of the benefits and pitfalls of

---

[35] *Regina v. Immigration Officer at Prague Airport and Another Ex parte European Roma Rights Centre and Others* [2004] UKHL 55.

this approach. Shachar mentions in a footnote programs that have established mechanisms to acquire visas in countries of origin or transit, among them a visa-processing facility opened in Haiti following the 2010 earthquake, which enabled Haitians to get special humanitarian visas in Port-au-Prince to travel to Brazil rather than rely on smugglers to get them there (p. 84, n 203). There is, in addition, a long history in the United States of in-country refugee processing, including in Vietnam, the former Soviet Union, Cuba, Central America, Haiti, and Iraq, which provides an opportunity to test how the severing of territorial arrival and the granting of protection status might work. I focus on Haiti below.

After Haiti's President Jean Bertrand Aristide was deposed, the George H. W. Bush administration lobbied for a regional solution, which proved inadequate for the number of Haitians fleeing; as discussed above, the administration then began to take them to the US naval base on Guantánamo, Cuba, where they were pre-screened for asylum in the United States. In May 1992, citing the surge of Haitians that month, Present Bush ordered the Coast Guard to intercept all Haitians in boats and return them without interviews, offering those repatriated the option of in-country refugee processing. What were the problems with this system? First, the existence of an in-country processing system was used to justify the policy of summarily returning all interdicted Haitians without screening by both President George H. W. Bush and President Bill Clinton. By May 1994, in-country processing was described as a complete sham and as a smokescreen for *refoulement*. At that point, 54,219 applications had been filed on behalf of nearly 106,000 people; 10,644 cases had been decided, of which 9,827 had been denied. In addition, the program provided no safety for applicants during the slow and highly visible procedure.[36]

Shachar notes the benefits of severing the relationship between territory and protection: such initiatives could "save lives, dry up the

---

[36] For these arguments and this history see Bill Frelick, 'In-Country Refugee Processing of Haitians: The Case against', *Refuge 21*, no. 4 (2003): pp. 66–72.

market for human smugglers, allow security screening of entrants prior to arrival, permit greater choice and agency for migrants themselves to select their destination country, and help alleviate fear of 'loss of control' among voters in the recipient countries" (p. 85, n 204). Yet such an approach also raises significant challenges. To conduct refugee processing outside the territory of destination countries clearly enables governments' efforts to limit the number and kind of persons arriving on their shores. How could one ensure that this processing was conducted in a way that would not diminish rights? Processing-at-a-distance suggests less oversight than processing on-shore; what is the guarantee that routinizing offshore processing would not invite a race to the bottom? Shachar would presumably respond with her important predicate: that her twofold strategy rests on a "lexical priority" (p. 88) of her two normative ideas: the idea that human rights protection follows the border takes priority over "relocating protection operations to where vulnerable migrants are" (p. 88), so that governments "do not use the latter as a fig leaf" (p. 88). But how would one muster the political will for this to happen? Political will is in part a product of legal obligation. Severing territory from asylum evades the mandate of *non-refoulement* and renders refugee processing an utterly discretionary activity. Given how governments today are furiously manipulating their borders to keep asylum seekers out, where is the evidence that governments, other than in occasional anomalous circumstances such as Canada and refugees from the Syrian conflict, would choose to bring the border to refugees in order to assist them, rather than to push them back?

Conclusion

States bleed in and push out their borders, disconnecting the legal border from physical territory. A close examination of such border manipulation in the United States raises various questions in response to *The Shifting Border* Should the threat of deportation be considered a form of borders "bleeding in"? Are "bleeding in" and "pushing out" equivalent forms of delinking legal protection from territory? And how likely is it that rights enhancement will accompany the moving border, particularly once the mandate of *non-refoulement* no longer applies? Shachar's rich description and provocative normative framework provide us with a conceptual road map, the charting of possible paths to follow, and new questions to explore, as we navigate an unsettling legal topography, that of the shifting border.

6

The law and politics of the "shifting border"

Chimène I. Keitner

My father tells the story of his family's clandestine escape from Hungary into Austria in 1956, after Soviet tanks and troops crushed an anti-communist uprising in his hometown of Budapest.[1] The border, which was not visibly demarcated at my grandparents' point of crossing, served as the boundary between two distinct political and legal regimes: on one side, subjection to the Hungarian police state; on the other, access to international protection. Austria's decision to recognize all fleeing Hungarians as refugees within the meaning of the 1951 Refugee Convention, and the relatively rapid resettlement of some 170,000 Hungarian refugees in third states, meant that the primary barrier to escaping Hungary and entering Austria was physical (based on one's willingness and ability to undertake the hazardous journey across the border) rather than legal (based on one's personal identity or status).

The Austrian response to the influx of Hungarian refugees in 1956–57, and the large number of third states willing to aid in resettlement, proved rather anomalous in recent history.[2] As Ayelet Shachar's lead essay describes, states have developed myriad techniques to deter and prevent (and, selectively, to facilitate and accelerate) entry by foreign nationals.

[1] For context, see Marjoleine Zieck, 'The 1956 Hungarian Refugee Emergency, an Early and Instructive Case of Resettlement', *Amsterdam Law Forum* 5, no. 45 (2013): pp. 45–63.
[2] See, for example, Amanda Cellini, 'The Resettlement of Hungarian Refugees in 1956', *Forced Migration Review* 54, no. 6 (2017): pp. 6–8, online www.fmreview.org/sites/fmr/files/FMRdownloads/en/resettlement/cellini.pdf.

The topic of migration is both timely and timeless, as politicians continue to use manufactured immigration "crises" to galvanize domestic support for their political platforms. The time-honored technique of blaming the "other" for social and economic ills, and the still elusive formula for building lasting civic solidarity in diverse societies, make it unsurprising that states interpret their legal obligations toward non-citizens narrowly. Perhaps more alarming are the exclusionary definitions of citizenship and national identity that undergird policies targeting immigrants who are, in many cases, would-be citizens. Shachar's lead essay focuses on these narrow interpretations and their accompanying enforcement strategies. Her essay is as important for what it does not address as for what it does. As she recounts, states seeking to deter entry have built and fortified physical barriers along their geographic borders.[3] They have also "externalized" border controls to "make it more difficult for vulnerable migrants to reach [destination countries] safely and exercise their legal rights."[4] And those who succeed in crossing the border may find themselves subject to an immigration-law regime that increasingly resembles criminal law enforcement.[5] Yet offering a critique of these strategies does not get us very far toward understanding, or attempting to alleviate, the structural and other factors that contribute to their adoption in the first place. The shifting border is a symptom, not the disease.

The selective reception of immigrants—particularly by countries surrounded by oceans that can more easily control physical entry—has deep historical roots. That said, the perception of a "refugee crisis" and the resurgence of immigrant-threat narratives have spurred additional

---

[3] See, for example, Moria Paz, 'Between the Kingdom and the Desert Sun: Human Rights, Immigration, and Border Walls', *Berkeley Journal of International Law 34*, no. 1 (2016): pp. 1–43, p. 7 (observing that "border walls are a predictable strategic response by States that seek to regain exclusion capabilities").

[4] Leon Prop, 'The Red Cross and the Externalisation of EU Migration Policy: Addressing the Humanitarian Challenges', in *Shifting Borders: Externalising Migrant Vulnerabilities and Rights?* (Bruxelles: Red Cross EU Office, 2013), pp. 5–6, p. 6, online https://redcross.eu/uploads/files/Positions/Migration/Shifting-borders-booklet/shifting-borders-externalizing-migrant-vulnerabilities-rights-red-cross-eu-office.pdf.

[5] See Jennifer M. Chacón, 'Managing Migration through Crime', *Columbia Law Review Sidebar 109* (2009): pp. 135–148.

measures designed to regulate and to restrict the movement of people across borders. The cumulative effect, as described by Anil Kalhan, is that "the *migration border*—the set of boundary-points at which nation-states authorize individuals to enter or be admitted, prevent or allow their entry or admission, or subject them to possible expulsion—has been decoupled from the territorial border and rendered 'virtual': layered, electronic, mobile, and policed by an escalating number of public and private actors."[6] To be sure, these developments merit serious attention, even if they are largely epiphenomenal.

Shachar contends that "we currently lack the basic conceptual language to capture, describe, and critique these rapid changes" (p. 7). Given the proliferation of academic and policy work documenting and responding to these changes, I am less persuaded that the core problem is one of conceptual under-development.[7] Rather, as Shachar notes with respect to Australia's externalization policies, "[d]espite domestic contestation and international condemnation, the major political parties in Australia have refused to reverse the policy of off-shore processing" (p. 48). It appears that the core problem is not a lack of conceptual tools, but a lack of political will.

Although Shachar acknowledges "the blurring lines between law and politics in the age of shifting borders" (p. 48), she focuses her attention on law. Yet law alone will not save us, at least in its current forms.

---

[6] Anil Kalhan, 'Immigration Surveillance', *Maryland Law Review 74*, no. 1 (2014): pp. 1–78, p. 9 (emphasis in original).

[7] Scholars from a range of disciplines, including those cited by Shachar, have grappled with the challenges posed by strategies of border externalization. Representative recent work includes David FitzGerald, *The Asylum Paradox: Remote Control of Forced Migration to the Global North* (forthcoming); Bill Frelick, Ian M. Keysel, and Jennifer Podkul, 'The Impact of Externalization of Migration Controls on the Rights of Asylum Seekers and Other Migrants', *Journal on Migration & Human Security 4* (2016): pp. 190–220; Cecilia Menjívar, 'Immigration Law beyond Borders: Externalizing and Internalizing Border Controls in an Era of Securitization', *Annual Review of Law & Social Sciences 10* (2014): pp. 353–369; Maribel Casas-Cortes, Sebastian Cobarrubias, and John Pickles, 'Riding Routes and Itinerant Borders: Autonomy of Migration and Border Externalization', *Antipode 47* (2015): pp. 894–914; Maribel Casas, Sebastian Cobarrubias, and John Pickles, 'Stretching Borders beyond Sovereign Territories? Mapping EU and Spain's Border Externalization Policies', *Geopolítica 2* (2011): pp. 71–90, online https://core.ac.uk/download/pdf/38816040.pdf.

Notably, as Guy Goodwin-Gill and others have emphasized, the 1951 Refugee Convention, and corresponding customary international law norms, do "not deal with the question of admission, and neither [do they] oblige a state of refuge to accord asylum as such" (p. 30, n 71).[8] I am thus less optimistic than Shachar that existing legal norms—which themselves are forged by deeply political compromises—can be activated to achieve the level of protection of non-nationals that the normative positions underpinning her approach appear to demand. As suggested below, even if more flexible interpretations of existing obligations were *legally* achievable, they would likely be unsustainable unless accompanied by a deep shift in *political* understandings. As Shachar notes, quoting Rainer Forst, "'[i]f we do not understand how norms and interests intermesh to generate and reproduce power, we are condemned to failure' in our efforts to understand political, legal, and normative orders, let alone transform them" (p. 93, n 218).[9]

Although it is natural for lawyers to look to law for answers, laws are necessarily embedded in existing political frameworks. In order to be effective, any reconceptualization of the scope and content of a state's domestic and international legal obligations must ultimately be accepted by the state itself, in addition to other relevant stakeholders. The first part of this essay briefly traces the regulatory shift from location to identity that lies at the heart of Shachar's account. The second part canvasses some of the persistent obstacles to states' acceptance of constraints on their ability to regulate entry by non-nationals. The third part suggests that what I refer to as governance models of migration regulation might ultimately be better suited than advocacy models to addressing contemporary challenges of global human protection.

---

[8] Quoting Guy Goodwin-Gill, 'The International Law of Refugee Protection', in Elena Fiddian-Qasmiyeh *et al.*, eds, *The Oxford Handbook of Refugee and Forced Migration Studies* (Oxford: Oxford University Press, 2014), pp. 36–45, p. 45.

[9] Quoting Rainer Forst, *Normativity and Power: Analyzing Social Orders of Justification* (Oxford: Oxford University Press, 2017), p. 143. See also Joseph H. Carens, 'Realistic and Idealistic Approaches to the Ethics of Migration', *The International Migration Review 30* (1996): pp. 156–170, p. 159.

The regulatory shift from location to identity

The idea that state sovereignty entails an absolute right to exclude foreigners has a relatively recent pedigree.[10] James Nafziger observed in 1983 that "it is only a slight exaggeration to note that authority today for the proposition absolving the sovereign of any legal duty to admit aliens is derived 'almost exclusively' from turn-of-the-century common law precedent, even in writings from some countries outside the common law tradition."[11] This understanding, which has become deeply entrenched, has had profound implications for immigration law and policy. As Shachar and others have described, states have intensified efforts to deny individuals the opportunity to enter. As Thomas Gammeltoft-Hansen and James Hathaway have observed, "the politics of *non-entrée* is based on a commitment to ensuring that refugees shall not be allowed to arrive."[12] The "shifting border" is created by the exercise of control at the moment of encounter between a state's authorities (or its proxies) and the immigrant, which might not coincide with the moment of encounter between the immigrant and the state's territorial border.[13]

Well-documented strategies of *non-entrée* mean that "in exercising sovereignty, states are shifting their focus from control over territory to control over people."[14] Consequently, as Alison Kesby has noted, "[t]he border is not that which is stable and delineated, but rather shifts in meaning, location, and the manner in which it is experienced."[15] In the

[10] See Vincent Chétail, 'Sovereignty and Migration in the Doctrine of the Law of Nations: An Intellectual History of Hospitality from Vitoria to Vattel', *European Journal of International Law 27* (2017): pp. 901–922, online http://www.ejil.org/pdfs/27/4/2697.pdf.

[11] James A. R. Nafziger, 'The General Admission of Aliens under International Law', *American Journal of International Law 77* (1983): pp. 804–847, p. 808.

[12] James C. Hathaway and Thomas Gammeltoft-Hansen, 'Non-Refoulement in a World of Cooperative Deterrence', *Columbia Journal of Transnational Law 53* (2015): pp. 235–284, p. 251.

[13] See Efrat Arbel, 'Shifting Borders and the Boundaries of Rights: Examining the Safe Third Country Agreement between Canada and the United States', *International Journal of Refugee Law 25* (2013): pp. 65–86, p. 78, online https://commons.allard.ubc.ca/cgi/viewcontent.cgi?article=1018&context=fac_pubs.

[14] Alison Kesby, 'The Shifting and Multiple Border and International Law', *Oxford Journal of Legal Studies, 27* (2007): pp. 101–119, p. 112.

[15] Ibid., p. 102.

evocative words of Marie-Laure Basilien-Gainche, "[t]he border is the migrant."[16]

Shachar sees a "deep paradox" in these developments (p. 8). On the one hand, "when it comes to controlling migration, states are willfully *abandoning* traditional notions of fixed and bounded territoriality, stretching their jurisdictional arm inward and outward with tremendous flexibility" (p. 8). Conversely, however, "when it comes to granting rights and protections, the very same states snap back to a narrow and strict interpretation of spatiality which limits their responsibility and liability, by attaching it to the (illusionary) static notion of border control" (p. 8). She critiques states' insufficient guarantees of protection for vulnerable migrants and also what she characterizes as states' willful hypocrisy.

Although Shachar faults certain states for actual non-compliance, her core critique involves states' arguable compliance with the letter— but not the spirit—of the legal commitments they have undertaken. In Shachar's view, states such as Canada, the United States, and Australia have walked too fine a line "between skirting their constitutional and human rights obligations and their declared commitment to upholding them" (p. 71). Litigants have framed this objection as one based on the interpretive principle of good faith, challenging "the lawfulness of measures that were taken to prevent [legal obligations] ever being triggered."[17] Migration control thus takes place in a border zone between lawful and unlawful state behavior that is constructed and contested through authoritative interpretations of applicable laws.

Shachar's account of the regulatory shift from location to identity "emphasiz[es] the core role of law and legal institutions in reinventing the border in the exercise of governmental authority . . . [and] explore[s] whether there are limits on such authority, and if so, how to activate

---

[16] Marie-Laure Basilien-Gainche, 'The EU External Edges: Borders as Walls or Ways?', *Journal of Territorial and Maritime Studies* 2 (2015): pp. 97–117, p. 107.

[17] *Regina v. Immigration Officer at Prague Airport and Another Ex parte European Roma Rights Centre and Others* [2004] UKHL 55, [2005] 2 AC 1 [57].

them and who should do so" (pp. 7–8). In so doing, she does not differentiate consistently among constitutional, statutory, and international sources of law. Yet the answer to "whether there are limits on such authority, and if so, how to activate them and who should do so" often turns critically on differences among these types of legal regimes.[18] In particular, the relative lack of judicial enforcement mechanisms at the international level means that "activat[ing]" legal limits on governmental authority requires identifying provisions that are enforceable in domestic courts, as described below (p. 61, n 150). Notably, although Shachar argues that "there is no inherent reason why the sovereign authority to control borders" ought to be free from judicial oversight (p. 76), she spends much more time on the extraterritoriality problem than on arguments for subjecting the immigration regime as a whole to more rigorous judicial review.

There is a deeper challenge that surfaces when the lens widens from "law and legal institutions" to encompass the social and political context in which laws are embedded and in which legal institutions operate. In addition to "activating" legal limits on governmental authority, we need to understand why that authority has been deployed to begin with. States are responsive to, and responsible for, their domestic constituencies. It is natural for activists to use the legal tools they currently have at their disposal and to interpret state obligations expansively, but it is also natural for states to interpret their legal obligations narrowly and to craft policies that respond to political incentives while avoiding legal liability. As Thomas Gammeltoft-Hansen has cautioned, a predictable result in the refugee context is that "courts' opinions that establish extraterritorial obligations under carefully circumscribed conditions may in some situations provide an indirect road map for executives to develop next generation deterrence

---

[18] See Chimène I. Keitner, 'Rights beyond Borders', *Yale Journal of International Law 36* (2011): pp. 55–114, online https://digitalcommons.law.yale.edu/cgi/viewcontent. cgi?article=1395&context=yjil, cited p. 76, n 184. See also Chimène I. Keitner, 'Framing Constitutional Rights', *Southwestern Law Review 36* (2011): pp. 617–633, online https://repository.uchastings.edu/cgi/viewcontent.cgi?article=2093&context=faculty_ scholarship.

measures creatively."[19] Long-term answers to the problems Shachar identifies cannot come from courts, but only from new political compromises within and among states.

The debate over extraterritorial obligations

Within the existing legal framework, the regulatory shift from location to identity raises the critical question of extraterritorial protection of migrants. Shachar advocates "expanding the extraterritorial reach of human rights" to address the lack of sufficient legal protections for non-nationals outside a state's border (pp. 74–75). In particular, she proposes a "hinge-like strategy" under which, "[w]here a country intentionally delinks migration-control activities from its geographical borders, a correlated expansion of rights and protections for the individual must follow" (p. 74). As well as expanding the extraterritorial reach of human rights, this would require "relaxing the fixation on territorial access as a precondition for securing refuge" (p. 75). The first part of this strategy calls for closing a protection "loophole" that states have identified by pushing human rights obligations out past a state's geographic border. The ECtHR increasingly has interpreted the geographic scope of the European Convention on Human Rights (ECHR) consistent with this proposal, although, as many have observed, one result has been that European states have outsourced migration controls to third states that are not bound by ECHR obligations. The second part would require going beyond what states have thus far agreed to do in the Refugee Convention, and would likely require securing political agreement as a precondition for implementation.

The clearest example of a doctrinal evolution toward functional, rather than strictly territorial, criteria for triggering a state's human rights obligations lies in the jurisprudence of the ECtHR, whose

---

[19] See Thomas Gammeltoft-Hansen, 'International Refugee Law and Refugee Policy: The Case of Deterrence Policies', *Journal of Refugee Studies 27* (2014): pp. 574–595, p. 588.

decisions are binding on states party to the ECHR.[20] Yet even the ECtHR's landmark *Hirsi Jamaa* decision could not invent an international right to asylum.[21] The Grand Chamber affirmed:

> Contracting States have the right, as a matter of well-established international law and subject to their treaty obligations, including the Convention, to control the entry, residence, and expulsion of aliens.... [T]he right to political asylum is not contained in either the Convention or its Protocols.[22]

That said, Article 3 of the Convention does "impl[y] an obligation not to expel" an individual to a country where there are substantial grounds to believe the person would face a real risk of being subjected to torture or to inhuman or degrading treatment or punishment (in this case, in the form of repatriation to Somalia and Eritrea).[23] In addition, Article 4 of Protocol 4 to the ECHR prohibits the collective expulsion of aliens. In the ECtHR's view:

> [Although] the notion of expulsion is principally territorial ... the special nature of the maritime environment cannot justify an area outside the law where individuals are covered by no legal system affording them enjoyment of the rights and guarantees protected by the Convention which the States have undertaken to secure to everyone within their jurisdiction.[24]

The ECtHR thus concluded in the *Hirsi Jamaa* case that Italy could not avoid its obligations under the ECHR by using Italian ships to intercept migrants at sea.

Shachar contrasts the ECtHR's approach to defining the scope of a state's obligations under the ECHR with that of the US Supreme Court in *Sale v. Haitian Centers Council*, which interpreted the legal obligations differently (p. 78). In *Sale*, Harold Hongju Koh—who later served

---

[20] For a list of relevant cases, see European Court of Human Rights Press Unit, 'Factsheet: Extraterritorial Jurisdiction of States Parties to the European Convention on Human Rights', online www.echr.coe.int/Documents/FS_Extra-territorial_jurisdiction_ENG.pdf.

[21] *Hirsi v. Italy*, [GC], App No. 27765/09, Eur. Ct. H.R. (2012). Discussed pp. 77–78.

[22] *Hirsi v. Italy* (n 34), 113.

[23] Ibid.

[24] Ibid., p. 178.

as Legal Adviser to the US Department of State—represented Haitians and Haitian organizations challenging an Executive Order directing the Coast Guard to intercept vessels outside the territorial sea of the United States that were transporting passengers illegally from Haiti to the United States, and to return those passengers to Haiti without first determining whether they qualified as refugees under the Immigration and Nationality Act (INA) or the Convention on Refugees.[25] Justice Stevens wrote the majority opinion, which found that neither the domestic statute nor the international treaty limited the President's authority to issue such an order because "[t]he INA offers . . . statutory protections only to aliens who reside in or have arrived at the border of the United States."[26] The majority concluded that neither the INA's provisions nor the Refugee Convention's *non-refoulement* obligation were "intended to have extraterritorial effect," notwithstanding "the moral weight of th[e] argument" to the contrary.[27]

Justice Stevens's opinion emphasized the voluntarist nature of treaty undertakings and the risk of a purposive interpretation in exceeding the parties' explicit commitments:

> The drafters of the Convention and the parties to the Protocol—like the drafters of [INA] § 243(h)—may not have contemplated that any nation would gather fleeing refugees and return them to the one country they had desperately sought to escape; such actions may even violate the spirit of Article 33; but a treaty cannot impose uncontemplated extraterritorial obligations on those who ratify it through no more than its general humanitarian intent.[28]

In addition to making a point about treaty interpretation, this passage encapsulates a broader concern about judicial interpretations outpacing political agreement. On the one hand, particularly in the context of individual and human rights, we rely on courts as a backstop for political actions that abrogate protections afforded by fundamental laws.

---

[25] *Sale v. Haitian Centers Council,* 509 U.S. 155, 155–208 (1993).
[26] Ibid., p. 160.
[27] Ibid., p. 179.
[28] Ibid., p. 183.

On the other hand, as the backlash against the ECtHR illustrates, the legitimacy and authority of courts, and the stability of the legal systems in which they operate, can depend on the exercise of a sufficient degree of judicial restraint.

Lord Bingham of Cornhill echoed this sentiment in his opinion for the UK House of Lords in *R. v. Immigration Officer at Prague Airport ex parte European Roma Rights Centre*: "However generous and purposive its approach to interpretation, the court's task remains one of interpreting the written document to which the contracting states have committed themselves."[29] In that case, and perhaps anticipating Shachar's critique of duplicitousness, Lord Bingham emphasized that "there is no want of good faith if a state interprets a treaty as meaning what it says and declines to do anything significantly greater than or different from what it agreed to do."[30] This meant declining to interpret the term "refugee" as including Czech nationals of Roma origin who were denied visas to enter the United Kingdom by UK immigration officers temporarily stationed at Prague Airport. Although the situation of visa denial is, on the face of it, quite different from maritime interdiction, the arguments in the *Prague Airport* case illustrate one possible version of Shachar's proposal to "relax[] the fixation on territorial access as a precondition for securing refuge" (p. 75). In rejecting this proposal as going beyond the requirements of existing law, Lord Bingham quoted Dr Nehemiah Robinson, director of the Institute of Jewish Affairs of the World Jewish Congress, who wrote at the time the Refugee Convention was drafted that "Article 33 concerns refugees who have gained entry into the territory of a Contracting State, legally or illegally . . . [I]f a refugee has succeeded in eluding the frontier guards, he [*sic*] is safe; if not, it is his hard luck."[31] One

---

[29] *Regina v. Immigration Officer at Prague Airport and Another Ex parte European Roma Rights Centre and Others* [2004] UKHL 55, [2005] 2 AC 1 [18]. Quoting *Brown v. Stott* [2003] 1 AC 681, 703 (indicating that "caution is needed 'if the risk is to be averted that the contracting parties may, by judicial interpretation, become bound by obligations which they did not expressly accept and might not have been willing to accept'").

[30] Ibid., p. 19.

[31] *Regina v. Immigration Officer at Prague Airport and Another Ex parte European Roma Rights Centre and Others* [2004] UKHL 55, [2005] 2 AC 1 [17]. Quoting Nehemiah

might disagree vehemently with this distinction and find it unjust or arbitrary, but one cannot simply wish it away.

This is not to say that one cannot interpret the Refugee Convention's *non-refoulement* obligation as applying extraterritorially, at least in certain circumstances. Notably, the Office of the UNHCR followed the Human Rights Committee's approach to the interpretation and application of the International Covenant on Civil and Political Rights (ICCPR)[32] and concluded:

> In determining whether a State's human rights obligations with respect to a particular person are engaged, the decisive criterion is not whether that person is on the State's national territory, or within a territory which is *de jure* under the sovereign control of the State, but rather whether or not he or she is subject to that State's effective authority and control.[33]

As indicated above, Shachar embraces this approach as an antidote to states' attempts—through strategies such as interdiction on the high seas and screening at foreign airports—to avoid incurring legal obligations toward refugees by deploying the coercive power of the state to prevent refugees from reaching the state's geographic border. Yet the UNHCR has espoused this more expansive approach for over a decade without persuading national courts to embrace it or legislatures to adopt it.

Regional human rights bodies have been more amenable to embracing purposive approaches; indeed, Lord Bingham endorsed the reasoning of the Inter-American Commission of Human Rights, which found that the United States had breached both the Inter-American Declaration of the

---

Robinson, *Convention Relating to the Status of Refugees: Its History, Contents and Interpretation: A Commentary* (New York City: Institute of Jewish Affairs, 1953).

[32] United Nations High Commissioner for Refugees, Advisory Opinion on the Extraterritorial Application of Non-Refoulement Obligations under the 1951 Convention Relating to the Status of Refugees and Its 1967 Protocol, January 26, 2007 (United Nations), p. 36. Quoting United Nations Human Rights Committee, *General Comment No. 31 on the Nature of the General Legal Obligations on States Parties to the Covenant* (U.N. Doc. CCPR/C/21/Rev.1/Add.13, 26 May, 2004), para. 10.

[33] Ibid., p. 35.

Rights and Duties of Man and the Refugee Convention in its treatment of Haitians who were—unlike the Czech Roma—"certainly outside Haiti, their country of nationality."[34] In Lord Bingham's assessment:

> There would appear to be general acceptance of the principle that a person who leaves the state of his nationality and applies to the authorities of another state for asylum, whether at the frontier of the second state or from within it, should not be rejected or returned to the first state without appropriate enquiry into the persecution of which he claims to have a well-founded fear. But that principle, even if one of customary international law, cannot avail the appellants, who have not left the Czech Republic nor presented themselves, save in a highly metaphorical sense, at the frontier of the United Kingdom.[35]

Lord Bingham reasoned that "the appellants' position differs by an order of magnitude from that of the Haitians, whose plight was considered in *Sale*" because "[t]he appellants were at all times free to travel to another country, or to travel to [the United Kingdom] otherwise than by air from Prague."[36] In his view, the appellants' encounter with UK authorities at Prague Airport could not be held to create legal obligations on the United Kingdom precisely because states have refused to accede to a regime for refugee protection triggered by anything short of presentation at the *physical* (rather than the "metaphorical") frontier.

What, then, lies in the way of Shachar's proposal to realign the legal frontier of protection with the "metaphorical" frontier of the encounter between an individual and the destination state's authorities or proxies, wherever that encounter takes place? As Shachar notes, the United States officially took the contrary position in 2007, rejecting the UNHCR's conclusion that the *non-refoulement* obligation in the 1951

---

[34] *Regina v. Immigration Officer at Prague Airport and Another Ex parte European Roma Rights Centre and Others* [2004] UKHL 55, [2005] 2 AC 1 [21] (Lord Bingham). Citing *The Haitian Centre for Human Rights et al. v. United States*, Case 10.675, Report No. 51/96, Inter-Am. C. H.R. (March 13, 1997), paras. 156–158 and 171.

[35] Ibid., p. 26 (Lord Bingham). The House of Lords did, however, find that the Prague operation violated the domestic and international prohibitions on discrimination.

[36] Ibid., p. 21 (Lord Bingham).

Convention and 1967 Protocol applies extraterritorially (p. 65, n 165). In his capacity as State Department Legal Adviser, Harold Koh subsequently prepared two legal memos endorsing the extraterritorial application of the ICCPR[37] and the *non-refoulement* obligation in Article 3 of the Convention Against Torture,[38] yet neither of these analyses was officially adopted by the US Government. Although more expansive interpretations of states' legal obligations have been endorsed by scholars and some regional and international bodies,[39] destination states themselves—including, by and large, their domestic judiciaries—have not followed suit. As Lord Hope of Craighead reasoned in the *Prague Airport* case, the Refugee Convention "does not require the state to abstain from controlling the movements of people outside its borders who wish to travel to it in order to claim asylum. It lacks any provisions designed to meet the additional burdens which would follow if a prohibition to that effect had been agreed to."[40] Absent an enlarged and more protective treaty regime, those seeking protection must argue that they are entitled to such protection under existing agreements. The conceptual and doctrinal tools for making such arguments have existed for quite some time; the challenge lies in persuading the relevant decision-makers to adopt them.

[37] Harold Hongju Koh, United States Department of State, Office of the Legal Adviser, Memorandum on the Geographic Scope of the International Covenant on Civil and Political Rights, October 19, 2010, online www.justsecurity.org/wp-content/uploads/2014/03/state-department-iccpr-memo.pdf.

[38] Harold Hongju Koh, United States Department of State, Office of the Legal Adviser, Memorandum Opinion on the Geographic Scope of the Convention against Torture and Its Application in Situations of Armed Conflict, January 21, 2013, online www.justsecurity.org/wp-content/uploads/2014/03/state-department-cat-memo.pdf.

[39] See, for example, Juan Méndez, United Nations Commission on Human Rights, Office of the High Commissioner, *Report of the Special Rapporteur on Torture and Other Cruel, Inhuman or Degrading Treatment or Punishment* (U.N. Doc. A/HRC/37/50, February 26, 2018), p. 53 (Advance Unedited Version) (emphasizing that "the principle of non-refoulement applies at all times, even when States operate or hold individuals extraterritorially, including on the high seas" and that it prohibits "rejections at the frontier" in the form of pushbacks or border closures because such measures "aim to exercise effective control over the physical movement of migrants" and therefore "bring affected migrants within the jurisdiction of the operating State for the purposes of the prohibition of refoulement").

[40] *Regina v. Immigration Officer at Prague Airport and Another Ex parte European Roma Rights Centre and Others* [2004] UKHL 55, [2005] 2 AC 1 [64] (Lord Hope).

Advocacy versus governance models
of transnational migration

When Shachar looks at the commitments states have already made toward vulnerable migrants, she sees a different picture from the one destination states purport to see. In her view, destination states "are proving endlessly enterprising in trying to 'release' themselves from the domestic, regional, and international legal protection obligations they have undertaken, *without* formally withdrawing from them" (p. 72). As explored above, she criticizes states for "attempt[ing] to skirt responsibility in a global system whereby the standard interpretation of access to protection is tied to a fixed interpretation of territoriality" (p. 59). Yet, the global legal system is, by and large, defined by the undertakings and understandings of *states*. To be sure, aspirational texts can, over time, become embedded in collective understandings and assume the status of binding commitments, just as expansive interpretations of existing commitments can, if accepted by states, prevail over narrower constructions. But, if anything, the current rise of "populist nationalism" in many destination states and the deployment of immigrant-threat narratives make such a process appear less, not more, likely to occur.[41] It might well be true that, as Shachar emphasizes, "international cooperation is possible" (p. 87). However, the ideological benefits associated with accepting refugees from Communist countries during the Cold War, for example, no longer exist in the post-Cold War era. The task is to identify other incentives that can be deployed to motivate countries to more evenly share the burdens associated with the transnational movement of people, and to address the underlying causes of displacement.[42]

---

[41] As Ralph Wilde notes, "[o]bjections to *non-refoulement* and extraterritorial applicability have to be understood, in part, as objections to the legal protection of rights for foreigners, especially given the xenophobic turn commentators have identified and are identifying for the period corresponding to that under present analysis, where *non-entrée* policies, extraterritorial migration-policy activities, and the backlash against human rights protection, have taken place." Ralph Wilde, 'The Unintended Consequences of Expanding Migrant Rights Protections', *American Journal of International Law Unbound 111* (2018): pp. 487–491, p. 490.

[42] This insight has motivated the rise of "global migration law" as a new field of scholarly inquiry, motivated by a recognition that "international migration law needs to be

In considering these broader questions, Shachar "beg[s] to differ" with Hannah Arendt's assessment that the problem of refugees is one of "political organization" rather than one of space (p. 70). Shachar argues that "the challenges posed by current migration flows encompass *both* our notions of space *and* political organization, and, as a result, any new answers will require addressing these combined factors in tandem." (p. 70). By way of example, she suggests thinking in "a more out-of-the-box fashion" about "the allotment of designated parcels of land for 'refugee nations' to rebuild their lost homes and political autonomy" (p. 88, n 209). Yet it is unclear what would lead us to expect a "refugee nation"—were an accessible and habitable parcel of land fortuitously available for resettlement—to avoid replicating the very policies of exclusion and *non-entrée* that current states exhibit.

It is worth considering Arendt's reflections in context. As Shachar notes, Arendt observed:

> What is unprecedented is not the loss of a home but the impossibility of finding a new one. Suddenly, there was no place on earth where migrants could go without the severest restrictions, no country where they would be assimilated, no territory where they could find a new community of their own. This, moreover, had next to nothing to do with any material problem of overpopulation; it was a problem not of space but of political organization.[43]

Arendt posited that the true "calamity of the rightless" was that "they no longer belong to any community whatsoever."[44] "Space" (a term she used quite literally to mean overpopulation) was, and is, not the problem preventing destination states from incorporating displaced persons into their respective political communities. Rather, as Arendt correctly identified, the problem was, and is, one of "political organization": the fact

radically redesigned." See Jaya Ramji-Nogales and Peter J. Spiro, 'Introduction to Symposium on Framing Global Migration Law', *American Journal of International Law Unbound 111* (2017): pp. 1–2, p. 1.

[43] Hannah Arendt, *The Origins of Totalitarianism*, 3rd edition (San Diego: Harcourt Brace, 1979), pp. 293–294.

[44] Ibid., p. 295.

that destination states remain, as a general matter, unwilling to absorb large migrant populations.[45] The United Nations has rightly made migration a top priority, but the prospects of a new framework for sharing responsibility for human security across borders—particularly absent the moral and political leadership of destination states—remain uncertain at best.[46]

Conclusions

Shachar recognizes that solutions to the problems she describes will require "daring political leadership, which is currently in short supply" (p. 90) and that "[a]ny sustainable solution or comprehensive response to migration pressures in an unequal world requires a wide-ranging approach that will facilitate development measures, expansion or addition of new definitions of people in need of protection, and the opening up of new legal channels of migration and mobility" (p. 91, n 215). We do not lack visions of what these solutions could look like; what we lack are effective strategies to combat the political mobilization of xenophobia, and programs to alleviate the deep and growing inequality within and between societies that drives destination states to implement restrictive measures to begin with. Rather than spending too much time decrying destination states as hypocritical, we should focus our attention on identifying and addressing the political pressures that produce narrow interpretations of existing legal obligations and inhibit states from undertaking new, broader commitments.

---

[45] As Moria Paz elaborates: "Strong states, rich with resources, may well refuse to sign on to such a law [providing refugees with a right to enter and to remain]. And leaders who do might be punished by their electorates." Moria Paz, 'The Incomplete Right to Freedom of Movement', *American Journal of International Law Unbound 111* (2018): pp. 514–518, p. 517.

[46] See Secretary General of the United Nations, United Nations General Assembly, Report of the Secretary-General: Making Migration Work for All (U.N. Doc. A/72/643, December 12, 2017).

7

The underrated premium of territorial arrival

Jakob Huber

Political theorists usually ask two kinds of questions when it comes to issues of refugees and asylum: who should be granted refugee status and which rights go along with it, on the one hand,[1] and how the burdens of refugee protection should be distributed among states,[2] on the other. Ayelet Shachar's essay, I believe, brings to the fore a third and much less frequently discussed puzzle: does it matter *from where* refugees seek protection? Shachar herself seems to be drawn to a negative conclusion. Questioning why the most needy would have to first get somewhere in order to claim protection and potentially life-saving assistance, she offers innovative proposals that would allow us to leave behind the "overrated premium" of territorial arrival (p. 71).

In this response, I want to explore whether we may not have principled reasons also to work toward *reconstituting* the tie between humanitarian claim-making and territorial presence rather than focusing primarily on *severing* it. Drawing on Kant's conception of cosmopolitan right (*Weltbürgerrecht*), I will defend a right of safe passage—that is, a

---

[1] Matthew Lister, 'Who Are Refugees?', *Law and Philosophy* 32, no. 5 (2013): pp. 645–671; Matthew Price, *Rethinking Asylum: History, Purpose, Limits* (Cambridge: Cambridge University Press, 2009); Andrew Shacknove, 'Who Is a Refugee?' *Ethics* 95, no. 2 (1985): pp. 274–284.

[2] David Owen, 'In loco civitatis: On the Normative Basis of the Institution of Refugeehood and Responsibilities for Refugees', in Sarah Fine and Lea Ypi, eds, *Migration in Political Theory* (Oxford: Oxford University Press, 2016), pp. 269–289; Matthew Gibney, 'Refugees and Justice between States', *European Journal of Political Theory* 14, no. 4 (2015): pp. 448–463; Joseph Carens, *The Ethics of Immigration* (Oxford: Oxford University Press, 2013), pp. 192–225.

particular kind of mobility right that allows refugees to travel safely and without unreasonable obstacles through transit states to the state where they wish to seek asylum. My aim is not to repudiate the considerations that lead Shachar to prioritize extraterritorial ways of protection, nor do I want to present these two strategies as mutually exclusive. My aim is simply to add to the picture a particular kind of (agency-based) perspective from which, I believe, the option of reconstituting the possibility of territorial access turns out to be more attractive than it may initially appear.

The argument unfolds as follows. In the first section, I argue that our answer to the shifting-border phenomenon is contingent on a deeper conceptual question concerning the relation between humanitarian claim-making and territorial presence. The second section turns to a related interpretive puzzle in the context of Kant's cosmopolitan right. Against the widespread "natural law" reading (which, I argue, obscures Kant's motivation for including in it a right to roam the earth's surface) I put forward an interpretation that characterizes cosmopolitan mobility as a form of political agency. This allows me, in the third section, to defend a right of safe passage as part and expressive of a broader shift aimed at acknowledging the *choice* and the *voice* of refugees.

Humanitarian claims and territorial presence

Shachar's argument unfolds on three interrelated argumentative levels (p. 13): diagnostic, interpretive, and prescriptive. On the diagnostic level, we get a description of the concrete phenomenon—that is, the "spatial and regulatory reinvention of borders" (p. 10) many states engage in with the aim of keeping unwanted migrants out. Shachar describes a variety of measures aimed at detaching border controls from specific physical frontier locations, flexibly shifting them to whatever location best suits their goal of restricting access. A variety of classic state functions (such as regulating entry, admission, settlement or demarcating membership) thus no longer take place within a fixed and clearly delineated geopolitical space (p. 95). In some cases, the border stretches inward, allowing states to refuse to legally acknowledge physical arrival as such (for instance, through the establishment of "excision" or "expedited removal" zones). In others, borders stretch outward beyond the edge of the territory, such that migrants can be stopped already on their way to the desired destination country (for instance, through preclearance systems and foreign transportation hubs or pushing back migrant boats on the open sea).

The sole purpose of these various strategies is to prevent would-be immigrants from reaching a territory. The reason this has come to be of highest priority to states, particularly in the refugee context, is a mechanism, deeply ingrained both in international law and many domestic legal codes, that directly converts physical presence into certain substantive and procedural (humanitarian) entitlements for newcomers: most importantly, to get a fair determination whether they satisfy the relevant criteria specified by the 1951 Refugee Convention. Detaching a polity's legal boundaries from the geographic borders of its territory thus serves states to prevent those who would be entitled to claim protection from ever reaching their territory in the first place; without a specific state's soil physically underfoot, their humanitarian rights remain "abstracted and un-actionable" (p. 60).

On the second, diagnostic level, Shachar zooms in on the wider ramification of these developments for our thinking about the nexus of membership, territory, and sovereignty. Here, she highlights how the paradigm shift entailed in the shifting-border phenomenon cannot be captured by two prominent frameworks. On the one hand, the traditional Westphalian model conceptualizes states as defined by clearly delineated and jurisdictionally exclusive territories. Migration and movement are thought to be regulated precisely at the physical barriers that stand at the frontier of a country's territory (the literal black lines we draw in our maps to divide up the world) (p. 4).

On the other hand, proponents of a post-Westphalian order have long announced the "demise of states" (p. 10), arguing that supra- and transnationalism will almost necessarily rid us of borders.[3] By contrast, Shachar takes the evidence to suggest that migration controls are not vanishing but simply being reinvented. States may very well be engaged in abandoning traditional notions of bounded territoriality; unlike the reinforced physical barrier, the shifting border is no longer fixed in time and place. In so doing, however, they regain control over a crucial realm of their allegedly waning sovereign authority (p. 5).

It is the third, *prescriptive* level that will be my main concern in what follows. Observing that the various measures do not only reconceptualize the relationship between law and territory on a descriptive level but also raise a number of normative issues anew, Shachar sets out to develop innovative democratic and institutional responses. But, first, we have to ask what (if anything) is problematic about the shifting-border phenomenon; why should we even look for ways to "tame [its] sting" (p. 20)?

Shachar provides a variety of resources to answer this question. To start with, there is the simple fact that states reliably harm vulnerable people by denying them the opportunity to even seek protection (p. 6). Plausibly, this wrong is further aggravated through the very contradiction—or, to put it more bluntly, the "organized hypocrisy"[4]—states are caught in when they insist on restricting their humanitarian obligations to those who make it inside some privileged space while *simultaneously* preventing would-be claimants from ever reaching that space (p. 9). From a democratic perspective, moreover, the new tactics problematically mean that border controls increasingly take place out of sight (and hence of scrutiny) of domestic audiences, empowering new and sometimes unaccountable actors such as airline officials, coastguards, and, somewhat ironically, smugglers and traffickers (p. 59).

---

[3] Shachar observes that this diagnosis is often welcomed as being likely to have emancipatory effects—for example, that it will improve human rights protections and mobility options. This hope, however, is undermined as "the idea of de-territorialized space and action . . . has been skillfully (and arguably repressively) 'hijacked' by law-and-order agencies seeking to restrict and police mobility" (p. 62).

[4] Matthew Gibney, *The Ethics and Politics of Asylum: Liberal Democracy and the Response to Refugees* (Cambridge: Cambridge University Press, 2004), p. 229.

Hence, while it may be a matter of contention whether states are in breach of international (humanitarian) law when attempting to evade responsibility for refugees simply by preventing their arrival,[5] I agree with Shachar that there can be no doubt that they are normatively problematic at least in some respects. The question then becomes how they should be answered. How should we (as theorists, citizens, activists, but also the wider international community) counter de-territorialized exercises of political authority intended to keep people away from a jurisdiction?

Shachar's guiding intuition in answering this question is that the dramatic reconception of the relation between law and territoriality that states are engaged in requires an equally radical response. She thus suggests that we conceive of the shifting-border phenomenon as an opportunity to come up with innovative strategies that were impossible to imagine under the classic—static—view of the border. Specifically, the idea is to "borrow a page from the shifting-border book, albeit subversively" (p. 74): as the exercise of political authority (increasingly) occurs extraterritorially, so should human rights protection.

In this spirit, Shachar puts forward two concrete strategies for challenging the relevant patterns. The first is to expand the extraterritorial reach of human rights, such that they effectively follow the border. The thought is that responsibility for refugees should be attributed on the basis on an "effective control" principle rather than territorially. This would mean that instances of protection become operative upon a claimants' contact with state officials or their delegates exerting binding migration-regulation authority *whenever* and *wherever* such authority is exercised (p. 76).

Her second proposal is to relax our fixation on territorial access by relocating protection operations to where vulnerable migrants are, rather than vice versa. There is a variety of ways in which states could provide access-from-afar to opportunities that are otherwise open only to those who can afford to reach the actual border (p. 83). For instance,

5   See also Lori Nessel, 'Externalised Borders and the Invisible Refugee', *Columbia Human Rights Law Review* 40 (2009): pp. 625–699.

claims could be processed in international asylum-processing centers, refugee-protection zones or internationally proclaimed safe areas located in countries within major regions of forced-migration outflow. Alternatively, states could open their embassies and consulates to process (or at least pre-screen) asylum claims in the refugee's country of origin, directly resettling successful applicants to the relevant territory.

Notice that both of these proposed strategies—expanding the extraterritorial reach of human rights, on the one hand, and relaxing the fixation on territorial access, on the other—involve severing the tie (that is a central feature of the contemporary refugee regime) between territorial presence and humanitarian claim-making. Given that the "train of extraterritorial border control has already left the station" (p. 95), Shachar argues, we should use the opportunity to revisit the relationship between space and political responsibility as a whole rather than merely reconstituting the status quo ante.

She does concede that, additionally, "recourse to territorial arrival must remain available to those seeking safety" (p. 72) and mentions a number of ways in which such a right of "safe passage" might be institutionalised, such as the interwar Nansen passport, domestic humanitarian visas, or single-journey entry permits. Yet it strikes me that her heart is with the more innovative proposals that get rid of any touching-base requirement. And, indeed, there is plenty of reason to presume, as Shachar does, that the "premium" of territorial access is "overrated" (p. 71). She rightly points to the sense in which the shifting-border phenomenon sheds light on the essentially Darwinian nature of the global refugee regime: only those who are able to embark (often with the dubious help of smugglers or traffickers) on a dangerous, costly journey and eventually "make it" somewhere—usually not even the most vulnerable, threatened, or deprived among those in need of protection—ever get to claim the requisite rights (p. 71). It seems that what should really do the work is the harm or hardship suffered by someone rather than their ability to move to a safe haven.

In fact, Shachar's argument to this effect strikes me as so convincing that, ultimately, it is not clear to me why the two strategies should even complement each other. For at least no principled reason seems to speak in favor of investing *any* efforts to reinforce the tie between touching base and humanitarian claim-making, rather than simply doing away with it altogether. It is precisely this kind of reason that I hope to provide in my response. Drawing on Kant's conception of cosmopolitan right, I want to defend the idea that, after all, there may still be a normatively relevant difference between having your case for asylum heard *somewhere* and having your case heard *period*.

Kant on cosmopolitan mobility

My discussion of the shifting-border phenomenon led us to a more fundamental puzzle concerning the relation between humanitarian claim-making and physical presence: to what extent (if any) should it matter *from where* claims to seek protection or asylum are made? I will now go on to connect this question to an interpretive puzzle in Kant's discussion of what he calls "cosmopolitan right" (*Weltbürgerrecht*). In order to make sense of Kant's insistence to include in it a "right to visit all regions of the earth,"[6] I will highlight the way in which roaming the earth's surface is a form of exercising cosmopolitan agency for Kant. This, I hope, will allow us to make headway with regard to the predicament of the shifting border.

Kant introduces the notion of cosmopolitan right in Perpetual Peace[7] and the Doctrine of Right[8] as one of three domains of public right alongside domestic right, which deals with the institutional relations between individuals and their state, and the right of nations, concerned with peaceful interactions among states. Cosmopolitan right, then, addresses interactions *across* borders—that is, between citizens of different states or states and non-citizens.

---

[6]   Immanuel Kant, 'The Doctrine of Right', in Royal Prussian Academy of Sciences, ed., *Gesammelte Schriften* (Berlin: G. Reimer, 1910–1955), 6:353, 1900ff.
[7]   Ibid., 8:357ff.
[8]   Ibid., 6:352ff.

What has first and foremost puzzled interpreters about the pertinent (surprisingly brief) discussion is the irritatingly restrictive content of cosmopolitan right, which Kant "limits" to the "conditions of universal hospitality"[9]—that is, the right of a foreigner "not to be treated with hostility because he has arrived on the land of another." The fact that visitors are granted a right of temporary sojourn (*Besuchsrecht*) but must not stay permanently or even settle unless expressly permitted to do so by their hosts tends to disappoint, in particular, interpreters who turn to Kant with an eye on matters of refugee and asylum.[10]

I do not intend to redeem Kant in this respect by somehow bridging this gap. My more modest aim is to clarify why Kant includes a mobility aspect (however sparse) in cosmopolitan right *at all*. To this effect, I shall focus on a further issue of interpretive contention, namely the *normative grounds* of cosmopolitan right. Interpreters agree that the notion of original common possession of the earth plays a crucial justificatory role in this context. It is "by virtue of the right of possession in common of the earth's surface on which, as a sphere, they cannot disperse infinitely but must finally put up with being near one another,"[11] Kant argues, that individuals are subjects of cosmopolitan rights. There is less agreement, however, how precisely this should be understood. I would like to suggest that the recent tendency to liken Kant's notion of original common possession to that prevalent in the natural-law tradition has obscured his motivation for affirming a right to visit.

Let me explain. According to a widespread view among interpreters,[12] Kant follows natural law theorists such as Grotius, Pufendorf, or Achenwall in employing the concept of original common possession as a

[9] Immanuel Kant, 'Toward Perpetual Peace', in Royal Prussian Academy of Sciences, ed., *Gesammelte Schriften* (Berlin: G. Reimer, 1910–1955), 8:357.
[10] See, for instance, Seylab Benhabib, *The Rights of Others* (Cambridge: Cambridge University Press, 2004).
[11] Kant, 'Toward Perpetual Peace' (n 28), 8:358.
[12] See. for example, B. Sharon Byrd and Joachim Hruschka, *Kant's Doctrine of Right: A Commentary* (Cambridge: Cambridge University Press, 2010); Pauline Kleingeld, *Kant and Cosmopolitanism* (Cambridge: Cambridge University Press, 2012); Alice Pinheiro Walla, 'Common Possession of the Earth and Cosmopolitan Right', *Kant-Studien 107*, no. 1 (2016): pp. 160–178.

distributive criterion in accordance with which individuals (and states) can bring parts of the common stock of land and resources under their exclusive control. The basic idea is that the notion expresses the way in which individuals are symmetrically located with regard to things that are of value to each of them, on the one hand, but which none of them contributed to bringing about (such that they would have a special claim), on the other. While individuals are thus licensed to appropriate from the global commons, a residual "right of necessity" ensures that latecomers can equally satisfy their needs by allowing them to take from the surplus of property holders in cases of extreme and unavoidable hardship.[13]

In the case of Kant, who departs from the wider needs-based framework central to the natural-law tradition,[14] the relevant resource is the finite space constituted by the earth's spherical surface. Consequently, the idea that "originally no one had more right than another to be on a place on the earth"[15] is taken to simultaneously *justify* and *limit* unilateral acts of occupying some place or other. On the one hand, we are licensed to appropriate a piece of land and claim it as subject to our exclusive control. On the other hand, original common possession accounts for the negative externalities of unilateral appropriation for excluded third parties by granting them a compensatory entitlement. They retain a residual right "to be wherever nature or chance (apart from their will) has placed them"[16] even in a scenario where the earth's surface is completely appropriated. To cite Kant's famous example, a shipwrecked person who is swept onto the shores of a foreign land where she would find herself illegally occupying already appropriated

---

[13] See, for example, Hugo Grotius, 'The Rights of War and Peace [De Jure Belli ac Pacis]', Richard Tuck, ed., *Indianapolis: Liberty Fund*, [1625] 2005), II.2.6.1–4.

[14] Notice that considerations of need are explicitly excluded from the domain of right, which is introduced as exclusively concerned with coordinating the choices of multiple agents as they relate to one another under spatial constraints constituted by the earth's spherical surface (Kant, 'The Doctrine of Right' (n 25), 6:230). This is why Kant is concerned with occupation of space rather than appropriation of resources more generally.

[15] Kant, 'Toward Perpetual Peace' (n 28), 8:358.

[16] Ibid., 'Doctrines of Right' (n 25), 6:262.

territory must be granted temporary sojourn if refusal would lead to her "destruction."[17]

The problem with this reading is that this (residual) right to be somewhere does not include a mobility aspect—that is, an entitlement (to continue to) roam the earth's surface. For once all available space is particularized, the original "right to be in a place other than the one an individual rightly occupies disappears, and with it the right to visit that other place."[18] Once the earth's surface is fully carved up and all the land effectively particularized, our presence at some place is juridically protected only insofar as it is inadvertent and involuntary. The residual right to be *somewhere* does not entitle one to being *anywhere* other than the place one happens to occupy.

Hence, in the reading at hand it remains obscure *why* Kant puts a premium on the mobility aspect of cosmopolitan right. In order to show how the right to visit can be "derived"[19] or "lingers"[20] from original common possession, the former would have to be linked to the rationale for introducing the latter. Given that this is impossible, however, Kant's motivation for granting juridical agents (who only need *somewhere* to be in) extensive entitlements to roam the earth's surface is unclear.

Distancing Kant more radically from the natural-law tradition, I thus want to propose an alternative interpretation that illuminates *why* it matters that we get to move and interact across boundaries. The basic thought is that original common possession is not meant to serve as a distributive criterion on the basis of which the earth's surface is to be carved up. Instead, it simply functions as a visual expression of what it means to exist as an embodied moral agent, together with other such agents, within limited space. In other words, Kant employs the notion to frame the very problem of global coexistence.[21]

---

[17] Ibid., 23:173.

[18] Byrd and Hruschka, *Kant's Doctrine of Right* (n 31), p. 207.

[19] Ibid.

[20] Liesbet Vanhaute, 'Colonists, Traders, or Settlers? Kant on Fair International Trade and Legitimate Settlement', in Katrin Flikschuh and Lea Ypi, eds, *Kant and Colonialism* (Oxford: Oxford University Press, 2014), pp. 127–145, p. 129.

[21] In this, I build on a line of argument developed in my 'Theorising from the Global Standpoint: Kant and Grotius on Original Common Possession', *European Journal of Philosophy* 25, no. 2 (2017): pp. 231–249.

The relevant argument starts from the observation that, as corporeal agents, we unavoidably claim a place on earth—we simply need to be somewhere in order to act. Kant then immediately proceeds to the normative consequences of this simple fact. The finitude of the globe "unites all places on its surface, for if its surface were an unbounded plane, people could be so dispersed on it that they would not come into any community with one another, and community would not then be a necessary result of their existence on the earth."[22] The thought, I take it, is the following: given that the piece of space we take up at every particular point in time cannot be taken up by any other person, and the option of getting out of each other's way once and for all is off the table, where and how we pursue our ends necessarily impacts where and how others can do so; the earth's spherical surface entails that "the choice of one is unavoidably opposed by nature to that of another."[23] Put differently, given that we can affect and constrain each other with our choices, we stand in a distinct kind of interdependence relation—one of "possible physical interaction."[24] The pertinent kind of community is thus not one of co-owners with originally equal claims to the earth's surface conceived as some fixed quantity of land. Instead, it is a community of those whose fates are inevitably bound up with one another merely by virtue of the fact that they concurrently exist on the earth's surface.

Consequently, original common possession does not provide a *solution* to the problem of unilateral acquisition of land, a distributive principle on the basis of which we could divide up the earth's spherical surface or derive pre-political entitlements from the global commons. It is better understood as encapsulating the *task* of coming to terms with unavoidable coexistence under spatial constraints. Kant's cosmopolitan agents, that is to say, have to find a way of normatively structuring the common space they share by bringing their external exercise of freedom under a system of universal laws.[25]

---

[22] Kant, 'Doctrines of Right' (n 25), 6:262.

[23] Ibid., 6:267.

[24] Ibid., 6:352.

[25] Brian Milstein, 'Kantian Cosmopolitanism beyond "Perpetual Peace": Commercium, Critique, and the Cosmopolitan Problematic', *European Journal of Philosophy 21*, no. 1 (2012): pp. 118–143, calls this Kant's "cosmopolitan problematic."

In contrast to the natural-law reading, then, the original right to be *anywhere* does not simply collapse into a right to be just *somewhere in particular* as the earth's surface is carved up—for individuals are thought to legitimately claim a place on earth not in the sense that they get to privatize from the commons, but in the sense that they assert their standing as equals when it comes to negotiating shared terms of coexistence. Put differently, the idea of a right to be somewhere expresses the way in which individuals who concurrently exist on the earth's spherical surface are symmetrically located with regard to one another rather than with regard to external objects of their choice; it does not ascribe to them substantive natural rights but a formal reciprocal standing vis-à-vis one another. Original common possession, Kant pointedly puts it, is not "a relation to the land (as an external thing) but to other humans in so far as they are simultaneously on the same surface."[26]

Given that the earth's surface constitutes the unavoidable (spatial) condition of human social relations rather than a resource repository for purposes of needs satisfaction, it must be maintained as such *in particular* in the face of individual claims to own particular pieces of land and collective claims to exercise jurisdiction over them. For only in roaming the earth's surface with the aim of establishing cultural, intellectual, economic, or political exchange, Kant believes, can individuals learn to critically relate to one another as well as the contingent institutions, boundaries, and loyalties that separate them. In other words, face-to-face encounters can bring distant strangers "'into understanding, community, and peaceable relations with one another, even with the most distant."[27] Consequently, the right to "try to establish community with all and, to this end, to *visit* all regions of the earth"[28] constitutes a necessary condition for solving the task of transforming

---

[26] Kant, 'Preparatory Works for the Doctrine of Right', in Royal Prussian Academy of Sciences, ed., *Gesammelte Schriften* (Berlin: G. Reimer, 1910–1955), 23:323.

[27] Kant, 'Toward Perpetual Peace' (n 28), 8:368.

[28] Kant, 'Doctrines of Right' (n 25), 6:353.

the community of original common possession into a rightful community of juridical subjects.[29]

It is crucial at this point for me to emphasize that I intend to take inspiration from this framework (as I have reconstructed it in this section) only in a very specific and limited respect, which concerns the very subjects of cosmopolitan right. Rather than passive recipients of goods from the (originally) common stock (or latecomers who are owed compensation), my proposed interpretation conceives of them as active agents capable of establishing relations across borders. Kant's notion of original common possession does not only formulate unavoidable coexistence as a cosmopolitan challenge: it also characterizes agents as having the ability and shared authority to meet that challenge. That is, it empowers individuals to see themselves and each other as agents of justice who can come together as free and rational beings in order to create mutually justifiable relations.[30] It is this picture of cosmopolitan agents "on the move" that I want to take into the final section.

The case for safe passage

My aim in returning from the exegetical puzzle to the contemporary context is to spell out how Kant's attempt to put the empowering aspect of cosmopolitan mobility rights front and center can help us formulate a response to Shachar's shifting-border phenomenon. Recall that we took the latter to problematize, on a more fundamental level, the centrality of touching base in the contemporary refugee regime: to what extent (if any) should it matter normatively where claims to protection are made? With Kant, I shall now argue that we have important agency-based reasons for reasserting the tie between physical presence and humanitarian claim-making, rather than severing it.

[29] Cosmopolitan mobility as such is, of course, not sufficient, for Kant is well aware that interactions among distant strangers may be exploitative, unjust, and violent. Hence, he argues that states must at the very least bind themselves to treat visitors hospitably and bind their citizens to comport themselves hospitably abroad.
[30] Milstein, 'Kantian Cosmopolitanism' (n 44), p. 125.

The most obvious way in which a right of safe passage empowers refugees is simply by acknowledging their choice in deciding where to go and seek protection. Notice that current practice establishes responsibility for a particular refugee based on their site of first arrival.[31] A right of safe passage, by contrast, makes it up to refugees themselves where they seek asylum. In so doing, it acknowledges that they have both legitimate *general* (to do with a state's capacity and disposition to ensure robust human rights protection) and *particular* (to do with proximity, language, religion, or family ties) reasons for preferring some states over others.[32]

To say that refugees get to decide where they make use of their unique legal capacity to "activate" the protection machinery of host states by virtue of territorial arrival is not to say, of course, that their choice should be the only or indeed the decisive consideration when it comes to the question of where they ultimately receive asylum. Given that some states would be heavily favored by refugees over others, a right of safe passage would need to be combined with a secondary distributive mechanism ensuring justice among recipient states. Yet I believe we have important agency-related grounds at least to heavily weight their preferences by granting a right to pass through any state on their way to the destination where they desire to apply for asylum.

Of course, other institutional solutions may also be able to take into account refugee *choice* in some way. Hence, it is particularly important for me to highlight the way in which a right of safe passage also acknowledges their *voice*. What I mean by this is that the fact that they are physically present somewhere allows refugees to *shape, contest,* and *resist* the norms, practices, and institutions to which they are subject. First, refugees can have an impact on how we conceptualize, understand, and discuss migration. Alex Sager, for instance, criticizes the fact

---

[31] This has naturally led to a situation in which the vast majority of the global refugee population are hosted by already-struggling, resource-strapped countries in close proximity to active conflict zones (p. 70).

[32] David Owen, 'Refugees and Responsibilities of Justice', *Global Justice: Theory, Practice, Rhetoric 11* (2018): pp 23–44, p. 27.

that refugees are rarely invited to participate in shaping the rhetoric and categories that we use to make sense of their lives.[33] Our thinking should reflect their understanding and experience not just as a matter of sound policy but ultimately of epistemic justice.

Sager focuses, in particular, on the language of a refugee "crisis," which has become the default category for understanding the movement of large numbers of migrants, primarily since 2015. On his view, this notion contributes to the dehumanization of migrants by reducing them to "flows" rather than agents responding to adversity. At the very least, Sager argues, a category such as that of a refugee crisis should not be imposed by international bodies, states, or humanitarian organizations but be developed in consultation with those forced to move. Allowing them to be physically present where the relevant discourses take place will at least increase the likelihood that refugees get to have a say or impact on how we represent them to ourselves and in policymaking.

Second, refugees with a right of safe passage are in a better position to actively contest the principles, institutions, and practices of global refugee governance to which they are subject. Here, I am picking up on David Owen's distinctly political conception of cosmopolitan mobility rights, which is built upon the assumption that individuals must be able to effectively shape and contest an exercise of political power over them for it to be legitimate.[34] Given that the global refugee regime has such a profound effect on their lives, he concludes, refugees should be given a say in it. Most importantly, they should be able to confront the relevant agents and institutions at the very sites where they exercise power: refugees must be able to demonstrate their dissent by assembling, protesting, and campaigning on the ground. By virtue of being physically present where the pertinent laws, policies, and decisions are made, they

[33] Alex Sager, 'The Uses and Abuses of "Migrant Cirisis"', in Theodoros Fouskas, ed., *Immigrants and Refugees in Times of Crisis* (European Public Law Organization, forthcoming).

[34] Along these lines, Owen ('Human Rights, Refugees and Freedom of Movement', *Journal for Human Rights/Zeitschrift für Menschenrechte* 8, no. 2 (2014): pp. 50–65, p. 62) presents internal freedom of movement as a membership right intended to "[block] those forms of public and private domination that may consist in, operate through, or take advantage of, state-based constraints on freedom of internal movement."

can "seek support, tell their story, build coalitions with other groups and generally engage in the forms of political activity required for an effective power to shape and contest that rule to which they are subject."[35]

Importantly, it also becomes much more difficult for the local public to turn a blind eye to the living conditions of refugees and the way they are dealt with, simply because they are *no longer invisible*. For what happens on our doorstep and to people who live among us is bound to be subject to a very different level of scrutiny. The domestic population is much more likely to register maltreatment, speak out against it, and feel solidarity with the victims. Experience shows that the danger in particular with extraterritorial models of protecting refugees or even processing their claims is precisely that they easily become centers of unaccountable power where states or international administrations (qua their formal and informal agents) act free from scrutiny of the public, including human rights groups and refugee advocates. At worst, refugee camps and international protection zones turn into "global slums"[36] or "little Guantanamos,"[37] located conveniently beyond the sight of Western publics.

Finally, a right of safe passage allows refugees to *resist* specific policies and decisions concerning their asylum status. A number of authors have recently suggested that would-be immigrants are permitted to resist or at least disobey the enforcement of immigration laws and decisions that are unjust[38] or illegitimate.[39] For instance, they may circumvent (the threat of) deportation by evasion, deception, and violent

---

[35] Ibid., p. 63.
[36] A notion used by Christoph Möllers in response to Ayelet Shachar at a conference on 'Global Constitutionalism and Critical Theory' in Berlin, December 2015.
[37] Matthew J. Gibney, 'A Thousand Little Guantanamos', in Kate E. Tunstall, ed., *Displacement, Asylum, Migration: The Oxford Amnesty Lectures 2004* (Oxford: Oxford University Press. 2006), pp. 139–175, p. 152.
[38] Javier Hidalgo, 'Resistance to Unjust Immigration Restriction', *Journal of Political Philosophy 23*, no. 4 (2015): pp. 450–470; Luis Cabrera, *The Practice of Global Citizenship* (Cambridge: Cambridge University Press, 2010), pp. 131–153.
[39] Caleb Yong, 'Justifying Resistance to Immigration Law: The Case of Mere Noncompliance', *Canadian Journal of Law and Jurisprudence 31* (2018): pp. 459–481. On his view, the presumptive legitimacy of immigration laws is defeated only if they are *egregiously* unjust.

resistance. Insofar as we take activities of this kind to be permissible under *any* circumstances, their feasibility presupposes physical presence. Unless refugees get to enter a state's jurisdiction, they cannot resist (or being supported in resisting) being deported from it.

I believe that these considerations nicely reverberate with Shachar's own concern with the new "space for democratic resistance and contestation" that the shifting border has also created by "stretching the boundaries of the political, both above and below the nation-state level" (pp. 72, 94). She observes how, around the world, local populations—from civil society activists to advocacy groups and institutions such as universities, local authorities, and churches—support migrants (who often remain invisible and voiceless)—for instance, by mobilizing protests, filing law suits, planning sit-ins, accompanying irregular migrants to their deportation hearings, offering shelter, food, legal aid, and medical care in houses of worship, or (as is currently the case across the United States) providing "sanctuary" in cities, campuses, and workplaces (p. 94). A right of safe passage would allow such acts of solidarity to be performed not just on behalf of refugees but jointly with them. Precisely when what we are after is "crafting participatory and contestatory political responses to, as well as legal remedies for, today's new paradoxes of border control" (p. 15), reasserting the tie between humanitarian claim-making and territorial presence may turn out to be a more attractive strategy than it initially appears.

Admittedly, I am trying to carve a narrow conceptual path when it comes to the *voice* aspect. For while the right of safe passage I have in mind would go beyond a mere right to "pass-through,"[40] it still conceptualizes refugees as transients without (formal) rights to participate politically or even become a full member of the host state. The thought, then, is that territorial presence alone has ramifications on a more

---

[40] Owen, 'Human Rights' (n 53), p. 17, who borrows the term from Adam Hosein, 'Immigration and Freedom of Movement', *Ethics & Global Politics* 6, no. 1 (2013): pp. 25–37. In contrast to what they advocate, the right I have in mind would entitle refugees to "hospitable" treatment in the form of fundamental protections and basic needs fulfillment for the duration of their journey.

informal level of political agency: namely, both with regard to citizens' conception of (and attitude toward) refugees and, relatedly, the latter's mediate involvement in political processes and discourses.

Conclusion

Let me emphasize again that my intention was not to pitch my case for a right of safe passage *against* Shachar's proposal to radically rethink the relation between space and political responsibility. She is correct to observe, I believe, that the shifting-border phenomenon leaves us normatively disoriented to some extent, "like travellers navigating a new terrain with the help of old maps" (p. 6). In this spirit, my tentative suggestion is simply that the agency-based considerations that I have highlighted may help to guide us as we venture into unchartered normative territory.

That said, let me also emphasize that my specific argument here may have ramifications that go way beyond the refugee context. For making the case for conceiving of mobility as effectively a form of agency invites us to reframe migration as a whole and conceive of it less as a problem than as a regular part of the human condition. I do certainly welcome this implication and so (I dare to speculate) would Ayelet Shachar.

Part III

Reply

8

The multiple sites of justice: a reply

Ayelet Shachar

The border—its regulation, legitimacy, materiality—has become one of the most salient issues of our time. From Donald Trump's campaign promise to build an "impenetrable, physical, tall, powerful, beautiful southern border wall" to the erection of more than 1,000 kilometers of barbed wire and fencing (more than six times the length of the Berlin Wall when it came down in 1989) to keep uninvited migrants out of Europe, the "static" Westphalian border appears to be on the rise across the world.[1] As wretched migrants seek a haven in affluent countries, this hard boundary serves to separate "us" from "them," here from there, the fortunate heirs of membership of rich nations from those who drew the short stick in the birthright lottery.[2] The surge in border walls began before the 2015 refugee crisis and has only accelerated in its aftermath, dashing the hopes of those who had predicted the "end of history" and the imminent arrival of a borderless world.[3] These physical manifestations of sovereign brazenness and governments' desire to control human mobility, coupled with the anti-immigrant populist backlash,

[1] For comprehensive data on new border walls in Europe, see Ainoha Ruiz Benedicto and Pere Brunet, *Building Walls: Fear and Securitization in the European Union* (Barcelona: Centre Delàs d'Estudis per la Pau, 2018). On development in North America, see, for example, Elizabeth Vallet, ed., *Borders, Fences and Walls: State of Insecurity?* (Abingdon: Routledge, 2014); Roy Koslowski, 'Addressing Side-Effects of Increasing Border Security Cooperation: A Global Perspective', in Ferrucio Pastore, ed., *Beyond the Migration and Asylum Crisis: Options and Lessons for Europe* 108 (Milan: Aspen Institute Italia, 2017).
[2] Ayelet Shachar, *The Birthright Lottery: Citizenship and Global Inequality* (Cambridge, MA: Harvard University Press, 2009).
[3] See, for example, Francis Fukuyama, *The End of History and the Last Man* (New York: Free Press, 1992).

are vitally in need of study. But the focus on the *visible*, fortified border may distract our gaze from an equally significant development: the surge of *invisible* borders—borders that rely on sophisticated legal techniques to detach migration-control functions from a fixed territorial location, creating a new framework that I have called the *shifting border*.

My account of this phenomenon is closely linked to my interest in the spatial dimensions of public law and in re-examining the conditions for the legitimate exercise of sovereign authority.[4] Unlike the traditional border—a reinforced physical barrier—the shifting border is not fixed in place; it is comprised of legal portals rather than fences, walls, and gates. As such, it tests our understanding of the relationship between state order and territorial control in an increasingly globalized world. The shifting border also calls attention to the global stratification of mobility: well-off countries make it more and more difficult for unin-vited and unauthorized migrants to enter, while wealthy migrants wishing to deposit their mobile capital in these very same countries find fewer and fewer restrictions to fast-tracked admission.[5] Pressed by current localist, nativist, and nationalist backlash on one side and by the still influential globalist narrative on the other, states are constantly transforming the locus and focus of migration control, freeing it from "immobile" frontier locations and facilitating ever more innovative techniques of tampering with time and space in order to selectively open *and* close the gates of admission, privileging the few and forbid-ding the many.

Moving beyond the recent surge of walls and barbed wire and the increasingly "weaponized" use of geography—including deserts, moun-tain peaks, rivers, remote islands, rough seas—to refuse access, I have sought to identify and analyze the more intricate, invisible, and ever

[4] The spatial dimensions of public law are explored in detail in Ran Hirschl and Ayelet Shachar, 'Foreword: Spatial Statism', *International Journal of Constitutional Law 17* (2019): pp. 1–52.
[5] For further discussion, see Ayelet Shachar, 'The Marketization of Citizenship in an Age of Restrictionism', *Ethics & International Affairs 32* (2018): pp. 3–13.

mobile tracks of the shifting border.[6] The framework of analysis I have developed requires us to pierce the black lines on the map, reified and naturalized as these lines may be, in order to expand the horizons of current debates. The shifting-border framework reveals the reach and grip of law and legal institutions engaged in *expanding* the domain of state power in migration control. To preserve their control in a world that is both interdependent and turbulent, states are proactively creating new legal spaces of exclusion and engaging in ever closer cooperation with trusted partners, including other nations, corporate service providers, and supranational and international organizations.[7]

For decades, some of the most creative geologists and paleomagnetists have attempted to imagine how the land mass of the earth might have looked hundreds of millions of years ago, before the present-day continents drifted apart, when they were connected in a supercontinent, known as Pangea. These thinkers literally reconfigured the earth's geography in order to account for new discoveries about the world's formation. Like these imaginative scientists, today's explorers of law, politics, and human geography—academics and migrants alike—are encountering new and increasingly sophisticated methods of re-bordering and imagining novel forms of resistance. They too must respond to the world they observe and in part create by marking out new visions of mobility and claim-making with their pens and their footpaths. *The Shifting Border*, a problem-driven exercise in theory building, offers one such vision.

My account relies on extensive real-world evidence to develop a new conceptual framework that allows us to identify how and why governments proactively engage in shifting-border policies, creating fluid and liminal spaces, free from traditional constraints of political accountability and judicial scrutiny. The shifting border extends the long arm

---

[6]   I am grateful to Derek Denman and the participants in the 'Border Landscapes: Material Boundaries of Stasis and Mobility' workshop for helpful discussions about the use of geophysical barriers as constraints on human mobility.

[7]   This tendency to collaborate is particularly pronounced among nations with relatively well-developed "state capacity," as defined by political scientists. These developments are discussed in detail in Hirschl and Shachar, 'Spatial Statism' (n 4).

of the state to regulate mobility half a world away while also stretching deep into the interior. As this power is almost boundless in its conceptual framing and spatial manifestation, it defies the familiar dichotomous categorization of a "soft" inside (where rights are extensively protected) and a "hard" outside (where protections typically do not apply), blurring the extraterritorial and the local, challenging and destabilizing the open-versus-closed border categorization that has become a core organizing tenet in philosophical debates. No longer fixed in place and time, *The Shifting Border* offers a hard look at this striking—yet little understood—nascent landscape, where borders, like people, have the capacity to move.

I am deeply grateful to my interlocutors for their insightful, sharp, and generous engagement with my work. I also wish to express my gratitude to Peter Niesen and David Owen for offering an intellectual home to this interdisciplinary multilogue under the auspices of the Critical Powers series. In the limited space allotted to my response, I cannot do justice to the many excellent points raised in the commentaries. There is much that I agree with in the responses, and it would have been a pleasure to simply sing the praises of these essays. I will try to do so wherever possible in the discussion that follows. However, the bulk of my response will be devoted to three core issues that I believe are important to address. For the sake of analytical clarity and succinctness, I will label these as: 1) shapeshifting migration control and illiberal leeway; 2) legal institutions, social change, and constraints on governmental power; and 3) the emancipatory power of ideas and political agency.

Shapeshifting migration control and illiberal leeway

The essays by Steffen Mau and Noora Lori bring to the fore a startling puzzle raised by the shifting border, connecting it to long-standing debates about state theory: is it an indication of something deeper and darker than simply a new method of governing migration control, surveillance, and territoriality? Might this shift indicate a "change [in] the character of the regime itself?" (p. 129). There are several different ways in which we can unpack this vitally important idea. For example, liberal regimes may drift into illiberal practices, causing a widening gap between their stated values and actual policies. All the commentators seem to accept this characterization of the shifting border. As Mau observes, "The shifting border could be understood as a reaction [by liberal states] to the challenge of doing justice to their own liberal ethics and related obligations, on the one hand, and, on the other, the interest of limiting and controlling migration and mobility" (p. 157). This tension between respecting rights and tightening migration controls is indeed central to the invention of the shifting border and the attempt to create special zones of heightened regulation, utilizing "legally under-determined control locations . . . [in] an attempt to create illiberal lee-way" (p. 157). This last point is crucial. It captures both the positive and the normative concerns that I have raised in *The Shifting Border*, and echoes the commitment of many activists and lawyers engaged in the struggle to bring the shapeshifting "monster" (to draw on Sarah Fine's brilliant imagery) under some degree of meaningful constraint.[8]

We can take the logic of the argument a step further by examining whether and, if so, under what circumstances the "very mechanisms of effective migration enforcement . . . [coupled with] a deepening surveillance state" (p. 138) come to generate the "conditions for a descent into authoritarianism" (p. 138). Lori investigates this trajectory by examining the laws and policies governing immigration in the Gulf states in general, and the United Arab Emirates in particular—a topic she has explored with nuance and depth in her comparative work on temporary migration schemes and the development of national identification programs.[9] She underscores how "the specter of migration as a national

---

[8] The scholarship of authors such as Cathryn Costello, Thomas Gammeltoft-Hansen, Itamar Mann, and Violeta Moreno-Lax, among others, is representative of this strand of literature. Many of these lawyers are also engaged in human rights litigation focusing on restraining the territorially unmoored shifting-border policies adopted by states and their delegates, private or public.

[9] For a comprehensive discussion beyond this volume, see Noora Anwar Lori, *Offshore Citizens: Permanent Temporary Status in the Gulf* (Cambridge: Cambridge University Press, 2019).

security threat played a key role in the emergence and consolidation of autocratic rule in the UAE" (p. 137). It is comforting for many to *assume* that liberal states are shielded from such processes. Lori, by contrast, challenges us to critically evaluate this taken-for-granted promise. She asks whether liberal and democratic states too could gradually "backslide" toward more autocratic patterns of executing their sovereign authority as they become "more and more 'effective' at migration enforcement" (p. 138). Even if such a correlation can be observed, it still does not tell us in which direction the arrow of causality moves. In other words, did the country first see greater autocratic tendencies and then adopt harsher and more restrictive immigration policies, or vice versa? These are fascinating questions, ripe for future research and further investigation.

The political and institutional effects of the shapeshifting border include the risks it creates not only in relation to "stretching out" policies but also "bleeding in" legal inventions that create constitution-lite zones in which some or all residents are deprived of their human rights and constitutional liberties. Thinking about these effects allows us to draw a connection between the set of concerns raised in *The Shifting Border* and a budding literature exploring patterns of democratic backsliding and the "coming demise of liberal constitutionalism."[10] In the world around us, these questions are anything but merely academic. In the current zeitgeist of "us first" populist nationalism, growing political distrust, and renewed calls to "take back control," we can expect an increasing number of countries to adopt and invent their own variants of the shifting border, making safety and mobility even more elusive for those not born as members, those deemed to not fully belong to the nation, or those lacking the financial might to buy their way in. A flurry of new laws, decrees, and executive orders not only blend together border control with tighter requirements for membership but also reveal the blatant

---

[10] This phrase is drawn from an article by Tom Ginsburg, Aziz Z. Huq, and Mila Versteeg, 'The Coming Demise of Liberal Constitutionalism?', *The University of Chicago Law Review* 85 (2018): pp. 239–255. See also Mark A. Graber, Sanford Levinson, and Mark Tushnet, eds, *Constitutional Democracy in Crisis?* (New York: Oxford University Press, 2018).

bypassing of standard democratic decision-making and growing con-
centration of power in the hands of the executive. While not, at present,
amounting to authoritarianism or autocracy, these heavy-handed policies straddle the liberal/illiberal divide in countries as diverse as Italy,
Poland, and the United States, among many others.

Take a look at Hungary, a member state of the European Union. In
the summer of 2015, with a surge in the number of asylum seekers trying to enter the European Union through this conduit state on its
perimeter, Hungary became the first country in Europe to build a fence
to keep out uninvited migrants, many of whom hailed from Muslim-
majority countries.[11] Constructing a razor-wire barrier to seal its border
with Serbia and Croatia (both non-EU states) was only the first salvo in
a multi-pronged suite of responses. Challenging the competence of
"Brussels bureaucrats" to manage the migration crisis, Hungary's governing party embraced what Rogers Brubaker has aptly described as a
"civilizational narrative," defining the refugee crisis as an existential
threat to the foundations of Europe.[12] To quote Prime Minister Viktor
Orbán: the "spirit, civilization, culture and way of thinking [that] define
the character of European countries [is at stake]. . . . This is why we
build fences, we protect ourselves and we don't allow migrants to flood
us."[13] Beyond fighting words, the government introduced an arsenal of

[11] Notably, fear of "loss of control," the lack of a coordinated response among European
countries, and the political and policy anxieties that followed the influx of refugees and
migrants also saw the reintroduction of internal borders within Europe's free-mobility
zone, known as the Schengen area, by Austria, Germany, Slovenia, Sweden, Norway, and
Denmark, disrupting over two decades of free mobility within Europe. For the full list of
resurrected internal border walls, see member states' notifications of the temporary reintroduction of border control at internal borders pursuant to Article 25 et seq. of the
Schengen Borders Code, online https://ec.europa.eu/home-affairs/sites/homeaffairs/
files/what-we-do/policies/borders-and-visas/schengen/reintroduction-border-control/
docs/ms_notifications_-_reintroduction_of_border_control_en.pdf.

[12] Rogers Brubaker, 'The New Language of European Populism: Why "Civilization" Is
Replacing the Nation', *Foreign Affairs*, December 6, 2017. This confrontation with Brus-
sels eventually reached the Court of Justice of the European Union, where Hungry and
Slovakia lost their case against the European Council. See Joined Cases C-643/15 and
C-647/15 *Slovakia and Hungary v. Council*, September 6, 2017.

[13] Zsolt Körtvélyesi and Balázs Majtényi, 'Game of Values: The Threat of Exclusive Constitutional Identity, the EU and Hungary', *German Law Journal 18* (2017): pp. 1721–1744,
p. 1736, n 51 (citing Orbán).

new legal rules and regulations, taking swift action by drawing upon the repertoire of shifting-border techniques—and it quickly refurbished the repertoire with new inventions.

To complement its newly built border wall, the country soon established "transit zones" in which the fiction of *non-arrival* applied. According to this fiction, those who physically reached the Hungarian land border without authorization—those who somehow managed to pass through all the barriers along the dangerous routes of clandestine passage to Europe and fulfilled the demands of "territorial arrival"—are nevertheless legally deemed to have *not* arrived. This newly created transit zone—a closed-off and tightly guarded area located on the internal rim of the Hungarian border—has been aptly described as a "no-man's land."[14] In this no-man's land, officials swiftly review an applicant's asylum claim to check whether she has already filed an asylum claim in another EU country or whether the application can be summarily rejected as manifestly unfounded. The process typically takes only a few hours and may last no more than fifteen days.[15]

Here, Lori's sharp observation about the manipulation of time—in addition to space—in the service of the shifting border is spot on (p. 126). Held in a sealed-off location and facing a tightly compressed timeline between filing a claim and having it assessed by a government official, it becomes almost impossible for these (non-)arrivals to seek legal assistance or meet representatives of aid groups. In theory, rejected asylum seekers may appeal the decision against them, but, in practice, this hardly ever happens. Instead, the transit zone becomes a one-way ticket for deportation *away* from Europe. As these applicants are deemed to have never reached Hungary (and, by extension, the European Union), they are pushed back to the external side of the fence—and formally barred from re-entry. The transit zone becomes a

---

[14] Bernd Riegert, 'Could Hungary's Transit Zones for Refugees Be a Model for Germany?', *Deutsche Welle*, July 4, 2018, online www.dw.com/en/could-hungarys-transit-zones-for-refugees-be-a-model-for-germany/a-44511989.

[15] Ibid.

no-passage zone, an almost impenetrable barrier prohibiting access to Europe, even for those who "touch base."

In 2016, the Hungarian government introduced another shifting-border technique, resembling the US-style expedited-removal procedure permitting swift removal of irregular migrants, whether or not they claim asylum, if they are arrested within 5 miles (8 kilometers) of the country's territorial border. The spatial reach of this provision was later expanded to apply *nationwide*, in effect turning the whole *interior* of the country into an *external* border. With the onslaught of a border-control regime that now applied everywhere—and at all times—in the territory, the government took an additional step to blur the liberal–illiberal line. In 2018, new legislation was passed that criminalizes certain practices of immigration NGOs if they occur within the original 5-mile/8-kilometer buffer zone, effectively preventing NGOs from delivering service to asylum seekers. The Minister of Immigration was further authorized to impose restraining orders against individuals approaching the 5-mile/8-kilometer buffer zone, if, in the Minister's opinion, they engage in activities that are contrary to the national interest, frequently interpreted as intertwined with "Hungary's self-identity and its Christian culture." Here, as elsewhere, the shifting border not only dramatically extends the spatial reach of migration control, but also erodes basic protections and partakes in redrawing the boundaries of membership—initially targeting only migrants and eventually applying to everyone, citizens included, especially those deemed "different."[16]

The Hungarian example, combining a slide toward authoritarianism with ever tighter migration control, is a concrete, made-in-Europe manifestation of the never ending, always present, everywhere-and-nowhere border scenario that I have described in *The Shifting Border*, which is proving to have arguably even more predictive power than I

---

[16] We can also suspect, as Lori importantly emphasizes in her comment, that although such regulations apply across the territory, their impact is not borne equally by all residents; racialized, ethnic, religious, and visible minorities are more heavily targeted and penalized by such measures (pp. 131–132). Similar concerns are echoed in Leti Volpp's response (p. 159).

foresaw.[17] The creation of these expandable transit zones, ballooning to cover whole countries—swallowing in their path core constitutional norms and constraints on governmental authorities—is a development that is unlikely to stop. It now extends well beyond the rich countries of the global north. Take Bangladesh. One of the world's poorest and most densely populated countries, Bangladesh welcomed more than 750,000 Rohingya refugees violently expelled from Myanmar; two years on, tensions have emerged between locals and the recent arrivals, leading the Bangladeshi government to ban aid groups from assisting the refugees, just like Hungary did. The government also plans to relocate tens of thousands of Rohingya refugees to a remote, uninhabited island off the Bay of Bengal, calling it a new temporary home for them, although there are signals from top officials that the refugees will end up stranded there. The only way off the island will be to repatriate to Myanmar or to be selected for asylum by a third country. Complementing the ample attention that has been paid to the outward expansion or externalization of the border (as the European policy jargon would have it), the framework of analysis that I have offered provides a more holistic conceptual map that connects the dots and makes transparent the multidimensionality of the shifting border, including the scantly studied inward seeping that enables "illiberal leeway" to take hold *within* democratic polities.

Action without accountability or transparency is not something that we typically associate with liberal-democratic societies. Constitutionalism and human rights protections are understood primarily as *restraining* authority, as indispensable limits to governmental power. It is here that Sarah Fine's creative and powerful invocation of Thomas Hobbes's *Leviathan*, that "protean beast," becomes highly relevant, suggesting that the concerns I have raised in *The Shifting Border* do not stop at the contemporary erosion of the liberal (p. 101). Fine invites us to conceive

---

[17] Hungary is not alone. Italy has taken similar steps to criminalize NGOs and to block the disembarkation of migrants saved from drowning at sea by aid groups' rescue vessels. In the United States, volunteers with humanitarian groups at the border were put on trial for leaving out water and food for unauthorized migrants who tried to cross the deadly Arizona desert, which has claimed thousands of migrants' lives.

of the shifting border as a "Leviathan for the twenty-first century" (p. 100). The malleable spatial and temporal reach of this creature has no beginning and no end (p. 101). Its ability to transform "to suit the evolving legal and political landscape" reflects a fundamental transformation whereby "states and sovereignty are morphing into different shapes too" (p. 101). For governments caught in the bind of formally adhering to fundamental rights but determined *not* to incur the accompanying obligations when it comes to uninvited migrants and asylum seekers, the temptation to rely on the beastly—unrestrained, unregulated, uncontested—shapeshifting border is hard to overstate. This set of developments is indeed "terrifying," to use Fine's colorful language.

I want to hold onto this thought and return to it later in the discussion. For now, I wish to connect Fine's Leviathan analogy to the alarming sense of a loss of control—not only in the acrimonious political debate over immigration but also in terms of something deeper: namely, the disappearance of institutional restraints that constitute the fundamentals of the rule of law, protecting individuals from the arbitrary will of those who rule. On this reading, the shapeshifting border is both a catalyst and a symptom of a "massive shift in governance—from rule-bound to discretionary" (p. 129). As we have seen, the shifting border allows the state to tighten migration control within and beyond its territorial limits, brilliantly utilizing the manipulation of space and time to achieve its goals. We have also seen that these maneuvers are in part designed to "free up" the shifting border and its architects (including, but not limited to, regulatory agencies, senior government officials, and private contractors) from democratic checks and ordinary processes of legislation and review by other branches of government—be they courts, ombudspersons, or elected representatives. This loss of transparency and accountability erodes our basic faith in legality, the possibility of contestation, and the prevention of absolute power through the use of "law and legal arguments to explain, justify, and contest acts and policies."[18]

---

[18] Ian Hurd, 'The Empire of International Legalism', *Ethics & International Affairs* 32 (2018): pp. 266–278, p. 266.

When the legislative and judicial branches exercise only very limited review powers over the shifting border, it is difficult not to be concerned about the unlimited authority of the sovereign and the possibility of a Hobbesian executive Leviathan (or President) claiming all power of judgment and legislation. The repertoire of political thought that Fine evokes helps explain the tendency identified by Lori toward absolutism in the exercise of migration-control powers by both democratic and authoritarian governments. In the name of safety and security—the basis for the social contract—governments license themselves to escape from legal constraints. Here, the risk of a downward spiral is as vast as it terrifying, for at stake are the basic principles of separation of power and the delicate system of check and balances constraining executive authority.

While the Orbáns and Trumps of the world may be the most explicit about their intentions to shake up the liberal order, even among countries and supranational entities that are outspoken *critics* of the anti-immigrant, anti-liberal, anti-human-rights backlash we see policies that undermine the human rights and protections of migrants, showing just how quickly basic rule-of-law tenets can be eroded in the process of "regaining" control over the border. Take the European Union. In the post-2015 era, the European Union has introduced a bewildering array of policy and funding instruments, relying on a "mix of positive and negative incentives and the use of all leverages and tools" to intensify cooperation with countries of origin and transit through which uninvited and unwanted migrants arrive in Europe. Instruments known as "compacts," "statements," and "memorandums of understanding" have been signed with a plethora of non-EU countries, including a number of repressive governments known to have breached extensively the legal protections of life and liberty that the European Union's own citizens and residents enjoy.[19] Because these compacts are negotiated and

---

[19] European Commission, Communication from the Commission, the European Parliament, the European Council and the European Investment Bank on establishing a new Partnership Framework with Third Countries under the European Agenda on Migration, COM(2016) 385, June 7, 2016. For a concise overview, see Mark Akkerman, *Expanding*

signed *outside* the official rule-bound processes of legislation and trea-
ty-making, they remain shielded from democratic accountability and
public deliberation. Operating on the spectrum of legal liminality, with
no formal status, they do not require approval by the European Parliament, the most democratic among the branches of the complex EU
institutional structure. This lack of transparency and oversight has led
members of the European Parliament, the only institution of the European Union that is directly elected by EU citizens, to issue a strongly
worded resolution cautioning against this "undemocratic way of working."[20] These hard-to-classify new compacts, statements, and memoranda, created under a cloud of secrecy, are less strictly regulated than
standard instruments of international law once in operation.[21] Their
often undisclosed details manifest a retreat from formal, visible law-
making, just as the shifting border represents the turn away from
visible walls, enlisting instead invisible and mobile legal portals that
transcend time and space in the service of border control and migration management.

This growing trend of informalization allows affluent countries to
deputize poorer and less stable countries as "outpost border guards" to
conduct the work of keeping uninvited migrants out. By insulating
these instruments from review by the legislative and judicial branches,
yet another invisible wall is erected, implicating separation-of-power
principles and basic notions of transparency and accountability in law
and governance. The agreement signed between the European Union
and Turkey in 2016 to "stem the flow" exemplifies the trend. Defined by
observers as "one of the most controversial policy steps taken by the EU
in recent years," it has substantively reduced the number of refugees
entering Europe based on the premise, challenged by many, that Turkey

---

the *Fortress: The Policies, the Profiteers and the People Shaped by EU's Broder Externalisation Programme* (Amsterdam: Transnational Institute, 2018), pp. 14–15.

[20] European Parliament Resolution of April 5, 2017 on Addressing Refugees and Migrant Movements: The Role of EU External Action (2015/2342(INI)).

[21] Ramses A. Wessel, "'Soft' International Agreements in EU External Relations: Pragma- tism over Principles?', presented at the ECPR SGEU Conference, Panel Hard and Soft Law in the European Union, Paris, June 13–15, 2018, p. 1.

is a safe third country for refugees and asylum seekers.[22] When this agreement was challenged before the General Court of the European Union, the Court dismissed the complaints, reasoning that this policy instrument, formally known as the EU–Turkey Statement, was *not* subject to the Court's review because it was not an act of EU institutions but rather of member states.[23] The murky status of these apparently non-justiciable agreements affirms the concerns raised by Lori, Fine, and Mau regarding the need to closely investigate the still under-explored hazards and causal links between the shifting border of migration control and the resulting "illiberal leeway."

In their ever creative attempts to bypass domestic and international obligations to which they have committed themselves, governments have also sought additional ways to gain greater flexibility by establishing a "wide degree of discretion when it comes to migration control" (p. 114). Perhaps the most striking example of this pattern at work is the interception and forcible "push back" of refugees at sea. That states will rely on spatial barriers to mobility to escape their obligations to refugees was a specter already raised at the drafting stage of 1951 Refugee Convention. At the time, it was *European* states with "contiguous frontiers with other countries from where the stream of refugees [came]" that bore a disproportionate burden of hosting the vast post-World War II refugee population. Countries such as Australia, Canada, and the United States, on the other hand, were shielded from similar humanitarian obligations because "[t]he ocean protects the[se] countries" from the spontaneous arrival of the stream of refugees; they had no contiguous

[22] Narin Idriz, 'Taking the EU–Turkey Deal to Court?', VERFBLOG, December 20, 2017, online https://verfassungsblog.de/taking-the-eu-turkey-deal-to-court/.
[23] Ibid. See Orders of the General Court in Cases T-192/16, T-193/16 and T-257/16 NF, NG and NM v European Council; T-192/16 NF v European Council, February 28, 2017; T-193/16 *NG v. European Council*, February 28, 2017; T-257/16 *NM v. European Council*, 2017. Such "scale-jumping," distinguishing EU-court jurisdiction from member-state jurisdiction and competences, also played a key role in a recent decision focusing on humanitarian visas, Case C-638 PPU, *X and X v État Belge*, March 7, 2017. In both cases, the painstaking technical legal maneuvers adopted by the architects of the shifting border proved vital to *blocking* the substantive protection of vulnerable migrants.

frontiers with the conflict zones.[24] As historian Gilad Ben-Nun has shown in his research, it was the countries that were *remote* from Europe (such as the United States, Canada, Australia, and Venezuela), the epicenter of the post-World War II displaced-persons crisis, that advocate[d] *non-refoulement*—the principle of non-return—at the time because "they did not have to bear its demographic and social consequences."[25] It is one of history's little ironies that this empirical assumption turned out to be deeply misguided, a realization that partly explains the invention of the shifting border as a response. Those operating under the classic "static" border conception had clearly failed to predict the entrepreneurial desperation that, in collaboration with the rise of a lucrative black market for human smuggling, has allowed at least *some* refugees and other people in need of international protection to "vote with their feet"—to take action to reach certain desired destinations and to express, as Jakob Huber emphatically observes, political agency. Once it became clear that "non-contiguous" countries such as the United States would have to deal with a large influx of uninvited refugees arriving from afar, they began to devise legal practices to avert such arrival in the first place.

In her insightful commentary, Leti Volpp focuses on one famous episode of denial of protection in the early 1990s, emphasizing the ominous exercise of executive power by the US President that authorized the administration to callously block Haitian refugees en route to safety, deploying notions of extraterritoriality and spatiality to achieve this exclusionary goal. The background is as follows. In response to concerns about escalating numbers of Haitians escaping their home country following a coup d'état, the Oval Office (initially under President George H. W. Bush and later under the Clinton administration) authorized US Coast Guard cutters to interdict and directly return boatloads of Haitians who tried to flee a repressive government. Those on-board the interdicted vessels

---

[24] Gilad Ben-Nun, 'The British-Jewish Roots of Non-Refoulement and Its True Meaning for the Drafters of the 1951 Refugee Convention', *Journal of Refugee Studies 28* (2015): pp. 93–117, p. 100.
[25] Ibid.

were forcibly turned back to Haiti, where they faced the risk of "detention, abuse and death."[26]

This push-back policy was highly controversial from its inception and has been subject to extensive rebuke by refugee-law experts and international tribunals who view it as a breach of one of the most basic norms of human rights. The policy contradicts the clear and plain language of Article 33 of the 1951 Refugee Convention, which imposes a flat *prohibition* against the "return (*refouler*) [of] a refugee in any manner whatsoever to the frontiers of the territories where his life or freedom would be threatened."[27] This *non-refoulement* principle is the core principle of the post-World War II international refugee-protection system. In addition to disregarding this basic humanitarian obligation, which is incorporated into US law, the direct-return policy also marked a critical moment in modern bordering: it was one of the earliest exemplars of the shifting border, creating what has been dubbed a "floating Berlin Wall." People returned under the push-back policy were not screened for credible fear, a basic procedural protection they would have received had they managed to reach US soil. If the migrants' rights and access to remedy had followed the border as it shifted out to meet them, a process I have proposed in my lead essay, the effect would have been to deflate the "floating" Berlin Wall.

This is not what happened. Instead, in the ill-famed *Sale* decision, the US Supreme Court deferred to presidential powers in foreign affairs and migration control and a legal theory—vigorously defended by government lawyers—according to which, "as long as the Haitians were in international waters, they had no rights at all."[28] Accordingly, the

---

[26] *Sale v. Haitian Centers Council*, 509 U.S. 155 (1993), p. 208 (dissenting, Blackman, J.).

[27] Article 33, Refugee Convention. The United States is a signatory to the 1951 Refugee Convention so bears this obligation under both international and domestic law. *Non-refoulement* is considered by many to have achieved *jus cogens* status in international law, a total prohibition, a norm from which no derogation is permitted. This principle was also incorporated into US domestic law with the passage of the Refugee Act of 1980.

[28] For a captivating account of this legal struggle, see Brandt Goldstein, *Storming the Court: How a Band of Law Students Fought the President—and Won* (New York: Scribner, 2005), p. 232.

Court concluded that it could offer no judicial remedy to the refugees challenging the direct-return policy. This contentious interpretation of the *non-refoulement* obligation, which absolves a leading destination country from *any* responsibility and accountability if the denial of rights it has authorized takes place beyond its static, territorial border, is still upheld today in the United States, despite being a striking outlier among democratic nations. Former presidential advisors and national security officials who were responsible for shaping the US government's position on direct return claimed that the administration was *not* intent on breaching rights, holding that "[w]e could always do the right thing," meaning, in this context, to "allow the refugees to flee their country."[29] The crucial point, as they saw it, was to maintain a "greater degree of flexibility. It's a rare senior executive official who will surrender that flexibility."[30]

It is precisely this broad, largely unregulated government discretionary power, defined behind closed doors with little democratic accountability, which raises the deepest concerns about the corrosive effects of the shifting border. Taming and contesting the "law-free zone" thinking that informs government policies of border expansion, both outward and inward, is one of the most pressing ethical, political, and legal challenges of our times, and a key motivation for my writing this book. If the shifting border is akin to a modern Leviathan, then what can we do about it? In her magnificently creative essay, Fine identifies three possible responses: admit defeat, tame the beast, or fight back. This lucid formulation allows us to connect the debate about the shifting border to broader questions about the relationship between law and social change, and, relatedly, the power of ideas and of political agency to contest entrenched, structural power hierarchies. I address these topics in the remainder of this response. But to set the stage, we need to step back in time.

[29] Ibid., p. 293 (quoting national security official Eric Schwartz).
[30] Ibid.

Legal institutions, social change, and constraints on governmental power

In 1927, five prominent female activists petitioned the Supreme Court of Canada with a simple question: are women "persons"? In a masterfully crafted twenty-eight-page constitutional-law ruling, the Court ruled unanimously that women were *not* "persons," and were therefore ineligible to hold office in the country's upper house, the Senate.[31] The Court held that the relevant governing act, the British North America Act of 1867, did not specify whether the term "persons" included women or not. In interpreting this legal text, the judges took a narrow, restrictive approach: they explored the original meaning of the term "persons" in 1867, the year the Act was passed, and concluded that at the time it referred only to men. At the time, the common law upheld the view that "[w]omen are persons in matters of pains and penalties, but are not persons in matters of rights and privileges."[32] Ergo, the court reasoned, women were legally disqualified from public office such as the Senate of Canada.[33] In the learned opinion of the Court, the decision to exclude women from public office was hardly subject to dispute, as it merely upheld the "policy of centuries."[34]

To the suffragists who challenged the status quo, the government's legal interpretation was nothing but an "excuse for stalling."[35] By the time the Court heard their petition, women in Canada had already secured the right to hold political office at the provincial level (with the exception of Quebec), but the federal government held firm, arguing that even though it "would like nothing better than to have women in the Senate . . . the British North America Act made no provision for women."[36]

[31] Reference re Meaning of Word 'Persons' in s. 24 of the B.N.A. Act, [1928] S.C.R. 276.
[32] Jonathan Hart, *Empires and Colonies* (Cambridge: Polity Press, 2008), p. 251.
[33] Reference re Meaning of Word 'Persons' (n 45), p. 290.
[34] Ibid, p. 301.
[35] Ibid.
[36] Tabitha Marshall and David A. Cruickshank, 'Persons Case', *The Canadian Encyclopedia* (2015), online www.thecanadianencyclopedia.ca/en/article/persons-case.

I was reminded of the *Persons Case* when I read the learned legal response to *The Shifting Border* penned by Chimène Keitner. She begins her essay with an observation about law and politics: namely, that law and legal institutions are "necessarily embedded in existing political frameworks" (p. 180). I am confident that this observation would have rung true for the female activists who were denied recognition by the Supreme Court of Canada. I would also venture to speculate that as engaged activists and reformers, they would have contended that existing political frameworks, especially those that perpetuate unjust power hierarchies, are never as stable as they may appear. In challenging a law that they saw as unjust and unjustifiable, they demonstrated their conviction that political frameworks must always be subject to contestation. They were fighting back.

When we challenge the "unchallenged power of ideas," to draw on Fine's terminology, we not only seek to destabilize their meaning but also to challenge their authority and legitimacy: who gains and who loses when we uphold existing political frameworks? What justifications are used to entrench structural inequality under color of law, and by whom? This also brings out one of the oldest debates in the study of law and society: is law ultimately a force that permits the "haves" (however defined) to preserve their privilege, or an emancipatory tool that permits change over time and the inclusion of the once excluded? In the *Persons Case*, the judges claimed to have merely affirmed the "policy of centuries"; they resisted change. For the Famous Five, as the Canadian suffragists were known, this framing of the issue was precisely the problem. Upholding the "policy of centuries" gave legal endorsement to an unjust gendered societal order that was hierarchical, harmful, and illegitimate, and, as such, deserved to be thrown into the dustbin of history. Their legal challenge offered a competing narrative of who counts as a full member with voice, agency, and real political influence, a seat at the proverbial table where political frameworks are set and contested.

Today, the basic political frameworks that undergird the Westphalian system—sovereignty, territoriality, membership boundaries—are in flux. There is hot political debate about the meaning of these basic concepts

234 Reply

and about who gets to define them. Global constitutionalists urge convergence on the "Trinitarian values" of human rights, rule of law, and democracy.[37] The populist anti-immigrant backlash puts "us first" and others last, reinstating the primacy of the national over the subnational, supranational, transnational, and international. We find competing scripts on offer within the legal system, too. The human rights perspective places human dignity and protection of the individual center stage. This is the foundation for several now canonical decisions in the field of human rights and migration law, such as the ECtHR's landmark *Hirsi* decision, which, in contrast with the US Supreme Court's *Sale* decision, held that human rights obligations apply extraterritorially when state agents exercise effective control over the people they have "pushed back" without providing them with a credible fear screening.[38] Upholding the state-sovereigntist perspective, by contrast, might lead judges and policymakers to adhere to the "policy of centuries," according to which "migration control is a fundamental sovereign right of states" (p. 112).

For Fine, this last assumption is the mother of all wrongs, the status-quo-shielding notion that prohibits us from resisting and fighting back against the disparities and injustices upheld by the current system. As she powerfully argues, this system reveals the "astonishing, terrifying, mighty—even deadly—power of a simple idea": namely, that states have the right to exclude non-members from their territory and from access to citizenship. "Every person who drowns in the sea, dies in the desert, suffocates in the back of a lorry, or freezes to death on clandestine migration journeys is a victim of this monster" (p. 113). This framing of the issue leads Fine to conclude that the only way to truly delegitimize existing political frameworks is to challenge their foundational logic and

[37] The Trinitarian mantra is drawn from Verena Frick and Oliver W. Lembcke, 'Constituent Power and the Quest for Democratic Authority in Global Constitutionalism' (on file with author). See also Jeffrey L. Duff et al., "Hard Times: Progress Narratives, Historical Contingency and the Fate of Global Constitutionalism," *Global Constitutionalism* 4 (2015): pp. 1–17, p. 11.

[38] The ECtHR was interpreting the scope of regional human rights obligations as defined by the European Convention on Human Rights. Its ruling may serve as a persuasive authority, but it has no binding effect on countries such as the United States which are not signatories to the ECHR.

legitimacy, to uncover the current system's "many dark sides, its deadly costs." In short, we must fight back by striking at the heart of the problem, the source of its immense resilience, by contesting the idea that "the right to exclude is and must be a legitimate part of state authority." (p. 115).

A principled commitment to fighting back may translate in practice to manifold strategies, from radical reconceptualization of the current world system to grassroots activism and anything in between. In this search for strategies to slay or tame the beast, I would not neglect the role of legal institutions, which offer the basic grammar and framework that governs our shared political life. As the *Persons Case* demonstrates, law is often used to preserve power inequalities, camouflaging them in a veil of respectability and authority. But it is also a tool for emancipation. After they had lost their case before the Supreme Court of Canada, the Famous Five kept up the fight. In addition to political activism at the domestic level, they sought transnational legal remedy by turning to the Judicial Committee of the Privy Council, which at the time acted as the highest legal authority, the court of last resort in the Commonwealth world, including Canada. And there, *finally*, their claim was vindicated. Women were recognized as what they always were: persons, fully capable of voting and standing for public office.[39]

In a world of shifting borders, where the tentacles of mobile migration control seem to know no beginning and no end, I share Fine's basic intuition that the only way to bring about meaningful, lasting change is to challenge the "power of unchallenged ideas" (p. 116). This is precisely what the Famous Five were doing, just as the abolitionists did before them, and what countless social movements that challenge the status quo—from the civil rights movement to the many LGBTQ+ movements to the fast-growing climate justice movement—are all engaged in. Informed by visions of justice that seek progress by expanding the range of recognized actors and voices, redefining who counts as an equal, worthy of dignity and respect, these activists are

---

[39] *Edwards v. Canada* (AG) [1930] AC 124, 1929 UKPC 86, usually called the "Persons Case."

foundationally challenging core aspects of the existing order and the structural injustice it constructs, upholds, and "naturalizes."[40]

Importantly, challenging the power of unchallenged ideas is only a first step. Even if we defy conventional wisdom about migration as a matter of sovereign prerogative, this move does not yet tell us whether—and, if so, within what limits—states may continue to hold a *qualified* legitimate interest (as opposed to an unqualified right) to regulate their borders and membership boundaries. Although it is merely a first step, the implications are potentially far-reaching; today's taken-for-granted background assumptions about the link between the power to exclude and sovereign prerogative will be exposed, tested, and challenged. Such a review may lead some to imagine and aspire to a world without states or borders. For others, myself included, the more important break-through is that such a rethinking permits shifting the burden of justification, opening up a debate about what is legitimate, under what circumstances, and according to which principles and values. We might also ask who is owed reasons by whom, at what level of governance, and within which deliberative contexts and institutional frameworks. Such a discussion is already prevalent in political and legal-theory circles, but it tends quickly to fall into the familiar dichotomy of open versus closed borders. What the current debate acutely lacks is an awareness of the new reality of *shifting* borders, the realization that old distinctions fail to account for the pervasive government power that hollows out obligations, manipulating territoriality to prevent access to rights and protections by "touching base," even to asylum seekers. Such is the gap this book addresses, treating it as fertile terrain for theorists and activists alike. Beyond the need to elucidate this landscape theoretically is the urgent call to develop concrete, hard-nosed, viable, and, yes, difficult new ways to "tame the monster," here and now. People are facing oppression today. They seek shelter now. If migrants and refugees escaping the horrors of their home countries were offered safe passage and

---

[40] For an extensive recent discussion of structural injustice in the international arena, building on the earlier work of Iris Marion Young, see Catherine Lu, *Justice and Reconciliation in World Politics* (Cambridge: Cambridge University Press, 2017).

humanitarian visas, for example, deaths could have been prevented, kept out of IOM's database of "missing migrants" that dryly records the thousands of migrant fatalities worldwide, with the most recent data reporting one migrant child dead or missing every day.[41]

The strategies for taming the monster and toppling it can be thought of as interlinked, although they operate on different timescales. We might need to tame the monster here and now, but this provisional compromise need not undermine a commitment to the ultimate demise of the idea that states can act capriciously, limitlessly, and without meaningful restraint when it comes to their expansive goals of keeping out unwanted migrants.[42] The path I resist is to convince ourselves that nothing can be done, as Keitner seems to suggest, because it is only "natural for states to interpret their legal obligations [toward vulnerable migrants] narrowly" (p. 178). It was similarly "only natural" for men to sustain their privilege over women, for "free white men" in America to deprive African Americans of their personhood and citizenship status, for slave owners to treat other human beings as mere property, and so forth. To accept these power interests as predetermined, fixed political frameworks is to give up the fight. In assenting and acquiescing to the statist perspective on migration control, Keitner blinds herself to competing local and global political frameworks of sanctuary and resistance. She also downplays progressive interpretations of the legal obligations to which sovereign states have already committed under current domestic, regional, and international human rights legal frameworks.[43]

Power is never ceded without contest, without an unmasking of its "naturalized" justificatory frameworks. The beneficiaries of existing political frameworks will always choose to interpret any obligations

[41] For detailed data, see online https://missingmigrants.iom.int/; on migrant children, see reporting from the International Organization for Migration's Global Migration Data Analysis Centre (GMDAC), in collaboration with the UN Children's Fund, UNICEF, online https://news.un.org/en/story/2019/06/1041521.

[42] Although governments often act in this fashion, their right to do so is no longer recognized, if it ever was; at least in non-authoritarian regimes, governments have extensive powers in foreign-affairs law, immigration, taxation, but not without limitation and not without constraint—legal, ethical, political.

[43] For a panoramic overview, see, for example, the multiple contributions to the 'Symposium on Framing Global Migration Law', *American Journal of International Law Unbound* (2018).

placing restrictions on them narrowly and prefer that *their* interests
and privileges go unchallenged. If we take Keitner's approach, we cannot explain why change *ever* occurs. It certainly seemed "natural" for
the common law to treat women as if they were not persons, or for the
US Constitution, prior to passing the Reconstruction Amendments, to
count slaves as three-fifths persons for purposes of apportionment in
Congress while altogether denying their personhood, their right to
vote, their ability to bring suit in federal court, their dignity, their equality, and their citizenship. Affirming, as Keitner does, that states have an
interest in exercising control, and in narrowly interpreting their obligations to migrants and refugees, does not provide an adequate justification for their actions. Nor does this interest require us to accept the
conclusion Keitner draws: namely, that no legal change is possible and
that any attempt to imagine or contemplate reform to currently reign-
ing structures is futile. She misguidedly conflates the descriptive (states
indeed have such interests) with the normative (they are *justified* in
pursuing such interests) and fails to see the strength of competing
political frameworks and the power of ideas, whether drawn from consequential or deontological theories, to be action-guiding, to motivate
resistance.

Any attempt to counter the deleterious effects of the shifting border's
ever expanding reach requires us to challenge this framework's pre-
sumed naturalness, draw its contours, reveal the vigor of this new Leviathan with its ever elastic muscle, expose the mobile biometric "eyes" it
places on the surveilled. Any attempt to challenge existing political
frameworks as deficient or illegitimate inevitably relies on developing
alternative vocabularies and visions of justice, just as the Famous Five
did in their *legal* fight against the policy of centuries. By contrast, Keitner's critical account is paradoxically self-defeating. It captures a slice of
the reality but all too readily accepts and accedes to the "power of
unchallenged ideas," leading her to conclude that no change is possible
by any political actors *other than states themselves*. This assumption
about the "proper" agents of change licenses the beneficiaries of the current system to continue to set the rules. It ignores the historical role of

non-state actors and deprives today's countless non-governmental organizations, activists, reformists, and the refugees themselves of a voice in challenging the status quo and defining narratives for the future.[44] Why allow the fat cats to watch the very few available barrels of milk? To draw on Fine's terminology, it is this line of thinking that "feeds the beast, gives it strength, and keeps us all in awe" (p. 112). By focusing on states as the only relevant agents that may bring about change, Keitner upholds a rather formalistic understanding of "the political," which stands in sharp contrast to the emphasis on political agency and resistance developed by Fine and Huber in their contributions to this volume. Unwittingly, Keitner adopts a defeatist approach, providing cover for today's power holders to continue to push the boundaries of legality, to establish the illiberal leeway they seek by deploying the almost boundless reach, scope, and intensity of shifting-border migration controls.

Importantly, we already have plenty of resources *within* existing political and legal frameworks to contest the worst excesses; we don't need to wait for a utopian tomorrow to act today. Basic rule-of-law principles holding that "the political branches ... [cannot] govern without legal constraints"[45] could prove a valuable ally to those seeking to challenge the power of unchallenged ideas. We may therefore insist that migration controls and various forms of executive powers held by states "are not 'absolute and unlimited,'"[46] despite the best efforts of the architects of the shifting border to convince us otherwise. Basic rights protections are not "turned on or off at will."[47] Interestingly, these statements are not drawn from the work of radical political theorists trying

---

[44] On the vital role played by non-state actors in tabling the draft proposal of the *non-refoulement* obligation, which eventually became Article 33 of the Convention, see the fascinating study by Ben-Nun, which reveals that Agudas Israel, an ultra-Orthodox Jewish non-governmental organization with accredited status to ECOSOC, tabled the draft proposal on the *non-refoulement* principle before the Ad-Hoc committee. See Ben-Nun, 'The British-Jewish Roots of Non-Refoulement' (n 38), pp. 100–108.

[45] *Boumediene v. Bush*, 128 S. Ct. 2229 (2008), p. 2259. In a concurring opinion in the travel ban case, *Trump v. Hawaii*, 585 U.S. (2018), Justice Kennedy of the US Supreme Court wrote that "even in the sphere of foreign affairs," in which government officials have broad discretion, free from judicial scrutiny, "[i]t is an urgent necessity that officials adhere to ... constitutional guarantees and mandates in all their actions ... so that freedom extends outward, and lasts."

[46] Ibid.

[47] Ibid.

to undo the current international system. They are drawn from none other than the US Supreme Court, the very same court that upheld the grave deprivation of refugees' basic rights and protections in *Sale*. Over time, even this apex institution could not ignore or avoid the debates about the extraterritorial reach of constitutional protections, a point that Keitner herself has commandingly shown in her previous writings. Alas, in her contribution to this volume, she takes a different stance.

Keitner has written a classic lawyer's brief to establish one of the most restrictive interpretations that I have seen in recent academic literature about the scope and reach of humanitarian and human rights duties when it comes to states exercising migration control beyond their territories.[48] She devotes significant attention to a small selection of national court cases, most notably the above-mentioned controversial US Supreme Court *Sale* decision that upheld the forced return of the Haitian refugees—this notwithstanding the fact that various other national courts and supranational tribunals (including the Inter-American Commission on Human Rights and the ECtHR) have reached diametrically opposed conclusions, flatly rejecting the US Supreme Court's narrow construal of the *non-refoulement* obligation (p. 190).[49]

Perhaps even more puzzling, for an essay that begins by couching law in a political context, Keitner's commentary offers a traditional blackletter and court-centric account. Unlike Huber and Fine, both of whom offer accounts that associate the political with forms of contestation and resistance that test and challenge state power—Fine by advocating a strategy of direct opposition and Huber by emphasizing the political agency of refugees—Keitner holds a view of politics as a game conducted primarily *by* and *for* self-serving states. The best we can hope for, in her grim view, are "political compromises within and among states" (p. 184). She has little faith in either fighting back or taming the beast,

---

[48] For equally learned legal accounts that begin from a critical perspective but have interpreted the core sources and decisions in the field as placing specific responsibilities and limits on states in the context of extraterritorial border controls, see, for example, the over-500-page-long opus by Violeta Moreno-Lax, *Accessing Asylum in Europe: Extraterritorial Border Controls and Refugee Rights under EU Law* (Oxford: Oxford University Press, 2017).

[49] Keitner notes these competing positions but describes them as futile rather than promising.

or in giving voice and legal standing to the individual who is caught in the meshed web of today's shifting-border migration controls and surveillance infrastructures. Instead, she resorts to the "policy of centuries," according to which states and only states are visible to the international lawyer. If I were a refugee intercepted at sea, or an undocumented migrant stripped of rights in the constitution-lite zone, Keitner's defeatism might well be just as dangerous to me as the policies that states seek to resolutely uphold. Like those judges in 1927 who denied women recognition as persons, she can wash her hands and claim that, while we would all wish for refugees and asylum seekers to receive the rights protection they are owed on account of law and justice, the current world system—consisting of powerful states—makes no provision for this. Of all the commentators, Keitner is the only one declaring defeat.

Volpp's essay advances the legal discussion in a different direction, placing it in a broader historical context. Her analysis links the shifting border to earlier tactics of colonial governance and legal "erasures" of those who did not count as equal or as worthy of membership of the political communities and territories in which they resided. This fascinating direction of inquiry builds upon Volpp's earlier work on the exclusion of racialized and gendered subjects. It also connects with current scholarly interest in "status non-citizens," who are physically present in the territory but exist without recognized legal status or a pathway to achieving access to membership, as Lori has shown in her contribution (pp. 121–130).[50] Given these earlier regimes of inclusion and exclusion, Volpp asks what *precisely* is distinctive and novel about the shifting border's capacity to restrict mobility. To push Volpp's point one step further, just as some have suggested that a limited number of archetypical plots inform all stories, one could argue that nothing is new under the sun when it comes to sophisticated migration techniques. I would beg to differ, however. The shifting border's rationale

---

[50]   On the growing interest in category, see, for example, Linda Bosniak, 'Status Non-Citizens', in Ayelet Shachar *et al* ., *The Oxford Handbook of Citizenship* (Oxford: Oxford University Press, 2017), pp. 314–336; Katherine Tonkiss and Tendayi Bloom, 'Th eorizing Noncitizenship: Concepts, Debates and Challenges', *Citizenship* Studies 19 (2015): pp. 837–852.

for controlling the movement of people and resources is certainly continuous with past regimes of selective inclusion and exclusion. However, instead of relying on what today we would call suspect categories
of discrimination, such as race, gender, ethnicity, and the like, the new
exclusion paradigm relies on facially neutral lines of legal geography, as
well as wealth and capital, to draw distinctions between the fortunate
few who may crack open the gates of admission and the vast many who
remain locked outside. These *invisible* borders rely on the valorization
of certain kinds of capital (human, material, symbolic) combined with
spatial and temporal techniques of mobility and entry control.

The brilliance of the shifting-border invention lies in its dexterity
and ability to do the sorting work of determining whom to include and
whom to exclude *without* having to rely on prohibited grounds of discrimination. The effects, alas, may overlap with racialized exclusion, as
in the preoccupation of the European Union and its member states
with averting immigration from Africa to Europe. The rapid proliferation of "moveable" legal barriers that can in theory be "dispatched" anywhere, but are in practice applied selectively and unevenly, with
fluctuating degree, intensity, and frequency of regulation, creates a shell
game that permits hardline policies to infringe migrants' rights in certain locations without appropriate oversight, while accelerating the
admission of high-net-worth individuals (HNWI, defined as those
with personal mobile capital in excess of 1 million US dollars), again
with little democratic review and accountability. By fine-tuning their
policies, prosperous countries are bifurcating their admission regimes,
turning to increasingly sophisticated measures of preclearance and biometric tracking (among other techniques) in their quest to fast-track
"desired" migrants while preventing "undesirable" migrants, including
asylum seekers, from accessing their ever harder-to-reach legal spaces
of heightened rights protection and relative safety and stability.

The shifting border's tremendous agility and grandiose sweep is fit for
a global age of stratified mobility, generating new forms of "governance,
control, and selection" (p. 143). It unsettles the classic Westphalian image
of the static border while simultaneously testing the demise-of-
sovereignty thesis. The climate of political pressure to "regain control,"

combined with the innovation with which the shifting border operates, challenges fixed notions of territoriality and creates instead a gamut of strategies to "affect, influence, or control resources and people, by controlling area" (p. 140).[51] The shifting border also relies heavily on experimental and advanced technologies that permit surveilling and tracking a person's movement from his or her point of embarkation until arrival, and increasingly thereafter, too. In his commentary, Mau evocatively uses the term "metamorphosis" to describe the copiousness of these inventions—bringing to mind Franz Kafka's masterpiece short story depicting a traveling salesman who inexplicably transforms overnight into a gigantic insect (*ungeheures Ungeziefer*). The metamorphosis image, like Fine's Leviathan monster, is yet another animating way to portray the perplexing new landscape and legal topography that I aimed to capture in *The Shifting Border*.

In the context of our discussion, the metamorphosis relates to the once static border turning into a whole new dynamic beast. To the various examples I have discussed, Mau adds several articulations of different facets of change brought about by the burgeoning shifting-border regime (p. 146). These developments do not represent an exhaustive list but are helpful illustrations of the ever growing range of "intervention in mobility" prior to arrival and far away from the territorial edges of desired destination countries. These examples include: pre-arrival visa-waiver programs, which, in contrast with the predictions about open borders, *deepen* the global mobility divide by making borders more permeable for citizens of wealthy democracies and more impenetrable for all others; the intensifying international and regional cooperation among affluent countries in shaping, managing, and exercising migration control;[52] and "macroterritorialization," the border-security protocols of states that have bundled their migration-control operations to establish a harder-to-penetrate external perimeter, which is often accompanied by the lifting of internal borders, a process that is best

---

[51] Quoting Robert David Sack, *Human Territoriality: Its Theory and History* (Cambridge: Cambridge University Press, 1986)).

[52] On such cooperative bordering, see Matthew Longo, *The Politics of Borders: Sovereignty, Security and the Citizen after 9/11* (Cambridge: Cambridge University Press, 2017).

evidenced in the European Union but is also emerging in other regions of the world. Lastly, Mau emphasizes the centrality of digitalization and new "data-based and algorithmic screening and sorting procedures . . . used for controls."[53] This added layer of regulation is critical for comprehending today's shifting-border ambitions and unprecedented reach.

The proliferation of shifting borders has coincided with the rise of big data and the creation of enormous databases that store detailed information about travelers' identities, making anyone on the official grid continuously "visible" through the scanning booth, the digital monitor, the algorithmic risk calculator, the biometric chip in our passports, and so on. These additional tiers of preclearance and information gathering create a powerful yet invisible mobile border that is operational in every place (adjusting itself to the location and risk profile of the traveler). Because the regulation of mobility begins at the earliest point in time and space, sequentially *preceding* our travel and arrival, it evokes what one scholar has aptly termed the "arts and science of logistics," here applied to *humans* rather than cargo.[54] The new-technology aspect of the shifting border permits governments, along with their private sector partners, to "see like a state" both *within* and *beyond* their own territories.[55]

From airline personnel tasked with screening identity documents to the firms developing the algorithms and risk-profile software used by "smart borders," to the companies selling the screening and monitoring hardware, the "business" of regulating mobility is booming on a global scale.[56] China, Australia, the United States, and the United Arab Emirates (UAE) are leading the way. Dubai International Airport has

---

[53] Ibid, p. 14.

[54] On the logistics argument, see the fascinating account offered by Debora Cowen, *The Deadly Life of Logistics: Mapping Violence in Global Trade* (Minneapolis: University of Minnesota Press, 2014).

[55] James Scott, *Seeing Like a State: How Certain Schemes to Improve the Human Condition Have Failed* (New Haven: Yale University Press, 1998).

[56] For further discussion, see, for example, Thomas Gammeltoft-Hansen and Ninna Nyberg Sørensen, eds, *The Migration Industry and the Commercialization of International Migration* (New York; Routledge, 2013). The turn to smart borders is also facilitated through various international agreements, such as the International Civil Aviation Organization's agreement on Machine Readable Travel Documents, and the Global Compact for Safe, Orderly and Regular Migration, a non-binding intergovernmental negotiated agreement, which was adopted by the UN General Assembly in 2018. A stated objective of the Global

recently introduced a pilot test of new "biometric borders"—known as smart tunnels—in its Terminal 3 and plans to implement the new technology in the remaining terminals by 2020. The smart tunnel identifies the passenger through a combination of scans of her iris and 3D face-scanning, which occurs as she walks through it, meaning that no human interaction is needed.[57] The information is then matched with the passenger's digital profile. Government officials foresee a future in which arriving and departing passengers will not require "any travel documents such as passport, ID cards or boarding cards."[58] Instead, our *body* will become our ticket of admission (or, conversely, denial of entry) as biometric borders expand their reach. As Lori reminds us, the management of mobility does not end there. Once in the UAE, every citizen and lawful resident, including those on work visas, must also carry a national ID card (known as the Emirates ID) at all times. The Emirates ID serves as a personal database of every resident, which can be checked and verified by government officials as well as private actors when opening a bank account, accessing medical care, renting a house, or crossing a border (pp. 138–139).[59] In these examples, measures of migration and population control become intertwined with new, powerful technologies of surveillance, and they bring us back full circle to concerns about the illiberal leeway that is opened up by the sweeping and all-encompassing reach of the shifting border.

Compact is to "manage borders in an integrated, secured and coordinated manner" (Objective 11 of the Global Compact) by improving biometric identification and documentation, managing borders in a "coordinated manner, promoting bilateral and regional cooperation," and establishing "appropriate structures and mechanisms for effective integrated border management by ensuring comprehensive and efficient border crossing procedures, including through pre-screening of arriving persons, pre-reporting by carriers of passengers, and use of information and communications technology." See Global Compact, §27 (a) and (b).

[57] For further information, see online https://airwaysmag.com/airports/dubai-international-tests-new-passport-control/.

[58] See Dean Wilkins, 'Enter the UAE with Just Your Face: DXB in World First Trial of Face Recognition Technology at the Border', *Time Out Dubai*, October 11, 2018, online www.timeoutdubai.com/dubai-airport/386146-enter-the-uae-with-just-your-face.

[59] See also government.ae, Emirates ID, online www.government.ae/en/information-and-services/visa-and-emirates-id/emirates-id; Edarabaia, All You Need to Know about the Emirates ID (2019 Guide), online www.edarabia.com/all-you-need-know-emirates-id/.

We can therefore summarily agree with Volpp that, while there is *some* continuity with past exercises of migration controls, the changes evident in today's and possibly tomorrow's shifting border are both remarkable and unsettling. As Volpp puts it, the "fact that 'our gates' no longer stand fixed at the country's territorial edges has *developed remarkably* in recent years" (p. 159). Volpp is alive to the significance of "drawing connections between governmental practices often studied in isolation . . . [and the ambition of *The Shifting Border*] to develop a conceptual road map to explain the delinking of law and territoriality, clarifying the consequences for both scholarly thought and policy debates" (p. 159).

I share with Volpp the conviction that putting legal spatiality center stage helps reveal the otherwise invisible challenges to our established theoretical frameworks, which have yet to catch up with the grand metamorphosis taking place on the ground. As we have seen, new techniques of bordering indicate a paradigm shift, altering existing structures of rights protection, eroding democratic accountability, and ushering in the illiberal leeway of the "law-free zone." It is this shift that I have analyzed and foregrounded in *The Shifting Border*.

The emancipatory power of ideas and political agency

The image of a *jiu-jitsu* move to describe my proposed response to the shifting border is playfully offered by Volpp in her commentary. As a black belt in karate, I could not have asked for a better compliment. But let me indulge in another image: let us imagine the migrant's quest as a board game, with the many forbidding manifestations of shifting-border authority drawing the migrant back toward square one as she struggles to reach her destination. If these dangerous regulatory traps are the "chutes," what I have proposed is to add a series of "ladders" to the board, helping the migrant to move more expeditiously—and safely— to the end of her travels.

In my lead essay, I argue that the shifting border must carry humanitarian responsibilities with it, and that its elasticity can and should be used as a resource for rights protections and safe passage. While "touching base" must always be sufficient to gain protection, it should not be necessary, as conventional legal thinking would have it. Perhaps the boldest aspect of this proposal is this: as enforcement authorities have extended their reach beyond the limits of territorial boundaries, intake efforts should be similarly mobilized.

As I have shown, states drastically expand the spatial and operational reach of their power to exclude by detaching migration control from a fixed territorial location, but this extravagantly emboldened exercise of sovereign authority has not been complemented, to date, by an equivalent expansion of the geographical reach of basic rights protections. While it is tempting to wish away the shifting border, given the changes in the world around us, I believe that doing so is ultimately a futile strategy. Instead, it is time to adapt to its agile and perplexing everywhere-and-nowhere logic, to explore how to "saddle" the shifting border with basic duties of accountability and responsibility, which would have been applicable as a matter of course if the encounter between the individual and the border officer had taken place at the once fixed territorial frontier. Combined with a commitment to digging new channels for migrants seeking protection to gain access to safety, we can begin to imagine a multi-pronged response that builds upon, rather than resists, the movement of borders.

The challenge is, alas, formidable. Governments have astutely created extraterritorial and intraterritorial spaces in which standard constitutional and humanitarian obligations, designed to respect the dignity of the person and restrain governmental action, evaporate into thin air. This hocus-locus-pocus, as I referred to it in my lead essay, relies on a tremendously sophisticated apparatus that permits erasing certain binding norms in certain spaces in reference to certain people. But how can rule-of-law societies committed to democratic and liberal values actually pull this trick? It is helpful to think about officials exercising authority in these shapeshifting terrains as if they are carrying the law in their backpacks. The ability to carry the law in their backpacks *enables* the daily operation of the shifting border. It is precisely the mobility of the border, the ability to carry the decree of national (or supranational) law in an unmoored fashion, which grants authorization to official agents, or their delegates, to make binding decisions even if the encounter takes place thousands of miles, or kilometers, away from the actual border of the access-denying state.

By incorporating the agility of the border into our analysis, new options emerge. Just as it is used today to restrict access and protection, the same technique of "carrying the law in their backpacks" can be deployed tomorrow in a rights-enhancing fashion that *restrains* the arbitrariness of governmental action, wherever it takes place. The volumes of law books and precedents that border agents metaphorically carry in their backpacks are not only about enforcement. They also include the legacy and history of challenging the status quo, of domestic, regional, and international charters of rights and freedoms that are part and parcel of the rule of law in contemporary societies. When seeking illiberal leeway, government "excise," as it were, these latter aspects of the law while upholding the power of unchallenged ideas: their sovereign authority to exclude. To topple the beast, the presumption that "when legal power is brought to bear, so too are legal protections" must apply.[60] To counteract the "excision" of hard-fought rights and protections that restrain governmental action, state officials and their delegates, exerting effective control while on the move, must simultaneously carry in their backpacks the full range of legal sources that are rights-enhancing rather than merely rights-restricting. If a person is denied a chance to make an asylum claim in her encounter—by air, land, or sea—with the shifting border, the fact that the person never reached the country's territory is immaterial. Her ability to make a protection claim—to call on the grand normative and legal commitments states have already made, and, more concretely, to seek a humanitarian

[60] Kal Raustiala, 'The Geography of Justice', *Fordham Law Review 76* (2005): pp. 2501–2560, p. 254.

visa, a protection-sensitive migration visa, a special visa waiver for asylum-seeking purposes, and the like—emerges from the *encounter* with official state power. This approach is functional and relational, rather than territorial. It enhances mobility and facilitates responsibility sharing as a fruitful way to address the pressing legal, political, and ethical challenges in a world of shapeshifting borders. Still, we might want to ask: how can we ensure that such "remote control" exercise of migration-regulation and protection practice does not diminish rights (p. 175)? How do we weigh the appropriateness of intake-oriented mobilization in comparison to more traditional approaches that rely on the standard requirements of "touching base" (p. 206)? Should we stick to the already tested set of alternatives on offer—the devil we know—or explore novel prospects for expanding and realigning the range of potential remedies to match up with the frenzied movement of the shifting border? These questions evade any simple or abstract answers. Some attempts at reform may fail miserably, while others may succeed brilliantly. But we must not allow the perfect to become the enemy of the good. It is tempting to assess new ideas at a tremendously high bar, but to do so may paralyze attempts even to contemplate resistance and contest the power of unchallenged ideas. While productive to the extent that it requires us to sharpen and illuminate any holes in our arguments, consistency requires a similarly high bar when we evaluate the current situation and its deep imperfections.

In order to illustrate this last point, I offer an analogy. Imagine a remote country which offers outstanding health care; the pinnacle of the system is its state-of-the-art medical facility. I will call this facility the Hospital on the Hill. The doctors there are highly proficient, the staff multilingual, the services top-notch. All who work there are committed to providing the best care available to all who enter. There is only one snag: the Hospital on the Hill is inside a well-guarded fortress, heavily fortified and surrounded by a crocodile-infested moat. Entry is impossible except by scaling the walls, swimming the moat, and evading the guards, perhaps employing the help of smugglers. For those who lack the strength to breach the defenses and the means to buy their way in, there is no hope of getting into the Hospital on the Hill. By contrast, those who can overcome these barriers, will, under the prevailing system's rules, secure the right to gain safety and protection. They eluded the frontier guards. They made territorial arrival. They are the fortunate ones. They will gain access to the Hospital on the Hill and receive treatment for their wounds. Everyone else will not qualify. This is not because their condition doesn't merit care and not because their case is not urgent; in fact, it is quite possible that *their* need is more acute and deserving of treatment than those who (somehow) made their way into the hospital.

Think of a man who, in his desperate attempt to reach the hospital, jumped into the moat, where he was met with crocodiles that injured him badly. This bleeding man will unlikely be able to cross the moat. His need is urgent. Indeed, he might perish in the waters if left unsaved, but since he has been stopped en route, he has no claim for entry, for protection, for treatment.

Few will approve of the moats and walls around the Hospital on the Hill. Some observers, morally appalled by this arrangement, will assert that the only appropriate response is to storm the gates, breach the moat, and tear the walls down. I am thinking here of Fine's "fighting back" strategy. By other accounts such as Keitner's, we might see this situation as unjust or arbitrary but concede that there is nothing we can do but wait until the powers that be find it in their interests to amend the situation. If someone wastes away at the gates, or is eaten by crocodiles in an attempt to swim the moat, it is their problem and not ours. As I have explained, I reject this latter line of thinking, and believe that neither the power of the privileged nor the statist desire to skirt responsibility can justify inaction in the face of such glaring human suffering.

As darkly fanciful as this imagined scenario may sound, it is closer to the current reality than we might be willing to acknowledge. Astonishingly, more than 90 percent of those who claim asylum in Europe have arrived via irregular means. Given no legal pathway to enter the European Union, to be eligible for protection or to activate the process of an asylum hearing, they must first scale walls and barbed wire, climb mountains (as when refugees try to enter Italy through the Alps) or cross moats (think of the Mediterranean as a large natural water barrier protecting Europe's shores)—or if they are trying to enter the United States, they must first survive the desert heat and overcome mounting "invisible" barriers—bureaucratic, technical, legal–construed to deter their arrival. We might imagine another system, less dystopian than the legal regime that we currently have in place, where the weakened, bleeding person trying to get in would be given support, a lifeline rather than a death sentence. Would it not be more plausible to suggest that the urgency of their claims—the severity of the risk they face—serves as the basis for priority criteria to determine whom to lift to safety, rather than focus, as we do today, on the question of *where* they were stopped? In an emergency-room setting, we expect triage to ensure that the most urgent cases will be dealt with first, rather than instruct the medical staff to only attend to those who have stormed the nurses' counter in desperation.

The purpose of my hospital analogy is to suggest that, even if we assume that states have the power to exclude, this does not justify exercising such authority in arbitrary or capricious fashion. States' capacity and responsibility to accept refugees and others in need of international protection, to provide care and shelter, need not be limited by their entry-preventing apparatuses, visible and invisible, in the same way that the Hospital on the Hill's fortifications prevent it from treating the most vulnerable. I have proposed that access to protection and other rights-enhancing remedies should be granted to those in need, according to the substantive merits of their claims, upon encounter with the omnipresent, effervescently versatile architecture of the shifting border. Instead, today's enforcement-centered mobility-restricting border apparatus clamps down on the vulnerable, dispatching its mobile feelers, actual or virtual, in the air, land, and sea to stop them as far away as possible from the promised lands of migration and refuge. States thereby enhance, rather than mitigate, the arbitrary power of their walls and moats, going out of their way to ensure that the sick and needy never reach the Hospital on the Hill.

Imagine, now, that the hospital adopts a new approach: it deploys a fleet of ambulances to provide out-of-hospital care where it is most urgently needed and to bring patients from the outside world into the hospital itself. These ambulances can reach the sick and injured where they happen to be, rather than placing the burden of access onto the unwell. The walls stay up and the moats stay full, at least for now, but the hospital manages to break out of the arbitrary boundary around it. It suddenly becomes possible for outsiders in need of care to receive it without having to pay prohibitive costs, in monetary terms or by facing great dangers. Returning to my real focus here, my proposals for rights enhancement along the shifting border and affirmative intake missions by migration officials operate the same way as the ambulances, mobilizing states' humanitarian responsibilities and commitments beyond their own bounded territories. Mobile protection is at the heart of my proposed approach, just as it was in the invention of the ambulance, the "mobile field hospital."[61] The growing interest in mobility-enhancing visas that allow safe, regulated, and authorized passage, which can be claimed from *outside* the territory by those with the most pressing protection needs, is a concrete example of how to apply the idea of rights-enhancing borders and state apparatuses that move, like an ambulance, to the place where remedy is most urgently called for.

Once we begin to think about ladders rather than chutes, it becomes clear that we have plenty of resources in our common vocabulary to imagine better solutions rather than simply continuing to stumble along the road we are on. The current system of immigration and mobility control is deeply flawed. To do nothing, or to assess all proposed reforms by perfectionist standards without implementing meaningful interim measures, is to declare defeat. The ultra-cautionary approach adopted by some of my commentators is unpersuasive. It leads to a paralysis that we cannot afford. Remember, the so-called "leader of the free world," the President of the United States, is doing everything he can to push back vulnerable migrants into the "burning houses they are

---

[61] The word "ambulance" is etymologically derived from the French *hôpital ambulant*—"mobile field hospital"—tracing back to the Latin form, *ambulant* or *ambulare*, meaning "walking" or "moving about."

escaping." [62] These efforts include measures such as the practice of "metering," making asylum seekers queue for weeks or months at the border before being given a chance to apply for asylum. This deployment of time as an attrition barrier is supplemented by recently introduced Migrant Protection Protocols, colloquially known as the "remain in Mexico" program. Under this program, those who queued up and finally reached a border guard at the gates of the Hospital on the Hill— those who *have managed* to fulfill the requirement of "territorial arrival"—are inspected at the border and then forced into removal proceedings to Mexico to await their proceedings there. The legal abracadabra performed here is subtle and extreme at once. The claim is not denied, so formal law is not breached, but the asylum seeker is not permitted into the country to present her case. This is a dark mirror image of legal arrangements favoring the global one percent, the über-rich, who can purchase citizenship with the click of a button, authorizing a hefty bank transfer, while remaining in the comfort of their homes, exempt from the requirement of setting foot on the territory.

Next, the Trump administration "incentivized" Mexico, under threat of heavy tariffs, to deploy its newly established National Guards on *its* southern border (gaining, as Volpp astutely observes in relation to an earlier program, strategic depth to the tune of 1,864 miles: the distance from the US southern border to Mexico's southern border). Following the path of constrictive precedent, and learning from the European "neighborhood" approach, the United States signed its first-ever regional compact, known as the "memorandum of cooperation."[63] The newly established regional approach will aim to reach even further: it will see the enforcement tentacles of the shifting border reach all the way south to Guatemala, El Salvador, and Honduras.[64]

---

[62] See online www.politico.com/story/2019/05/30/asylum-restrictions-trump-central-america-1489012 (citing Pili Tobar, deputy director of America's Voice, an immigration advocacy group).

[63] US Department of Homeland Security, Press Release, *Secretary Nielsen Signs Historic Regional Compact with Central America to Stem Irregular Migration at Source, Confront U.S. Border Crisis* (March 28, 2019), online www.dhs.gov/news/2019/03/28/secretary-nielsen-signs-historic-regional-compact-central-america-stem-irregular.

[64] Ibid.

Washington tried to take another page from the EU–Turkey script by putting pressure on Mexico to sign a safe-third-country agreement that would, barring special circumstances, oblige migrants from Central America (or anywhere else) to apply for asylum in Mexico, not the United States, if they passed through Mexico's territory prior to arrival to the United States. Mexican officials have to date refused to budge, although they eventually were strong-armed to "host" asylum seekers on Mexican territory while they await news of their claims from the United States. Finding the "weakest link," US officials secretly negotiated a bilateral cooperation agreement with the Guatemalan government; the details of this cooperation agreement are unclear and its meaning opaque. It was initially dubbed a safe-third-country agreement by US officials, a characterization denied by the Guatemalan counterparts. Despite this uncertainty, the highest official of the US Department of Homeland Security declared that the United States is pursuing "similar agreements" with Honduras and El Salvador as part of the drive to "turn the region into a buffer zone for U.S.-bound migrants."[65]

The administration has further introduced a rule that bans from applying for asylum anyone *passing through* another country before reaching the US–Mexico border. To implement this new rule (initially suspended by a preliminary court ruling, which was eventually overruled), border officials would have to "track" the often clandestine movement of the individuals whose protection it bars, creating a tailor-made "map" of their movements across the territory of *other* countries and treating such movement as reason enough to deny eligibility for protection. On this Kafkaesque logic, "safe passage," or *mere* passage, becomes a booby trap, a dangerous, explosive burden on both the individual and the country through which she passes. If such a sweeping overhaul of asylum procedures were implemented on a regional scale, a person escaping gender violence in Honduras would have to seek asylum in Guatemala if she passed through that country before reaching

---

[65] Sofia Menchu, 'After Guatemala, U.S. Seeks Migration Deals with Honduras, El Salvador', *Reuters*, August 1, 2019. Such an agreement for "cooperation in the examination of protection claims" was signed with El Salvador on September 20, 2019.

Mexico and ultimately the United States. Here again, scale-jumping from the national to the regional *constricts* rights rather than protecting them. Whereas the "physical, tall, powerful" border wall that President Trump promised has yet to materialize, his administration has proven effective in constructing an "invisible wall" to deter uninvited migrants. The invisible wall creates procedural, regulatory, and administrative hurdles to mobility and entry, the bulk of which were introduced without Congressional input or approval, highlighting concerns about "informalization" and democratic backsliding.

While not yet fully molded, the US approach of treating neighboring countries as buffer zones seems to be harsher than comparable cases. It focuses on passing through a third country, without requiring it be to be "safe"; it strong-arms countries to make concessions and commitments; it does not provide basic safeguards or exceptions for vulnerable migrants; and, perhaps most dramatically, it altogether *abolishes* the option of seeking asylum upon territorial arrival. This is the worst of all worlds: an ever more bloated Leviathan, with no constraint on its powers or strings attached to the exercise of migration-control authority. The border extends and stretches inward and outward, but the individual caught in this swollen, shapeshifting legal space is only subject to more rights-restricting enforcement powers and *not* offered any rights-enhancing protections. These are alarming variations on the theme elaborated in *The Shifting Border*.

It appears the wardens now governing the Hospital on the Hill believe the way forward is to build ever more impenetrable walls: physical, bureaucratic, reconnoitering, temporal, spatial, fiscal, anything to stop those who seek to get in, irrespective of the merits of their claims. They call this project the "regional approach," a label that conceals its glaring shortcomings: namely, the lack of any joint standards or responsibility-sharing mechanism. If the United States slams the door shut, it risks creating both chain-*refoulement* and chain expulsion. Mobility will become retrograde, in effect, forcing people back to where they came from. Instead, we need ambulances, we need bridges, we need fresh ideas. The necessity of mobile remedies and geographically flexed rights protections is blindingly, painfully obvious.

We can imagine—and recount—alternative narratives to closure and clampdown. Brazil's response to the recent refugee crisis in Venezuela is a telling example. Fleeing political instability, hyperinflation, and human rights abuses, thousands of Venezuelans have sought safety in Brazil, most of them making the crossing by land. This refugee influx, estimated at nearly a quarter of a million entrants, proved overwhelming for the already cash-strapped border towns and host communities. Despite a tradition of welcoming asylum seekers from near and far, including inviting more than 65,000 Haitians to find refuge in Brazil following the devastating Haiti earthquake in 2010, and pledging to accept 100,000 Syrian refugees (a promise that eventually did not materialize), the lack of shelter, sanitation, and capacity to absorb new entrants in the host towns on the Brazilian side of the border reached breaking point. Brazil could have declared an emergency and taken action to stem the flow, following in the footsteps of many European countries' response to the 2015 migration crisis. But local politicians and civil society organizations, supported by the UNHRC and other UN agencies, such as the IOM and the UN Development Program, chose a different path. They developed an innovative relocation program to reduce the pressure on the border regions in the poorer north by recruiting cities and municipalities across Brazil, many of them in the richer south, to commit themselves to accepting the refugees, despite not having "contiguous frontiers" with Venezuela. With the relocation program in place, eligible beneficiaries were asked to specify their preferences regarding *where* they wanted to move. The respective cities established priority criteria and created integration opportunities, while also factoring in modalities of family reunion and employment opportunities, echoing the Swiss model of "matching" allocations. The Brazilian air force then dispatched airplanes to Boa Vista, the capital of the northern Brazilian state where many of the Venezuelan refugees had arrived, to airlift them to their new home communities.

This swift, nimble, well-coordinated relocation response offers a refreshing alternative to naysaying and fearmongering. Instead of closing the border, raising the draw bridges, infesting the moats with crocodiles, and separating families (as was done by US border guards in response to the arrival of the migrant "caravans" from Central America), Brazil tried a different tack. The border was kept open. Wealthier counterparts in the rest of the country took action to relocate and resettle the Venezuelan refugees from the poorer border towns, which could not cope with the strain. Ambulances and airplanes were dispatched, instead of mobile borders to halt admission. Translating such interstate distribution mechanisms, which were modeled on the new UN global compacts, to different countries and regions will require tremendous skill and innovation. The beast will not surrender easily. But the writing on the wall is clear. Proactive, imaginative "mobile" protection responses offer our best hope for addressing the real, pressing, multilayered—yet not insurmountable—challenges we face in an age of ever tighter migration regulation across the vast and fluctuating terrains of the shifting border.

Even in Europe, following years of bickering and kick-the-can inaction, a proposed migrant-distribution mechanism for those saved in the Mediterranean—Europe's vast and forbidding "moat"—has been agreed by core EU states. Germany will take in 25 percent of the migrants, France another 25 percent, Italy 10 percent, and the remaining 40 percent will be allocated to other partners in the bloc. For the plan to succeed, it is estimated that twelve to fifteen member states will need to actively accept migrants; those who refuse to do so on nationalistic or related grounds will have to show other forms of solidarity. This is no panacea; a more fundamental reform is required to ensure a fair distribution of humanitarian obligations. But it a step in the right direction: it cracks open the barricades around the Hospital on the Hill.

Fine observes that "[a]s lawyers must maintain some faith in the power of the law, so philosophers continue to have faith in the power of ideas (for good or ill)" (p. 117). Having faith in the power of ideas, of political agency, is the linchpin of change, resistance, contestation. Providing remedies that move along or "track" the agility of the shifting border is not a silver bullet but a new mindset. Obviously, assurances need to be introduced to address concerns about the potential arbitrariness of review processes and to develop proper oversight. I share these concerns, but I believe they speak to the level of implementation rather than principle. We would not suggest that ambulances should not be deployed because we worry that emergency health-care workers providing relief outside the hospital might not follow protocol while treating a patient in an ambulance. Rather, we would aim to develop proper procedures to provide care on the move, to invest in training, and to monitor its implementation, making amends as required and periodically reviewing these protocols. This is not rocket science. Such reviews are embedded into any regulatory or administrative agency's protocol in the modern era. Given the tremendous logistical and conceptual reach of the shifting border, and the already proven constitutional and democratic deficits in reining it in, a new approach is urgently needed, even if it does not offer a perfectly satisfying response. "Incompletely theorized arguments," to draw on Cass Sunstein's terminology, are vital for producing results and motivating action under conditions where we lack full information or have not yet fully theorized all aspects of the studied phenomenon.[66]

Accepting the direction of my proposed remedies, Mau seeks to push them a step further. Once a suite of "mobile" rights-protection instruments attaches to "[s]tate actors or those acting on their behalf [who] would take the legal obligations 'with them,'" he asks, why limit its application only to humanitarian migration (p. 155)? This is an excellent point. Theorists and lawyers often develop their analyses around the hardest and most pressing cases, such as those relating to refugees and asylum seekers. This does not preclude addressing more "standard" cases such as those seeking to enter on tourist visas, based on family relations, or for employment opportunities. If the shifting-border paradigm obliges them to encounter pre-emptive border controls prior to arrival, far away from the destination country, then

[66] Cass R. Sunstein, 'Incompletely Theorized Arguments Commentary', *Harvard Law Review 108* (1994): pp. 1733–1772.

why not also offer them basic assurances that they will be treated fairly and equitably in their encounters with the state, including the provision of reasons for their denial of entry and the right to challenge such decisions in a timely fashion? I welcome this friendly amendment to my proposal. It seamlessly follows the logic of the "as if" approach I have advanced. It allows us to treat the migrant procedurally *as if* she had already arrived. The idea is to make the shifting border "mimic" the actual protections that one receives after reaching the territorial border.[67]

Legally, the range of instruments that comes closest to a "ladder" (returning to the board-game analogy) is known as protected-entry schemes, which waive the precondition of territorial arrival in order to provide urgent relief.[68] While still few and far between, these are the kinds of measures that offer an alternative to the insistence on "touching base" as the make-or-break precondition for activating the "machinery" of protection (itself increasingly elusive, as we saw earlier). Combined with the growing effectiveness of intertwined networks of bilateral and multilateral return and readmission agreements, the shifting border of enforcement creates a dense yet invisible system of "moveable" barriers that *lock out* the very people they were designed to protect—those who have a robust claim for asylum on substantive grounds. They are excluded not due to any principled consideration, but because affluent and powerful states have invented a system whereby legal spatiality fractures access to protection: if you manage to scale the wall and cross the moat, you are in—the hospital will treat you, the destination state will hear the merits of your case and is forbidden from sending you back to face the risk of persecution or serious harm. But if you are too sick to travel, too fragile, too poor to collect the funds required to pay your way in, you will not gain access to the guarded fortress, to the relative safety available to those who have managed to find a way to duck the authorities around these "islands" of heightened protection.

---

[67] In practice, there would likely be additional place-specific remedies that would need to be developed to address encounters with border officials, or their delegates, who stop migrants en route.

[68] Such schemes are based on the logic of severing the need to reach the territory as a pre-condition for claiming asylum.

Alas, if you are unsuccessful in eluding the everywhere-and-nowhere shifting border, with its varied enforcement agents, it is your "hard luck."

I believe that if we stood behind a Rawlsian veil of ignorance, none of us would have freely chosen the present system of allocating protection and relief, sophisticated and commanding as it may appear in the current era. This brings us back to Fine's core question: how can we respond to this "magnificent and terrifying" shapeshifting border—taking into account its malleability and endless creativity in altering form and function depending on who approaches? For Fine, the only viable answer is to attack the source of the monster's immense potency: the very presumption at the heart of the current international system of migration regulation: namely, the powerful idea that states have an unqualified right to exclude non-members and to control and to police their territorial and membership boundaries. Huber takes a different track. He does not contest the basic idea that states command legitimate authority over controlling borders, so long as a *residual* right of safe passage is reserved for individuals in need of asylum. Huber defines this right of safe passage as a "particular kind of mobility right that allows refugees to travel safely and without unreasonable obstacles through transit states to the state where they wish to seek asylum" (p. 195). Whereas Fine summons the all-powerful Hobbesian monster to elucidate the potency of today's shifting border and to explain why she sees no choice other than taking the path of fighting back, Huber's taming strategy is informed by Kant's concept of cosmopolitan right, which famously defines the duties owed by states to non-citizens facing immediate danger, or "destruction" in Kant's terms.[69] While some might insist that Huber's innovative account overstretches the notoriously narrow and restrictive Kantian category of cosmopolitan right, I find his reconstruction, which focuses on mobility and spatiality, attractive for the project of rethinking and re-crafting the relationship between states and individuals on the move.

---

[69] For an illuminating account, which also aims to expand the scope and application of Kantian cosmopolitan law, see Pauline Kleingeld, *Kant and Cosmopolitanism* (Cambridge: Cambridge University Press 2012), pp. 74–81.

Huber's analysis, following Kant, focuses on individuals as embodied corporal agents coexisting within a physical universe in which certain spatial constraints require us to find ways to peacefully coexist on the face of the earth. I share and endorse the commitment to providing safe passage and to giving greater weight to the choices and voices of refugees, asylum seekers, and other people in need of protection claiming a stake for their "place on earth." These suggestions are attractive, but they also pose significant puzzles. Can a person pass through as many safe third countries as she wishes on her way to a desired destination? If she no longer faces immediate danger, or "destruction," on what grounds should her *want* (not need) to proceed to another polity override the political agency of the residents of those countries through which she would like to transfer, especially if significant jurisdictional responsibilities attach to permitting such entry?[70] Does the strength of the individual's claim for safe passage diminish the farther away she gets from her country of origin, where she faced danger, and the more countries she traverses on her journey? David Miller has argued that once a person reaches a country that offers adequate protection for her human rights, it is not clear that she can press a claim of justice for asylum in another jurisdiction.[71] The agent-centered account favored by Huber is more demanding, giving greater weight to the voices and interests expressed by refugees. It seems closer to the rationale of free-movement arguments than to the highly restrictive Kantian idea of preventing destruction. As such, it may require an altogether separate argument or justification to hold.

Another query relates to methodological issues. The programmatic part of my argument sought to offer a combined positive and normative account that highlights power relations, inequalities, and unfairness in

---

[70] On such jurisdictional responsibilities, see Michael Blake, 'Immigration, Jurisdiction, and Exclusion', *Philosophy and Public Affairs 41* (2013), pp. 103–130. Most safe-third-country agreements and the Dublin rules recognize family reunification as a protected interest of individuals, treating it as a need rather than want, and thus giving greater agency to the affected individuals.

[71] David Miller, 'Justice in Immigration', *European Journal of Political Theory 14* (2015), pp. 391–408.

the apparatus of migration control in an age of shifting borders, while at the same time seeking to say something not only about how things *are* but how they *ought* to be. This quest for prescription, not just description, I share with Fine and Huber. As recent debates about the "realistic turn" have emphasized, normative political theory with such aspirations "needs to be firmly rooted in an understanding of human experience and political possibility that is genuinely plausible, if it is to have something serious to say about *politics*, as we know it."[72]

While lucidly argued, it remains unclear at what level of analysis Huber's discussion is pitched and what kind of empirical background conditions inform it. If states were to grant an expansive right for individuals to pass through their territories, as Huber calls for, then we will no longer operate in a world where migration and mobility are tightly regulated, as they are today. In such a world, the motivation for states to invent and ever more creatively enforce the shifting border will evaporate, because, contrary to what Huber suggests, territorial access will no longer be dispositive. It will instead become only one among many factors, prime among them the choice of the individual to reach a *particular* destination country in which to make an asylum claim. If, by contrast, one begins with the reality of borders that are increasingly tightly shut and apply in ever more remote and distant locations and instantiations, then it is difficult to make a leap of faith and simply wish away this reality by proposing that the individual pass freely through as many countries as she wishes until she reaches her favorite destination as an expressive act of political agency. There is no doubt that this is a wonderful, powerful expression of her will, but how precisely does it respond to the kind of real-world boundless, limitless use of "greater degrees of flexibility" sought by potent states that are doing everything in their power to prevent such entry in the name of their legitimate sovereign authority?

If we were to break the spell of "locking in" the first country of arrival into binding protection obligations toward the individual arriving on its shores (or mountains, or deserts), then the whole system of refugee

---

[72] John Horton, 'What Might It Mean for Political Theory to Be "Realistic"?', *Philosophia* 45 (2017), pp, 487–501, p. 488.

protection would look quite different. Why? Because mobility would then become the norm, not the prohibited "secondary movement" that it is today. If Italy were not "burdened" with the obligations to host the refugees on-board the Sea Watch, the migrant rescue NGO vessel that docked in Lampedusa's port after defying a prohibition to enter Italy's territorial waters, Italy would have had no reason to object to such a landing in the first place. Because we presently have no proper distribution mechanism among countries to share the burden, or responsibility, of protecting vulnerable migrants, the magic requirement of "touching base" remains legally and politically deeply loaded. It is the make-or-break condition. If this connection were removed, or relaxed, as I have argued for in *The Shifting Border*, then proposals like Huber's, which emphasize mobility and individual choice, would have a much greater chance to succeed. We can also speculate that if such a link were relaxed and humanitarian responsibilities were more equitably distributed, then governments would no longer have to go through the tremendous investment (material, conceptual, symbolic) involved in averting such arrival by inventing the mega-apparatus of the shifting border.

If fixed assumptions like territorial arrival were removed, then questions of fair allocation would gain greater traction. While the traditional international approach is to seek "pledges" from different countries, a new generation of thinkers and policymakers are pushing the envelope and seeking new solutions by pragmatically redefining the present impasse as a set of "matching" problems (as economists would put it). For the techie optimist, placement algorithms can be developed and sophisticated ranking systems can be put in place to encourage *both* individuals *and* states to rank their preferences. The more countries and the more individuals are involved, the greater the chance of a "positive" match that best fits the choices and ranking specified by the involved parties. While any such matching mechanism will inevitably "flatten" the rich variety of human experience, it permits us to take into account the versatile needs, histories, expressed wills, and unique circumstances of the individuals in need of international protection, *wherever* they happen to be while making the asylum claim. This is

certainly an improvement on the Darwinian mechanism we now follow, which places the burden of territorial arrival on the needy and vulnerable. Several teams of researchers, such as those working at the
Immigration Policy Lab, with branches in Stanford and Zurich's ETH,
are developing a placement algorithm for improving the integration of
refugees once they are in a country—for example, by allocating new
arrivals in a way that "gives each person the best possible match" in
relation to each possible resettlement location. This new matching
algorithm will be piloted by the Swiss government. Its adoption can be
seen as representing part of the big-data revolution in migration management, here manifesting an emancipatory prospect of tailor-made
opportunities for newcomers rather than helping states keep them out.
These multivariable matching and relocation schemes are not materi-
ally or practically dependent upon territorial arrival. They rely on data
that can in principle be collected anywhere in the world, and they might
prove to be the ambulances of the future, the new virtual ladders that
help overcome the shifting border's hazardous and treacherous chutes.

Keeping the focus on the individual, Huber's analysis also suggests
that territorial presence will enhance the political standing of refugees.
Just as women and other status groups were long excluded from the
franchise, today's refugees are unrecognized as full-fledged political
agents (at least so long as they do not have permanent status); their
voices and multiplicity of opinions are typically not factored into the
laws and regulations that deeply shape and affect their lives. This returns
us full circle to the concerns raised by Lori: presence on the territory,
even if it extends for many long years through waiting in vain for a
status determination, does not automatically translate into access to
membership and democratic decision-making processes. On this frontier,
Huber's account has much in common with the work of migration scholars highlighting what Engin Isin has called "acts of citizenship."[73] This
term refers to political acts of resistance that non-citizens pursue in
order to "*shape, contest*, and *resist* the norms, practices, and institutions

---

[73] See, for example, Engin F. Isin and Greg M. Nielsen, eds, *Acts of Citizenship* (Chicago:
University of Chicago Press, 2008).

to which they are subject" (p. 207). Here, too, the maverick philosopher might be aided by a healthy dose of evidence drawn from the more empirical social sciences. Huber *assumes* (without providing evidence to support his assumption) that the physical proximity of refugees, the presence of "strangers in our midst," is important not only to empower refugees to engage in various forms of political activity but also to evoke in the local public a greater sense of commitment to the cause of refugees, who are "*no longer invisible*" (p. 209).[74] As he sees it, when newcomers live among us, the "domestic population is much more likely to register maltreatment, speak out ... and feel solidarity with the victims" (p. 209).

Perhaps. This is clearly one possible outcome of such interaction, and it would be highly illuminating to investigate in a systemic fashion the conditions that foster such solidarity. Alas, the political realities in many European countries in the aftermath of the 2015 summer of migration (or "refugee crisis") also reveal other, less sanguine results, whereby proximity, real or imagined, to the "invaders" who entered without permission may ignite the rise of xenophobic, chauvinistic, anti-immigrant sentiments among voters who are galvanized to "take back control." The emotive power of us-first policies is that they allow members of the majority to deploy the language of deprivation, anxiety, and existential threat to the nation to "reclaim"—politically, culturally, and economically—what they see as having been unfairly taken from them, the "true" and "authentic" insiders, by undeserving and untrustworthy outsiders.[75] In Germany, refugees were initially welcomed with a tremendous outpouring of support in the summer of 2015. Today, however, study after study shows that "xenophobia is becoming increasingly widespread throughout the country," especially in the eastern parts, where almost half the population (47 percent) agrees with statements such as

---

[74] The term "strangers in our midst" is drawn from David Miller, *Strangers in Our Midst: The Political Philosophy of Immigration* (Cambridge, MA: Harvard University Press, 2016).

[75] For an elaboration of the majoritarian "cultural defense" line of claims, see Liav Orgad, *The Cultural Defense of Nations: A Liberal Theory of Majority Rights* (Oxford: Oxford University Press, 2015).

"foreigners take advantage of the welfare state." Perhaps even more damning to the assumption that proximity breeds solidarity are findings that more than half of the nation's population (55 percent) now agrees with the statement "due to the many Muslims here, I sometimes feel like a foreigner in my own country."[76] The backlash against minorities and the re-emergence of *majority* nationalism in Germany, as elsewhere, has been accelerated by the perception of "loss of control" over borders, of unregulated and uncontrolled entry of migrants who show up uninvited. Under such circumstances, proximity may breed fear, hatred, and bigotry, rather than empathy, care, and solidarity.

Huber, again building on Kant's analysis, further emphasizes the significance of face-to-face encounters to building trust and community (p. 205). This demand might have been relevant in Kant's day (although even that is questionable), but it seems artificially restraining in a globalizing context in which transnational activism and digital communication permit *distant strangers* to bond together for a common cause. How many of us have come face-to-face with Greta Thunberg? Very few. Has that prevented her from inspiring a fast-growing grassroots climate-justice resistance movement among the millions who have taken to the streets in more than 150 countries? Does the absence of "local," "domestic," "corporeal," or "embodied" encounters (all terms emphasized by Huber) forbid us from paying attention to and comprehending the political and ethical challenges of climate change, or the tragedy of migrants drowning on clandestine escape routes because no legal routes of entry are available to them?

The approach for which I advocate does not elevate proximity to a pedestal. Instead, it rests on the conviction that portable mechanisms for facilitating entry and movement—including, but not limited to, safe-passage visas, humanitarian visas, protection-sensitive migration visas, refugee travel documents, emergency resettlement options, and the like—must be included in the "backpacks" that border agents or

---

[76] These statements are drawn from the Leipziger Autoritarismus-Studie 2018; a summary in English can be found in The Local, 'Anti-Foreigner Attitudes on the Rise in Germany, Study Finds', November 8, 2018, online www.thelocal.de/20181108/anti-foreigner-attitudes-on-the-rise.

their delegates carry with them on the ever mobile tracks of the shifting borders. If such a proposal were adopted, asylum seekers and others in need could activate the "machinery" of protection, without having to reach the actual, territorial border. The proposed alternative implores that humanitarian protection follows the agility and kinesis of the de-territorialized shifting border. In so doing, it provides a much needed corrective. It permits rebalancing the shifting border's enormous enforcement powers with a robust catalogue of rights protections, opening up legal portals of inclusion rather than exclusion, ladders in lieu of chutes. The innovative streak here is to take on the basic rationale of the shifting border—namely, that immigration control is no longer attached to fixed location—and "subvert" it (as I have argued in *The Shifting Border*) by putting it to use in the service of those individuals who are currently most exposed to its punishing mobility restrictions, thereby offering them "mobile" entry procedures that become operational upon contact with the beast. Such nimble responses counter the shifting border's maverick program to escape humanitarian obligations with equally portable protection mechanisms. Mobility-enabling procedures avert the cruelty of the territorially fixed admission procedures that we now follow. They *expand* access to protection and enlarge the "pie" of actors and stakeholders, responding to the "growing international interest in humanitarian visas and safe pathways to protection."[77]

For Huber, the central image of the "corporeal body" refers to individuals roaming the earth's surface, "voting with their feet." While he is rare among philosophers in paying heed to the spatiality dimension, Huber's account seems to rely implicitly on a background assumption of able-bodied individuals who express their agency and choice by "deciding where to go and seek protection" (p. 207). For critical migration scholars, it is precisely this assumption which is the cause of concern, as it arbitrarily rewards "individuals who can *physically* approach

---

[77] Claire Higgins, 'How a Visa for Asylum Could Grant Safe Passage to Europe', *Refugees Deeply*, January 18, 2019.

the state." [78] Their physical capacity allows them to cross the moat and to scale the wall—to fulfill the make-or-break prerequisite of territorial arrival—whether to the Hospital on the Hill or the destination country they wish to reach, overcoming along the way those who are not similarly endowed. This system is the result of the insistence on territorial arrival as the precondition for activating protection. It benefits those who are stronger, who run faster, who jump higher. While the motto of *citius, altius, fortius* fits the rationale of the Olympic Games, it seems radically out of place when it comes to protection of the vulnerable. Again, we can imagine that behind a veil of ignorance, a different set of principles and institutions could have been designed, one that focuses on assessing eligibility on account of the harm and risk people face, even if they are *not* able-bodied or are otherwise unfit to take the dangerous, clandestine journey to the shores of well-off jurisdictions.

We are, alas, not behind a veil of ignorance. In the real world around us, in the current anti-immigrant political environment, I am unequivocally in favor keeping the option of "touching base" open and available to those who make it to the territory. However, I would equally strongly resist, as Huber does, the idea that this should be the *only* connecting factor activating the responsibility to protect. Placing a premium on territorial arrival, as our current laws do, gives states an irresistible, structural incentive to perfect their methods of shifting borders and gain greater "degrees of flexibility" to restrict access and prevent unwanted admission.

Like Huber, Volpp emphasizes *The Shifting Border*'s "wealth of corporeal metaphors that depict the state's manipulation of borders. The border 'contracts', 'protrudes', 'pushes out', 'bleeds inwards', and 'penetrates deeply'" (p. 160). The long arm of the state moves and reconfigures, across space and time, to selectively open or close the gates of admission. Volpp further underscores the relationship between "state and body, or body politic, particularly in a context where the national body is described as invaded, penetrated, and violated by migrants" (p. 160). Her analysis offers valuable clues to why the presence of the

---

[78] Moria Paz, 'The Incomplete Right to Freedom of Movement', *American Journal of International Law Unbound 111* (2018), pp 514–518, p. 518 (emphasis added).

feared "outsider" may lead to the polar opposite of solidarity. Fine's account also brings up the image of the body—not that of the mobile individual or detested newcomer but rather of the omnipotent Sovereign King. Recall that that the frontispiece of *Leviathan* vividly depicts a giant, crowned figure that represents the potency of the absolutist, almighty sovereign, whose torso and arms are composed of hundreds of tiny human figures. Above the figure, as in Fine's essay, we find a quote from the Book of Job: "There is no power on earth compared to him." This element of fear and invincibility, its paralyzing persistence, is exactly the power which Fine militates against.

Placed under increasing political pressure with the surge of anti-immigrant sentiment, governments, especially in Europe, deploy the shifting border deeper and deeper into the territories of transit countries and source countries. At the same time, they also seek to create new institutional architectures that will "shield" Europe from irregular migration. One option that has been floated by European officials is to establish a system of so-called regional disembarkation platforms, whereby smuggled migrants who are caught in the Mediterranean will be towed to reception centers in transit states, mostly in North Africa, and wait *there* as their asylum claims are assessed in Europe. These plans were flatly rejected by the member states of the African Union but deserve our critical attention nonetheless, for at least two reasons.

First, this proposal reveals the dangerous transnational mobility of *constrictive* ideas (pp. 64–67). Tested by Australia in its offshore centers, the idea of deputizing third countries as the waiting ground for refugees who are declined entry has recently also been adopted by the United States, which used the threat of heavy sanctions to pressure Mexican officials to agree to "host" Central American migrants on Mexican soil while they await the results of their asylum claims, processed in the United States. While wealthy migrants can now (literally) purchase citizenship by transferring hefty sums of money without setting foot in the passport-issuing country, fast-tracking their application in the process, the asylum seeker faces the opposite trajectory. The asylum claim, the legal file describing a person's unique life circumstances as the basis for substantiating her humanitarian claim seeking protection, is mobile: it "crosses" the border. By contrast, the person making the claim is denied entry, locked outside of the promised land, potentially lavishing for weeks, months, or years as the slow wheels of the determination process grind. These combined temporal and spatial exclusion mechanisms are the hallmark of the shifting border, whether seeping inwards (as in Lori's discussion of perpetual denial of membership) or stretching outward.

The sweeping "cooperation agreements" recently signed by the United States with Guatemala and El Salvador may altogether deny asylum protection in the United States. If these controversial and legally vague agreements pass judicial muster, they could potentially authorize the United States to transfer asylum seekers from *any* country, save Guatemala and El Salvador, to be processed there rather than in the United States. Talks are underway with Honduras to secure a similar agreement. If the rapid transnational diffusion of constrictive ideas continues, we might witness further coercion and the erosion of basic freedoms, not only of migrants but of those trying to assist them, just as we saw in Hungary. In Australia, the government introduced the Border Force Act in 2015, making the disclosure of information about conditions inside the remote, offshore centers an offence punishable by up to two years in prison. Democratic backsliding through tactics such as these, which silence opposition and impair the ability to challenge executive action or hold it to account, seem to go hand in hand with ruthlessly restrictive immigration measures.

Second, such disembarkation platforms would force refugees into "encampment," into *im*mobilization, confining them in gigantic no-man's-land zones, and potentially forcing them to submit to biometric identification methods (such as iris scans), which are now tested in refugee camps in Jordan as part of the implementation of UN-supported pilot-project uses of blockchain technologies for dispensing humanitarian aid, exacerbating concerns about the "see all" brand of migration control and surveillance in the age of shifting border.

Like the tsunami of restrictive policies spearheaded by the Trump administration, the proposed disembarkation platforms would harden exclusion and foster the illiberal leeway. They are the arch-rival of the ambulance-like remedies that *move along* with the shapeshifting border. Recalibrating the shifting border to offer the migrant protection, rather than placing upon her the burden of scaling the wall, swimming the moat, and evading the ever shifting locations and technologies of migration control, is a first, small step toward breaking away from the survival-of-the-fittest ordinance. This simple but radical rethinking performs a *jui-jitsu*-like move, using the shifting border's own movement to subvert the exclusionary objectives it has historically served, redirecting the beast's energy toward fostering inclusion and human rights. The border's very mobility thus becomes a potent resource for offering relief and refuge for those who need it most.

In the Jewish tradition, and in many other analogues, the concept of *Tikkun Olam* (in Hebrew עוֹלָם תִּיקוּן, repair of the world) points to the importance of creating lasting change by tackling systemic and structural injustice and taking action to address tangible problems in the world around us. What I have proposed is to address the present, worldwide problem of unaccountable anti-mobility regulation, and the harm it does, in the spirit of *Tikkun Olam*. The situation requires attention here and now. We cannot wait for perfection before we turn to counter preventable harm, death, and injustice. At the same time, we should not be afraid to contemplate robust, long-term solutions to the vexing problems of unfettered power, systemic exclusion, and official indifference to migrants' rights, safety, and dignity. If we do not wish to declare defeat, or merely tame the monster, we might need to think about ways to tie down Leviathan, like Gulliver, with a million tiny ropes: threads of law, social mobilization, and political resistance, stretching both near and far, with as much flexibility and elasticity as the moving monster they seek to restrain—the shifting border itself.

Bibliography

Abizadeh, Arash, 'Democratic Theory and Border Coercion: No Right to Unilaterally Control Your Own Borders', *Political Theory 36* (2008): pp. 37–65.

ACLU, 'The Constitution in the 100-Mile Border Zone', online www.aclu.org/know-your-rights-constitution-free-zone-map.

Agnew, John, 'The Territorial Trap: The Geographical Assumptions of International Relations Theory', *Review of International Political Economy 9* (1994): pp. 53–80.

Akakpo, Crispino E.G. and Patti T. Lenard, 'New Challenges in Immigration Theory: An Overview', *Critical Review of International Social and Political Philosophy 5* (2014): pp. 493–502.

Akkerman, Mark, *Expanding the Fortress: The Policies, the Profiteers and the People Shaped by EU's Broder Externalisation Programme* (Amsterdam: Transnational Institute, 2018).

Aleinikoff, T. Alexander et al., eds, *Immigration and Citizenship: Process and Policy*, 5th edition (Eagan: West, 2003).

Aliverti, Ana, 'Enlisting the Public in the Policing of Immigration', *British Journal of Criminology 55* (2015): pp. 215–230.

Al-Khouri, Ali, 'The Challenge of Identity in a Changing World: The Case of GCC Countries', in *2010 Exeter Gulf Studies Conference* (Exeter: University of Exeter, July 7, 2010).

Amoore, Louise, 'Biometric Borders: Governing Mobilities in the War on Terror', *Political Geography 25* (2006): pp. 336–351.

Anderson, Bridget, *About Time Too*, 2018 (manuscript on file with author).

Anderson, James and Liam O'Dowd, 'Borders, Border Regions and Territoriality: Contradictory Meanings, Changing Significance', *Regional Studies 33* (1999): pp. 593–604.

Anderson, James, Liam O'Dowd, and Thomas M. Wilson, eds, *Culture and Cooperation in Europe's Borderlands. European Studies: An Interdisciplinary Series in European Culture, History and Politics* (Amsterdam and New York: Rodopi, 2003).

Anderson, Malcolm and Didier Bigo, 'What Are EU Frontiers for and What Do They Mean?' in Kees Groenendijk, Elspeth Guil, and Paul Minderhoud, eds, *In Search of Europe's Borders* (Den Haag: Brill, 2002).

Appelby, Kevin, 'Strengthening the Global Refugee Protection System: Recommendations for the Global Comact on Refugees', *Journal on Migration and Human Security 5* (2017): pp. 780–799.

Arbel, Efrat, 'Shifting Borders and the Boundaries of Rights: Examining the Safe Third Country Agreement between Canada and the United States', *International Journal of Refugee Law 25* (2013): pp. 65–86.

Arendt, Hannah, *The Origins of Totalitarianism* (New York: Schoken, 2004).

Arendt, Hannah, *The Origins of Totalitarianism*, 3rd edition (San Diego: Harcourt Bace, 1979).

Aronica, Valentina, 'Italy, the Mediterranean as a Political Space, and Implications for Maritime Migration Governance', PhD dissertation, Oxford: University of Oxford.

Australian Government, 'Australia by Boat? No Advantage', online http://malaysia.highcommission.gov.au/files/klpr/No%20Advantage%20flayer.pdf.

Australian Government, Department of Immigration and Multicultural Affairs, Fact Sheet 71: Border Measures to Strengthen Border Control (Consequential Provisions Act) 2001 (Australia).

Avbelj, Matej, 'Theorizing Sovereignty and European Integration', *Ratio Juris 27* (2014): pp. 344–363.

Baird, Theodore, 'Carrier Sanctions in Europe: A Comparison of Trends in 10 Countries', *European Journal of Migration and Law 19* (2017): pp. 307–334.

Balibar, Étienne, *Politics and the Other Scene* (London and New York: Verso, 2002).

Basaran, Tugba, 'Legal Borders in Europe: The Waiting Zone', in J. Peter Burgess and Serge Gutwirth, eds, *A Threat against Europe: Security, Migration and Integration* (Brussels: VUB Press, 2001), pp. 63–74.

Basaran, Tugba, *Security, Law and Borders: At the Limits of Liberties* (New York: Routledge, 2011).

Basilien-Gainche, Marie-Laure, 'The EU External Edges: Borders as Walls or Ways?', *Journal of Territorial and Maritime Studies 2* (2015): pp. 97–117.

BBC Technology, 'Accenture and Microsoft Plan Digital IDs for Millions of Refugees', June 20, 2017, online www.bbc.com/news/technology-40341511.

Benedicto, Ainoha Ruiz and Pere Brunet, *Building Walls: Fear and Securitization in the European Union* (Barcelona: Centre Delàs d'Estudis per la Pau, 2018).

Ben-Nun, Gilad, 'The British-Jewish Roots of Non-Refoulement and Its True Meaning for the Drafters of the 1951 Refugee Convention', *Journal of Refugee Studies 28* (2015): pp. 93–117.

Benhabib, Seyla, *The Claims of Culture: Equality and Diversity in the Global Era* (Princeton: Princeton University Press, 2002).

Benhabib, Seyla, 'Political Geographies in a Global World: Arendtian Reflections', *Social Research 69* (2002): pp. 539–566.

Benhabib, Seyla, *The Rights of Others: Aliens, Residents, and Citizens* (Cambridge: Cambridge University Press, 2004).

Bergeron, Claire, 'Temporary Protected Status after 25 Years: Addressing the Challenge of Long-Term "Temporary" Residents and Strengthening a Centerpiece of US Humanitarian Protection', *Journal on Migration and Human Security 2* (2014): pp. 22–43.

Betts, Alexander, *Survival Migration: Failed Governance and the Crisis of Displacement* (Ithaca: Cornell University Press, 2013).

Bhattacharya, Aveek, 'Does Justice Require a Migration Lottery?' *Global Justice 5* (2012): pp. 4–15.

Bigo, Didier, 'Frontier Controls in the European Union: Who Is in Control?', in Didier Bigo and Elspeth Guild, eds, *Controlling Frontiers: Free Movement into and within Europe* (Aldershot: Ashgate, 2005), pp. 49–99.

Bigo, Didier and Elspeth Guild, eds, *Controlling Frontiers: Free Movement into and within Europe* (Aldershot: Ashgate, 2005).

Bigo, Didier and Elspeth Guild, 'Policing at a Distance: Schengen Visa Policies', in Didier Bigo and Elspeth Guild, eds, *Controlling Frontiers: Free Movement into and within Europe* (Ashgate, 2005), pp. 233–263.

Blake, Michael, 'Immigration, Jurisdiction, and Exclusion', *Philosophy and Public Affairs 41* (2013), pp. 103–130.

Border Angels, 'Border Water Drop', online www.borderangels.org/desert-water-drops/.

Bosniak, Linda, 'Being Here: Ethical Territoriality and the Rights of Immigrants', *Theoretical Inquiries in Law 8* (2007): pp. 389–410.

Bosniak, Linda, *The Citizen and the Alien: Dilemmas of Contemporary Membership* (Princeton: Princeton University Press, 2008).

Bosniak, Linda, 'Status Non-Citizens', in Shachar, Ayelet et al., *The Oxford Handbook of Citizenship* (Oxford: Oxford University Press, 2017), pp. 314–336.

Bossong, Raphael and Helena Carrapico, 'The Multidimensional Nature and Dynamic Transformation of European Borders and Internal Security', in Raphael Bossong and Helena Carrapico, eds, *EU Borders and Shifting Internal Security: Technology, Externalization and Accountability* (Berlin: Springer, 2016), pp. 1–21.

Brezger, Jan, Andreas Cassee, and Anna Goppel, 'The Ethics of Immigration in a Non-Ideal World: Introduction', *Moral Philosophy and Politics 3* (2016): pp. 135–140.

Brouwer, Andrew and Judith Kumin, 'Interception and Asylum: When Migration Control and Human Rights Collide', *Refuge 21* (2003): pp. 6–24.

Brown, Wendy, *Walled States, Waning Sovereignty* (Cambridge: Zone Books, 2010).

Brubaker, Rogers, 'The New Language of European Populism: Why "Civilization" Is Replacing the Nation', *Foreign Affairs*, December 6, 2017.

Brysk, Alison and Gershon Shafir, eds, *People out of Place: Globalization, Human Rights, and the Citizenship Gap* (New York: Routledge, 2004).

Burdett, Anita, *British Records of the Emirates 1961–1965* (Slough: Archive Editions Limited, 1963).

Burnett, Christina D., 'A Convenient Constitution? Extraterritoriality after Boumediene', *Columbia Law Review 109* (2009): pp. 973–1046.

Byrd, Sharon and Joachim Hruschka, *Kant's Doctrine of Right: A Commentary* (Cambridge: Cambridge University Press, 2010).

Cabrera, Luis, *The Practice of Global Citizenship* (Cambridge: Cambridge University Press, 2010).

Canada Border Services Agency, '2008–2009 Report on Plan and Priorities', online www.tbs-sct.gc.ca/rpp/2008-2009/inst/bsf/bsf02-eng.asp.

Canada Border Services Agency, *Department Performance Report 2008–09* (Ottawa: CBSA, November 5, 2009).

Carens, Joseph H., 'Aliens and Citizens: The Case for Open Borders', *The Review of Politics 49* (1987): pp. 251–273.

Carens, Joseph H., *The Ethics of Immigration* (Oxford: Oxford University Press, 2013).

Carens, Joseph H., 'Realistic and Idealistic Approaches to the Ethics of Migration', *The International Migration Review 30* (1996): pp. 156–170.

Casas-Cortes, Maribel, Sebastian Cobarrubias, and John Pickles, 'Stretching Borders beyond Sovereign Territories? Mapping EU and Spain's Border Externalization Policies', *Geopolítica 2* (2011): pp. 71–90, online https://core.ac.uk/download/pdf/38816040.pdf.

Casas-Cortes, Maribel, Sebastian Cobarrubias, and John Pickles, 'Riding Routes and Itinerant Borders: Autonomy of Migration and Border Externalization', *Antipode 47* (2015): pp. 894–914.

Celikates, Robin, Regina Kreide, and Tilo Wesche, eds, *Transformations of Democracy: Crisis, Protest and Legitimation* (London: Rowman & Littlefield, 2015).

Cellini, Amanda, 'The Resettlement of Hungarian Refugees in 1956', *Forced Migration Review 54*, no. 6 (2017): pp. 6–8.

Chacón, Jennifer M., 'Managing Migration through Crime', *Columbia Law Review Sidebar 109* (2009): pp. 135–148.

Chétail, Vincent, 'Sovereignty and Migration in the Doctrine of the Law of Nations: An Intellectual History of Hospitality from Vitoria to Vattel', *European Journal of International Law 27* (2017): pp. 901–922.

Chung, Erin, *Immigration and Citizenship in Japan* (Cambridge and New York: Cambridge University Press, 2006).

Citizenship and Immigration Canada, *Comparable ICO Network Models, Review of the Immigration Control Office Network – Final Report* (2001), Appendix A.

Cohen, Elizabeth F., 'The Political Economy of Immigrant Time: Rights, Citizenship, and Temporariness in the Post-1965 Era', *Polity 47* (2015): pp. 337–351.

Cohen, Elizabeth F., *The Political Value of Time: Citizenship, Duration, and Democratic Justice* (Cambridge: Cambridge University Press, 2018).

Collinson, Sarah, 'Visa Requirements, Carrier Sanctions, "Safe Third Countries" and "Readmission": The Development of an Asylum "Buffer Zone" in Europe', *Transactions of the Institute of British Geographers 21* (1996): pp. 76–90.

Cook-Martin, David and David FitzGerald, 'Culling the Masses: A Rejoinder', *Journal of Ethnic and Racial Studies 38* (2015): pp. 1319–1327.

Council of the European Union, A Strategy for the External Dimension of JHF: Global Freedom, Security and Justice, 14366/1/05, November 24, 2005 (European Union).

Council of the European Union, Integrated Border Management Strategy Deliberations 13926/06 Rev 3, November 21, 2006 (European Union).

Cover, Robert M., *Justice Accused* (New Haven: Yale University Press, 1975).

Cover, Robert M., 'Violence and the Word', *Yale Law Journal 95* (1986): pp. 1601–1629.

Cowen, Debora, *The Deadly Life of Logistics: Mapping Violence in Global Trade* (Minneapolis: University of Minnesota Press, 2014).

Cox, Adam B., 'Three Mistakes in Open Borders Debates', in Jack Knight, ed., *NOMOS: Immigration, Emigration, and Migration* (New York: NYU Press, 2017), pp. 51–68.

Crépeau, François, *Regional Study: Management of the External Borders of the European Union and Its Impact on the Human Rights of Migrants* (UN Doc. A/HRC/23/46, April 24, 2013).

Crépeau, François and Delphine Nakache, 'Controlling Irregular Migration in Canada: Reconciling Security Concerns with Human Rights Protection', *Immigration and Refugee Policy Choices 12* (2006).

Crock, Mary, ed., *Migrants and Rights* (Abingdon: Routledge, 2015).

Curl, Joseph, 'Homeland Security Secretary Kirstjen Nielsen: "Well Coached" Illegal Aliens Using Children to Pose as Families', *The Daily Wire*, June 18, 2018.

Davidson, Robert A., 'Spaces of Immigration "Prevention": Interdiction and the Nonplace', *Diacritics 33* (2003): pp. 3–18.

Dench, Janet, 'Controlling the Borders: C-31 and Interdiction', *Refuge 19* (2001): pp. 34–40.

Department of Homeland Security Press Office, 'DHS Announces 11 New Airports Selected for Possible Preclearance Expansion Following Second Open Season' (4 November 2016), online www.dhs.gov/news/2016/11/04/dhs-announces-11-new-airports-selected-possible-preclearance-expansion-following.

Department of Homeland Security Press Office, 'DHS Announces Intent to Expand Preclearance to 10 New Airports' (May 29, 2015), online www.dhs.gov/news/2015/05/29/dhs-announces-intent-expand-preclearance-10-new-airports.

Diner, Alexander C. and Joshua Hagan, *Borders: A Very Short Introduction* (Oxford: Oxford University Press, 2012).

Directive (EU) 2016/681 of the European Parliament and of the Council, O.J. (L 119/132), May 4, 2016 (EU).

Dowd, Rebecca and Jane McAdam, 'International Cooperation and Responsibility-Sharing to Protect Refugees: What, Why, and How?', *International and Comparative Law Quarterly 66* (2017): pp. 863–892.

Duff, Jeffrey L. et al., 'Hard Times: Progress Narratives, Historical Contingency and the Fate of Global Constitutionalism', *Global Constitutionalism* 4 (2015): pp. 1–17.

Dumbrava, Costica, 'Citizenship and Technology', in Ayelet Shachar et al., eds, *The Oxford Handbook of Citizenship* (Oxford: Oxford University Press, 2017), pp. 767–788.

Edwards, Alice, 'Human Rights, Refugees, and the Right "to Enjoy" Asylum', *International Journal of Refugee Law 17*, no. 2 (2005): pp. 293–330.

Egelko, Bob, 'Court Denies Immigrants Right to Attorney in Expedited Deportations', *SFGate*, February 7, 2017, online www.sfgate.com/nation/article/Court-denies-immigrants-Sright-to-attorney-in-10915296.php.

El Qadim, Nora, 'The Symbolic Meaning of International Mobility: EU–Morocco Negotiations on Visa Facilitation', *Migration Studies 6* (2018): pp. 279–305.

Elden, Stuart, *The Birth of Territory* (Chicago: The University of Chicago Press, 2013).

European Commission, Migration and Home Affairs, 'Reforming the Common European Asylum System and Developing Safe and Legal Pathways to Europe', online https://ec.europa.eu/home-affairs/what-is-new/news/news/2016/20160406_2_en.

European Court of Human Rights Press Unit, 'Factsheet: Extraterritorial Jurisdiction of States Parties to the European Convention on Human Rights', online www.echr.coe.int/Documents/FS_Extraterritorial_jurisdiction_ENG.pdf.

European Parliament, Resolution of April 5, 2017 on Addressing Refugees and Migrant Movements: The Role of EU External Action (2015/2342(INI)).

Eurostat, *Record Number of over 1.2 Million First Time Asylum Seekers Registered in 2015* (Eurostat News Release 44/2016, March 4, 2016), online http://ec.europa.eu/eurostat/documents/2995521/7203832/3-04032016-AP-EN.pdf/790eba01-381c-4163-bcd2-a54959b99ed6.

Fine, Sarah, 'The Ethics of Immigration: Self-Determination and the Right to Exclude', *Philosophy Compass 8*, no. 3 (2013): pp. 254–268.

Fitzgerald, David, *The Asylum Paradox: Remote Control of Forced Migration to the Global North* (forthcoming).

Fitzgerald, David, 'The History of Racialized Citizenship', in Ayelet Shachar et al., eds, *The Oxford Handbook on Citizenship* (Oxford: Oxford University Press, 2017).

Forst, Rainer, *Normativity and Power: Analyzing Social Orders of Justification* (Oxford: Oxford University Press, 2017).

Freedom House, 'Freedom in the World 2018: Methodology', online https://freedomhouse.org/report/methodology-freedom-world-2018.

Frelick, Bill, 'In-Country Refugee Processing of Haitians: The Case Against', *Refuge 21*, no. 4 (2003): pp. 66–72.

Frelick, Bill, and Barbara Kohnen, 'Filling the Gap: Temporary Protected Status', *Journal of Refugee Studies 8* (1995): pp. 339–363.

Frelick, Bill, Ian M. Keysel, and Jennifer Podkul, 'The Impact of Externalization of Migrant Controls on the Rights of Asylum Seekers and Other Migrants', *Journal on Migration and Human Security 4* (2016): pp. 190–220.

Fukuyama, Francis, *The End of History and the Last Man* (New York: Free Press, 1992).

Gallagher, Anne T. and Fiona David, *The International Law of Migrant Smuggling* (Cambridge: Cambridge University Press, 2014).

Gammeltoft-Hansen, Thomas, *Access to Asylum: International Refugee Law and the Globalization of Migration Control* (Cambridge: Cambridge University Press, 2011).

Gammeltoft-Hansen, Thomas, 'Extraterritorial Immigration Control and the Reach of Human Rights', in Vincent Chétail and Céline Bauloz, eds, *Research Handbook on International Law and Migration* (Cheltenham: Edward Elgar, 2014), pp. 113–131.

Gammeltoft-Hansen, Thomas, 'International Refugee Law and Refugee Policy: The Case of Deterrence Policies', *Journal of Refugee Studies 27* (2014): pp. 574–595.

Gammeltoft-Hansen, Thomas and Ninna Nyberg Sørensen, eds, *The Migration Industry and the Commercialization of International Migration* (New York: Routledge, 2013).

Ghezelbash, Daniel, *Refuge Lost: Asylum Law in an Interdependent World* (Cambridge: Cambridge University Press, 2018).

Ghosh, Bimal, 'Toward a New International Regime for Orderly Movements of People', in Bimal Ghosh, ed., *Managing Migration: Time for a New International Regime?* (Oxford: Oxford University Press, 2000), pp. 6–26.

Gibney, Matthew J., *The Ethics and Politics of Asylum: Liberal Democracy and the Response to Refugees* (Cambridge: Cambridge University Press, 2004).

Gibney, Matthew J., 'Refugees and Justice between States', *European Journal of Political Theory 14* (2015): pp. 448–463.

Gibney, Matthew J., 'A Thousand Little Guantanamos', in Kate E. Tunstall, ed., *Displacement, Asylum, Migration: The Oxford Amnesty Lectures 2004* (Oxford: Oxford University Press. 2006).

Giddens, Anthony, *The Nation-State and Violence: Volume Two of A Contemporary Critique of Historical Materialism* (Berkeley: University of California Press, 1985).

Ginsburg, Tom, Aziz Z. Huq, and Mila Versteeg, 'The Coming Demise of Liberal Constitutionalism?', *The University of Chicago Law Review 85* (2018): pp. 239–255.

Giugni, Marco and Florence Passy, eds, *Political Altruism: Solidarity Movements in International Perspective* (London: Rowman and Littlefield, 2001).

Glenn, H. Patrick, 'Persuasive Authority', *McGill Law Journal 32* (1987): pp. 261–287.

Goldenziel, Jill I., 'Displaced: A Proposal for an International Agreement to Protect Refugees, Migrants, and States', *Berkeley Journal of International Law 35* (2017): pp. 47–89.

Goldstein, Brandt, *Storming the Court: How a Band of Law Students Fought the President—and Won* (New York: Scribner, 2005).

Goodman, Sara, *Immigration and Membership Politics in Western Europe* (Cambridge: Cambridge University Press, 2014).

Goodwin-Gill, Guy, 'The International Law of Refugee Protection', in Elena Fiddian-Qasmiyeh, Gil Loescher, Katy Long, and Nando Sigona, eds, *The Oxford Handbook of Refugee and Forced Migration Studies* (Oxford: Oxford University Press, 2014), pp. 36–45.

Government Accountability Office, *Border Patrol: Checkpoints Contribute to Border Patrol's Mission, but More Consistent Data Collection and Performance*

Measurement Could Improve Effectiveness (Washington, DC, GAO 09-824, 2008) (United States).

Government of Canada, 'Preamble, Canada US Statement of Mutual Understanding (SMU)', online www.canada.ca/en/immigration-refugees citizenship/corporate/mandate/policies-operational-instructions-agreements/agreements/statement-mutual-understanding-information-sharing/statement.html.

Graber, Mark A., Sanford Levinson, and Mark Tushnet, eds, *Constitutional Democracy in Crisis?* (New York: Oxford University Press, 2018).

Grotius, Hugo, 'The Rights of War and Peace [De Jure Belli ac Pacis]', Richard Tuck, ed. (Indianapolis: Liberty Fund, [1625] 2005).

Guiraudon, Virginie and Gallya Lahav, 'A Reappraisal of the State Sovereignty Debate: The Case of Migration Control', *Comparative Political Studies 33* (2000): pp. 163–195.

Gulf Labour Markets and Migration, Demographic and Economic Database, online https://gulfmigration.org/gcc-total-population-and-percentage-of-nationals-and-non-nationals-in-gcc-countries-national-statistics-2017-2018-with-numbers/.

Gülzau, Fabian, Steffen Mau, and Natascha Zaun, 'Regional Mobility Spaces? Regional Integration and Visa Waiver Policies', *International Migration 54* (2016): pp. 164–180.

Günter, Klaus, 'World Citizens between Freedom and Security', *Constellations 12* (2005): pp. 379–391.

Hammar, Tomas D., *Democracy and the Nation State: Aliens, Denizens, and Citizens in a World of International Migration*, Research in Ethnic Relations Series (Aldershot: Gower Pub. Co., 1990).

Hansen, Randall, *Constrained by Its Own Roots: How the Origins of the Global Asylum System Limit Contemporary Protection* (Washington, DC: Migration Policy Insitute, 2017).

Hart, Jonathan, *Empires and Colonies* (Cambridge: Polity Press, 2008).

Hassner, Ron E. and Jason Wittenberg, 'Barriers to Entry: Who Builds Fortified Boundaries and Why?', *International Security 50* (2015): pp. 157–190.

Hathaway, James C. and Thomas Gammeltoft-Hansen, 'The Emerging Politics of "Non-Entrée"', *Refugees 91* (1992): pp. 235–284.

Hathaway, James C. and Thomas Gammeltoft-Hansen, 'Non-Refoulement in a World of Cooperative Deterrence', *Columbia Journal of Transnational Law* 53 (2015): pp. 235–284.

Herz, John H., 'Rise and Demise of the Territorial State', *World Politics*, 9 (1957): pp. 473–493.

Hidalgo, Javier, 'Resistance to Unjust Immigration Restriction', *Journal of Political Philosophy 23* (2015): pp. 450–470.

Higgins, Claire, 'How a Visa for Asylum Could Grant Safe Passage to Europe', *Refugees Deeply*, January 18, 2019.

Hollifield, James F., 'Offene Weltwirtschaft und nationales Bürgerrecht: Das liberale Paradox', in Dietrich Thränhardt and Uwe Hunger, eds, *Migration im Spannungsfeld von Globalisierung und Nationalstaat* (Wiesbaden: Westdeutscher Verlag, 2003), pp. 35–57.

Hollifield, James F., 'Sovereignty and Migration', in Matthew J. Gibney and Randall Hansen, eds, *Immigration and Asylum from 1900 to the Present* (Santa Barbara: ABC-CLIO, 2005), pp. 574–576.

Home Office, *Securing the UK Border: Our Vision and Strategy for the Future* (United Kingdom: March 2007).

Hirschl, Ran and Ayelet Shachar, 'Foreword: Spatial Statism', *International Journal of Constitutional Law 17* (2019): pp. 1–52.

Horton, John, 'What Might It Mean for Political Theory to Be "Realistic"?', *Philosophia 45* (2017), pp, 487–501.

Hosein, Adam, 'Immigration and Freedom of Movement', *Ethics & Global Politics 6* (2013): pp. 25–37.

Hu, Margaret, 'Algorithmic Jim Crow', *Fordham Law Review 86* (2017): pp. 633–696.

Huber, Jakob, 'Theorising from the Global Standpoint: Kant and Grotius on Original Common Possession', *European Journal of Philosophy 25* (2017): pp. 231–249.

Human Rights Watch et al., *NGO Background Paper on the Refugee and Migration Interface* (2001), online http://repository.forcedmigration.org/pdf/?pid=fmo:5415.

Idriz, Narin, 'Taking the EU–Turkey Deal to Court?', VERFBLOG, December 20, 2017, online https://verfassungsblog.de/taking-the-eu-turkey-deal-to-court/.

International Organization for Migration's Global Migration Data Analysis Centre (GMDAC), in collaboration with the UN Children's Fund, UNICEF, online https://news.un.org/en/story/2019/06/1041521.

Isaacs, Mark, 'The Intolerable Cruelty of Australia's Refugee Deterrence Strategy', *Foreign Policy*, May 2, 2016, online http://foreignpolicy.com/2016/05/02/australia-papua-new-guinea-refugee-manus-nauru/.

Isikel, Turkuler, *Europe's Functional Constitution: A Theory of Constitution beyond the State* (Oxford: Oxford University Press, 2016).

Isin, Engin F. and Greg M. Nielsen, eds., *Acts of Citizenship* (Chicago: University of Chicago Press, 2008).

Jackson, Robert, *Sovereignty: The Evolution of an Idea* (Cambridge: Polity Press, 2007).

Jacobson, David, *Rights across Borders: Immigration and the Decline of Citizens* (Baltimore: John Hopkins University Press, 1996).

Jellinek, Georg, *Allgemeine Staatslehre* (Berlin: O. Häring, 1914).

Joppke, Christian, 'Citizenship in Immigration States', in Ayelet Shachar et al., eds, *The Oxford Handbook on Citizenship* (Oxford: Oxford University Press, 2017), pp. 385–406.

Joppke, Christian, 'Why Liberal States Accept Unwanted Immigration', *World Politics 50* (1998): pp. 266–293.

Kalhan, Anil, 'Immigration Surveillance', *Maryland Law Review 74* (2014): pp. 1–78.

Kant, *Gesammelte Schriften*, Royal Prussian Academy of Sciences, ed. (Berlin: G. Reimer, 1910–1955).

Kanter, James and Andrew Higgins, 'E.U. to Offer Turkey 3 Billion Euros to Stem Migrant Flow', *The New York Times*, November 29, 2015, online www.nytimes.com/2015/11/30/world/europe/eu-offers-turkey-3-billion-euros-to-stem-migrant-flow.html.

Kapiszewski, Andrzej, United Nations Secretariat, Population Division, Department of Economic and Social Affairs, *Arab versus Asian Migrant Workers in the GCC Countries* (Beirut: UN/POP/EGM/2006/02, United Nations Expert Group Meeting on International Migration and Development in the Arab Region, Beirut, 2006).

Kasimis, Demetra, 'The Tragedy of Blood-Based Membership: Secrecy and the Politics of Immigration in Euripides's Ion', *Political Theory 41* (2013): pp. 231–256.

Keitner, Chiméne I., 'Framing Constitutional Rights', *Southwestern Law Review* 36 (2011): pp. 617–633.

Keitner, Chiméne I., 'Rights beyond Borders', *Yale Journal of International Law* 36 (2011): pp. 55–114.

Kesby, Alison, 'The Shifting and Multiple Border and International Law', *Oxford Journal of Legal Studies 27* (2007): pp. 101–119.

Kleingeld, Pauline, *Kant and Cosmopolitanism* (Cambridge: Cambridge University Press, 2012).

Knight, Stephen M., 'Defining Due Process Down: Expedited Removal in the United States', *Refuge 19* (2001): pp. 41–47.

Knop, Karen, 'Statehood: Territory, People, Government', in James Crawford and Martti Koskenniemi, eds, *The Cambridge Companion to International Law* (Cambridge: Cambridge University Press, 2012), pp. 95–116.

Koh, Harold Hongju, 'The Haitian Refugee Litigation: A Case Study in Transnational Public Law Litigation', *Maryland Journal of International Law 18* (1994): pp. 1–20.

Komlosy, Andrea, 'Migration und Freizügigkeit. Habsburger Monarchie und Europäische Union im Vergleich', in Joachim Becker and Andrea Komlosy, eds, *Grenzen Weltweit. Zonen, Linien, Mauern im historischen Vergleich* (Wien: Promedia und Südwind, 2004).

Koslowski, Roy, 'Addressing Side-Effects of Increasing Border Security Cooperation: A Global Perspective', in Pastore, Ferrucio, ed., *Beyond the Migration and Asylum Crisis: Options and Lessons for Europe* 108 (Milan: Aspen Institute Italia, 2017).

Körtvélyesi, Zsolt and Balázs Majtényi, 'Game of Values: The Threat of Exclusive Constitutional Identity, the EU and Hungary', *German Law Journal 18* (2017): pp. 1721–1744.

Krygier, Martin, 'Transformations of the Rule of Law: Legal, Liberal and Neo-', in Ben Golder and Daniel McLoughlin, eds, *The Politics of Legality in a Neoliberal Age* (Abingdon: Routledge, 2018).

Kumin, Judith, 'Orderly Departure from Vietnam: Cold War Anomaly or Humanitarian Innovation?', *Refugee Survey Quarterly 27* (2008): pp. 104–117.

Kyle, David and Rey Koslowski, eds, *Global Human Smuggling: Comparative Perspectives*, 2nd edition (Baltimore: John Hopkins University Press, 2011).

L3 Research Center, 'iBorderCtrl', online www.l3s.de.

Lambert, Hélène, Jane McAdam, and Maryellen Fullerton, eds, *The Global Reach of Europe's Refugee Law* (Cambridge: Cambridge University Press, 2013).

Lane, Melissa, 'Response to Gibney', in Kate Tunstall, ed., *Displacement, Asylum, Migration: The Oxford Amnesty Lectures 2004* (Oxford: Oxford University Press, 2006), pp. 170–175.

Laube, Lena, *Grenzkontrollen jenseits nationaler Territorien. Die Steuerung globaler Mobilität durch liberale Staaten* (Frankfurt am Main: Campus Verlag, 2013).

Laube, Lena and Andreas Müller, 'Warum die Kontrolle abgeben? Die Delegation von Migrationskontrolle aus der Prinzipal–Agent-Perspektive', *Berliner Journal für Soziologie 25* (2015): pp. 255–281.

Lee, Erik and Christopher Wilson, eds, *The US–Mexico Border Economy in Transition* (Washington, DC: Wilson Center, 2015).

Lee, Esther Yu Hsi, 'Immigrant Families Aren't Getting Their Day in Court', *ThinkProgress*, May 20, 2016, online https://thinkprogress.org/immigrant-families-arent-getting-their-day-in-court-f7edc1026c2c/.

Leitner, Helga and Christopher Struck, 'Spaces of Immigrant Advocacy and Liberal Democratic Citizenship', *Annals of the Association of American Geographers 104* (2014): pp. 348–356.

Lippert, Randy K. and Sean Rehaag, eds, *Sanctuary Practices in International Perspectives: Migration, Citizenship and Social Movements* (Abingdon: Routledge, 2013).

Liste, Philip, 'Transnational Human Rights Litigation and Territorialized Knowledge: *Kiobel* and the "Knowledge of Space"', *Transnational Legal Theory 5* (2014): pp. 1–16.

Lister, Matthew, 'Who Are Refugees?', *Law and Philosophy 32* (2013): pp. 645–671.

Longo, Matthew, *The Politics of Borders: Sovereignty, Security, and the Citizen after 9/11* (Cambridge: Cambridge University Press, 2018).

Lori, Noora, *Offshore Citizens: Permanent Temporary Status in the Gulf* (Cambridge University Press, 2019).

Lu, Catherine, *Justice and Reconciliation in World Politics* (Cambridge: Cambridge University Press, 2017).

Marshall, Tabitha and David A. Cruickshank, 'Persons Case', *The Canadian Encyclopedia* (2015), online www.thecanadianencyclopedia.ca/en/article/persons-case.

Martin, Philip L., *There Is Nothing More Permanent than Temporary Foreign Workers, Backgrounder* (Center for Immigration Studies, 2001).

Mau, Steffen, *Das metrische Wir: Über die Quantifizierung des Sozialen* (Berlin: edition suhrkamp, 2017).

Mau, Steffen, 'Mobility Citizenship, Inequality, and the Liberal State. The Case of Visa Policies', *International Political Sociology 4*, no. 4 (2010): pp. 339–361.

Mau, Steffen, 'Die Politik der Grenze. Grenzziehung und politische Systembildung in der Europäischen Union', *Berliner Journal für Soziologie 16* (2006): pp. 115–132.

Mau, Steffen and Heike Brabandt, 'Visumpolitik und die Regulierung globaler Mobilität. Ein Vergleich dreier OECD-Länder', *Zeitschrift für Soziologie 40* (2011): pp. 3–23.

Mau, Steffen et al., 'The Global Mobility Divide: How Visa Policies Have Evolved over Time', *Journal of Ethnic and Migration Studies 41* (2015): pp. 1192–2213.

Mau, Steffen et al., *Liberal States and the Freedom of Movement* (Basingstoke: Palgrave Macmillan, 2012).

McNevin, Anne and Neumann, Klaus, *Who Is Speaking* (quoting Australia's Attorney-General Robert Menzies), paper presented at the 2017 APSA Annual Meeting, San Francisco.

Mehta, Uday, 'Liberal Strategies of Exclusion', in Frederick Cooper and Ann Laura Stoler, eds, *Tensions of Empire: Colonial Cultures in a Bourgeois World* (Berkeley, Los Angeles and London: University of California Press, 1997).

Menchu, Sofia, 'After Guatemala, U.S. Seeks Migration Deals with Honduras, El Salvador', *Reuters*, August 1, 2019.

Méndez, Juan, United Nations Commission on Human Rights, Office of the High Commissioner, *Report of the Special Rapporteur on Torture and Other Cruel, Inhuman or Degrading Treatment or Punishment* (U.N. Doc. A/HRC/37/50, February 26, 2018).

Menjivar, Cecilia, 'Immigration Law beyond Borders: Externalizing and Internalizing Border Controls in an Era of Securitization', *Annual Review of Law & Social Sciences 10* (2014): pp. 353–369.

Menjivar, Cecilia, 'Liminal Legality: Salvadoran and Guatemalan Immigrants' Lives in the United States', *American Journal of Sociology 111* (2006): pp. 999–1037.

Meron, Theodor, 'Extraterritoriality of Human Rights Treaties', *American Journal of International Law 89* (1995): pp. 78–82.

Mezzadra, Sandro and Brett Neilson, *Border as Method, or, the Multiplication of Labor* (Durham: Duke University Press, 2013).

Miller, David, 'Justice in Immigration', *European Journal of Political Theory 14* (2015), pp. 391–408.

Miller, David, *Strangers in Our Midst: The Political Philosophy of Immigration* (Cambridge, MA: Harvard University Press, 2016).

Milstein, Brian, 'Kantian Cosmopolitanism beyond "Perpetual Peace": Commercium, Critique, and the Cosmopolitan Problematic', *European Journal of Philosophy 21* (2012): pp. 118–143.

Minister for Immigration and Multicultural Affairs, Press Release, *Joint Statement with Minister for Justice and Customs: Government Strengthens Border Integrity* (MPS 161/2001, September 17, 2001).

Moreno-Lax, Violeta, *Accessing Asylum in Europe: Extraterritorial Border Controls and Refugee Rights under EU Law* (Oxford: Oxford University Press, 2017).

Motomura, Hiroshi, 'Haitian Asylum Seekers: Interdiction and Immigrants' Rights', *Cornell International Law Journal 26* (1993): pp. 695–717.

Mountz, Alison, 'Embodying the Nation State: Canada's Response to Human Smuggling', *Political Geography 23* (2004): pp. 323–345.

Nafziger, James A. R., 'The General Admission of Aliens under International Law', *American Journal of International Law 77* (1983): pp. 804–847.

Nail, Thomas, *A Theory of the Border* (Oxford: Oxford University Press, 2016).

Nasr, Leila, 'The Extraterritoriality of the Principle of Non-Refoulement: A Critique of the Sale case and Roma case', *LSE Human Rights*, online http://blogs.lse.ac.uk/humanrights/2016/02/09/the-extraterritoriality-of-the-principle-of-non-refoulement-a-critique-of-the-sale-case-and-roma-case/.

Nessel, Lori, 'Externalised Borders and the Invisible Refugee', *Columbia Human Rights Law Review 40* (2009): pp. 625–699.

Neuman, Gerald L., 'The Extraterritorial Constitution after Boumediene v. Bush', *Southern California Law Review 82* (2009): pp. 259–290.

Neumayer, Eric, 'Unequal Access to Foreign Spaces: How States Use Visa Restrictions to Regulate Mobility in a Globalized World', *Transactions of the Institute of British Geographers 31* (2006): pp. 72–84.

Ngai, Mae, *Impossible Subjects: Illegal Aliens and the Making of Modern America* (Princeton: Princeton University Press, 2004).

Nixon, Ron, 'Homeland Security Goes Abroad. Not Everyone is Grateful', *The New York Times*, December 26, 2017.

Nolen, Stephanie, 'Southern Exposure: the Costly Border Plan Mexico Won't Discuss', *Globe and Mail*, June 16, 2016, online www.theglobeandmail.com/news/world/the-costly-border-mexico-wont-discuss-migration/article30397720/.

Oakley, Sharon, 'Accelerated Procedures for Asylum in the European Union', Sussex Migration Working Paper No. 43 (Sussex: Sussex Centre for Migration Research, 2007).

OECD, *International Migration Outlook 2017, Summary* (Paris: OECD 2017).

Office of the Auditor General of Canada, *Report of the Auditor General of Canada to the House of Commons, Ch. 5: Citizenship and Immigration Canada—Control and Enforcement* (FA1-2003/1-5E, 2003).

Ohmae, Kenichi, *The Borderless World* (London: Collins, 1990).

Oltermann, Philip, 'UK May Allow the US Security Checks on Passengers before Transatlantic Travel', *The Guardian*, September 11, 2014, online www.theguardian.com/uk-news/2014/sep/11/uk-us-security-checks-passengers.

Orgad, Liav, *The Cultural Defense of Nations: A Liberal Theory of Majority Rights* (Oxford: Oxford University Press, 2015).

Ormsby, Eric A., 'The Refugee Crisis as Civil Liberties Crisis', *Columbia Law Review 117* (2017): pp. 1191–1229.

Owen, David, 'Human Rights, Refugees and Freedom of Movement', *Journal for Human Rights/Zeitschrift für Menschenrechte 8* (2014): pp. 50–56.

Owen, David, 'In Loco Civitatis: On the Normative Basis of Refugeehood and Responsibilities for Refugees', in Sarah Fine and Lea Ypi, eds, *Migration in Political Theory: The Ethics of Movement and Membership* (Oxford: Oxford University Press, 2016), pp. 269–289.

Owen, David, 'Refugees and Responsibilities of Justice', *Global Justice: Theory, Practice, Rhetoric 11* (2018): pp. 23–44.

Paik, Naomi, 'Abolitionist Futures and the US Sanctuary Movement', *Race and Class 59* (2017): pp. 3–25.

Paik, Naomi, *Rightlessness: Testimony and Redress in U.S. Prison Campus since World War II* (Chapel Hill: UNC Press, 2016).

Panizzon, Marion, 'Readmission Agreements of EU Member States: A Case for EU Subsidiary or Dualism', *Refugee Survey Quarterly 31* (2012): pp. 101–133.

Parliament of Australia, Department of Parliamentary Services, *Excising Australia: Are We Really Shrinking!* (Research Note No. 5, 2005–2006, August 31, 2005).

Parliament of Australia, Research Paper Series 2016–2017, Elibritt Karlsen, *Australia's Offshore Processing of Asylum Seekers in Nauru and PNG: A Quick Guide to Statistics and Resources* (Canberra: Parliamentary Library, December 19, 2016).

Parmar, Alpa, 'Policing Belonging: Race and Nation in the UK', in Mary Bosworth, Alpa Parmar, and Yolanda Vázquez, eds, *Race, Criminal Justice, and Migration Control: Enforcing the Boundaries of Belonging* (Oxford: Oxford University Press, 2018), pp. 108–124.

Paz, Moria, 'Between the Kingdom and the Desert Sun: Human Rights, Immigration, and Border Walls', *Berkeley Journal of International Law 34* (2016): pp. 1–43.

Paz, Moria, 'The Incomplete Right to Freedom of Movement', *American Journal of International Law Unbound 111* (2018): pp. 514–518.

Paz, Moria, 'The Law of Walls', *European Journal of International Law 28* (2017): pp. 601–62.

Perju, Vlad F., 'Constitutional Transplants, Borrowing, and Migrations', in Michel Rosenfeld and András Sajó, eds, *The Oxford Handbook of Comparative Constitutional Law* (Oxford: Oxford University Press, 2013).

Pinheiro Walla, Alice, 'Common Possession of the Earth and Cosmopolitan Right', *Kant-Studien 107* (2016): pp. 160–178.

Price, Matthew, *Rethinking Asylum: History, Purpose, and Limits* (Cambridge: Cambridge University Press, 2009).

Prop, Leon, 'The Red Cross and the Externalisation of EU Migration Policy: Addressing the Humanitarian Challenges', in *Shifting Borders: Externalising Migrant Vulnerabilities and Rights?* (Brussels: Red Cross EU Office, 2013), pp. 5–6, online https://redcross.eu/uploads/files/Positions/Migration/Shifting%20borders%20booklet/shifting-borders-externalizing-migrant-vulnerabilities-rights-red-cross-eu-office.pdf.

Ramji-Nogales, Jaya and Peter J. Spiro, 'Introduction to Symposium on Framing Global Migration Law', *American Journal of International Law Unbound 111* (2017): pp. 1–2.

Raustiala, Kal, 'The Geography of Justice', *Fordham Law Review 73* (2005): pp. 2501–2560.

Red Cross, *Shifting Borders: Externalising Migrant Vulnerabilities and Rights* (Brussels: Red Cross EU Office, 2013), online https://redcross.eu/uploads/files/Positions/Migration/Shifting%20borders%20booklet/shifting-borders-externalizing-migrant-vulnerabilities-rights-red-cross-eu-office.pdf.

Refugee Council of Australia, 'Australia's Offshore Processing Regime', online www.refugeecouncil.org.au/getfacts/seekingsafety/asylum/offshore-processing/briefing/.

Refugee Council of Australia, 'Turnbull and Dutton Must Guarantee the Safety of the Men They Have Kept Trapped on Manus', *Relief Web*, November 23, 2017, online https://reliefweb.int/report/australia/turnbull-and-dutton-must-guarantee-safety-men-they-have-kept-trapped-manus.

Registrar of the Court, Press Release, European Court of Human Rights, *The Immediate Return to Morocco of Sub-Saharan Migrants who Were Attempting to Enter Spanish Territory in Melilla Amounted to a Collective Expulsion of Foreign Nationals, in Breach of the Convention* (ECHR 291 (2017), October 3, 2017).

Rickerd, Chris, 'Customs and Border Protection's (CBP's) 100-Mile Rule', online www.aclu.org/sites/default/files/assets/14_9_15_cbp_100-mile_rule_final.pdf.

Riegert, Bernd, 'Could Hungary's Transit Zones for Refugees Be a Model for Germany?', *Deutsche Welle*, July 4, 2018, online www.dw.com/en/could-hungarys-transit-zones-forrefugees-be-a-model-for-germany/a-44511989.

Robinson, Nehemiah, *Convention Relating to the Status of Refugees: Its History, Contents and Interpretation; A Commentary* (New York: Institute of Jewish Affairs, World Jewish Congress, 1953).

Ryan, Bernard and Valsamis Mitsilegas, eds, *Extraterritorial Immigration Control: Legal Challenges* (Leiden: Martinus Nijhoff, 2010).

Sack, Robert David, *Human Territoriality. Its Theory and History* (Cambridge: Cambridge University Press, 1986).

Sager, Alex, 'The Uses and Abuses of "Migrant Crisis"', in Theodoros Fouskas, ed., *Immigrants and Refugees in Times of Crisis* (European Public Law Organization, forthcoming).

Salter, Mark B., 'Governmentalities of an Airport: Heterotopia and Confession', *International Political Sociology 1* (2007): pp. 49–66.

Salter, Mark B., 'Passports, Mobility, and Security: How Smart Can the Border Be?', *International Studies Perspectives* 5 (2004): pp. 71–91.

Samers, Michael, 'An Emerging Geopolitics of "Illegal" Immigration in the European Union', *European Journal of Migration and Law* 6 (2004): pp. 27–45.

Sampson, Robyn, 'Embodied Borders: Biopolitics, Knowledge Mobilization, and Alternatives to Immigration Detention', PhD dissertation, La Trobe University (2013).

Sassen, Saskia, *Losing Control? Sovereignty in an Age of Globalization* (New York: Columbia University Press, 1996).

Schmidt, Michael S., 'U.S. Security Expands Presence at Foreign Airports', *The New York Times*, July 13, 2012.

Scott, James, *Seeing Like a State: How Certain Schemes to Improve the Human Condition Have Failed* (New Haven: Yale University Press, 1998).

Shachar, Ayelet, *The Birthright Lottery: Citizenship and Global Inequality* (Cambridge: Harvard University Press, 2009).

Shachar, Ayelet, 'Citizenship for Sale?' in Ayelet Shachar et al., eds, *The Oxford Handbook of Citizenship* (Oxford: Oxford University Press, 2017).

Shachar, Ayelet, 'The Marketization of Citizenship in an Age of Restrictionism', *Ethics & International Affairs* 32 (2018): pp. 3–13.

Shachar, Ayelet, *Multicultural Jurisdictions: Cultural Differences and Women's Rights* (Cambridge: Cambridge University Press, 2001).

Shachar, Ayelet, 'Selecting by Merit: The Brave New World of Stratified Mobility', in Sarah Fine and Lea Ypi, eds, *Migration in Political Theory: The Ethics of Movement and Membership* (Oxford: Oxford University Press, 2016), pp. 175–202.

Shachar, Ayelet, and Ran Hirschl, 'On Citizenship, States and Markets', *Journal of Political Philosophy* 22 (2014): pp. 231–257.

Shacknove, Andrew, 'Who Is a Refugee?' *Ethics* 95 (1985): pp. 274–284.

Shamir, Ronen, 'Without Borders? Notes on Globalization as a Mobility Regime', *Sociological Theory* 23 (2005): pp. 197–217.

Silvey, Rachel, 'Borders, Embodiment, and Mobility: Feminist Migration Studies in Geography', in Lise Nelson and Joni Seager, eds, *A Companion to Feminist Geography* (Oxford: Blackwell, 2015), pp. 138–149.

Sitkin, Lea, 'Coordinating Internal Migration Control in the UK', *International Journal of Migration and Border Studies* 1 (2014): pp. 39–56.

Slaughter, Anne-Marie, *A New World Order* (Princeton: Princeton University Press, 2005).

Soja, Edward W., *Postmodern Geographies: The Reassertion of Space in Critical Social Theory* (London: Verso, 1989).

Song, S., 'Why Does the State Have the Right to Control Immigration?', in Jack Knight, ed., *NOMOS: Immigration, Emigration, and Migration* (New York City: NYU Press, 2017), pp. 3–50.

Soysal, Yasemin N., *Limits of Citizenship: Migrants and Postnational Membership in Europe* (Chicago: University of Chicago, 1994).

Standing Committee on Citizenship and Immigration, *Immigration Detention and Removal* (June 1998) (Canada), online http://cmte.parl.gc.ca/Content/HOC/committee/361/citi/reports/rp1031513/citirp01/09-rec-e.htm.

Sunstein, Cass R., 'Incompletely Theorized Arguments Commentary', *Harvard Law Review 108* (1994): pp. 1733–1772.

Sunstein, Cass R., 'On the Expressive Function of Law', *University of Pennsylvania Law Review 144* (1996): pp. 2021–2053.

Taylor, Paul et al., 'Unauthorized Immigrants: Length of Residency, Patterns of Parenthood', *Pew Research Center*, December 1, 2011, online www.pewhispanic.org/2011/12/01/unauthorized-immigrants-length-of-residency-patterns-of-parenthood/.

Taylor, Peter J., 'The State as Container: Territoriality in the Modern World-System', *Progress in Human Geography 18* (1994): pp. 151–162.

The Local, 'Anti-Foreigner Attitudes on the Rise in Germany, Study Finds', November 8, 2018, online www.thelocal.de/20181108/anti-foreigner-attitudeson-the-rise.

Tonkiss, Katherine and Tendayi Bloom, 'Theorizing Noncitizenship: Concepts, Debates and Challenges', *Citizenship* Studies *19* (2015): pp. 837–852.

Torpey, John, 'Coming and Going: On the State Monopolization of the Legitimate "Means of Movement"', *Sociological Theory 16* (1998): pp. 239–259.

Torpey, John, *The Invention of the Passport—Surveillance, Citizenship and the State* (Cambridge: Cambridge University Press, 2000).

Toshkov, Dimiter and Laura de Haan, 'The Europeanization of Asylum Policy: An Assessment of the EU Impact on Asylum Applications and Recognitions Rates', *Journal of European Public Policy 20* (2013): pp. 661–683.

Triandafyllidou, Anna and Angeliki Dimitriadi, 'Migration Management at the Outposts of the European Union', *Griffith Law Review 22* (2013): pp. 598–61.

UN General Assembly, *Convention Relating to the Status of Refugees*, July 28, 1951, United Nations, Treaty Series, vol *189*, online www.refworld.org/docid/3be01b964.html.

UN General Assembly, Report of the Secretary-General: Making Migration Work for All (U.N. Doc. A/72/643, December 12, 2017).

UN General Assembly, *Universal declaration of human rights*, 217 [III] A, Paris, 1948.

UNHCR, 'Global Trends Report—Forced Displacement in 2014: World at War', online http://unhcr.org/556725e69.html.

UNHCR, *Resettlement Handbook* (Geneva: UNHCR, 2011).

UNHCR, Standing Committee, *Interception of Asylum-Seekers and Refugees: The International Framework and Recommendations for a Comprehensive Approach* (10, U.N. Doc. EC/50/SC/CPR.17, June 9, 2000).

UNHCR, 29th Session, *Statement by Mr. François Crépeau, Special Rapporteur on the Human Rights of Migrants* (Geneva, June 15, 2015) (United Nations).

UNHCR, 'Worldwide Displacement Hits All-Time High as War and Persecution Increase', online www.unhcr.org/news/latest/2015/6/558193896/worldwide-displacement-hits-all-time-high-war-persecution-increase.html.

United States Customs and Border Protection, 'Preclearance Locations', online www.cbp.gov/border-security/ports-entry/operations/preclearance.

United States Department of Homeland Security, Press Release, *Fact Sheet: Secure Border Initiative* (November 2, 2005).

United States Department of Homeland Security, Press Release, *Secretary Nielsen Signs Historic Regional Compact with Central America to Stem Irregular Migration at Source, Confront U.S. Border Crisis* (March 28, 2019), online www.dhs.gov/news/2019/03/28/secretarynielsen-signs-historic-regional-compact-central-america-stem-irregular.

United States Department of State, *Observations of the United States on the Advisory Opinion of the UN High Commissioner for Refugees on the Extraterritorial Application of Non-Refoulement Obligations under the 1951 Convention Relating to the Status of Refugees and its 1967 Protocol* (US Department of State Archive January 20, 2001 to January 20, 2009, December 28, 2007), online https://2001-2009.state.gov/s/l/2007/112631.htm.

Urry, John, 'Globalization and Citizenship', *Journal of World-Systems Research 5* (1999): pp. 311–324.

Vallet, Elizabeth, ed., *Borders, Fences and Walls: State of Insecurity?* (Abingdon: Routledge, 2014).

Vanhaute, Liesbet, 'Colonists, Traders, or Settlers? Kant on Fair International Trade and Legitimate Settlement', in Katrin Flikschuh and Lea Ypi, eds, *Kant and Colonialism* (Oxford: Oxford University Press, 2014).

Vogl, Anthea, 'Over the Borderline: A Critical Inquiry into the Geography of Territorial Excision and the Securitisation of the Australian Border', *University of New South Wales Law Journal 38* (2015): pp. 114–145.

Volpp, Leti, 'The Citizen and the Terrorist', *UCLA Law Review 49* (2002): pp. 1575–1600.

Volpp, Leti, 'Imaginings of Space in Immigration Law', *Law, Culture and the Humanities 9*, no. 3 (2012): pp. 456–474.

Walzer, Michael, 'The Politics of Resistance', *Dissent*, March 1, 2017, online www.dissentmagazine.org/online_articles/the-politics-of-resistance-mi-chael-walzer.

Wasem, Ruth Ellen, *US Immigration Policy on Haitian Migrants*, Congressional Research Service (RS2149, January 15, 2010), online http://trac.syr.edu/immigration/library/P4230.pdf.

Weil, Patrick and Itamar Mann, 'We Need a New Orderly Departure Program', Opinion, *Al Jazeera America*, September 9, 2015.

Wellman, Christopher Heath, 'Immigration and Freedom of Association', *Ethics 119* (2008): pp. 109–141.

Wessel, Ramses A., '"Soft" International Agreements in EU External Relations: Pragmatism over Principles?', paper presented at the ECPR SGEU Conference, Panel Hard and Soft Law in the European Union, Paris, June 13–15, 2018.

Wilde, Ralph, 'The Unintended Consequences of Expanding Migrant Rights Protections', *American Journal of International Law Unbound 111* (2018): pp. 487–491.

Wilkins, Dean, 'Enter the UAE with Just Your Face: DXB in World First Trial of Face Recognition Technology at the Border', *Time Out Dubai*, October 11, 2018, online www.timeoutdubai.com/dubai-airport/386146-enter-the-uae-with-just-your-face.

Yong, Caleb, 'Justifying Resistance to Immigration Law: The Case of Mere Noncompliance', *Canadian Journal of Law and Jurisprudence 31* (2018): pp. 459–481.

Zieck, Marjoleine, 'The 1956 Hungarian Refugee Emergency, an Early and Instructive Case of Resettlement', *Amsterdam Law Forum 5* (2013): pp. 45–63.

Zolberg, Aristide R., 'Matters of State: Theorizing Immigration Policy', in Charles Hirschman, Philip Kasinitz, and Josh DeWind, eds, *The Handbook of International Migration: The American Experience* (New York: Russell Sage Foundation, 1999), pp. 71–93.

Zolberg, Aristide R., *A Nation by Design: Immigration Policy in the Fashioning of America* (New York: Russell Sage Foundation, 2006).

Zürn, Michael, Martin Binder, and Matthias Echer-Ehrhart, 'International Authority and Its Politicization', *International Theory 4* (2012): pp. 69–106.

Legal sources

Legislation and regulation

Aliens Act 2000 (Spain).

Chinese Exclusion Act 1882 (United States).

Commission Implementation Regulation (EU) No 118/2014, O.J. (L 39/1), February 8, 2014 (EU) Consolidated versions of the Treaty on European Union and the Treaty on the Functioning of the European Union, 2012/C 326/01 (EU).

Convention Implementing the Schengen Agreement of June 14, 1985, O.J. September 22, 2000 (EU).

Department of Homeland Security, Designated Aliens for Expedited Removal, 69 Fed. Reg. 58.877, 11 August 2004. (United States).

Directive (EU) 2016/681, O.J. (L 119/132) May 4, 2016 (EU).

Executive Order 13767, Border Security and Immigration Enforcement Improvements, 82 Fed. Reg. Presidential Documents 8793, January 27, 2017 (United States).

Executive Order 13768, Enhancing Public Safety in the Interior of the United States, 82 Fed. Reg. Presidential Documents 8799, January 30, 2017 (United States).

German Bundespolizeigesetz [BPolG] [Federal Police Law], October 19, 1994, BGBl. I at 2987, § 2, last amended by Art. 3 of Gesetz, 26 July, 2016, BGBl. I at 1818 (Ger.).

Government of Canada, Preamble, Canada US Statement of Mutual Understanding (SMU) (Canada), online www.canada.ca/en/immigration-refugees-citizenship/corporate/mandate/policies-operational-instructions-agreements/agreements/statement-mutual-understanding-information-sharing/statement.html.

Human Rights Committee, *General Comment No. 31 on the Nature of the General Legal Obligations on States Parties to the Covenant* (U.N. Doc. CCPR/C/21/Rev.1/Add.13, May 26, 2004).

Immigration and Nationality Act (United States).

Member States' Notifications of the Temporary Reintroduction of Border Control at Internal Borders Pursuant to Article 25 *et seq.* of Regulation 562/2006 of the European Parliament and of the Council of 15 March 2006 establishing a Community Code on the Rules Governing the Movement of Persons across Borders (Schengen Borders Code), 2006 O.J. (L 105) 1 (EU), online https://ec.europa.eu/home-affairs/sites/homeaffairs/files/what-we-do/policies/borders-and-visas/schengen/reintroduction-border-control/docs/ms_notifications_-_reintroduction_of_border_control_en.pdf.

Migration Act 1958 (Australia).

Migration Amendment (Excision from Migration Zone) Act 2001 (Australia).

Migration Amendment (Unauthorised Maritime Arrivals and other Measures) Act 2013 (Australia).

Migration Legislation Amendment (Regional Processing and Other Measures), Act 2012 (Australia).

Regulation (EU) 2016/1624 of the European Parliament and of the Council on the European Border and Coast Guard, O.J. (L 251/1) September 16, 2016 (EU).

Regulation (EU) 604/2013 of the European Parliament and of the Council, O.J. (L 80/31), June 29, 2013 (EU).

Regulation 562/2006 of the European Parliament and of the Council of March 15, 2006 establishing a Community Code on the Rules Governing the Movement of Persons across Borders (Schengen Borders Code), 2006 O.J. (L 105) 1 (EU).

Return Directive, 2008/115/EC of the European Parliament and of the Council, O.J. (L 348/98) December 16, 2008 (EU).

United Nations General Assembly, Resolution Adopted by the General Assembly on September 19, 2016, New York Declaration for Refugees and Migrants, A/Res/71/1, October 3, 2016 (United Nations).

United Nations High Commissioner for Refugees, Advisory Opinion on the Extraterritorial Application of Non-Refoulement Obligations Under the 1951 Convention Relating to the Status of Refugees and Its 1967 Protocol, January 26, 2007 (United Nations).

United States Department of State, Office of the Legal Adviser, Memorandum on the Geographic Scope of the International Covenant on Civil and Political Rights, October 19, 2010 (United States), online www.justsecurity.org/wp-content/uploads/2014/03/state-department-iccpr-memo.pdf.

United States Department of State, Office of the Legal Adviser, Memorandum Opinion on the Geographic Scope of the Convention against Torture and Its Application in Situations of Armed Conflict, January 21, 2013 (United States), online www.justsecurity.org/wp-content/uploads/2014/03/state-department-cat-memo.pdf.

Cases

Australia

CPCF v. Minister for Immigration and Border Protection [2015] 255 CLR 514.

Plaintiff M61/2010E v. Commonwealth of Australia and Plaintiff M69 of 2010 v. Commonwealth of Australia [2010] 243 CLR 319.

Plaintiff M70/2011 v. Minister of Immigration and Citizenship [2011] 244 CLR 144.

Plaintiff S156/2013 v. Minister for Immigration and Border Protection [2014] HCA 22.

Ruddock v. Vadarlis [2001] 110 FCR 49.

Canada

Reference re meaning of the word "Persons" in s. 24 of the British North American Act, [1928] S.C.R. 276.

Singh v. Minister of Employment and Immigration [1985] 1 S.C.R. 177.

Court of Justice of the European Union (CJEU)

A.S. v. Slovenia, Case C-490/16, EU:C:2017:585, Eur. Ct. Justice (2017).

Adil, Case C-278/12 PPU, ECLI:EU:C:2012:508, Eur. Ct. Justice (2012).

Case C-9/16, ECLI:EU:C:2017:483, Eur. Ct. Justice (2017).

Melki and Abdeli, Cases C-188/10 and C-189/10, ECLI:EU:C:2010:36, Eur. Ct. Justice (2010).

NF, NG and NM v European Council, Cases T-192/16, T-193/16 and T-257/16, February 28, 2017; *NF v European Council*, Case T-192/16, February 28, 2017; *NG v. European Council*, Case T-193/16, February 28, 2017; *NM v. European Council*, Case T-257/16, February 28, 2017.

Slovakia and Hungary v. Council, Joined Cases C-643/15 and C-647/15, September 6, 2017.

X and X v Etat Belge, Case C-638 PPU, March 7, 2017.

Judicial Committee of the Privy Council

Edwards v. Canada (AG) [1930] AC 124, 1929 UKPC 86.

European Court of Human Rights

Amuur v. France, App. No. 19776/92, Eur. Ct. H.R. (1996).

Hirsi v. Italy, App. No. 27765/09, Eur. Ct. H.R. (2012).

Issa and others v. Turkey, App. No. 31821/96, Eur. Ct. H.R. (2004).

Khlaifia and others v. Italie, App. No. 16483/12, Eur. Ct. H.R. (2015).

N.D. and N.T. v. Spain, App. Nos 8675/15 and 8697/15, Eur. Ct. H.R. (2017).

Saadi v. UK, App. No. 13229/03, Eur. Ct. H.R. (2008).

Papua New Guinea

Namah v. Pato [2016] PGSC 13, S.C. 1497.

United Kingdom

Brown v. Stott [2003] 1 AC 681.

Regina v. Immigration Officer at Prague Airport and Another Ex parte European Roma Rights Centre and Others [2004] UKHL 55.

United States

Boumediene v. Bush, 553 US 723 (2008).

Hulilun Centers Council Inc. v. McNary, 807 F. Supp. 928 (E.D.N.Y. 1992). *cert. granted, Haitian Centers Council v. McNary*, 506 US 814 (1992).

Kaplan v. Tod, 267 US 228 (1925).

Kiobel v. Royal Dutch Petroleum, 569 US 108 (2013).

Knauff v. Shaughnessy, 228 US 537 (1950).

Sale v. Haitian Centers Council, 509 US 155 (1993).

Shaughnessy v. United States ex rel. Mezei, 345 US 206 (1953).

U.S. v. Peralta Sanchez, 868 F.3rd 852 (9th Cir. 2017).

United States ex rel. Knauff v. Shaughnessy, 338 US 537 (1950).

United States v. Martinez-Fuerte, 428 US 543 (1976).

United States v. Verdugo-Urquidez, 494 US 259 (1990).

Zadvydas v. Davis, 533 US 678 (2001).

Index

Note: page numbers in *italics* refer to illustrations; footnotes are indicated by page numbers followed by n and the number of the footnote.